THE NEUROPSYCHOLOGY OF

DEGENERATIVE BRAIN DISEASES

Robert G. Knight

**University of Otago
New Zealand**

1992

LAWRENCE ERLBAUM ASSOCIATES, PUBLISHERS
Hillsdale, New Jersey   Hove and London

Lawrence Erlbaum Associates, Inc., Publishers
365 Broadway
Hillsdale, New Jersey 07642

Library of Congress Cataloging-in-Publication Data

Knight, Robert G.
   The neuropsychology of degenerative brain diseases / Robert G.
Knight.
        p.   cm.
   Includes bibliographical references and index.
   ISBN 0-8058-0927-9
   1. Brain—Degeneration.   2. Neuropsychological tests.   3. Clinical
neuropsychology.   I. Title.
   [DNLM: 1. Brain Diseases.   2. Nerve Degeneration.
3. Neuropsychology.   WL 359 K71h]
RC394.D35K65   1992
616.8—dc20
DNLM/DLC
for Library of Congress   91-38177
                                                                   CIP

Printed in the United States of America

10 9 8 7 6 5 4 3 2 1

To Ione,

and Kieran and Jamie

Contents

PREFACE

The last two decades have seen a dramatic increase in the number of published neuropsychological studies. Nowhere is this more evident than in the investigation of the psychological consequences of degenerative brain diseases. Studies on the biological, neuropsychological, and social changes resulting from such disorders as Alzheimer's disease, multiple sclerosis, and Huntington's disease abound. This book is primarily a survey of the neuropsychological research focused on these chronic neurological conditions. My objective is to make this research more accessible to clinicians who work with patients who have degenerative brain diseases and to students encountering these patients in the course of their training.

The motivation to review this work came from my involvement in studies of the cognitive function of patients with brain disorders. Much of our present knowledge of cognitive systems and functional neuroanatomy comes from the experimental study of patients with brain lesions. However, from the outset it must be acknowledged that my perspective is that of a clinical psychologist, concerned with all aspects of the impact of brain damage on the lives of those affected. Consequently, I have interpreted neuropsychology in a broad way to allow inclusion of studies of the psychosocial consequences of brain changes for both patients and their caregivers. All clinicians involved with the management of brain-injured clients in any capacity will be aware that there is more to working with such clients than documenting their cognitive deficits. The neuropsychological consequences of brain disorders need to be placed in the psychosocial context of individual clients and their families if interventions and support are to be effectively planned. I have endeavored to make this a significant theme of each chapter.

In the first part of this book, the range of neuropsychological measures available for the assessment of patients with degenerative brain diseases are introduced. In Part 2, research involving patients with degenerative diseases is considered. The biological basis of each disorder, and the consequent neuropsychological and psychosocial deficits, are reviewed in turn. Each of the diseases reviewed herein has its own unique clinico-pathological character, causing different psychological effects, and providing different adaptive challenges. Alzheimer's disease causes a pervasive dementia, and a progressive loss of insight, but few motor or physical deficits. In amytrophic lateral sclerosis and progressive supranuclear palsy, the loss of motor abilities is profound, but the cognitive changes are often minimal. Parkinson's disease has features of both Alzheimer's disease and progressive supranuclear palsy, but is dominated by the progression of involuntary motor activity and rigidity. Many of the psychosocial consequences of Huntington's disease arise from its genetic transmission; the unpredictable course and onset in early adulthood gives multiple sclerosis its special psychosocial features. Although there are unique consequences for individual patients, there are also elements of a common experience with each disease. The emphases within each chapter have been determined by the way in which different diseases have been studied.

In Part 3, the process of adaptation to the disease is discussed. The focus here is not only on the patients, but also on their caregivers. In the final chapter I present a model of adjustment that is intended to make explicit the way in which understanding the effects of any neurological condition for individual patients, and all those involved in their care, necessitates taking account of all the changes that follow the onset of the disorder.

Finding an appropriate, inclusive label for the disorders reviewed in this book was problematic. At best the term *degenerative* can only be applied loosely. In this case it is intended to denote those diseases that cause a progressive destruction of brain structures with a consequent decline in psychological functioning. Neurological conditions resulting from infections, trauma, or cerebrovascular changes have been excluded. The diseases covered are those degenerative disorders whose effects have been most widely studied because of their potential to elucidate brain-behavior relationships. Most of the diseases surveyed would usually be classified as degenerative, for example, Alzheimer's disease, Parkinsonism, and Huntington's disease. Multiple sclerosis is often listed as a demylinating disease. Korsakoff's disease is more exceptional in that the degeneration has a known etiology and, although irreversible, is not necessarily progressive. It is, however, difficult to exclude Korsakoff's disease from consideration because of the frequent comparison of alcoholic Korsakoff patients with other dementing subjects.

Preparation of this book would have been impossible without the help of very many people. At the outset I would like to acknowledge a special sense of gratitude to my colleagues Hamish Godfrey, Barry Longmore, Nigel Marsh, and Fiona Partidge for their support, insights, and work over the past few years. I am also grateful to the many colleagues and students who have worked with us: Samir Bishara, Jocelyn Burke, Oliver Davidson, Michael Feehan, Tom Gati, Sara-Jane Ivory,

Fiona Longmore, and Lynley Stenhouse. I would also like to express my appreciation to my colleagues in the department of Psychology at the University of Otago for creating an environment in which research and scholarship can thrive, and particularly to Geoffrey White for his enthusiastic and practical support of our endeavors. Many thanks also to Russell Phillips for his help with the Archimedes. Finally, I would like to record my thanks to Norma Bartlett and Isabel Campbell for their willing, cheerful, and professional approach to preparing the manuscript. Without their efforts, completion of this project would have been all but impossible.

R.G.K.

PART 1

ASSESSMENT

Chapter 1

ASSESSING THE DEMENTING PATIENT

In the process which we call dementia, the clinical picture is usually dominated by intellectual disintegration, but feeling and striving are always affected. The general features of the syndrome show a fairly consistent pattern which is varied in the individual case according to the premorbid personality, the age of onset, the nature of the cause, and any local preponderance in the early lesions. The impairment of memory for recent events, which is the earliest change, may be effectively compensated for a considerable time by a surprising ingenuity in concealment, adherence to a rigid daily routine and the use of a notebook. This adjustment breaks down as intellectual grasp weakens and thinking becomes slow, labored and ill defined. Attention is now aroused and sustained with difficulty, the patient tires easily, particularly with any unaccustomed task, and he is prone to become lost in the middle of an argument or sentence. Poverty of thought supervenes in a once richly stored, flexible mind: it shrinks to a small core of ever-recurring, rigidly held ideas and re-evoked memories of the remote past, which may long remain vivid and clear.
(Mayer-Gross, Slater, & Roth, 1969, p. 491)

Introduction

Nearly every professional contact with a client who has a degenerative brain disease, whether for clinical or research purposes, incorporates some level of formal or informal evaluation of the client's current functioning. Accordingly, it is helpful to begin with a brief review of some of the procedures used in constructing an understanding of the neuropsychological consequences of degenerative brain diseases for individual patients.

Some degree of cognitive failure or functional decline is associated with almost all the degenerative diseases reviewed in this book; these changes are given the generic label of *dementia*. The *Diagnostic and Statistical Manual of Mental Disorders*, 3rd ed., rev. (DSM-III-R; American Psychiatric Association 1987) describes dementia as resulting in a deterioration in memory functioning, abstract thinking, judgment, personality, and other higher-order cortical functions, such as language, perception, constructional skills, and conceptual learning. Dementia is invariably present in some disorders, such as Alzheimer's disease (AD), but is less common in others, for example, Parkinson's disease (PD). Studies comparing groups of patients with dementia associated with different degenerative diseases, suggest that there may be variations in the pattern of cognitive disturbance as a consequence of differing distributions of neurological damage. Whether dissimilar profiles of cognitive performance can or cannot be distinguished in patients with diseases of different pathology, in practice the assessment of dementing patients proceeds in much the same way. Selection of appropriate assessment procedures depends more on the severity of the dementia than on the nature of the diagnosis.

The appropriate selection of measures for use with dementing patients depends to a large extent on the purpose of the particular assessment being undertaken. This might be screening for the presence of dementia or documenting consequent changes in performance, both important objectives in the evaluation of clients with degenerative neurological conditions. The valid measurement of the presence or degree of dementia is also important in the process of describing samples of patients used in research. Specific tests will be useful in some circumstances and entirely inappropriate in others. When planning to use standardized measures in research with neurologically impaired clients or for the assessment of individual patients in a clinical setting, it is vital to have the assessment goals clearly defined. Some of the specific objectives of testing are listed here:

Diagnosis. This includes the detection of the onset of a dementing process and, under some circumstances, contributing a more precise diagnosis, such as Alzheimer's disease or multi-infarct dementia. Although physical techniques such as computed tomography (CT) scans have an increasingly important part to play in diagnosis, no amount of scanning can specify exactly what a patient is capable of achieving as far as social or cognitive performance is concerned. Formal psychometric testing may also contribute to differential diagnosis by eliminating alternative explanations for poor cognitive performance, such as depression or concurrent psychiatric disturbance.

Documenting the extent, severity, or stage of the dementing disorder. Frequently a diagnosis has already been established, and the aim of testing is to determine a patient's current level of functioning. In clinical practice, testing is important in planning case management. Knowledge of the severity of the disorder is a prelude to planning rehabilitation, a long-term care strategy, and the mobilization of appropriate support. Necessarily, case management requires the comprehensive assessment not only of cognitive functioning, but also of personality, behavior, social support, and adaptive skills.

Monitoring the effects of treatment or disease progression. Assessing changes in personal functioning or cognition as a consequence of intervention, particularly pharmacological treatment, but also psychosocial remediation, is another objective of testing. Evaluating the rate of deterioration (or in disorders like multiple sclerosis, the degree of remission) is another important clinical task. In this situation, the measures used need to be sensitive to change and relevant to the aims of the treatment or care strategy.

Experimental research. A major use of standardized measures of impairment is the accurate description of groups of patients for research purposes. This includes demonstrating that diagnostic statements are well-founded and establishing the severity of the impairments of the patient tested. This serves to facilitate comparison between the results of different research groups.

Epidemiological research. Planning health services and testing etiological theories that involve environmental risk factors necessitate appropriate community screening and follow-up diagnostic testing to determine the prevalence and incidence of the diseases under consideration.

Numerous published rating scales, objective performance tests, and interview schedules are available to perform the functions just outlined. A selection of these are reviewed in this chapter. There are some advantages to using published scales that have been standardized on relevant samples of patients. One benefit is the enhanced opportunity for integrating research from different laboratories using common procedures. In addition, the process of test construction is laborious; thus, using measures with known psychometric credentials can save time and unnecessary duplication of effort. On the other hand, measures developed by other researchers may not be sufficiently precise or accurate for use in some circumstances. Although the development of a better or more specific test may be time-consuming, the dividends from doing so can be considerable. For example, many clinicians devote considerable time to planning and executing an innovative treatment program, but pay little attention to monitoring the outcome. Use of inappropriate or imprecise outcome measures may preclude the demonstration of a strong treatment effect; in this case failure to spend time constructing powerful measures of treatment efficacy may render the effort expended in treatment worthless.

The choice of particular measures of dementia to meet specific clinical or research goals is obviously dependent on the relevance and scope of the content of scale items. However, there are also other important factors. For example, the usefulness of a test for detecting dementia depends on its *discriminatory power*. In psychometric terms, discriminatory power depends on test reliability and the difficulty of the items. Increases in reliability can be achieved by making the items more homogeneous or by lengthening the test. The difficulty level of items is something that needs to be considered carefully when selecting or developing a measure for demented patients. Tests with too many easy items may be of little use for discriminating normal from mildly impaired patients, but an excellent way of documenting severity in the moderate range of disability. A more difficult test may be useful for describing deficits in mildly impaired patients, but may be totally beyond the capacity of more demented patients. The discriminatory power or sensitivity of a particular test needs to be carefully considered in relation to the level of deficit a client or group of research subjects may display.

In the remainder of this chapter I present a survey of a representative selection of measures developed primarily for use with dementing patients. Because some of these measures are multipurpose batteries, it is not a simple matter to classify the range of standardized inventories available in terms of either content or function. Some measures are designed to be administered as tests of the instrumental skills of patients, others are based on relatives' ratings, or on the observations of a trained interviewer. Accordingly, the categorization of measures presented here, which is based largely on test function, must be regarded as somewhat arbitrary.

Mental Status Examinations

The initial clinical examination of psychiatric or neurological clients often involves asking a set of relatively standard questions designed to screen for the presence of an acquired impairment in cognition. A number of these lists of mental status questions, which focus primarily on memory and orientation, have been published and have found widespread use in clinical and research practice. Usually the items employed in mental status examinations involve simple cognitive operations, well within the capability of the healthy elderly person, and failure on one or more of the test items raises the question of dementia. A typical set of items that might be used to assess mental status in dementing patients is presented in Table 1.1.

Table 1.1: Items Frequently Used to Assess Mental Status in Dementing Patients

Orientation
    Time (year, season, date, day, month)
    Place ("Where are we?," city, town, hospital, ward)
    Person

Concentration and attention
    Serial sevens (count back from 100 in 7s)
    Counting from 1 to 20
    Counting from 20 to 1
    Months of the year backward

Memory
    Memory Span, repetition of digits (digit span)
    Learn names of three objects (number of trials)
    Delayed recall of same three objects (5-minute delay)

Remote Memory
    Date of birth, place of birth, schools attended, occupation
    Names of siblings, wife, and children
    Names of employers
    Name of mayor, president, date of World War 2
    Knowledge of current events

Abstract thinking
    Explain proverbs (e.g., "Don't cry over spilled milk.")
    Similarities (e.g., lion - tiger)

Language
    Name common objects (pen, book, coin)
    Repeat a complex sentence
    Follow a three-stage command

Apraxia
    Copy a geometric design

Orientation for place, person, and time is almost always tested in the course of a mental status examination. Some general knowledge or informational items, which assess remote memory for autobiographical information ("When did you go to school?") or public events ("Who was the president of the United States during World War 2?"), are also usually included. Memory performance is particularly sensitive to the effects of dementia, and the failure to remember three or more items or paired-associates after a delay of up to 5 minutes, is suggestive of impairment. Concentration and attention is often tested by having the client count backward from a fixed number in threes or sevens. Another test often regarded as assessing concentration is repetition of strings of digits, a measure of memory span. The Digit Span subtest from the Wechsler Adult Intelligence Scale (WAIS) is often used for this purpose. Some examinations also include brief measures of constructional abilities, language, and abstract thinking.

Mental status tests vary considerably in length and in the range of abilities tested. The focus is on assessing cognition using verbal questions, although sometimes performance skills (copying or writing) are screened. The main use of mental status questionnaires is to screen for dementia in the clinic, or to provide evidence for the presence or absence of dementia in research samples. The items are relatively easy, thus these brief assessments do not provide a good documentation of the neuropsychological impairments in mildly demented patients. They may, however, be useful in characterizing the severity of dementia in patients whose impairment is in the moderate range. In addition, such measures are often the only way of assessing the residual capacity of moderately to severely demented patients. In sum, mental status tests will be most successful when used to distinguish patients with moderate impairments from healthy controls; at the early stages of a disorder like Dementia of the Alzheimer's type (DAT), classification based on mental status testing tends to be less accurate (Fillenbaum, 1980).

Table 1.2 lists some of the mental status examinations in general use. This list includes measures that provide brief assessments of a range of cognitive functions. Comprehensive batteries, comprising neuropsychological tests that are more sensitive to subtle changes in cognition (e.g., Dementia Assessment Battery; Teng et al., 1989) are considered later.

One of the most popular dementia screening tests is the Mini Mental State Examination (MMSE; M. F. Folstein, S. E. Folstein, & McHugh, 1975). This measure evaluates a variety of cognitive functions and has a score range of 0-30. The test-retest reliability of the MMSE is in the region of .8 - .95 (J. C. Anthony, LeResche, Niaz, Von Korff, & M. F. Folstein, 1982; Dick, Guiloff, Stewart, Blackstock, Bielawska,

Table 1.2: **Standardized Mental Status Measures Used With Dementing and Geriatric Patients**

Scale	Content
Mental Status Questionnaire (Kahn et al., 1960)	Orientation, information, calculation
Information-Memory-Concentration test (Blessed et al., 1968)	Orientation, information, attention
Mini Mental State Examination (M. F. Folstein et al., 1975)	Orientation, registration, attention, calculation, memory, language, copying
Short Portable Mental Status Questionnaire (Pfeiffer, 1975)	Orientation, attention, information
Clifton Assessment Scale (Pattie & Gilleard, 1975)	Orientation, information, concentration, writing, reading, psychomotor performance
Dementia Rating Scale (Mattis, 1976)	Orientation, attention, initiation and perseveration, construction (copying), conceptualization, memory
Alzheimer's Disease Assessment Scale (Rosen et al., 1984)	Orientation, memory, language, construction
Extended Mental Status Questionnaire (Whelihan et al., 1984)	Orientation, information, calculation, remote memory
Cambridge Cognitive Examination (CAMCOG; Roth et al., 1986)	Orientation, language, memory, construction skills, attention, abstract thinking, perception, calculation
Severe Impairment Battery (SIB; Saxton et al., 1990)	Orientation, social interaction, visuo-perception, construction, language, memory, praxis, attention

Paul, & Marsden, 1984; M. F. Folstein et al., 1975). The sensitivity of this examination to dementia is good, despite its brevity. For example, J. C. Anthony et al. (1982) found that 87% of a group of clinically diagnosed demented patients were correctly detected using a cutting score of 23 and below as indicating dementia.

The sensitivity of the MMSE does, however, decline noticeably when mildly impaired patients are tested. Kay, Henderson, R. Scott, J. Wilson, Rickwood, and Grayson (1985) found that classification accuracy fell to 59% when the test was used to detect mild dementia. Similarly, Galasko, Klauber, Hofstetter, Salmon, Lasker, and Thal (1990) reported that the MMSE correctly detected only 50 of 74 community-dwelling demented patients, using a cutoff score of 23. Galasko et al. (1990) found that the sensitivity of the MMSE to a mild degree of dementia was determined primarily by performance on just two items — orientation for place and delayed recall of three items. Raising the cutoff point to 27 increased the sensitivity of the test for detecting dementia from 67% to 93%, while misclassifying only one of the 74 controls. However, their sample was described by the authors as "well-educated," and they conclude that raising the cutoff to 27 is likely to overdiagnose cognitive impairment in general population surveys that include people with less education.

Research with the MMSE has revealed its limitations, and those of similar questionnaires. The majority of the items are not sufficiently difficult for the test to be highly sensitive to cognitive changes in the early stages of dementia. This is a fundamental problem of the test and can only be remedied by revising the items to provide a great range of difficulty. However, to do so would compromise the usefulness of the test with more severely impaired patients. Therefore, in cases of suspected dementia, more comprehensive neuropsychological testing will usually be called for to establish a diagnosis; in these circumstances, the MMSE is best regarded as an initial screening test. In addition, because of the brevity of many of the items, the MMSE does not provide valid information about specific cognitive functions; for example, the language assessment provided by most mental status questionnaires is particularly superficial. It is also important to bear in mind that the items are not matched for difficulty level. This means, for example, that the language test may not be comparable in difficulty to the memory items. Thus, comparing scores on these items from different groups may confound genuine differences in the severity of symptoms displayed by patients with different diseases, with differences in the discriminatory power of the individual items.

The Short Portable Mental Status Questionnaire (SPMSQ; Pfeiffer, 1975) has 10 items and a score range of 0-10. It is a reliable measure (e.g., R. L. Kane, Bell, Reigler, A. Wilson, & R. A. Kane, 1983; Pfeiffer, 1975), and because of its brevity, has been widely used in community surveys and routine clinical assessment. The sensitivity of the SPMSQ is high for the detection of moderate to severe dementia, but considerably poorer when used for separating mild dementia from intact functioning (Fillenbaum, 1980). Overall, the SPMSQ and the earlier and similar Mental Status Questionnaire (MSQ; Kahn et al., 1960) are most useful for the detection of moderate to severe dementia; the difficulty level of the items is too low to detect mild degrees of cognitive impairment.

The Dementia Scale (DS) of Blessed, Tomlinson, and Roth (1968) is made up of two parts: the first a rating of adaptive functioning, the second a series of mental status items. The second section has often been used in its own right as a means of quantifying cognitive changes in dementing patients. The mental status portion of the DS, the Memory-Information-Concentration test (MIC) consists of 13 items (with a score range of 0-33 errors), similar in content to SPMSQ. A modification of the test has been developed by Fuld (1983) and found to have good retest reliability (Thal, Grundman, & Golden, 1986). Kay (1977) reported that using 17 as a cutting score, 90% of a group of demented patients could be correctly identified. In a longitudinal study using the original Blessed DS, Katzman and colleagues (1988) found that for patients with error scores less than 24, the mean annual rate of change on the scale was 4.4. Notably, they found that once the patients became severely impaired (error scores greater than 33), the test was less sensitive to individual differences between patients. Similar ceiling effects operate at the most impaired end of the score-range on most mental status questionnaires (P. B. Davis, J. C. Morris, & Grant, 1990). A six-item version of the MIC, with a score range from 0-28, has also been validated (Katzman, T. Brown, Fuld, Peck, Schechter, & Schimmel, 1983) and found to be at least as effective as the SPMSQ.

A more detailed appraisal of the cognition of demented patients is provided by the Dementia Rating Scale (DRS; Mattis, 1976). Administration takes about 30 to 40 minutes (Salmon, Kwo-on-Yuen, Heindel, Butters, & Thal, 1989). The DRS was primarily designed to be sensitive to individual differences between dementing patients and provides a more substantial picture of the range and severity of impairment than, for example, the MMSE. Salmon and associates (1989) used this measure to discriminate between groups of patients with DAT and Huntington's disease (HD). Squire and his colleagues (Shimamura & Squire, 1989) have also used this test to screen for the presence of dementia in amnesic patients. The Severe Impairment Battery (SIB) of Saxton, McGonigle-Gibson, Swihart, V. J. Miller, and Boller (1990) is a similar measure employing simplified versions of neuropsychological tests used with less impaired patients. The SIB takes 20 to 30 minutes to administer and preliminary psychometric data are encouraging.

There are three other commonly used mental status scales each of which forms part of a more comprehensive set of assessment procedures. The Clifton Assessment Procedures for the Elderly (CAPE) contains the Cognitive Assessment Scale (CAS; Pattie & Gilleard, 1975), made up of 12 Orientation-information questions, and items testing reading, writing, recitation of the alphabet, and the ability to count quickly. There is also a psychomotor task that requires the subject to trace a path through a spiral maze without touching a number of small black circles scattered along the path. The Cambridge Mental Disorders of the Elderly Examination (CAMDEX) also contains a number of cognitive tests (CAMCOG; Roth et al., 1986) designed to assess the extent and severity of cognitive impairment in the elderly. CAMCOG consists of the items of the MMSE and additional items testing perception, remote and recent memory, and recognition and recall of newly learned information. CAMCOG is highly correlated with the MIC (-.7) and with clinicians' ratings of severity (-.83; Roth et al., 1986). A third measure is the Alzheimer's Disease Assessment Scale (ADAS), which was designed to assess the symptoms most frequently seen in patients with DAT. It includes brief subtests assessing memory, language, orientation, and constructional skills, as well as rating scales for depression, agitation, psychosis, and vegetative signs (W. G. Rosen, Mohs, & K. L. Davis, 1984). Administration time with demented patients takes about 45 minutes and the reliability of the scale has been found to be high.

Finally, an entirely different approach to assessing cognitive decline in the elderly has been proposed by Jorm and Korten (1988). Jorm and his colleagues (Jorm, R. Scott, & Jacomb, 1989) developed a brief 26-item questionnaire, which can be used with an informant to determine whether any noticeable changes in a patient's cognitive skills have occurred. The emphasis is on the assessment of the changes in the subject's memory and intellect over the past 10 years. The scale has a high degree of internal consistency and correlates highly (.78) with MMSE scores in demented patients (Jorm et al., 1989). The informant interview offers a useful alternative or supplement to objective mental status tests.

Summary. Mental status questionnaires vary in their length and the range of abilities sampled. The DRS, ADAS, and CAMCOG provide the most detailed output, but still fall short of providing the depth and breadth of information that would emerge from a detailed neuropsychological assessment. Mental status testing is most validly used for the detection of moderately impaired patients or for the quantification of global capacity reduction in patients in the moderately to severely impaired range. The items are not usually sufficiently taxing to separate intact and healthy elderly people from mildly demented patients. On the other hand, the items are often beyond the ability of the severely demented patient. Mental status testing often provides a useful initial screening procedure, but it is usually only a starting point for a more detailed evaluation.

Assessment of Behavior Problems

Behavioral disturbances and changes in personality are a common consequence of neurological diseases. Several studies, primarily with Alzheimer patients, have identified dementia-related behavioral problems as being both prevalent and stressful to caregivers (e.g., Baumgarten, R. Becker, & Gauthier, 1990; Swearer, Drachman, O'Donnell, & Mitchell, 1988; Teri, Borson, Kiyak, & Yamagishi, 1989). Much of this work is reviewed in Chapter 9; behavioral changes are especially associated with DAT. In Table 1.3 a representative selection of scales used to quantify behavior problems in dementia have been listed.

Table 1.3:   Scales Used for the Assessment of Behavioral and Personality Changes Associated With Dementia

Scale	Reference
Stockton Geriatric Rating Scale	Meer & I. A. Baker (1965)
Behavior Rating Scale	Gilleard & Pattie (1977)
Behavior and Mood Disturbance Scale	Greene et al. (1982)
Memory and Behavior Problem Checklist	S. H. Zarit et al. (1980)
Behavior Problem Checklist	Teri et al. (1989)
Dementia Behavior Disturbance Scale	Baumgarten et al. (1990)

The Memory and Problem Behavior Checklist (MPBC; S. H. Zarit, Reever, & Bach-Peterson, 1980) is perhaps the best known of these scales. A caregiver or informant is asked to rate the frequency of occurrence of 29 potential problem behaviors or signs of cognitive deterioration in their demented relative or patient. Dura, Bornstein, and Kiecolt-Glaser (1990), using a principal components analysis, found that the scale decomposed into eight significant factors, yielding in turn three higher-order factors: self-care and self-maintenance functions; memory problems and psychiatric symptoms associated with dementia; and communication problems and agitation. High positive correlations were found between level of adaptive functioning and dementia severity, and the frequency of problems on the MPBC.

Another scale designed to be administered in an interview format is the 28-item Dementia Behavior Disturbance scale (Baumgarten et al., 1990). The scale has been shown to be reliable, and the items focus specifically on behaviors; there are no items assessing cognition or mood directly. The most common behavioral symptoms reported in the initial validation study were repetitive questioning, losing or hiding things, nocturnal wakefulness, unwarranted accusations, and excessive daytime sleeping. Greene et al.'s (1982) Behavior and Mood Disturbance (BMD) scale samples a broader range of symptoms (emotional, behavioral, and psychopathological) using an informant interview rating procedure. Factor analysis of the BMD has identified three subscales that can be scored separately: Apathetic-withdrawn; Active-disturbed; and Mood Disturbance.

Teri et al. (1989) used a checklist (the Behavior Problems Checklist) to survey 56 DAT patients' and their caregivers to determine the frequency of 48 emotional and behavioral problems. Informants were asked to rate each item on a five-point frequency scale and Teri and colleagues found that the items with the highest rate of occurrence were: loss of memory, confusion, and disorientation. Neither occurrence nor duration of the problems was related to level of cognitive impairment as assessed by the DRS (Mattis, 1976).

One of the older scales that has been influential is the 31-item Stockton Geriatric Rating Scale (GRS; Meer & I. A. Baker, 1965), which was originally developed for use with elderly patients at the Stockton Hospital in California. Ratings of patients behavioral deficits can be reliably made by staff using this measure. Four subscale scores can also be determined: physical disability, apathy, communication failure, and socially irritating behavior. A shortened 18-item version was normed for use in the United Kingdom by Gilleard and Pattie (1977). This form of the GRS was subsequently included in the CAPE battery as the Behavior Rating Scale. The four subscales of the original version have been retained and can be scored independently.

Assessment of Adaptive Functioning Level

A number of scales have been constructed that are devoted largely, or in part, to the assessment of the functional skills of demented patients. The content of such scales is typically focused on both self-care and instrumental skills (such as the ability to use the telephone or prepare a meal). Decline in instrumental skills tends to be related to cognitive deterioration and to be an early problem in demented patients (Teri et al., 1989). Loss of self-care skills and deterioration in manners, on the other hand, tend to occur at a later stage in the disease. Adaptive functioning is typically assessed either by informant interview or by observing the patient complete a series of standard behavioral tests.

Rating Scales. The Instrumental Activities of Daily Living (IADL; Fillenbaum & Smyer, 1981) is an example of the informant interview approach to determining adaptive level. The IADL is comprised of 15 items, 8 that measure instrumental skills and 7 that measure self-care skills (eating, dressing, personal hygiene, walking, bathing, toileting, and continence). Each activity is rated on a three-point scale (0 = unable, 1 = some help needed, 2 = able to perform without help). The scale has good reliability and validity, is easy to use, and the clear distinction between self-care and instrumental skills is useful.

Other informant-based interview schedules that focus on functional skills include the Index of Independence in the Activities of Daily Living (Katz, Ford, Moskowitz, Jackson, & Jaffe, 1963), the rating section of the Blessed DS, and the Performance Activities of the Daily Living Scale (Kuriansky & Gurland, 1976). The Crichton Geriatric Behavior Rating Scale (Cole, 1989) and the Physical and Mental Impairment-of-Function Evaluation in the aged (PAMIE; Gurel, M. W. Linn, & B. S. Linn, 1972) also contain items relating to self-care and other adaptive skills, but these are presented together with items assessing psychiatric disturbance, affective symptoms, and behavior problems. Some further scales that include items that can be used to assess functional status are the Geriatric Rating Scale of Plutchik, Conte, Lieverman, Bakur, Grossman, and Lehrman (1970), the Sandoz Clinical Assessment-Geriatric (SCAG; Shader, Harmatz, & Salzman, 1974), and the Rapid Disability Rating Scale-2 (M. W. Linn & B. S. Linn, 1982). The Plutchik et al. scale was developed at the Bronx State Hospital. It consists of 31 items rated on a three-point frequency scale, and the content focuses on self-care, behavior problems, and instrumental skills. The Rapid Disability Rating Scale-2 is a revision of an earlier form, and assesses self-care skills, degree of disability (communication, continence, sensory problems), and degree of special problems (confusion, depression, and cooperativeness). The scale is quick, reliable, and valid, and has been used in pharmacological trials. The SCAG was primarily constructed as a brief rating scale for use in geriatric pharmacology research. Judges are asked to rate 18 symptoms on a seven-point scale. Factor analysis has revealed four factors that describe the content of the scale: Cognitive Dysfunction, Mood-Depression, Agitation-Irritability; Withdrawal-Apathy (Overall, 1989).

Performance Tests. Another approach is to test patients' skills directly using standardized performance tasks. Skurla, J. C. Rogers, and Sunderland (1988) described four role-playing procedures, which they used to compare the functional abilities of DAT and healthy subjects. The situations they employed were: dressing for a cold and wet day; making a cup of instant coffee; telephoning to find out pharmacy hours; and using money to purchase a snack and a pair of gloves. In each case the role-play was initiated using appropriate props and standard prompts. Scoring involved breaking the four situations down into a series of subtasks (there were 11 for telephone task), each of which was scored on a 0-4 scale depending on the degree of prompting required. Performance by the DAT patients on this measure of instrumental skill correlated with cognitive skill and with rated severity of disease. The Direct Assessment of Functional Status (DAFS) is a similar performance-based procedure (Loewenstein et al., 1989), but tests a wider range of abilities. To give some idea of the possible range of skills assessed by a functional measure, the content of the items of the DAFS are presented in Table 1.4. Loewenstein and colleagues presented evidence of satisfactory reliability and validity for the DAFS, including a correlation of .59 with scores on the Blessed Dementia Scale.

Summary. Behavioral tests of functioning have several important advantages over interview-based scales. They test functional capacity directly in domains of performance that are relevant to clients' everyday life. The skills tested tend to be ones that are not biased by cultural, language, educational, or social factors. The deficits revealed by a test like the DAFS permit the formulation of appropriate goals for rehabilitation or behavioral intervention and performance of the various tasks is likely to be sensitive to changes over time. However, testing in this manner is likely to be time-consuming, and under many circumstances information from caregivers may be a more efficient means of evaluating functional status. It is, however, prudent to bear in mind that actual level of skill at home may be masked by the patient's apathy, depression, or poor motivation, and appraisal by caregivers can be unintentionally distorted or misperceived by the interviewer. Direct assessment in the clinic, with appropriate support and encouragement, can lessen the likelihood that failure will be wrongly attributed to actual loss of skill, rather than to interpersonal or motivational problems.

Table 1.4: **Activities Assessed in the Direct Assessment of Functional Status (DAFS; Loewenstein et al., 1989)**

Time orientation (16 points)
        Telling the time from clock model
        Orientation to date

Communication (14 points)
        Use of push-button telephone
        Preparation of letter for mailing

Transportation (13 points)
        Response to roadsigns

Financial (21 points)
        Identification of currency
        Counting out change
        Writing a check
        Balancing checkbook

Shopping (16 points)
        Memory for grocery items (delayed recall)
        Selecting groceries
        Checking change

Grooming (14 points)
        Brushing teeth
        Washing face
        Brushing hair
        Putting on coat
        Adjusting clothes

Eating (10 points)
        Use of utensils
        Pouring water, drinking from glass

Comprehensive Diagnostic Interview Schedules

There are several interview-based schedules that have been developed primarily for the detection of dementia in community surveys of the elderly, as well as in clinical examinations. The Geriatric Mental State (GMS; Copeland et al., 1976) is one such interview measure. The GMS is a semi-structured interview based largely on items from the Present State Examination (Wing, J. E. Cooper, & Sartorius, 1970) and Spitzer, Fleiss, Burdock, and Hardesty's (1964) Present Status Schedule, and intended for use in classifying and describing psychopathology in elderly people. The GMS was used in the US/UK diagnostic project, which compared the prevalence of mental disorders amongst the elderly in New York and London. The interview takes 30 to 40 minutes to complete and has been shown to be a valid method of separating patients with organic brain disorders from those with functional psychoses; however, it does not provide a distinction between dementias of different etiologies. A computer program providing a diagnostic formulation on the basis of GMS ratings (AGECAT) has also been developed. A shorter 40-item version of the GMS has been constructed and its reliability and validity as a diagnostic tool found to be acceptable (Henderson, Duncan-Jones, & Finlay-Jones, 1983).

The Comprehensive Assessment and Referral Evaluation (CARE; Gurland, Kuriansky, Sharpe, Simon, Stiller, & Birkett, 1977) is a substantial development of the GMS and is similarly designed for use in community surveys. The scale has a broad scope. It covers psychiatric-emotional, medical, nutritional, economic, and social difficulties making it suitable for a wide range of uses in the assessment of geriatric patients. The CARE semi-structured interview is lengthy, taking some 90 minutes to complete on average. The format used in the PSE and GMS has been retained, with mandatory questions being followed by contingent questions as necessary. The schedule is designed for administration by a trained interviewer and covers a wide variety of issues relevant to people over the age of 65. The diagnostic emphasis is on distinguishing pervasive dementia from other psychiatric conditions, and there is evidence that it can be applied in a reliable manner (Gurland, Dean, Copeland, Gurland, & Golden, 1982). It is, however, a broad-based measure, and cognition and behavior problems relevant to dementing disorders are covered in less depth than would be required under some circumstances (Overall, 1989).

CAMDEX, which its authors (Roth et al., 1986) describe as "a standardized instrument for the diagnosis of mental disorder in the elderly with special reference to the early detection of dementia" (p. 698), is a comprehensive examination with a more detailed focus on dementia than the CARE scale. CAMDEX consists of three sections: "(1) A structured clinical interview with the patient to obtain systematic information about the present state, past history and family history; (2) a range of objective cognitive tests that constitute a mini-neuropsychological battery; (3) a structured interview with a relative or other informant to obtain independent information about the respondent's present state, past history and family history" (Roth et al., 1986, p. 698). Section 2 is CAMCOG, which was introduced in the discussion of mental status testing. CAMDEX incorporates a scale for differentiating DAT from multi-infarct dementia (MID) the Hachinski ischemic score (Hachinski et al., 1975) and the rating section of the Blessed DS. CAMDEX takes about 80 minutes to administer (Huppert & Tym, 1986), is reliable, and can be used in community survey research.

Staging Scales

There are two scales that are widely used primarily to quantify severity of dementia and to provide a classification of patients in terms of the stage of the disease. These scales are designed for use with patients who have a primary dementing disorder such as DAT, but they could be appropriately applied to most patients with evidence of cognitive impairment. There are, however, specific staging scales available for other degenerative disorders, for example the Hoehn and Yahr (1967) scale for categorizing patients with Parkinson's disease, which target the particular symptoms of the disorder more precisely.

The Clinical Dementia Rating (CDR; Berg, 1984, 1988; Berg, Hughes, Coben, Danziger, R. L. Martin, & Knesevich, 1982) instructs clinicians to consider severity of impairment on six dimensions: Memory, orientation, judgment and problem solving, community affairs, hobbies and home, and personal care. After a semistructured interview focusing on these areas, an overall level of impairment is provided on the following scale: 0 = no impairment; 0.5 = questionable; 1 = mild; 2 = moderate; 3 = severe. The Global Deterioration Scale (GDS) developed by Reisberg and his colleagues (e.g., Reisberg, Ferris, deLeon, & Crook, 1982, 1988) is a similar measure. This scale has also been widely used to classify patients with primary degenerative dementia, particularly those with DAT. There are seven stages ranging from 1 (no cognitive decline) to 7 (very severe cognitive decline), and patients are assigned an impairment rating following an interview evaluation of memory, orientation, and instrumental self-care skills. The reliability of the categorizations based on the CDR and GDS has been found to be high and both have been widely used in research work to define disease severity in patients with Alzheimer's disease. Both these scales are discussed further in Chapter 4.

Conclusions

The accurate assessment of patients with degenerative brain diseases is critical to their management. It should be emphasized that much of this process of evaluation does not involve formal testing. A great deal of information is gathered from the client, family, and other sources by means of interviews and informal observation. In particular, understanding the psychological and social effects of the disease necessitates a review of the patient's coping resources and insight, and the effectiveness with which the family is coping with the stress of caring for someone with a chronic disease. These issues are discussed in later chapters. At this stage, however, it is important to bear in mind that the use of the formal tests and measures described in this chapter takes place against a background of less structured, but equally important, informal assessment procedures.

The selection of tests to be administered to clients in clinical practice and research depends on how the results will be used and the severity of client's impairment. This is an obvious statement to make, but it is surprising how little thought is sometimes given to the objectives of testing individual patients. For instance, if the aim is to provide data of use for the rehabilitation or management of a client with memory loss, then it is important to locate measures that will best suit this purpose. If the aim is to detect a deficit, then it is vital to employ tests sufficiently sensitive to do so. For example, as discussed in Chapter 5, bed-side mental status testing is not an effective method of detecting cognitive deficits in many people who have multiple sclerosis. The sensitivity and discriminatory power of a particular test needs to be considered in relation to the severity of an individual client's impairments.

In this chapter numerous scales that have been constructed to detect and measure cognitive, behavioral, emotional, and psychiatric changes in patients with varying degrees of dementia have been reviewed. Most have been validated on patients with Alzheimer's disease, but can be used with clients who have dementia arising from other diseases. Mental status tests are widely used in the assessment of dementing clients. These vary considerably in complexity and the lengthier scales tend to be abbreviated neuropsychological test batteries. Shorter scales, like the MMSE, tend to be relatively ineffective in detecting dementia in the early stages, and where dementia is suspected on clinical grounds, more detailed neuropsychological testing of cognitive functioning is usually warranted. This is the focus of Chapter 2.

In addition to the assessment of cognitive status, there is an increasing emphasis on quantification of changes in the dementing patient's adaptive functioning. Frequently, it is the behavioral and emotional changes that provide the greatest challenges to case management. In most cases, systematic evaluation of these changes and the client's actual level of functioning are important factors in the practical business of planning for a patient's care.

Chapter 2

NEUROPSYCHOLOGICAL ASSESSMENT

The psychological assessment techniques currently available for the elderly are open to criticism. They are often too difficult, too long, and too stressful—exposing the patient to many failures. They emphasize deficits rather than abilities, contain inappropriate material, and are too insensitive to change. (Woods, 1982, p. 93)

Although the last decade has seen the publication of many new and improved neuropsychological tests for use with elderly, it is perhaps apposite to begin this chapter with Woods's (1982) rather chastening comment. From the perspective of the elderly or impaired patient, testing may be a stressful and unnecessary intrusion on their time. Many patients with chronic degenerative diseases have short attention spans and are easily fatigued, and several testing sessions may be necessary to administer a test like the WAIS. In clinical practice, the necessity for the administration of a comprehensive neuropsychological battery needs to be considered in terms of the possible distress to the client and the usefulness of the outcome. Savage, Britton, Bolton, and Hall (1973) provided an interesting commentary on the response of some 1,000 healthy community-dwelling elderly people to being administered the WAIS subtests. They tested their subjects in their homes rather than in the clinic, and noted that testing often took three to four sessions to complete. Administration of neuropsychological tests to the elderly requires patience and sensitivity.

In what follows, some of the neuropsychological tests used in clinical practice and research studies are reviewed. The objective is to introduce these measures; it is beyond the scope of this chapter to consider the full range of neuropsychological tests available. The interested reader is referred to Lezak (1983).

Intelligence

Loss of intellectual power is a common consequence of brain disease. Neuropsychological assessment of the patient with a degenerative neurological condition often incorporates the administration of an individual intelligence test. The most widely used measure of intelligence is the

Wechsler Adult Intelligence Scale (WAIS) and the revised version, the WAIS-R. Scores from the WAIS and WAIS-R are featured throughout this book. Recently J. J. Ryan, Paola, and Brungardt (1990) prepared normative WAIS-R IQ tables for persons over the age of 75. Results from 130 healthy volunteers are presented for the age ranges 75-79 and 80 and above. These norms provide an important supplement to those available in the WAIS-R manual, which extend only to the age of 74. J. J. Ryan et al. sounded one note of warning: "The lowest IQ's for the elderly are 55 on the Verbal Scale, 64 on the Performance Scale, and 52 on the Full Scale. . . . This limited floor effect suggests that the total WAIS-R will not provide a meaningful evaluation of many persons with moderate to severe dementia" (p. 410). They suggested that mental status questionnaires may be more appropriate measures of intellectual functioning with such patients.

The Wechsler intelligence scales will be familiar to most clinicians working with neurological patients. Lezak (1983) prepared a thorough discussion of the accumulated clinical and interpretative material available for these tests. However, the use of the WAIS-R in clinical practice to test for acquired organic impairment in cases of suspected neurological damage requires some introduction. At issue is the interpretation of the pattern of subtest or IQ-scale scores as evidence of intellectual deterioration.

The output from a standardized test of intelligence is essentially a score that reflects current level of functioning relative to some appropriate normative group; the score itself cannot be directly used to infer any change of functioning. If someone has an IQ score of 112, there is no way of knowing from the score itself whether this represents some diminution of intellect or whether they have always had an IQ at that level. To establish the presence of an acquired deficit, it is necessary to compare the present score with some indication of past or premorbid functioning. This is often very difficult. On rare occasions, a patient has had a previous assessment in the course of military service or education. More commonly, however, it is necessary to estimate premorbid functioning indirectly. In contrast, although mental status tests lack sensitivity, they are more readily interpreted in terms of acquired impairment. This is a consequence of constructing items set at a difficulty level that is unlikely to result in failure for the majority of healthy individuals; most people can draw intersecting pentagons or remember three items. Thus failure on any item, and certainly failure on several items, raises the question of impairment. The WAIS-R subtests are made of items with a range of difficulty levels and so failure on any particular item does not necessarily imply deficit. There are a number of procedures that have been used for estimating premorbid Wechsler IQ scores;

none of which have proved to be entirely successful. The estimation of premorbid IQ is, however, of considerable significance when testing people with progressive degenerative diseases. It is important to be aware of the limitations of these commonly applied methods.

Use of Demographic Variables

On an informal basis, discrepancies between current IQ and past levels of achievement can provide evidence of impairment. A person with a college education and a professional employment history, who is found to have a current Full-Scale IQ (FSIQ) of 85, can reasonably be assumed to have suffered some decline in performance. However, usually the discrepancy is not that dramatic. Regression formulas for estimating premorbid IQ scores based on demographic characteristics have been developed for the WAIS (R. S. Wilson, Rosenbaum, G. Brown, Rourke, Whitman, & Grisell, 1978) and the WAIS-R (Barona, Reynolds, & Chastian, 1984; Eppinger, Craig, Adams, & Parsons, 1987). These formulas provide only approximate estimates. This is apparent from the large standard errors (Barona et al., 1984), 11.79 (Verbal IQ; VIQ), 13.23 (Performance IQ; PIQ), and 12.14 (FSIQ), and the low multiple correlations between actual and the estimated IQ scores: .38 (VIQ), .24 (PIQ), and .36 (FSIQ).

Furthermore, the regression weights for the predicted Wechsler scores were based on data from the U.S. standardization samples, and are of dubious value outside the United States. Even within the United States these formulas should be used cautiously. In a recent report, Sweet, Moberg, and Tovian (1990) found that the use of the Barona formulas to predict the IQ range of their subjects was no better than chance. They concluded that "in general, these formulas may be useful in research (i.e., matching subjects) or when cautiously used in conjunction with previous records (e.g., school or military). However, they should not be used in isolation with individual patients" (p. 43-44). Crawford, Stewart, Cochrane, Foulds, Besson, and Parker (1989) produced similar demographic regression equations for predicting WAIS IQ for use in the United Kingdom. The standard errors are in the range from 9 to 10, and like the Barona equations, these formulas should be applied cautiously.

Subtest/Test Comparison Methods

An alternative method of indirectly determining premorbid IQ is to base the estimate on the best performance achieved by the client during the testing process. Underlying this approach is the assumption that intelligence is a global capacity, reflected in the performance of a variety of tasks. Injury may influence abilities on some tasks, but not others, and consequently scores on those tasks that produce the best performance are an indication of the past intellectual capacity of an impaired client. One approach is to look at the scatter of WAIS-R subtest scores. For example, a patient may have scores of 15 on the vocabulary subtest and 16 on both Information and Comprehension, but an overall IQ of 92 because of low scores on most of the performance subtests. In this case the high subtest scores suggest that the patient was functioning at a much higher level in the past than suggested by the current score of 92.

Examination of subtest scatter and the use of the best subtest performance to estimate premorbid IQ is fraught with problems. Most of these arise from the unreliability of the subtest scores; measurement is not perfectly accurate, so large differences between subtest scores can be expected on the basis of measurement error alone (for a more detailed discussion of the standard errors of WAIS-R indices see Brophy 1986; R. G. Knight, 1983; Kramer, 1990). R. G. Knight and Godfrey (1984a) and Kramer (1990) prepared tables for interpreting differences between subtest scores that, if used cautiously, provide some indication of the statistical reliability of subtest scatter. Matarazzo and Prifitera (1989), however, drew attention to the considerable subtest scatter that occurs in normal healthy volunteers. They examined subtest scatter in the WAIS-R standardization sample, and found that the average discrepancy between the highest and lowest subtest scores was 6.7 points. They also discovered that the amount of scatter increased with increases in IQ level; Subjects with higher IQ's tended to have larger subtest discrepancies than those with lower IQ scores. Matarazzo and Prifitera (1989) issued the following warning:

> We hope that (our data) will underscore for clinicians the need for caution in interpreting scatter to determine premorbid IQ. In isolation and without other corroborating evidence, a finding of a sizable degree of scatter in a WAIS-R record cannot be used ipso facto either (a) to estimate (using the highest scale scores) the examinee's supported "premorbid" level of intellectual function or (b) to identify areas (using the lowest scale scores) of current cognitive impairment. (p. 191)

Comparing sets of aggregated WAIS-R subtest scores is a more robust method of detecting IQ deterioration. This is primarily because a score resulting from the combination of a number of subtests is likely to be more reliable than the score from any one subtest. The most obvious contrast is between the verbal and performance IQ scale scores (VIQ-PIQ differences). Tables for assessing these differences have been published elsewhere (R. G. Knight, 1983). In routine clinical practice it is worth bearing in mind that relatively large discrepancies are to be expected in healthy nonimpaired individuals. Ten percent of normal elderly people in the age range 70-74 years have VIQ-PIQ discrepancies of 19, 5% of 23, and 1% of 30. In addition, there is a factor that confounds the interpretation of VIQ-PIQ differences in the demented elderly: In these patients, WAIS-R subtest scores are often uniformly depressed, so that as the disease progresses, and the dementia becomes more pronounced, VIQ-PIQ discrepancies may actually diminish.

Another method of aggregating subtests is on the basis of factor analysis. The WAIS-R standardization sample data have been submitted to several factor analytic investigations (e.g., N. C. Beck, Horwitz, Seidenberg, Parker, & Frank, 1985; O'Grady, 1983; J. J. Ryan, Rosenberg, & De Wolfe, 1984; Waller & Waldman, 1990). Various factor solutions have been proposed; the differences in the outcome are largely attributable to the variations in the techniques and assumptions used. Waller and Waldman (1990) concluded that a three-factor solution may best account for the relationship between the WAIS-R subtests. Their solution is much the same as that proposed by J. Cohen (1952) for the Wechsler-Bellevue and WAIS. The following are the three factors, with the subtest factor loadings in parentheses.

Factor 1   *Verbal Comprehension*: Information (.86), Vocabulary (.92), Comprehension (.81), Similarities (.79)

Factor 2   *Perceptual Organization*: Picture Completion (.74), Picture Arrangement (.66), Block Design (.78), Object Assembly (.69)

Factor 3   *Freedom from Distraction*: Digit Span (.66), Arithmetic (.81), Digit Symbol (.61)

Another means of predicting premorbid Wechsler IQ scores in dementing patients is to test an ability unlikely to be severely affected by dementia. An example of the application of this procedure is the National Adult Reading Test (NART; H. E. Nelson, 1982). Here the subject is asked to read aloud 50 words with irregular pronunciation (thyme, ache). The ability to pronounce words correctly is not lost until a late stage in dementia and underlying this procedure is the assumption that the number of pronunciation errors reflects past learning capability or intelligence. There are a number of limitations with this method. A regression method is used to estimate premorbid WAIS IQ scores with a sizeable standard error of prediction of 9.4 for PIQ, and 7.6 for VIQ. The range of possible estimated IQ scores does not extend beyond a maximum of 128 and a minimum of 86. It is important to be aware that it is WAIS IQs that are predicted, not WAIS-R, so differences between current IQ (based on the WAIS-R) and premorbid IQ (based on NART WAIS estimates) are likely to be misleading. The NART also depends on subjects having had the opportunity to learn the words in the past, and it may therefore be sensitive to educational background and related social economic factors. Crawford, Stewart, Cochrane, Foulds, Besson, and DeLacy (1989) combined the original NART standardization sample data with results from a cross-validation study to provide revised regression equations for WAIS IQ estimates. These new formulas should be substituted for those provided in the test manual.

From the previous discussion it becomes apparent that no satisfactory way of estimating premorbid IQ from current functioning is available for use with clients suspected of dementia. Clinical judgment and the combination of data from several sources is necessary in the application of any procedures already discussed. One of the most useful functions of WAIS-R testing in clinical practice may be in comparing changes in scores with repeated testing. Any downward drift of IQ scores of a reasonable magnitude (four or more IQ points) is likely to be indicative of deterioration: Repeated testing of healthy volunteers even after a lengthy retest interval usually results in an increase in performance attributable to practice effects.

Finally, where testing of intelligence is limited by the time available or patient fatigue is an issue, short-forms of the WAIS-R are often administered. A number of 4- and 2-subtest versions of the WAIS-R have been proposed (Cyr & Brooker, 1984; Silverstein, 1982). Clinicians may choose to administer only those parts of the WAIS-R that are likely to give a true reflection of the patient's ability. For example, as discussed in Chapter 6, administering subtests that require manual dexterity to patients with Parkinson's disease is likely to lead to a substantial underestimate of their global cognitive abilities. Another method of shortening the WAIS was proposed by Satz and Mogel (1962). This involves administering every third item of the Vocabulary and Picture Completion subtests (starting with the usual introductory item), and every odd item on the remaining subtests. The subtests scores are then multiplied by three or two to produce an equivalent scaled score. IQ scores can be determined in the usual manner. Osato, Van Gorp, Kern, Satz, and Steinman (1989) compared full WAIS-R scores with Satz-Mogel scores and reported encouraging evidence for the usefulness of this short-form with demented elderly patients.

Memory

The memory performance of patients with degenerative disorders has been extensively studied. A number of the standardized scales and clinical procedures that have been widely used are featured in the chapters that follow and these are introduced here.

Memory Tests

Wechsler Memory Scale (WMS). Without a doubt the WMS (Wechsler, 1945) has been the most widely used measure of memory performance in clinical research and practice. In a survey of studies with Korsakoff patients, R. G. Knight and B. E. Longmore (1991) found that this measure was the most commonly used test for documenting severity of impairment in amnesics. The long-awaited revision, the WMS-R, will certainly occupy an important place in memory assessment in the future.

The WMS is comprised of several subtests: Information and Orientation, Mental Control, Logical Memory, Digit Span, Visual Reproduction, and Paired Associate Learning. Subtest scores are combined to produce an age-corrected Memory Quotient (MQ), which has come to be an important criterion for defining degree of anterograde amnesia in research. The difference between (WAIS) FSIQ and MQ has also been employed as a means of determining degree of impairment and the specificity of an acquired memory defect. A large IQ-MQ discrepancy (in excess of 12-15 points) suggests that memory decline has occurred relative to a preserved intellectual capacity. For example, the famous amnesic H. M. has an IQ of 112 (comparable to his premorbid IQ), but an MQ of 67, a very large discrepancy, strongly suggestive of a profound and circumscribed amnesia. Comparison of MQ and IQ scores is based on the assumption that they are highly correlated and memory loss can occur without a concurrent decline in intelligence. These assumptions tend to be generally tenable.

There have been a number of major reviews of the WMS (D'Elia, Satz, & Schretlen, 1989; Erickson & M. L. Scott, 1977; Prigatano, 1977) and the problems with this scale are well-known. Norms from the initial standardization sample of 200 subjects aged between 25 and 50 were described as preliminary nearly 50 years ago. Since then, supplementary normative data have been reported (see D'Elia et al., 1989), but are not easy to use systematically. There is also a composite set of WMS norms in Lezak (1983). Further difficulties include the absence of any cross-validation for the regression equations used for the derivation of the MQ values and the range of skills tested by the WMS tends to be restricted.

There are also major problems with using the IQ-MQ index. The distribution of the index is not known, and the magnitude of the difference that distinguishes memory-impaired from normal subjects is largely a matter of opinion. The recent publication of the WAIS-R raises further difficulties and it is clear that comparing a WAIS-R FSIQ with an MQ from the WMS is invalid (Prifitera & Barley, 1985).

The WMS and MQ scores reappear in subsequent chapters and an appreciation of their limitations is important. The new WMS-R (Wechsler, 1987) corrects many of the faults of its predecessor and is likely to become the standard memory test for research and clinical purposes, at least for patients under the age of 75. Improvements to the WMS in the revised version include the addition of extra items in the Information/Orientation subtest, elimination of the speed bonus from Mental Control, and minor revisions to the Digit Span and Logical Memory subtests. Three new subtests have been added : Figural Memory, which assesses recognition of abstract visual patterns; Visual Paired-Associates (a visual analog of the Verbal Paired-Associates); and Visual Memory Span (a visual test corresponding to the Digit Span subtest). Some revisions have also been made to the Associate Language (which is now the Verbal Paired-Associates subtest) and Visual Reproduction subtests. A major innovation is the introduction of a delayed recall trial for Logical Memory, Visual Paired-Associates, Verbal Paired-Associates, and Visual Reproduction. The scoring procedures for Logical Memory and Visual Reproduction have been extensively revised, and are far more detailed and easy to use. Rather than a single MQ, there are five composite scores derived from the various subtests that have been scaled to have a mean of 100 and standard deviation of 15. These are labeled: General Memory, Attention and Concentration, Verbal Memory, Visual Memory, and Delayed Recall. Information and orientation scores are presented separately.

The standardization sample was chosen "to represent the normal population of the United States" (Wechsler, 1987, p. 43) and the norms are more acceptable than those available for the WMS. However, the standardization sample was made up of 50 cases in each of 6 age groups, but for 3 age ranges "ages 18-19, 25-34, and 45-54, norms were derived by an estimation procedure" (Wechsler, 1987, p. 43). Therefore, although the norms have been presented in the manual for 9 age ranges from 16 to 74, an interpolation process was used for 3 of the age groups. It is important to note that the upper age limit of 74 places a restriction on the use of the test with many elderly patients. Finally, Wechsler (1987) drew attention to the fact that the average IQ of the standardization sample was 103.9 and noted that "it is likely that the norms developed for the WMS-R are anchored at a slightly higher level than would be ideal; however, the effect is of a relatively low magnitude (.26 SD units) and is judged not to be of practical or clinical significance" (p. 49).

Atkinson (1991) calculated the magnitude of the discrepancies between WMS-R indices and WAIS-R IQ scales scores necessary to reach statistical significance. This allows the clinician to assess change in memory performance relative to IQ in much the same way as IQ-MQ differences were used previously. For people in the age range 55-74, the size of the difference between the WMS-R General Memory Index and WAIS-R FSIQ necessary to reject the hypothesis that difference is entirely due to measurement error is in the range 12-15 points. Atkinson noted that differences in the normative samples between the two tests and the fact that the statistical procedure used to calculate the significance of the differences does not take account of possible regression effects limit the accuracy of these computations. Nevertheless, these results provide a useful guide to clinical decisions.

Further validation research for the WMS-R is beginning to emerge (Butters et al., 1988; Loring, Lee, Martin, & Meador, 1989) Loring et al. (1989) found that the Verbal and Visual Memory indices did not predict side of lesion following unilateral temporal lobectomy and expressed caution about making inferences about the laterality of damage on the basis of WMS-R index scores.

Selective Reminding Procedure (SRP). The SRP does not have a standard set of items or set number of trials, and differs in its application from the usual serial word list learning test. The SRP requires the examiner to only remind the subject of those words not recalled on the immediately preceding trial (except, of course, on the first trial, when the full list is presented; (Buschke, 1973; Buschke & Fuld, 1974). As Kraemer, Peabody, Tinklenberg, and Yesavage (1983) noted, the structure of the test is based on a three-stage learning model. Items on the test can be either nonencoded (in which case they will not be recalled), in an intermediate stage where they are sometimes recalled without reminding, or in long-term storage, from where they can be recalled without reminding. The SRP has been used extensively with clinical subjects, including patients with dementia (e.g., Kraemer et al., 1983).

Ruff, Light, and M. Quayhagen (1988) provided norms for two alternate 12-item SRP forms. The normative sample comprised 202 female and 190 male volunteers with an average IQ of about 110, between the ages of 16 to 70 years. The lists were administered until either the 12 items had been recalled on two consecutive occasions, or 12 trials had elapsed. A further trial was administered after a one-hour delay. A similar set of four equivalent 12-word lists has been prepared by Hannay and H. S. Levin (1985). Selective reminding tests have definite appeal because they can be administered in a variety of forms to suit particular needs, and because they partition learning performance into separate components of memory. The validity of these components has, however, been questioned (Loring & Papanicolaou, 1987). Reliability estimates range from modest (.48 - .65; Hannay & H. S. Levin, 1985) to acceptable (.73; Ruff et al., 1988).

California Verbal Learning Test (CVLT). The test authors stated that the CVLT is "one of the first assessment instruments to quantify and provide normative data reflecting the multifactorial ways in which examinees learn, or fail to learn, verbal material" (Delis, Kramer, Kaplan, & Ober, 1986, p. iii). The normative sample for the research edition of this test consists of 273 healthy subjects ranging in age from 17 to 80. The test employs two shopping lists, A and B. List A is administered five times, followed by a trial with List B. Free and cued recall of A are then tested, and subsequently, after a 20-minute delay, free recall, cued recall, and recognition of List A are tested again. This process provides measures of recall and recognition, serial position effects, rate of learning, the effects of interference, indices of recognition performance, perseveration, intrusions in recall, and the use learning strategies.

There is good evidence for the validity of the various facets of learning performance assessed by this test and the clinical usefulness of the test has been demonstrated in studies with dementing patients (Delis, Freeland, Kramer, & Kaplan, 1988). The CVLT is undoubtedly the most comprehensive and best standardized of the verbal learning tests available. Although administration takes in the region of 45 minutes, it is a relatively straightforward test and patients with suspected or mild dementia can take it without distress.

Rey Auditory Verbal Learning Test (RAVLT). The best account of the RAVLT is provided by Lezak (1983). In structure it is similar to the CVLT. A list of 15 words is administered five times, a further trial is given with a different list of words, and then there is a sixth trial with the first list. This procedure allows assessment of memory span, serial position effects, interference, and rate of learning. The test takes about 10 to 15 minutes to administer and parallel versions have been prepared (Crawford, Stewart, & Moore, 1989; J. J. Ryan, Geisser, Randall, & Georgemiller, 1986). Some composite norms are available in Lezak (1983). Norms for elderly subjects (over age 55) have been prepared by

Ivnik, Malec, Tangalos, R. C. Peterson, Kokmen, and Kurland (1990). The RAVLT has been extensively used with brain injured subjects in research and is useful where a valid, sensitive, but quick measure of verbal learning is needed.

Russell's Version of Wechsler Memory Scale (RWMS). Prior to the publication of the WMS-R, a version of the WMS involving immediate and delayed recall of the Logical Memory and Visual Reproduction subtests was developed by E. W. Russell (1975, 1982). This procedure rapidly became a popular assessment tool in clinical research studies. Scores on the immediate and 30-minute delayed recall trials, and a measure of percentage retained, are expressed in the terms of the average impairment rating derived from the Halstead-Reitan battery. Updated norms for the test have been provided by E. W. Russell (1988). The RWMS is a well accepted procedure. However, it is important to be aware that several varying criteria are in use for the scoring of the Logical Memory subtest (Loring & Papanicolaou, 1987), which differ from the procedures used by Wechsler (1945). The advent of the WMS-R with its published scoring criteria and more detailed norms is likely to render the use of the RWMS less common.

Other Memory Tests. Details of other commonly used memory assessment tests are provided by Lezak (1983) and Poon (1988). Table 2.1 describes a number of other tests used in research and practice with neurological patients. The Rey Figure Test is often employed in studies involving unilateral brain damage and is a useful adjunct to the RAVLT. One of the more recent additions to clinical testing is Warrington's (1984) Recognition Memory Test. This measure has the advantage of directly comparing verbal and nonverbal memory. The stimuli used are 50 words and 50 faces and after the presentation of each set of 50 items, a two-choice procedure is used to test recognition.

One of the few memory tests actually constructed for use with the elderly is the Kendrick Object Learning Test (KOLT). In combination with the Digit Copying Test, the KOLT forms a two-part measure (the Kendrick Cognitive Tests; Kendrick, 1985), designed to screen for dementia. The Kendrick tests are also useful for distinguishing between demented, depressed, and healthy elderly. Test cards with 10-25 line-drawings of common objects are exposed to the subject for a brief time and then recall tested. The norms extend from age 55 upward.

Table 2.1:   Additional Psychometric Tests Used to Assess Memory in Neurological Patients

---

Modified New Word Learning Test (Walton & Black, 1957)
  Ability to learning the means of 10 words unknown to the subject.

Recurring Figures Test (Kimura, 1963)
  Recognition of previously exposed geometric or irregular designs.

Benton Visual Retention Test (Benton, 1974)
  Immediate or delayed recall of geometric designs.

Rey Complex Figure Test (Osterreith, 1944)
  Immediate or delayed recall of a complex design.

Memory-for-Designs (Graham & Kendall, 1960)
  Immediate recall of 15 geometric figures.

Recognition Memory Test (RMT; Warrington, 1984)
  Two-choice recognition of 50 faces and 50 words.

Guild Memory Test (Crook, J. G. Gilbert, & Ferris, 1980)
  Test battery comprising measures of digit span, prose recall, paired-associate recall, and design recall. Prose and paired-associate retention is tested on immediate and delayed trials.

Fuld Object-Memory Evaluation (Fuld, 1981)
  Object learning using a selective reminding procedure.

Kendrick Object Learning Test (Kendrick, 1985)
  Recall of objects after brief exposure.

In the Fuld Object-Memory Evaluation, 10 common objects are given to the subject to identify both visually and tactually. A series of five recall trials are then administered using a selective reminding procedure. Each recall trial alternates with a 30 or 60s distraction task. Delayed recall and recognition are tested after a five-minute delay. La Rue (1989) investigated the usefulness of the test for distinguishing between depressed and dementing elderly patients. No selective pattern of deficits was identified that might help distinguish depressed from demented subjects, however, the demented patients tended to show more profound memory impairments. La Rue concluded,

> Overall, the outcomes indicated that the Object-Memory Evaluation is a useful test for characterizing and differentiating memory impairments in elderly inpatients. Its primary value is in distinguishing between depression and primary degenerative disorder, on a quantitative as opposed to qualitative basis, but it may also be useful in detecting the additive impairments which result from the coexistence of these conditions. (p. 421)

Practical Assessment of Memory

Neuropsychologists use standardized measures of memory performance to confirm the presence of an impairment and to give a preliminary indication of severity. However, tests like the WMS-R have their limitations. It is not easy to translate test scores into a form that conveys something useful to all the professionals involved in handling an individual case. It can also be difficult to communicate exactly what to expect from a patient, simply by quoting a set of test scores and their normative values. This is a consequence of the fact that most memory tests are not criterion referenced in a way that is particularly useful in case management. Even a neuropsychologist who is familiar with the WMS-R and the range of index scores will have difficulty answering detailed questions about a patient's actual ability to perform a particular task. Furthermore, the range of skills assessed by such tests is typically narrow and based on laboratory measures developed for experimental purposes.

There are, however, some more practical methods for assessing memory in clinical practice.

Self-report Memory Questionnaires. One noticeable difference between amnesics is the degree of insight or awareness they have of their problems. Many Korsakoff patients display a marked lack of awareness of (or indifference to) an often profound degree of memory loss. This is also typical of DAT patients, who often show little awareness of the true extent of their problems. The depressed elderly, in contrast, often show a different pattern. The number of memory and other cognitive complaints they report is often abnormally high, even when their actual test performance is close to normal (e.g., M. J. Feehan, R. G. Knight, & Partridge, 1990; Popkin, Gallagher, L. W. Thompson, & Moore, 1982).

A number of self-report memory questionnaires have been developed that assess patients' perception of their current abilities. They include the Subjective Memory Questionnaire (Bennett-Levy & Powell,

1980), the Cognitive Failures Questionnaire (Broadbent, P. F. Cooper, Fitzgerald, & Parkes, 1982; Sunderland, Harris, & Baddeley, 1983), and the Memory Assessment Clinics Self-rating Scale (Crook & Larrabee, 1990). Another recent measure is the Self-rating Scale of Memory Functions (Squire & Zouzounis, 1988). This is comprised of 18 items that ask subjects to compare their present ability with their ability before their "memory problems began" (p. 730). Typical items in this test are "My ability to search through my mind and recall names I know is . . ." and "My ability to recall things when I really try is . . ." Squire and Zouzounis found that depressed patients and depressed persons treated with electro-convulsive therapy (ECT) had an overall equivalent level of self-reported memory impairment. The depressed patients (not given ECT), however, showed a uniform degree of impairment across all the test items. Korsakoff and ECT-treated patients reported more severe difficulties on some items than on others. The KD patients tended to underestimate their memory problems relative to the control subjects.

Measures of subjective memory complaint have considerable limitations. There is something ironic about asking memory-impaired patients to remember the severity of their memory loss. Level of subjective cognitive complaint has often been found to be unrelated to actual level of impairment in the memory-impaired elderly (e.g., Sunderland et al., 1983). This is in part a consequence of the tendency of DAT patients to deny, mask, or appear unaware of the extent of their cognitive decline. Also, subjective questionnaires may tap the subject's sense of loss of function, which is dependent on level of premorbid ability, rather than absolute level of current memory functioning. Thus perceived memory loss and objective performance may be totally unrelated. Subjective memory questionnaires therefore are perhaps best used to assess awareness of self-perception of deficit. This often reveals clues about insight and may be important in separating depressed from demented patients, because depressed patients often have normal memory but a high degree of subjective complaint.

Practical Memory Tasks. Functional testing of memory is a direct and useful way of determining the practical limits of a patients memory skills. Tests relevant to an individual client's circumstances can often be devised . Such tests can serve to answer the kind of fundamental questions that need to be addressed in a rehabilitation program. Can patients carry out a set of simple instructions? Can patients find their way around a familiar route? Can patients draw a map of their living environment? Although such tests have no norms they effectively reveal that a patient is capable of doing in a familiar environment or learning in a new one. Over the years, it is apparent that clinicians have been moving toward using more face valid tests of memory deficits. The shopping list procedure used in CVLT is a compromise between practical and laboratory measures. It is worth remembering, however, that in real life most people write down lists: The important skill to test may be how a person responds to the need to remember a list. Learning a list by rote memory is something that has little ecological validity.

One of the best developed set of everyday memory problems is the Rivermead Behavioral Memory Test (RBMT; B. Wilson, Cockburn, Baddeley, & Hiorns, 1989). B. Wilson and her colleagues constructed a 12-item measure that has good face validity as a series of practical tests of memory, is reliable, and is sensitive to changes over time. A brief description of the 12 items is presented in Table 2.2. Four parallel forms of this test are available, and a version suitable for use with children is being prepared.

Crook and Larrabee (1988) described a set of computer-based memory tests designed to simulate learning and retention in everyday life. The subjects' responses can be recorded using a touchscreen and the visual stimuli used are stored and presented using laser disks. These procedures are most ingenious, and could be used in a variety of clinical settings. The test battery includes measures of:

Memory Span. This is tested by asking subjects to read aloud a telephone number and then dial it immediately on a telephone connected to the computer. Numbers of different lengths are presented successively. This is a test of memory span couched in functional terms (Crook, Ferris, McCarthy, & Rae, 1980).

Recall of Names and Faces. In this task, subjects are shown video recordings of actors introducing themselves stored on a disk. Recall is assessed by showing actors again, in a different order, and asking for the name of each individual. Testing is repeated after a 40-minute delay.

Detection of Repetition. A series of photographs of faces are presented on the computer monitor and the subject's task is to indicate whether the face has appeared earlier in the series. A delayed retesting takes place 40-minutes later.

Delayed Matching to Sample, Facial Recognition. In this procedure, starting with a single facial photograph, an additional face is added on each of 24 subsequent trials and the subject asked to identify the novel face.

Memory for Misplaced Objects. Subjects are asked to place the computer representations of 12 everyday objects somewhere in a computer simulation of the interior of a house. One object is placed in each room. The testing phase takes place 40-minutes later, and subjects are instructed to indicate the rooms in which they left the objects.

Narrative Recall. Subjects are asked to watch a 6-minute sequence of TV news and to respond to 25 multiple-choice questions.

Crook, Larrabee, and associates (Crook, Youngjohn, & Larrabee, 1990a, 1990b; Larrabee & Crook, 1989) have now assembled a considerable amount of evidence for the feasibility, reliability, and validity of computer-assisted memory testing with brain-impaired subjects.

Observation. Patient's impairments can also be documented using ratings made by family or ward staff. We have used this procedure with memory-impaired alcoholics (Inpatient Memory Impairment Scale; R. G. Knight & Godfrey, 1984b). Data from a group of alcoholic Korsakoff patients using this measure are presented in the next chapter. B. Wilson et al. (1989) outlined a similar measure called the Memory Checklist, which was designed for use with patients in a rehabilitation facility.

Remote Memory Tests

The assessment of retrograde amnesia involves asking patients to recall personal or public information about the past. Often this is done informally, for example, by asking patients to recall six presidents of the U.S. (Hamsher & Roberts, 1985). However, such procedures may not be especially sensitive when subjected to experimental scrutiny. Assessing recall of autobiographical information is often problematic because knowledge of the correctness of answers may not be available to the examiner. Standardized measures of remote memory typically employ questionnaire items about famous people or events (e.g., M. S. Albert, Butters, & J. Levin, 1979; Squire, 1974). Items may use simple recall (Who was Mary Jo Kopechene?) or multichoice recognition [Who was convicted of killing Martin Luther King, Jr? (a) James Ed Brown (b) Frank Lloyd Wright (c) Norman Vincent Peale (d) James Earl Ray]. Items specific to particular decades are selected and recall of public events over an extended period of the past can be tested.

Table 2.2:   Brief Description of the Items of the Rivermead Behavioral Memory Test (from B. Wilson et al., 1989)

Item	Brief Content
Name recall	Remembering the name of a person portrayed in a picture.
Hidden belonging	Delayed recall of the location of an item belonging to the patient hidden by the examiner.
Appointment	Delayed recall of an instruction (e.g., to arrange the next appointment).
Picture recognition	Two-choice delayed recognition of 10 line drawings.
Newspaper article	Immediate and delayed recall of a newspaper prose passage.
Face recognition	Two-choice delayed recognition five faces.
Memory for route (immediate)	Recall of the route around points in a room.
Memory for route (delayed)	Route recall after a 10-minute delay.
Message delivery	Picking up and delivering a message while retracing the route in the previous item.
Orientation	Test of orientation for time and place.
Date	Recall of present date.

There are many problems to overcome when constructing a remote memory test, including ensuring that learning about an event or person took place at a particular time, and only at that time. Some famous people have such enduring fame (or notoriety) that they are known to people who were not alive at the time when their fame was at its height. A question like "Who was Adolf Hitler?" is of little use in testing remote memory. It is hard to construct decade-specific subtests that contain homogeneous items and are of equal difficulty. This is important because if items from the 1920s are easier for healthy 70-year-olds to answer than items from the 1960s to 1980s, then misleading conclusions might be drawn about decline in remote memory. That is, it might look as if more distant memories were better preserved than more recent memories; if the subtests measuring recall of events from specific decades are not equally difficult, however, such a conclusion is unwarranted.

It is also hard to know whether people fail items because they were never exposed to the opportunity to learn about the content tested or because they have actually forgotten. Some people have no interest in sports and so they have never learned of bygone sporting legends. Information and remote memory tests do not transfer well from one country to another. For example, most North Americans would be unable to answer the question "Who was Hone Heke?", an item that features in a New Zealand version of the WAIS-R Information Subtest. Many English and Australian subjects have similar problems with the comparable American WAIS-R items.

Language

Disturbances in language function are a frequent consequence of the dementing process. Aphasia is commonly associated with the progression of Alzheimer's disease, but is also reported in patients with other degenerative conditions, notably Parkinson's disease and multiple sclerosis. Most comprehensive neuropsychological examinations of patients with dementing conditions involve some tests of the integrity of communication functions.

There are a variety of standardized procedures for the assessment of aphasia. Most of the aphasia tests comprise a collection of tasks designed to identify deficits in the patient's receptive and expressive language, nonverbal communication, reading, and writing. The different channels through which communications may be received, interpreted, and responded to, are systematically evaluated using a variety of standardized clinical tests. The difficulty level of these tests is typically within the scope of most people with suspected or mild to moderate levels of dementia. Comprehensive aphasia test batteries do, however, take some time to administer and may take multiple sessions to complete with elderly and impaired clients. Many neuropsychologists use selected subtests from such batteries or abbreviated measures in their routine testing practice. The in depth analysis of language function is often the province of speech therapists or speech pathologists, who have a detailed knowledge of aphasiology.

Table 2.3 lists some of the aphasia batteries and screening procedures in common use. One of the best-known of the aphasia batteries is the Boston Diagnostic Aphasia Examination. This measure provides a detailed evaluation of the communication skills of aphasic patients. The 34 subtests take at least an hour to administer and almost certainly longer with the demented elderly. The quantitative assessments are supplemented by a series of qualitative ratings of prosody, fluency, articulation, grammatical level, paraphrasia, and word-finding ability based on the tape-recorded sample of continuous free speech. The Boston Diagnostic Aphasia Examination was standardized on some 200 aphasics and the authors have related common aphasic syndromes to typical test profiles, enhancing its use as a diagnostic instrument. This measure provides the clinician with a detailed evaluation of communication dysfunction presented in terms of traditional nomenclature and diagnostic distinctions. The Western Aphasia Battery (Kertesz, 1979) is a development and extension of the Boston test.

Hildred Schuell's Minnesota Test for Differential Diagnosis of Aphasia (MTDDA) is the most systematic and lengthy aphasia battery in common use. It consists of some 47 subtests and testing time is said to range from 2 to 3 hours; with elderly patients testing is likely to be spread over several sessions. Unlike the Boston test, the emphasis in the MTDDA is not on the identification of the usual aphasic syndromes nor on the precise definition of the cognitive changes that have occurred. Instead, Schuell's intention was to construct a procedure that provides a diagnosis with prognostic validity. This diagnostic system involves classifying patients in terms of the severity of their language problems and their prospects for rehabilitation. This gives the test its major advantage: an emphasis on testing for active rehabilitation and case management. However, many clinicians find the length of testing time required and the unfamiliar classificatory system inconvenient.

Eisenson's (1954) Examining for Aphasia is now a rather dated test, although it does provide a thorough and flexible approach to testing communication skills. In contrast, the Porch Index of Communicative Abilities (PICA) measures a circumscribed range of language functions is highly standardized, precise, and reliable manner. Each of the 18 subtests of the PICA requires the use of the same 10 objects (key, fork, comb, etc.) and the resulting 180 test items can usually be administered in 60 to 120 minutes (Porch, 1971). Porch placed considerable emphasis on the careful training of the test administrator (at least 40 hours training is recommended). He concluded that "studies thus far indicate that, in the hands of a well-trained tester, this battery and the aphasic patients yield consistent results. Once the tester achieves reliability in his [her] administration and scoring, the tests are sensitive to small changes in the patient's performance" (p. 1).

Table 2.3:   Aphasia Batteries and Tests

Comprehensive Test Batteries

> Boston Diagnostic Aphasia Examination (Goodglass & Kaplan, 1972).
> Examining for Aphasia (Eisenson, 1954).
> Minnesota Test for the Differential Diagnosis of Aphasia (Schuell, 1972).
> Multilingual Aphasia Examination (Benton & Hamsher, 1976).
> Neurosensory Center Comprehensive Examination for Aphasia (Spreen & Benton, 1969).
> Porch Index of Communicative Ability (Porch, 1967).
> Western Aphasia Battery (Kertesz, 1979).

Screening Tests

> Aphasia Screening Test (Halstead & Wepman, 1959).
> Token Test (De Renzi & Vignolo, 1962).
> Very Short Version of the Minnesota Aphasia Test (Powell, Bailey, & E. Clark, 1980).

The Neurosensory Center Comprehensive Examination (NCCE; Spreen & Benton, 1969) has frequently been used in research with dementing patients. This battery is comprised of 24 brief and easily administered subtests. Although this test is not as sensitive to mild aphasic problems as some of the batteries considered earlier, it is useful with more impaired patients. The brevity and simplicity of the NCCE subtests makes it ideally suited for use with dementing patients. The Multilingual Aphasia Examination also comprises subtests that are often selected for use with dementing clients. In particular, the word fluency test (Controlled Oral Word Association) is often used independently.

Aphasia screening tests are often employed as part of a neuropsychological battery as a routine test of language. Although they do not provide a fine-grained analysis of communication skills, they may provide a preliminary indication of the presence of language deficits. The Aphasia Screening Test of Halstead and Wepman (1959) is one such measure. Developed as part of the Halstead-Reitan Neuropsychological Test Battery, the Halstead-Wepman Scale comprises 51 items and can usually be administered in 30 to 60 minutes. The Token Test (De Renzi & Vignolo, 1962) is simple to administer and a particularly sensitive measure of linguistic dysfunctions. Test materials comprise 20 tokens cut from plastic, wood, or heavy paper, that vary in shape (circular or square), color (yellow, red, blue, green, or white), and size (big or small). The test consists of 62 oral commands of the following form:

Touch the yellow circle and the red square.
Put the red circle on the green square.
Before touching the yellow circle, pick up the red square.

A short-form of this measure is included in the NCCE (Spreen & Benton, 1969). A short screening measure is Powell, Bailey, and E. Clark's (1980) very short version of the Minnesota Aphasia Test. This uses four subtests from the MTDDA and is designed only to detect aphasia. A more detailed diagnostic formulation requires the administration of the full test.

Other Cognitive Functions

Dementia, as reflected in the quotation at the head of Chapter 1, is usually seen by clinicians as a global deterioration in intellectual and memory capacity. However, the neuropsychological assessment of patients with degenerative brain diseases typically involves testing a range of cognitive skills. Tests of spatial abilities, visuomotor impairments, and measures of frontal lobe functioning are not considered in this chapter. Many of the tests commonly employed to assess other cognitive functions will be encountered as the neuropsychological impairments seen in the various degenerative diseases are described. One exception, however, is the Wisconsin Card Sorting Test (WCST). The WCST is possibly the most commonly employed measure of frontal lobe damage. It is also frequently administered to dementing patients, so some introduction is in order.

The WCST assesses the ability to acquire a new rule and to change it when conditions alter. It is therefore a measure of conceptual learning and the ability to make self-directed changes in mental set, functions often ascribed to the frontal cortex. The subjects' task is to sort a set of cards on each of which are printed one, two, three or four symbols in one of four colors (yellow, green, red, or blue). Four shapes are used for the symbols: star, circle, cross, or triangle. The cards can be sorted according to three principles—color, shape of the symbol, or number of symbols. Four stimulus cards are placed before the subjects—one red triangle, two green stars, three yellow crosses, and four blue circles. Subjects are then instructed to sort the cards according to a rule known only to the examiner. As the cards are placed one by one under the four stimulus cards, subjects are given feedback about the correctness of each response. Their task is to deduce the rule the examiner is using, from the pattern of feedback they are receiving. The first rule is to sort according to color, and ignore shape and number. Once the rule has been learned, the examiner changes to a new rule (based on the number of symbols) without directly informing the subjects. The testees must learn from the change in responses from the examiner that a shift in the sorting principle has occurred and learn the new rule. Up to a maximum of 6 rule changes can be made using 2 decks of 64 cards each.

The most common indicators of performance are the number of categories (or changes in rule) learned and the number of perseverative errors. Perseveration is defined as the continued use of an old rule after a change to the new one has been made. Poor performance on the WCST has most commonly been attributed to frontal lobe damage (Lezak, 1983).

Depression and Cognition

The measurement of depression in elderly patients is the most frequent formal assessment of personal functioning undertaken by clinicians. Knowing something of a patient's current emotional status is often an important part of a neuropsychological assessment for a variety of reasons. First, depression may present as a reaction to the onset or progression of a chronic neurological condition and provide an indication of failure to adapt or cope. Such a reactive depression is treatable and the circumstances leading to its development need to be explored. Depression has been particularly associated with Parkinson's disease, although it can occur in conjunction with any of the disorders considered in this book. In addition, elderly patients may be so severely depressed that their cognition is impaired, and they be mistakenly diagnosed as having an organic dementia. Depressed patients often report severe cognitive deficits, which may be taken as a sign of dementia, however, in practice, many depressed elderly patients who consent to testing usually have scores on memory and intelligence tests in the normal range. The process of assessment may help to elucidate diagnosis in such cases. Finally, depression and dementia may coexist, and the depressive symptoms may serve to accentuate the degree of cognitive disability.

It is beyond the scope of this chapter to discuss these issues in detail; excellent reviews exist elsewhere (Jorm, 1986; L. W. Thompson, 1988). Some of the major depression scales that can be used with patients with degenerative disorders are listed in Table 2.4. Of the interviewer scales, perhaps the Hamilton Rating Scale of Depression has been most frequently used. The Beck Depression Inventory has been the self-report instrument of choice in many studies. However, the Geriatric Depression Scale is a simple and straightforward instrument well suited to use with depressed elderly people.

Table 2.4: Depression Scales

Interview-based

Schedule for Affective Disorders and Schizophrenia (Spitzer & Endicott, 1978). Structured interview for making DSM diagnoses.

Hamilton Rating Scale for Depression (Hamilton, 1967). Clinician rating of depressive symptom severity.

Self-report

Beck Depression Inventory (BDI; A. T. Beck et al., 1961). Intensity of depressive symptoms.

Center for Epidemiological Study—Depression (Radloff, 1977). A 20-item measure of frequency of depressive symptoms.

Geriatric Depression Scale (Yesavage et al., 1983). A 30-item scale designed to discriminate the depressed from the healthy elderly.

Zung Self-rating Depression Scale (Zung, 1965). Measure of severity of depressive symptoms.

Neuropsychological Assessment and
Research Methodology

Conducting neuropsychological research with patients who have degenerative brain diseases presents many methodological challenges. In particular, difficulties in constituting and describing samples of patients used in research abound. In Part 2 of this book, some of the specific ways in which researchers have attempted to overcome these problems are outlined. At the conclusion of this chapter, however, it is useful to review some of the general problems confronting neuropsychological researchers designing an appropriate testing strategy.

Diagnosis

The last 20 years have seen an increasing concern with the development and standardization of research diagnostic criteria for neurological diseases. This is an important step in the comparison and integration of results from different laboratories. Nevertheless, the accurate diagnosis of degenerative brain diseases is often fraught with difficulty. For example, in the case of multiple sclerosis, although reliable diagnostic standards have been established (Poser et al., 1983), diagnosis in the early stages of the disease remains problematic, particularly where the onset is marked primarily by cognitive changes (Rao, 1986). Similarly, although Alzheimer's disease can be diagnosed clinically with some degree of certainty, the diagnosis can only be confirmed on autopsy. In general, this means that research samples typically comprise subjects with uncomplicated and unequivocal diagnoses, and may not be truly representative of the population of patients as a whole.

A related problem is the difficulty of establishing the stage of the disease and the severity of impairment. Although staging scales for most degenerative conditions have been formulated, these often lack sufficient precision for research work. In addition, the disease stages tend to be based on physical and neurological signs and symptoms, and place less reliance on mental and psychological impairments. Neuropsychologists have also contributed to problems in this area by using different batteries of tests to establish the presence and severity of cognitive changes. In his review of testing the elderly, Woods (1982), observed that "Clinical psychologists are as idiosyncratic in their choice of tests as they are in their attitudes to assessment" (p. 91). Researchers are similarly inconsistent, thereby making the comparison of outcomes from different studies more difficult than necessary. There are hopeful signs that neuropsychologists are beginning to work together to construct standard batteries of neuropsychological tests suitable for use with different neurological disorders. This can only help to facilitate the process of integrating research findings.

Control Groups

The selection of an appropriate comparison sample is of the utmost importance in the accurate identification of deficits in a pathological group. The most commonly used matching variables are age and education. Determining that contrasted groups have equivalent premorbid intellectual capacity is more problematic. As we have seen in the section reviewing methods of estimating premorbid IQ, procedures that rely on current test performance are likely to underestimate the premorbid competence of patients with moderate to severe dementia (Larrabee, Largen, & H. S. Levin, 1985). There is no simple solution to the problems of matching for premorbid IQ. It is advisable to collect multiple indicators of premorbid functioning and to interpret those based on concurrent testing (for example, NART estimates of WAIS FSIQ estimates) with considerable caution.

It is also important to acknowledge that the use of normal healthy volunteers as a control group does not allow for the possible debilitating effects of institutionalization and coping with chronic degenerative illness. When investigating the psychosocial consequences of neurological conditions it is particularly important to control for these potential effects.

Concurrent Disabilities

In addition to those changes directly attributable to a specific degenerative disease process, many patients suffer from other, often unrelated disabilities. For example, many dementing elderly people suffer from coronary heart disease or systemic conditions. It is not unusual for patients to have more than one neurological disorder—for example, Parkinsonism complicated by the effects of stroke. The changes associated with other diseases, together with the effects of any treatment given, can be a factor in the cognitive or emotional disturbances the patients display. In other instances, an affective disorder may be superimposed on neurological symptoms. Depression and dementia frequently coexist.

Another possible confounding factor is the use of psychoactive medications. Antidepressants and anxiolytics may have an acute or long-term influence on cognition. The precise effects of such medication on particular tests is usually unknown, and it is necessary to act cautiously in the interpretation of test data from patients receiving drug treatments.

Finally, it is imperative that testing strategies take due account of the likely influence that sensory or motor deficits may have on measures of cognition. In those diseases causing considerable motor disability or loss of sensory acuity, tests and research tasks must be selected and administered in a way that minimizes these problems. The testing of patients in clinical practice usually permits the use of flexible assessment strategies. In research, however, where standard procedures are applied to groups of patients, if patients with significant concurrent disabilities are excluded, there can be considerable difficulties in recruiting a representative sample.

Conclusions

In this chapter we have reviewed a selection of the standardized dementia scales and neuropsychological tests commonly employed with patients who have degenerative brain diseases. We encounter these measures repeatedly in the following chapters. However, out of necessity this survey has been limited. Other tests are introduced as we proceed. For example, measures of motor disability and frontal lobe impairment are featured in the chapter on Parkinsonism.

Most centers that routinely assess patients who may be or are dementing, develop a comprehensive battery of neuropsychological measures that suit their particular purposes. Such batteries are likely to incorporate the dementia scales we reviewed in the earlier part of this chapter supplemented by formal neuropsychological and personality tests as necessary. Several batteries of neuropsychological tests have been described in the literature. For example, Storandt and Hill (1989) used the Wechsler Memory Scale, a word fluency test, subtests from the WAIS, the Trail-Making Test, and a letter-cancellation task, to assess patients with a diagnosis of DAT. Teng et al. (1989) outlined a similar neuropsychological test battery with four parallel forms. To illustrate the range of tests that neuropsychologists consider appropriate for testing patients with suspected or mild-moderate dementia, the content of their battery is listed in Table 2.5.

Similarly, a recent attempt to standardize cognitive assessment in patients with Alzheimer's disease has resulted in the Consortium to Establish a Registry for Alzheimers Disease (CERAD; J. C. Morris, Heyman, Mohs, et al., 1989) neuropsychological battery. This battery contains measures of memory disturbance, category fluency, confrontation naming, constructional praxis, and the MMSE. The learning-memory procedures involve testing word-list learning, delayed recall, and delayed recognition. One important aim in the development of the battery has been to encourage the consistent use of psychometric measures with patients with Alzheimer's disease to facilitate cross-study comparisons (Welsh, Butters, Hughes, Mohs, & Heyman, 1991).

Table 2.5:   Neuropsychological Test Battery (Teng et al., 1989)

Finger Tapping	Rate of tapping with the index finger
Digit Span (Forward)	WAIS-R measure of memory span
Boston Naming Test	A measure of confrontation naming using line drawings
Verbal Memory	Nine items, three learning-recall trials, a delayed recall trial, a delayed recognition trial
Visual Memory	Immediate recall of geometric designs
Token Test	Assessment of receptive language
Number Cancellation	Perceptual-motor speed
Word Fluency	Generation of words starting with a designated letter
Symbol-Digit Substitution	Simplified version of the WAIS Digit-Symbol Test
Copying Designs	Ability to reproduce geometric designs

Most of the measures we have considered so far focus on quantifying changes and disabilities from the perspective of the clinician. There are few comparable scales assessing the psychosocial impact of chronic and progressive brain diseases. This is changing, however, and scales that measure change and adaptation from the patient's or caregiver's viewpoint are being developed and used. We encounter scales relevant to measuring such psychosocial factors as perceived stress and burden, coping skills, and social support in later chapters.

PART 2

NEUROPSYCHOLOGICAL RESEARCH

Chapter 3

KORSAKOFF'S DISEASE

Jim is a retired sawmiller. He never married, and he has lived and worked all over the country. He is 62 years old now and he spends most of his time sitting and smoking. He rarely asks questions and seldom spontaneously volunteers anything much. He likes a game of pool, but most of the time he seems content with his own company. Jim can be readily engaged in conversation. He describes his life as a sawmiller and recounts stories from his war service. He is always willing to be involved in psychological testing or experimental sessions, but displays no great interest in what he is being asked to do. On first acquaintance there is nothing remarkable about him at all; he seems out of place in one of the long-stay wards of a psychiatric hospital.

It is only when he is asked about his present life that his diffi-culties become obvious. He seems not to know the names of any of the other people in the hospital dayroom, even though he has shared a dormitory with some of them for several years. "People come and go here" he says "it's not worth learning their names." When asked, he is unable to give the name of the charge nurse who has been working on the ward since Jim was admitted three years ago, although "it is on the tip of his tongue". In fact, Jim can remember very little of what has happened since he came to the hospital; indeed he has almost no recollection of things that have happened over the past 15 years. Although he watches television every evening he is unable to name any of the programs he has seen, nor does he have any knowledge of current affairs. If he were to leave the room for just a few minutes in the middle of a psychological test, on his return he is most likely to have completely forgotten what he was doing and to deny ever having seen the test mate-rials before. In short, his capacity to learn anything new seems to have almost totally vanished. Surprisingly, Jim never complains of having a poor memory. When his inability to

*recall something becomes obvious he is likely to brush off his
failure with a superficial response such as "It's not the sort of
thing you remember" or "I didn't take any notice."*

*Yet on occasions, Jim will obviously recognize a nurse rostered
back to the ward after an absence of several weeks. He has
learned his way around the ward and provided he follows the
same route, does not get lost walking around the hospital
grounds. He has not lost the skills he learned long ago—he
has no difficulty setting up the colored balls for a game of
snooker. However, a major event on the ward, like a special
trip or a fight, seems to be forgotten moments after it happened.
The ward staff describe his major problems as a "failure of
short-term memory" and a constant state of "apathy." With
respect to the latter, although he was once a very heavy drink-
er, he now has no apparent urge to leave the hospital to find a
bar. Sometimes staff bring newly admitted alcoholics to see
Jim and some of his fellow patients as part of an alcohol education program. "If you don't stop drinking" the alcoholics are
told, "you could finish up in here, a Korsakoff like them."*

Background

Korsakoff's disease (KD) is a disorder characterized by a profound and
irreversible amnesia, without the clinical symptoms of dementia or any
other major disturbances of higher cognitive functioning. Frequently KD
is preceded by a period of acute confusion, known as Wernicke's encephalopathy. The label Korsakoff's disease is sometimes used to describe
any severe amnesic condition, regardless of etiology. In this chapter,
however, the term will be used to refer to amnesia consequent on chronic
alcohol abuse.

Korsakoff's disease is unlike the other neurological conditions
reviewed in this book. For one thing, the etiology is known, for another,
the course of KD tends to be stable as long as the patient abstains from
drinking alcohol. However, because of the severity of the disorder,
patients with KD are often managed in facilities catering to patients with
chronic progressive neurological conditions. In addition, there are many
neuropsychological studies in which the deficits of KD are contrasted
with those of other conditions such as Alzheimer's disease, Huntington's
disease, and Parkinsonism. Hence KD is reviewed in this book.

The patient with an alcoholic amnesic disorder is often first encountered on admission to the hospital in a delirious and confused state. An acute episode of delirium (Wernicke's encephalopathy) is not, however, a necessary antecedent to the development of KD, and many patients with Wernicke's encephalopathy recover completely and never become chronically amnesic. In contrast, patients with KD are typically in a stable and lucid state. As is the case with Jim, the patients' marked amnesia may not be immediately apparent and it is their lack of initiative and spontaneity that is often more immediately striking.

Historically, the clinical description of the acute and chronic phases of this alcohol-induced neurological disorder proceeded independently. In 1881, Carl Wernicke (1973) described the symptoms of three cases of profound neurological disturbance characterized by severe oculomotor disturbances, disorientation, ataxia, and delirium leading to a progressive deterioration, stupor, and death. One of these cases was a 20-year-old seamstress with sulphuric acid poisoning, the other two were chronic alcoholics. On the basis of the autopsy examinations, Wernicke concluded that he had uncovered a new clinical entity, which he called acute hemorrhagic superior encephalitis. He proposed,

> *We are dealing with an independent, inflammatory acute nuclear disease in the region of the ocular nerves which leads to death within 10 to 14 days. The focal symptoms consist of corresponding ocular motor palsies which develop rapidly, progress and finally lead to almost total paralysis of the ocular musculature... . The patient's gait becomes staggering, and shows a combination of stiffness and ataxia, reminiscent of the ataxia of the alcoholic. The general appearance is very striking. It consists of impairment of consciousness, which is either somnolence from the outset or a terminal stage of somnolence preceded by a longer period of agitation.* (p. 48)

Although similar cases were reported by a number of other clinicians who were contemporaries of Wernicke, his name has come to be associated with the disease.

Some 6 years later, Korsakoff presented the first detailed description of the chronic amnesic syndrome that has since been linked with his name. He described 20 cases in which peripheral nerve disease (a common consequence of alcoholism) was accompanied by mental changes. He believed these changes were a consequence of the toxic effects of alcohol and proposed that the new disease be labeled cerebropathia psychica toxaemica. The diagnostic label *Korsakoff syndrome* was first used by Jolly in 1897 (Victor, R. D. Adams, & Collins, 1971), who suggested that this term be used to describe irreversible amnesia, without reference to the presence of peripheral neuritis. Other clinicians introduced the terms *Korsakoff's psychosis* or *Korsakoff's disease*, and these labels have been used interchangeably with the term syndrome since the early 1900s. Sometimes the acute and chronic phases are linked and the disease is called Wernicke-Korsakoff syndrome. In this chapter our focus is on the chronic stage of the disorder; hence the term *Korsakoff's disease* is preferred.

Wernicke and Korsakoff did not appreciate that there might be a relationship between the two disorders. Indeed, the clinical and neuroanatomical study of the two diseases followed a parallel path for several decades before beginning to converge in the 1920s. One factor contributing to this separation was the difference in the proposed neuropathology of the two disorders. Wernicke's encephalopathy was regarded as a consequence of acute lesions in the grey matter bordering the third and fourth ventricles, with later reports implicating other diencephalic structures, notably the thalamus and mamillary bodies. Korsakoff, however, regarded cortical atrophy as primarily responsible for the memory impairments in his cases. Pathological changes in the cortex, particularly in the frontal lobes (Carmichael & R. D. Stern, 1931), were regarded as the most probable cause of amnesia in KD until the 1940s (Lishman, 1981).

In the 1930s and 1940s similarities in the etiology of Wernicke's and Korsakoff's diseases were reported. The earliest descriptions of both diseases had included cases in which the cardinal etiological factor involved the inability to properly ingest food. Patients with a carcinoma of the stomach, persistent vomiting during pregnancy, or severe malnutrition had been observed to develop Wernicke's encephalopathy. Eventually, lack of vitamins, primarily thiamine, was established as an important causative factor in the lesions producing both Wernicke's encephalopathy and Korsakoff's disease. R. A. Peters (1936) demonstrated lesions similar to those seen in Wernicke encephalopathy cases in the midbrain of thiamine-deprived pigeons. Subsequently, Jolliffe, Wortis, and Fein (1941) found that thiamine treatment resulted in significant and rapid improvement in the oculomotor symptoms and confusion displayed by Wernicke encephalopathy patients. Similar, although less dramatic improvements were found in KD cases (Bowman, Goodhart, & Jolliffe, 1939). These findings were reinforced by DeWardener and Lennox's (1947) report on the occurrence of Wernicke's encephalopathy in 52 prisoners of war held in Singapore. These men, many with severe amnesia and oculomotor disorders, responded well to thiamine. Eventually it became apparent that the high incidence of KD among alcoholics was a consequence of their poor nutrition and the lack of thiamine in their main dietary intake—alcoholic beverages.

Once nutritional insufficiency was found to be a common etiological factor, it came to be gradually accepted that the pathology of the two disorders was similar. The view that cortical atrophy caused Korsakoff amnesia was replaced by the current opinion that midbrain lesions, located similarly to those seen in Wernicke's encephalopathy, were critical in producing memory loss (Victor et al., 1971). Victor and colleagues' report on a series of 186 alcoholic patients with Wernicke-Korsakoff syndrome was especially important in establishing the similarities in brain pathology displayed by Wernicke and Korsakoff patients. They found that 84% of their Korsakoff patients had developed the disease subsequent to an episode of acute confusion.

This brief historical review allows the introduction of two important background variables that need to be considered when reviewing a patient with KD. First, such patients tend to have a pronounced degree of cortical atrophy in addition to any amnesia-producing lesions of the midbrain. This should alert the clinician to the expectation that the amnesia displayed by KD patients will not be totally circumscribed, but will frequently be accompanied by other, often subtle, cognitive changes. Second, the acuteness of the symptomatology of KD patients can vary considerably. In the initial stages of their presentation, prior to multivitamin treatment, many KD patients are acutely disturbed, and this often masks the presence of severe amnesia. Periodic drinking binges in KD can produce episodes of acute disturbance and further cognitive deterioration.

Diagnosis

Korsakoff's disease is categorized in the *DSM-III-R* as Alcohol Amnestic Disorder. The essential features of this diagnostic category are:

1. Impairment in short- and long-term memory "following prolonged, heavy ingestion of alcohol" (p. 133). The memory impairment persists when the patient is not delirious.

2. No evidence of dementia, that is, the patient does not display "impairment in abstract thinking or judgement," and has "no other disturbances of higher cortical function, and no personality change" (p. 109).

3. The memory disturbance is "not due to any physical or any other mental disorder" (p. 133).

These criteria capture the essential features of the disorder and are sufficient for most clinical purposes. However, neither the degree of memory impairment nor the method of determining whether a person displays an "impairment in abstract thinking or judgement" are specified. The *DSM-III-R* requires only that the memory impairment be "quite severe" and it is observed that "life-long custodial care may be necessary" (p. 133). Many studies have shown that chronic alcohol abusers show subtle impairments in higher cognitive functioning without being either profoundly amnesic or demented (M. S. Goldman, 1983; C. Ryan & Butters, 1983). It is likely that many Korsakoff patients, most of whom have been addicted to alcohol for many years, have acquired some degree of impairment in higher cognitive functioning that extends beyond their memory deterioration. Indeed there are a number of studies showing that Korsakoff patients have impairments in their problem-solving skills and are less efficient on visuomotor tasks (e.g., Oscar-Berman, 1973). Consequently, researchers are faced with the difficult task of deciding how severe memory impairment has to be before it can be called amnesia, and how to exclude from study amnesic patients who have other significant cognitive deficits. This is an important issue, central to the debate about what constitutes the obligatory deficits of amnesia, and is touched on later.

It is perhaps useful to conclude this section by examining in detail how one prominent group of researchers defines their amnesic sample. In a recent study, Shimamura and Squire (1989) assessed 12 amnesics, 6 of whom had alcoholic Korsakoff's syndrome. To establish that their amnesic patients had a severe and specific impairment of memory, they reported that:

> [The 12 amnesic patients] ... had an average Wechsler Adult Intelligence Scale-Revised IQ (WAIS-R) score of 103.3. On the Wechsler Memory Scale-Revised (WMS-R), they scored 95.8 on Attention and Concentration, 74.0 on Verbal Memory, 76.1 on Visual Memory, 68.5 on General Memory, and 56.7 on Delayed Memory. The WAIS-R and WMS-R are standardized with a mean of 100 and a standard deviation of 15. Thus these patients scored within the normal range on the WAIS-R and on the Attention and Concentration Index of the WMS-R. Yet, every patient scored at least 2 standard deviations below average on the Delayed Memory Index. (p. 722)

The severity of the memory impairment was confirmed by Shimamura and Squire using the Rey-Osterreith Complex Figure Test, the Rey Auditory Verbal Learning Test, immediate and delayed recall of a prose passage, 2-choice yes-no recognition of 15 nouns, and a 10-item paired-associate learning test. Shimamura and Squire also noted,

> Neuropsychological screening and independent neurological examination indicated that memory impairment was the only remarkable deficit of higher cortical function. The amnesic patients averaged 133.2 points out of a possible 144 points on the Dementia Rating Scale (Coblentz et al., 1973), losing most of their points on the memory subportion of the test. All patients could draw a cube and a house in perspective, and none had aphasia or apraxia. (p. 722)

Although not all research groups studying amnesics use the same measures to establish severity of memory dysfunction and exclude patients with other neuropsychological defects, most use similar criteria. Comparison of scores on the Wechsler Memory and Intelligence Scales is a method commonly used to establish the specificity of amnesia, and two standard deviations below a memory test mean is often taken as an index of severe amnesia. However, the fact that there is no universally acknowledged standard for defining a case of circumscribed amnesia adds considerably to the problem of comparing results from different laboratories (R. G. Knight & B. E. Longmore, 1991).

Symptoms

Amnesia is the defining symptom of KD, but it is frequently accompanied by other neurological features. Most of these additional signs of neurological disturbance are seen most severely during an acute episode of Wernicke's encephalopathy. It is useful therefore to review the major features of that disease. Table 3.1 lists the major symptoms of a Wernicke's episode. Those associated with the chronic Korsakoff phase are also indicated.

Most Wernicke's cases present with severe confusion, and their awareness of where they are may be disturbed and variable. On occasion, seeing the nurses, beds, and white coats, the patients may acknowledge they are in a hospital. This awareness can evaporate almost at once, and if questioned again they will answer that they are in a boarding house or an army camp. When asked about the present date, often patients will name a time years past, and if they asked their age they can rarely give an accurate response. They display no knowledge of prominent public figures or events in the last few years or even decades, and their thinking and speech are often illogical, unfocused, and contradictory. They may appear distressed, agitated, and perplexed. This confusion resolves gradually over a period of 6 to 50 days, and often leaves a starkly apparent, profound amnesia. The dimensions of the memory loss may not be obvious during the acute phase when the patient is typically unable to participate meaningfully in any formal or even informal assessment of memory.

Table 3.1:   Major Presenting Symptoms of Wernicke's Encephalopathy and Korsakoff's Disease

Wernicke's Encephalopathy	Korsakoff's Disease
Severe confusion, delirium	Lucid
Disoriented for time and place	May be disoriented, particularly for time
Severe amnesia; may be masked by delirium	Severe and disabling amnesia
Spontaneous confabulation may be encountered	Confabulation uncommon but patient is often unaware of amnesia
Staggering ataxic gait very common	Signs of ataxia may remain
Oculomotor disturbance very common	Oculomotor disturbance uncommon
Peripheral nerve disease very common	Symptoms of peripheral nerve disease may remain
Alcohol withdrawal symptoms (seizures, hallucinations) may occur	Withdrawal from alcohol is complete

Confabulation is a common feature of the amnestic disturbance during the Wernicke's episode. This is an interesting phenomenon, which is difficult to define and presents in a number of different ways.

Confabulation refers to the erroneous fabrication of memories. Patients with Wernicke's encephalopathy sometimes spontaneously respond to questions with detailed accounts of events that have not taken place, apparently without any awareness of their amnesic problems. Confabulation is difficult to explain satisfactorily. Certainly, the quality of the confabulation does not give the impression to the interviewer that the patient is deliberately constructing a story to disguise memory failings. Talland (1965) described confabulation in the Wernicke patient as follows:

> *Wernicke patients ... rarely admit ignorance, and freely invent answers on the spur of the moment. Do they invent answers in order to avoid embarrassment, to satisfy a need, to resolve a tension? Possibly so, even though a patently absurd reply would hardly serve that purpose in normal conversation, and can satisfy them only because they are unaware of its inadequacy. It certainly does not sound like a contrived fabrication or distortion of a true event. Neither is it done to humor the interviewer or to bolster their own self-esteem. These patients are too apathetic or agitated to care about either.* (p. 43)

Only a small proportion of KD patients confabulate. It is worth observing that confabulation is not simply a result of being amnesic. Many severely amnesic KD patients show no signs of confabulation. Rather than confabulate, KD patients are more likely to be evasive or noncommittal when confronted with their memory problems. For example, when asked about a recent news event such a patient might reply "I'm not interested in the news" or "I don't watch TV." These responses are in themselves indicative of either a lack of awareness of or lack of concern about having a memory deficit. The issue of lack of awareness of deficits, of which confabulation may be an extreme and special instance, is something considered further.

The other principal symptoms of Wernicke's encephalopathy are primarily somatic. *Ataxic gait* refers to the broad-based staggering walk that is sometimes also seen in chronic alcoholic patients. At its most severe, the patient stands with feet well spread, leaning forward, and can only walk with assistance. Those ataxic patients who are able to walk unsupported, tend to take short shuffling steps and appear to stagger forward. Ataxia is typically the consequence of the alcohol-related damage to the cerebellum and often occurs in alcoholics who show no signs of cognitive impairment. In Victor et al.'s (1971) series of Wernicke-Korsakoff patients, 107 patients with ataxia were followed up. In 38% the ataxia had disappeared, 35% showed an impairment but were left with a noticeable ataxic gait, and 27% showed no improvement after treatment. It is therefore common to find Korsakoff patients with residual ataxia.

Nearly all Wernicke cases show signs of ocular abnormalities. In 232 cases studied by Victor and associates, found only 4% who had no ocular problems. These symptoms are the result of the paralysis or weakness of the oculomotor muscles that control eye movement. The paralysis of one or more of the eye muscles may cause a squint (strabismus) or an inability to move one of the eyes. Frequently patients cannot move the eyes smoothly together (conjugate gaze disturbance). Some patients also show horizontal, vertical, or rotary uncontrolled, rhythmical eye-movements (a symptom known as *nystagmus*). Resolution of the ocular symptoms is usually complete and may begin within hours of treatment.

Polyneuropathy or peripheral nerve disease is common in alcoholics and therefore is frequently seen in Wernicke and KD cases. Wernicke patients have varying degrees of peripheral nerve damage. Recovery is typically slow and in the most severe cases there may be a long-term inability to walk, weakness, and loss of reflexes. The most common features of alcoholic peripheral neuropathy are:

Loss of sensation, typically in the lower limbs.
Loss or reduction of ankle or knee reflexes.
Weakness or muscle wasting in the limbs.
Pain, either dull and aching, or paroxysmal, in the limbs.
Complaints of excessive sensitivity in the lower limbs (making contact with bedclothes or walking unpleasant).

Finally, enforced abstinence may induce alcoholic withdrawal delirium. The symptoms of this condition include vivid hallucinations (often tactile or visual), and autonomic hyperactivity characterized by profuse sweating or tachycardia. The withdrawal symptoms usually resolve quickly (in 3 to 5 days) with appropriate treatment.

Course and Etiology

The lesions typical of KD are usually attributed to nutritional insufficiency. Thiamine depletion is largely responsible for the characteristic lesions in the region of the midbrain seen in both Wernicke's encephalopathy and KD. However, it is important to stress that nutritional problems are not the only disorders to which alcoholics are prone. Lishman (1981) drew attention to the possibility that subacute attacks of encephalopathy resulting from the systemic diseases and the liver problems endemic in alcoholics can cause a range of long-term brain impairments. Similarly, as Butters (1985) noted, alcohol has a direct toxic effect on the central nervous system irrespective of the nutritional regime of the chronic alcohol abuser, causing cumulative damage over time. This gradual damage will be superimposed on any specific amnesia-producing lesions. The cortical atrophy seen in many Korsakoff patients presumably results in part from their experience of being chronic alcoholics.

The course of the disease is also variable. Some patients have a long drinking history, a gradual onset of severe amnesia, and no evidence of a Wernicke's episode. In other patients, the drinking history is short, often just a matter of months, and the Korsakoff phase is clearly initiated by an episode of Wernicke's disease. This suggests that there is more than one pathway to a diagnosis of KD. Cutting (1978) conducted a retrospective study of 50 KD patients divided into two groups on the basis of the acuteness of the onset of their amnesia. He found that the acute onset group was less likely to be globally impaired than the chronic group, which was more likely to show pervasive neuropsychological deficits. The gradual-onset Korsakoff patients showed a degree of intellectual impairment similar to patients classified as having alcoholic dementia.

In summary, patients diagnosed as having an alcohol-induced amnesia vary in the amount of concurrent intellectual deficit they display. Those patients with a gradual onset and an extensive history of chronic alcoholism are more likely to have other deficits. Alcoholic KD patients also differ in the severity of their memory deficit. R. R. Jacobson and Lishman (1987) assessed the intellectual decline and memory loss of a group of 38 KD patients. They found that the patients were distributed over a continuum ranging from relatively pure and severe memory loss to memory loss plus intellectual deterioration, serving to emphasize the heterogeneity of the clinical presentation of patients with KD.

The Neuroanatomy of Memory

Much of what is known about the neuroanatomical basis of human memory comes from the study of clinical cases of amnesia. The largest group of patients with a relatively circumscribed and profound amnesia are alcoholic Korsakoffs and they have therefore played an important part in research into the underlying biological basis of amnesia. To understand the significance of the lesions that cause amnesia in KD, and also to highlight differences between patients with KD and other amnesics, it is helpful to review the structures and fiber systems in the brain believed to be involved in memory.

In Table 3.2, the various neurological disorders that cause severe amnesia and the regions of the brain associated with the amnesia are listed. Perhaps the best-known case of amnesia is the patient H.M., whose impairments were described in a number of eloquent reports by Brenda Milner and her colleagues at the Montreal Neurological Institute (Milner, Corkin, & Teuber, 1968; Scoville & Milner, 1957). H.M. was rendered densely amnesic after the bilateral neurosurgical resection of portions of the medial temporal lobe, an operation performed to relieve his intractable epilepsy. H.M. represents a prototypical case of severe circumscribed amnesia in the presence of intact intellectual functioning.

Table 3.2: Summary of the Neuroanatomical Basis of Disorders Commonly Causing Severe Amnesia

Neurological Disorder	Major Site of Lesions
Temporal lobectomy	medial temporal lobe
Herpes simplex encephalitis	temporal lobe
Anoxia	hippocampus
Alcoholic Korsakoff's disease	diencephalon, particularly mamillary bodies, thalamus
Midline tumors	diencephalon
Alzheimer's disease	basal forebrain, diffuse cortical atrophy
Rupture and repair of anterior aneurysms	basal forebrain and frontal lobes
Thalamic cerebrovascular infarctions	thalamus

The surgical procedure that H.M. underwent involved bilateral removal of part of the hippocampus and the amygdala, as well as other structures and tracts in the medial temporal lobe. The consequent amnesia H.M. displayed located part of the memory system in this region.

There have been a number of other cases that confirm the importance of temporal lobe damage in the production of amnesia. For example, herpes simplex encephalitis can cause bilateral medial temporal lobe damage, leaving other critical structures, such as the midbrain diencephalon untouched (Cermak, 1976).

Anoxia, an occasional complication of surgery, may also cause specific hippocampal lesions causing memory impairments (Hirst, 1982; Zola-Morgan, Squire, & Amaral, 1986). Evidence from surgical cases suggests that profound amnesia is the result of bilateral lesions to both the hippocampus and the amygdala (or adjacent regions; Zola-Morgan, Squire, & Amaral, 1989). Damage to the amygdaloid complex alone does not seem to produce memory impairment in humans and although bilateral lesions in the hippocampus produce a degree of memory loss, severe amnesia seems to occur only after bilateral damage to both the amygdala and hippocampus.

Clinical evidence also implicates other brain structures in memory processing. It is lesions in the diencephalon, along the midline of the brain, that are usually held to be responsible for the amnesia of alcoholic KD. In particular, damage to parts of the thalamus and mamillary bodies are of critical importance (Victor et al., 1971). There are other cases that confirm the importance of lesions in the diencephalon in cases of amnesia including amnesics with thalamic damage produced by circumscribed infarctions resulting from strokes. Another notable case of amnesia is N.A. (Teuber, Milner, & Vaughan, 1968), who sustained a degree of memory impairment after a stab wound with a fencing foil. The damage N.A. sustained involved the left thalamic nuclei, and possibly other midbrain structures (Weiskrantz, 1985).

A third region of the brain suspected of involvement in memory functions is the basal forebrain. This area is implicated because Alzheimer's disease, which causes profound intellectual and memory deterioration, is associated with degeneration of the cholinergic neurotransmitter system. The nucleus basalis of Meynert is the principal source of cholinergic innervation of the cerebral cortex and this is located in the basal forebrain area. Patients with Alzheimer's disease (and also patients with KD and Parkinsonism) tend to have a marked reduction in the number of neurons in this nucleus (T. Arendt, Bigl, A. Arendt, & Tennstedt, 1983). Another group of patients who may show memory impairments consequent on lesions that are neither medial temporal nor diencephalic, are surgical cases who have undergone the rupture and repair of an aneurysm arising from the anterior circulation (Alexander & Freedman, 1984; Gade, 1982). Aneurysms are small blisterlike dilations of the cerebral blood vessels that may suddenly burst, causing a subarachnoid hemorrhage. The long-term consequence is often a degree of infarction in the basal forebrain or frontal lobes. There have been several reports of amnesic states, mostly with an accompanying dementia, created by this process (e.g., Alexander & Freedman, 1984).

The clinical evidence summarized here suggests at least two and possibly three regions of the brain are involved in learning and memory. However, basing an anatomical model of memory on the study of patients with naturally occurring lesions does have limitations. Brain injury is rarely circumscribed, is usually hard to delineate exactly, and the patient's performance is frequently compromised by a variety of extraneous factors. A series of lesion studies in macque monkeys carried out by Mishkin and his colleagues (e.g., Mishkin, 1982) provided more precise data on which to base an anatomical model of memory, and the outcome of these studies corresponds closely to the results available from clinical research. Mishkin developed a visual discrimination learning task that he called *delayed nonmatching to sample*. In this task the monkey is presented with an unfamiliar object beneath which a reward is hidden. Having found the reward, there is a delay and then the monkey is confronted with two objects, one the same as in the previous trial, the other unfamiliar. The monkey is rewarded if it moves the novel or unfamiliar object. In this way, over a series of learning trials, the monkey is taught to detect novel stimuli after a variable delay.

Mishkin then conducted a number of ablation studies designed to determine the lesions that would disrupt learning on this task. He began by establishing that bilateral lesions to both the hippocampus and the amygdala were needed to produce severe global memory loss (Mishkin, 1978). Damaging either of these structures alone had only a small effect on the monkey's visual memory. This particular result was the starting point for Mishkin's proposal that learning at a biological level is dependent on two separate neuroanatomical memory circuits. Mishkin then went on to ablate structures in the diencephalic region that receive input from the amygdala and hippocampus. Again, lesions to both the points of termination, in the region of the dorsomedial nucleus and the anterior nuclei of the thalamus, were needed to produce severe visual memory loss (Aggelton & Mishkin, 1983).

At this stage, it is helpful to refer to a diagram of Mishkin's dual memory circuit model (Fig. 3.1). The first part of the model involves the elaboration of visual input (the process of perception), which follows from the visual cortex to the amygdala and hippocampus. These two structures have independent routes to the thalamus. The thalamus in turn has substantial links with the basal forebrain and prefrontal cortex. Mishkin proposed that a complex of cholinergic connections between these frontal regions and the sensory cortex completed the memory system (Bachevalier & Mishkin, 1986), and found that lesions in the basal forebrain and prefrontal cortex of monkeys also produced learning impairments.

In general, the results of clinical research with amnesics and Mishkin's lesion studies with macque monkeys have produced a consistent picture of the anatomical structures involved in learning and memory. Mishkin's dual circuit model implies that profound damage to both circuit pathways is needed to produce amnesia. This is a matter of some importance when it comes to understanding how amnesia occurs in KD.

Of what importance is this research on the neuroanatomical basis of amnesia for the clinician? First, the model has been widely used to provide an explanation for the neurobiology of amnesia, and to explain why memory loss is a consequence of several different disorders causing different patterns of lesions. Although more than likely this model will prove to be inadequate, it has the virtue of organizing the available clinical literature in a coherent and heuristic manner. In addition, this model alerts us to the fact that widely distributed brain structures cooperate to accomplish learning and memory. This helps explain why some degree of memory impairment accompanies most forms of brain injury, and also why profound amnesia is relatively uncommon. On the latter point, it is apparent that to produce global amnesia, it may be necessary to destroy two distinct circuits bilaterally. For example, because of their spatial separation, bilateral damage to both the amygdala and hippocampus is likely to be a rare event. This suggests that in most patients, amnesia is likely to be less than complete, and there will be residual memory skills that can be exploited in any rehabilitation program.

Biological Basis of KD

The site of the lesions critical to producing amnesia in KD is a matter of some controversy. Most researchers assert that it is the medial diencephalic damage that causes memory failure in these patients. However, the view that the critical damage is confined to the diencephalon is not universal. Butters (1985), drawing attention to T. Arendt et al.'s (1983) demonstration that KD patients (like patients with Alzheimer's Disease) sustain cell loss in the nucleus basalis of Meynert, raised the possibility that the critical lesions may be elsewhere. This nucleus is the source of the cholinergic innervation from the basal forebrain to the cortex, and this finding raises the possibility that cholinergic system degeneration plays at least some part in augmenting or causing amnesia in KD patients.

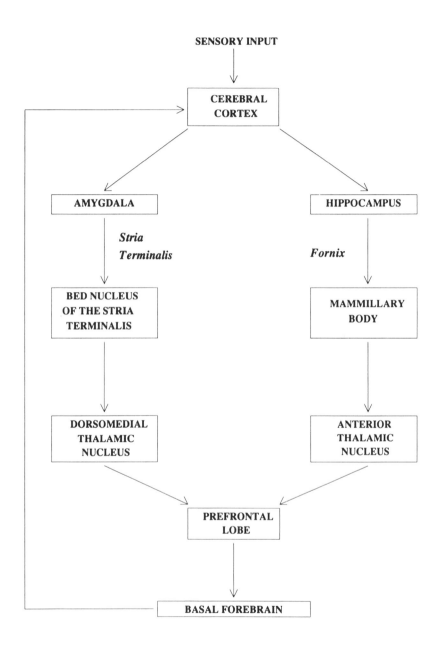

Figure 3.1. Schematic representation of Mishkin's dual circuit model of the neuroanatomy of memory.

Postmortem studies of the brains of KD patients have led to the formulation of at least three competing hypotheses concerning the possible diencephalic structures involved. One proposal purports that the critical lesions lie in the medial thalamic nuclei, in particular, the dorsomedial nuclei (Victor et al., 1971). The boundaries of the nuclei in this region are not well defined, and the precise location of the lesions of critical significance is a matter of contention (Mair, Warrington, & Weiskrantz, 1979; Markowitsch & Pritzel, 1985; Mayes, Meudell, Mann, & Pickering, 1988). According to a second view, degeneration of the mamillary bodies alone is sufficient to cause amnesia. And a third hypothesis, based on Mishkin's dual circuit model, asserts that specific bilateral lesions to both the medial portions of the thalamus, and to the mamillary bodies are necessary to cause amnesia. It is apparent from Fig. 3.1 that if both these lesions were to occur, this would disrupt both of the memory tracts arising from the amygdala and the hippocampus. It is also possible that an extensive bilateral thalamic lesion involving both the dorsomedial nuclei and the anterior thalamus (see Fig. 3.1) would be sufficient to cause profound amnesia.

Mayes et al. (1988) examined the brains of two Korsakoff patients who came to postmortem and found degeneration of the mamillary bodies together with damage to a region they labeled paratenial, adjacent to the dorsomedial nucleus. This finding provides some support for destruction of both Mishkin's proposed memory circuits as being the basis of severe amnesia in KD. This issue is, however, far from conclusively resolved. It is unequivocal, however, that the neuropathology of KD is variable. The amount of cortical atrophy, damage to the basal forebrain, and frontal lobes is likely to vary from one patient to the next. This is reflected in their extensive deficits and individual differences in performance on cognitive tests.

Amnesia in Korsakoff's Disease

Experimental Study of Memory

Before turning our attention to the clinical description of memory impairment, it is helpful to review briefly the terminology and descriptive models that have dominated experimental memory research. This is important because human experimental studies of memory have had a considerable influence on the study of amnesia in patients with KD and other disorders. It was William James who introduced into psychology the term *primary memory*, which he used to characterize the transient information and thoughts that we hold in the "specious present." James (1890), also stated that "memory proper, or secondary memory as it might be styled, is the knowledge of a former state of mind after it has already once dropped from consciousness; or rather *it is the knowledge of an event, or fact*, of which meantime we have not been thinking, *with the additional consciousness that we have thought or experienced it before*" (p. 648). There is a general although not universal acceptance that the primary-secondary memory dichotomy is of value, and it underlies much of memory research that has been conducted in the last 30 years.

Primary memory or *short-term memory* (STM) refers to memory for events that last for some 30 seconds. The classic measure of short-term memory is the memory span task, exemplified by the Digit Span subtest of the Wechsler Intelligence scales. STM and primary memory are virtually synonymous, however, the use of short-term by clinicians is frequently ambiguous. For example, the *DSM-III-R* refers to amnestic alcoholics as having "both short-term and long-term memory impairments," and defines short-term memory impairment as the "inability to learn new information" (p. 109). This confusion of short-term memory impairment with anterograde amnesia illustrates the problem with the use of the term short-term memory outside the experimental literature. A preference for the use of primary rather than short-term memory has become evident in the literature recently, and the primary-secondary dichotomy has the virtue of being less easily misapplied.

Initial research into STM processes was stimulated by demonstrations by J. A. Brown (1958) and L. R. Peterson and M. J. Peterson (1959) that limited amounts of information, well within a normal subject's memory span, were quickly forgotten if rehearsal was prevented. The Peterson-Brown distractor task involves presenting the subject with three consonants or words for a brief period of time (2-4 seconds) and then interfering with rehearsal (prior to testing recall) for periods of up to 60 seconds, by instructing the subject to perform a distracting task. For normal subjects there is a steep decline from 100% recall at 0-second delay down to 30 to 40% correct recall of three-items after a 30-second distraction filled delay.

Another important impetus for STM research was Broadbent's (1958) model of how information was processed in the primary memory system. This model involved two subsystems, one capable of storing parallel sensory inputs very briefly before they passed to a second stage, a limited capacity information-processing system. Information was assumed to be transferred from storage in the short-term system to a more permanent place in the long-term system as a consequence of rehearsal. The distinction between long- and short-term memory was explored in numerous studies in the 1970s; the validity of dividing memory in two parts was vigorously debated (for an excellent review of this work and of the evolution of recent approaches to memory models, see Baddeley, 1986). Neuropsychological studies made some contribution to this discussion. Many amnesics with profound secondary or long-term memory losses were found to perform normally on STM tasks. Conversely, Shallice and Warrington (1970) reported data from case K.F., who had a grossly defective STM, but was not amnesic. These results lent credence to the meaningfulness of the splitting memory into two major storage systems.

By the early 1970s numerous structural models of memory had emerged. B. B. Murdock (1974) noted that most of them had essentially the same features: a sensory buffer store and a limited capacity short-term store, from which inputs passed to a long-term store. Baddeley (1986), following Murdock's suggestion, referred to this generic three-stage storage system as the *modal model*. This general model stimulated much of the experimental work with amnesics in 1970s. However, numerous problems with the modal model emerged over the next decade and its influence, for a variety of reasons, had waned by the early 1980s (e.g., Crowder, 1982). In 1972 Craik and Lockhart presented an alternative model that moved the emphasis away from Broadbent-style structural models and toward understanding memory in terms of encoding and control processes. Craik and Lockhart's (1972) levels of processing approach proposed that acquiring new information involved processing the new input through a series of stages, from sensory analysis through to semantic elaboration, and the deeper the level of processing, the more likely the information was to be retained. Although the distinction between primary and secondary memory was not discarded, it was de-emphasized and research focused on the way memories came to be consolidated in the long-term store. Their work was to have an influence on amnesia research, particularly on Cermak's encoding deficit hypothesis, which was explored using the levels of processing paradigm. Problems with the levels of processing model, however, became apparent, and although it remains a useful way of understanding some of the memory research literature, there has been a gradual resurgence of interest in structural models and in the processes underlying primary memory.

One significant attempt to present an alternative to the modal model of STM is Baddeley and Hitch's (1974) Working Memory Model. This model and its research development is described in Baddeley (1986). The Working Memory Model comprises a limited capacity Central Executive, which has two slave systems. One of these slave systems is involved in the processing of language: the Articulatory Loop. The other is specialized for visuospatial memory and is called the visual-spatial scratchpad or sketchpad. The Central Executive system is of special interest. Its function is described as "initiating and modulating the dif-

ferent mental processes associated with working memory and has a high
degree of complexity which might make it especially vulnerable to the
effects of dementia" (R. G. Morris & Baddeley, 1988, p. 284). Morris
and Baddeley hypothesized that it is deficits in this central control system
that underlie the primary memory problems of demented patients.

The Working Memory Model is of particular importance in the
study of the way cognition is compromised in dementia; it is reintroduced
in the chapter on Alzheimer's disease. The present discussion of amnesia
in KD, however, takes a more traditional approach. First, the clinical
presentation of amnesia in KD is reviewed using the terms more commonly favored by clinicians—*anterograde* and *retrograde amnesia*.
Next, from a largely historical perspective, the experimental investigation of amnesia, much of which was conducted within the general
framework of the modal model is traced.

Clinical Presentation

The clinical description of amnesia typically involves a distinction between *anterograde amnesia (AA)* or the loss of capacity to learn new
information, and *retrograde amnesia (RA)*, which is the inability to retrieve information acquired before the onset of the brain injury. This
distinction can be most readily illustrated by the performance of patients
who have sustained a severe head injury. For a period immediately after
the injury, noncomatose patients are often confused and unable to
remember events that have just taken place. They will perform poorly
on memory tests that are sensitive to anterograde amnesia. In addition,
they will be unable to remember events that occurred prior to the acci-
dent that caused the injury. This is retrograde amnesia, and may extend
back for some years. Indeed on occasion patients may not even recognize
their spouse or children. KD patients have a profound anterograde
amnesia and, in addition, they show a variable degree of retrograde
memory loss.

As we have seen in the previous section, memory tasks are categorized by psychologists in a variety of ways. Tests that document or
uncover anterograde amnesia assess long-term memory. The only
measures in wide clinical use that directly assess short-term memory are
essentially memory span tests. The Digit Span and Visual Memory Span
subtests of the WMS-R are examples of STM tests. The Logical
Memory and Paired-Associate Learning subtest of the WMS-R are
examples of long-term memory tests. Tests of long-term memory need
to be distinguished from measures of retrograde amnesia, which are best
termed *remote memory* tests. A remote memory test questions patients
about public or personal events that have occurred over the whole range

of the patient's life since early childhood. KD patients show evidence of retrograde amnesia on such tests, although the precise quality of this memory loss is a matter of some debate (Squire, 1986; Weiskrantz, 1985). Descriptions of some experimental memory tests and procedures that have been traditionally used in the study of amnesia are presented in Table 3.3. The next section looks at the performance of Korsakoff patients on a variety of experimental memory tasks that reveal the range and depth of their amnesia.

Table 3.3: Distinctions Between Experimental Memory Testing Procedures

Memory Category	Testing Procedure
Short-term Memory or Primary Memory	Recall of items after a delay of 0-60 seconds with interpolated tasks preventing rehearsal (Peterson-Brown technique). Digit Span Tests.
Long-term Memory	Tests that assess recall of items that exceed in number the normal span of apprehension.
Remote Memory	Tests assessing memory for public or autobiographical events over the decades of the patient's life span (Famous Faces Test, M. S. Albert et al., 1979).

Anterograde Amnesia

The alcoholic Korsakoff patient's anterograde amnesia is the most striking feature of his memory disorder. He is unable to learn new verbal and nonverbal information from the time of onset of his illness. Learning the name of his physician, nurses, the name of the hospital, and even the location of his bed, may require weeks or months of constant repetition and rehearsal. Events that occurred hours or even minutes before will be lost... . Not only does he fail to learn the names of important people and places, but often he will not remember previous encounters with these individuals. If the patient spends three hours completing a number of psychometric tasks, he will fail to recall the entire test session two hours after it ended. Experimentally, this severe anterograde problem is exemplified by the severe difficulty the Korsakoff patient has in learning even short lists of five or six verbal paired associates. (Butters & Brandt, 1984)

In Table 3.4, there is a list of the memory skills that are impaired in KD. The first section comprises tests that assess anterograde amnesia; the range of Korsakoff memory deficits is obviously very considerable.

There are many examples of the severity of the anterograde amnesia in KD in the literature. For example, on the Rey Auditory Verbal Learning Test, the Korsakoff patient can recall 4 out of 14 words on the first trial, and by the end of 5 trials have learned on average only one more word (Squire & Shimamura, 1986). In contrast, we have found that severely head-injured people tested 6 months after discharge would be expected to score on average 12 out of 15 after 5 trials (Godfrey, Partridge, R. G. Knight, & Bishara, 1991). By the end of the 5th trial, elderly laborers (70-90 years) learn 9.5 words on average (Lezak, 1983). Similarly, D. N. Brooks and Baddeley (1976) presented 8 paired associates made up of high frequency words (e.g., cabbage-ink; tiger-desk) "chosen to exclude obvious associations" (p. 112) to a group of KD patients. After 4 trials, the controls had learned the association between 7.0 of the pairs, the KD patients had managed on average to learn only 2.5 pairs.

In short, on verbal and nonverbal tests, regardless of modality of presentation (visual, auditory, or tactile), and irrespective of whether retention is tested by free recall or recognition, patients with KD show major impairments. Their amnesia is profound and global.

Retrograde Amnesia

KD patients generally have extensive RA. Their recall of events that happened prior to the onset of severe amnesia is likely to be poor. Often it is as if events in the past 10 to 15 years had not happened at all. There is usually some temporal grading; elderly KD patients with an excellent recall of personal and public events during the World War 2, have no recollection of the Vietnam War, nor of world leaders since the 1950s. There are several experimental studies in the literature describing the retrograde amnesia of patients with KD (e.g., M. S. Albert et al., 1979; Sanders & Warrington, 1971; Shimamura & Squire, 1986b).

Table 3.4: Tasks on which Alcoholic KD Patients Show Deficits Relative to Chronic Alcoholics

Task	Representative Studies
Anterograde Amnesia	
Delayed free recall of verbal material	Baddeley & Warrington, 1973; Warrington & Weiskrantz, 1968
Recall of prose passages	Squire & Shimamura, 1986
Delay recall of visual location	Warrington & Baddeley, 1974
Learning verbal paired associates	D. N. Brooks & Baddeley, 1976; Cutting, 1978
Recognition of pictures, words, sentences, and meaningless designs	Cutting, 1978; Squire & Shimamura, 1986; Warrington & Weiskrantz, 1968
Memory for complex designs	Riege, 1977; Squire & Shimamura, 1986
Retrograde Amnesia	
Remote memory for famous people, events, and faces	M. S. Albert et al., 1979; Shimamura & Squire, 1986b
Memory-related experimental tasks	
Short-term memory; Recall of word triads after 9-60 seconds distraction	Cermak et al., 1971; Leng & Parkin, 1989; B. E. Longmore & R. G. Knight, 1988
Repetition priming: Acquiring new verbal associations	Shimamura & Squire, 1984, 1989
Release from proactive interference	Cermak et al., 1974; Squire, 1982.
Measures of sensitivity to proactive interference	Mayes et al., 1987; Warrington & Weiskrantz, 1970, 1978
Judgments of temporal order	Squire, 1982
Metamemory: Knowledge of memory function	Parkin et al., 1988
Metamemory: Accuracy of feeling of knowing judgments	Shimamura & Squire, 1986a
Source amnesia: Knowledge of where and when information was acquired	Schacter et al., 1984

One of the most detailed case studies of RA of a Korsakoff patient was presented by Butters and Brandt (1984). The patient was P.Z., an eminent scientist and academic, who developed KD at the age of 65. He was the author of several hundred scholarly articles and had prepared an autobiography in 1982, some 3 years prior to the onset of an episode of Wernicke's encephalopathy. He was subsequently diagnosed as having alcoholic KD and was found to have an extensive degree of RA. His retrograde amnesia was assessed using a measure comprising the names of 75 famous scientists well known to P.Z. before the onset of his disorder. P.Z. was asked to identify their areas of expertise and scientific contributions. His performance was compared to those of an age-matched colleague of similar eminence. It was apparent on the "Famous Scientist" test, P.Z. had developed a loss of knowledge about his scientist colleagues over all the temporal periods sampled, extending back over 30 to 40 years. However, his memory loss was most dramatic for scientists coming to prominence since 1965.

Butters and Brandt proposed that the deficits shown by alcoholic KD patients are the result of two factors. One is the effect of chronic alcohol abuse prior to the onset of amnesia on the acquisition of memories. There is some evidence that alcoholics show a progressive loss of remote memories for recent events (M. S. Albert, Butters, & Brandt, 1980). This implies that alcoholic KD patients will have greater difficulty remembering the recent past than the more remote past and thus a temporally graded remote memory test performance will emerge. The other factor is a generalized, ungraded loss of remote memories, which may be a consequence of an episode of Wernicke's encephalopathy. If these two factors are combined, KD patients will show a generalized memory loss across all time periods relative to age-matched controls, with a more pronounced loss of memories for recent decades. This was the kind of pattern revealed by P.Z. However, KD remote memory performance is variable. In Fig. 3.2, two KD cases from our research (F. J. Longmore, R. G. Knight, & B. E. Longmore, 1990) are presented, and their performance compared with that of age-matched controls. Patient KD01 shows a marked temporal gradient; the performance of KD02 is more variable, but also shows some temporal decline.

It is of interest that cases of amnesia with diencephalic lesions not resulting from alcohol abuse often have an extensive ungraded RA similar to that of alcoholic KD patients (Parkin, 1984). In contrast, H.M., who has medial temporal lesions, has a strongly graded RA. This suggests that it may not be the alcohol abuse or poor nutrition that causes the more extensive RA in KD. Rather, it may be either region of the brain affected or the more diffuse lesions and possible concurrent dementia that cause the more ungraded and extensive RA in Korsakoff patients.

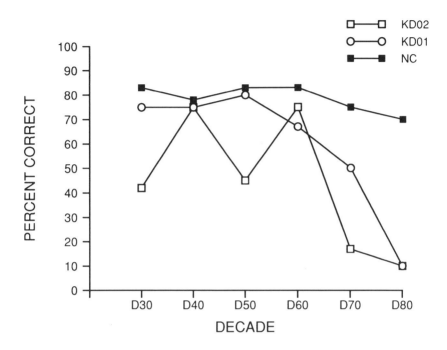

Figure 3.2. Remote memory performance in two patients with Korsakoff's disease (KD01, KD02) and a group of normal controls (NC).

Experimental Investigation of Amnesia

Table 3.4 also contains a list of the experimental tasks on which KD patients have shown deficits. Much of the research listed was focused on developing an understanding of cognitive processes damaged in amnesia. During the period from about 1968 to the early 1980s, there was considerable debate about whether amnesia was a defect of *consolidation* or *retrieval*. Consolidation failure referred to the inability to encode or register new memories and this initially seemed the most likely explanation of amnesia. Retrieval, on the other hand, is the ability to access previously stored memories. There are a number of comprehensive reviews of this period of research (e.g., Cermak, 1982; R. G. Knight & Wooles, 1980). Our main concern in this context is to look at how amnesia was studied, and the impact that this has had on later formulations of the cognitive basis of amnesic disorders.

In a series of important experiments, Warrington and Weiskrantz (1968, 1970) showed that amnesic patients (most of whom had KD), could recall verbal material and line drawings provided they were tested using a cuing method they called *partial information*. The first partial information procedure they used involved fragmented pictures. They prepared five versions of each line drawing or word ranging in a graduated series of steps from unaltered to extremely degraded, and used these stimuli to test learning. The most altered stimulus was presented first and then each of the other four versions was presented successively, in order of completeness, until the subject recognized the word or drawing. Unimpaired subjects gradually learn to recognize the fragmented pictures earlier in the sequence of presentation; the fragmented pictures therefore act as a cue for recognizing the complete word. Warrington and Weiskrantz found that their amnesic patients could learn to recognize these fragmented pictures normally. They went on to show (Warrington & Weiskrantz, 1970) that the same benefits of partial information could be shown in amnesic performance if patients were cued using the three initial letters of the word to be recalled.

Results from Warrington and Weiskrantz's studies, which compared different memory testing procedures, are shown in Table 3.5. Each test required subjects to read 8 words aloud. This was followed by a 1-minute distractor-filled delay. In the free recall condition, subjects were simply asked to recall as many words as they could. The recognition test involved asking subjects to respond yes or no to a list of 16 words, 8 of which had been presented on the learning trial, and 8 that were new. In the fragmented word condition, the degraded stimuli were presented as cues; in the partial information condition, recall was cued by the first 3 letters. As shown in Table 3.5 the amnesics were impaired on the free recall and recognition tests, but performed normally on the cued recall trials. The conclusion from these results was important: Method of retrieval determined the amount that amnesics could remember.

Warrington and Weiskrantz (1970) used these results to support their hypothesis that amnesia was not the result of consolidation failure. They concluded that "the fact that information in long-term memory is available even after learning by conventional methods, if a particular retrieval method is used, is further evidence that it is inappropriate to characterize the amnesic syndrome as being a failure of registration or consolidation" (p. 629).

**Table 3.5:   Recall of Words (Maximum Score 24) Using Different
Methods of Testing Retrieval**

Procedure	Controls	Amnesics	*p*
Free Recall	13.0	8.0	.02
Yes - No Recognition	18.7	16.5	.001
Fragmented words	11.1	11.4	ns
Initial letter cued recall	16.0	14.5	ns

Note. From Amnesic Syndrome: Consolidation or Retrieval?
By E. K. Warrington, & L. Weiskrantz, 1970. *Nature, 228,*
pp. 628-630. Copyright (c) 1970 McMillan Magazines Ltd.
Reprinted by permission.

If consolidation is unaffected in amnesics then their initial encoding, registration, and rate of decay from STM should be normal. Results from immediate memory (Digit Span) tasks support this view. Further evidence comes from a study by Baddeley and Warrington (1970). They asked amnesic subjects to recall as many items as they could from a list of 10 words. When probability of recall is graphed against serial position, normally two components emerge. Normal and amnesic serial position curves are illustrated in Fig. 3.3. There is a long-term memory component (a primacy effect, or the first part of the controls' curve in Fig. 3.3), which is reflected in the high probability of recall of the first few list items, and an STM (or recency) effect, apparent in the high probability of recall of the last few items. If amnesics have an unimpaired STM then the recency component should be normal, although the long-term-memory would be expected to be affected. This is indeed what Baddeley and Warrington found. As in Fig. 3.3, there were clear signs of an LTM deficit for the amnesics, but the STM component was quite normal. This result supported the view that consolidation was normal in amnesia.

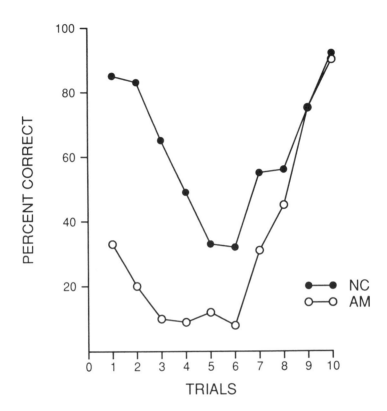

Figure 3.3. Probability of word recall as a function of serial position in amnesic (AM) and normal controls (NC) subjects.

However, the assertion that amnesic STM is normal has not been universally accepted. At issue are results from the performance of KD patients on the Peterson-Brown distractor task. There are several variations in this task, but one typical method (Cermak, Butters, & Goodglass, 1971) involves initially presenting the subject with 3 words. The subject is then signaled to begin a distracting activity designed to prevent rehearsal (e.g., counting backward in threes from a randomly selected 3-digit number). After a specified time has elapsed (0-60 seconds) the subject is asked to recall the three words. Probability of correct recall can be graphed against the delay time to give a measure of rate of decay from STM.

Results from this task have not been consistent. Baddeley and Warrington (1970) and Kopelman (1985) found normal performance by amnesic patients on this task, thereby supporting the contention that consolidation is normal in amnesia. On the other hand, Cermak et al. (1971) and B. E. Longmore and R. G. Knight (1988) found that KD patients perform more poorly than alcoholic controls. This discrepancy may be attributable to minor differences in experimental procedure or to the greater degree of diffuse cerebral impairment in some groups of Korsakoffs than others (Butters & Cermak, 1974). It is clear that amnesics differ in their performance of this task and the reason for this variation is not entirely clear. It is certainly fair to conclude, however, that at least under some circumstances KD patients show more rapid STM decay than do matched controls.

In support of their competing contention that KD amnesics show a degree of consolidation failure, Cermak et al. (1974) presented results from a release from proactive interference (PI) task. One of the simplest ways of illustrating release from PI was developed by Craik and Birtwistle. The general procedure is outlined in Table 3.6.

Table 3.6: Diagrammatic Representation of a Release from PI Procedure

Condition	Trial 1	Trial 2	Trial 3	Trial 4	Trial 5
Shift	10 animals	10 animals	10 animals	10 animals	10 cars
No-shift	10 tools	10 tools	10 tools	10 tools	10 tools

On each trial, subjects are given 10 words to read and then asked to recall as many as they can. In the shift condition the first four trials use words from one category, and then there is a shift to a new taxonomic category on the fifth trial. On the first four trials, recall gradually deteriorates but on the fifth there is usually a dramatic lift in performance with the introduction of a new category of words. In the no-shift condition, performance continues to deteriorate as PI builds up over the five trials.

KD patients have generally shown no improvement after a taxonomic shift (Cermak et al., 1974; B. E. Longmore & R. G. Knight, 1988; Squire, 1982; Warrington, 1982). Cermak et al. argued that the inability to detect conceptual changes was the result of an impairment of the capacity to encode new information. However, Warrington (1982) disputed this conclusion. Interestingly, Winocur, Kinsbourne, and Moscovitch (1981) showed that under at least one circumstance, KD patients do release normally. In their study, the number of trials was increased to nine, and category shifts were instituted on both the fifth and ninth trials. In this case, KD patients failed to release on the first occasion but did on the second. This suggests that once the expectation of shifting has been created, KD patients may release from PI normally.

Another test of the consolidation/encoding failure hypothesis involved investigating the effects of increasing the level of initial processing on amnesic performance (e.g., Cermak & Reale, 1978; DeLuca, Cermak, & Butters, 1976). The basic approach in these studies was to require amnesics to process information to a greater depth, thereby enhancing their naturally deficient encoding abilities. Table 3.7 presents the different levels of processing based on Craik and Lockhart's (1972) approach, together with a relevant question designed to ensure processing at that level.

Table 3.7: **Examples of Stimuli Used in Levels of Processing Studies**

Level	Stimulus Question	Yes Response	No Response
Semantic	Does this fit in the sentence: "The rain fell from the ..."	Sky	INK
Acoustic	Does this rhyme with cat?	MAT	Cabbage
Physical	Is this in uppercase letters?	DOG	Cat

The KD patients were shown 20 questions that required semantic analysis to provide an answer, 20 that required acoustic (rhyming) analysis, and 20 that required only the analysis of the physical features of the word. The 60 sentences were presented in random order, and then recall of the 60 response words was tested. Cermak proposed that if KD patients are forced to analyze material to the greatest possible degree, that is to conduct a full semantic analysis, then their recall should improve to normal levels. However, the procedure was only partly successful. It was not possible to demonstrate a marked improvement in performance as a consequence of increased depth of processing. Cermak and Reale (1978) concluded their article with a compromise:

> The fact that Korsakoff patients' recognition memory for verbal material can be affected by the level for which they process that information under certain conditions lends some support to the contention that Korsakoff patients' anterograde amnesia might stem, in part, from a tendency not to perform semantic analyses of to-be-retained verbal information. However, since instructions did not improve retention under all conditions, it must be concluded that other factors, such as level of retrieval search, must be explored as further contributors to the patients' overall memory problem. (p. 173)

By the early 1980s the retrieval-consolidation debate had lost momentum. Attention turned to how the cognitive experimental study of amnesia might contribute to the understanding of the neuroanatomical basis of memory loss. For example, Warrington and Weiskrantz (1982) suggested that the fundamental cause of amnesia at a functional level was a failure to engage in "cognitive mediation" during the learning process. By cognitive mediation they were referring to "cognitive elaboration, use of imagery, embellishment, manipulation, and organization" (p. 242). They proposed that the ability to use cognitive mediation was not actually lost, and that amnesics still had a normal semantic memory (i.e., their language skills were preserved), but these two functions were disconnected. Hence amnesics could comprehend, but not elaborate input. The biological basis for this disturbance was tentatively attributed to disconnection of the temporal lobes (containing the semantic memory store) and the frontal lobes (the cognitive mediation and elaboration area), caused by the destruction of the fornix-mamillary body fiber systems that connect the two areas.

When marshalling evidence for their model of amnesia, Warrington and Weiskrantz placed considerable stress on the reasons why amnesics might show profound anterograde amnesia and yet still perform some memory-related tasks quite normally. Since 1980 there has been considerable interest in the learning and memory skills that seem to be preserved in amnesia. Another issue that has received attention is the wide individual differences in the performance of memory tests by amnesics of different etiologies. Research has been concerned with the possibility that there may be more than one form of amnesia. We turn our attention first, however, to considering preserved memory in KD.

Preserved Memory Skills

The patient was a woman hospitalized at Asile de Bel-Air. She was 47 at the time of the first experiment, 1906... . When one told her a little story, read to her various items of a newspaper, three minutes later she remembered nothing, not even the fact that someone had read to her; but with certain questions one could elicit in a reflex fashion some of the details of those items. But when she found those details in her consciousness, she did not recognize them as memories but believed them to be something "that went through her mind" by chance, an idea she had without knowing why... .

I carried out the following curious experiment on her: to see whether she would better retain an intense impression involving affectivity, I stuck her hand with a pin hidden between my fingers. The light pain was as quickly forgotten... . But when I again reached out for her hand, she pulled it back in a reflex fashion, not knowing why. When I asked her for the reason, she said in a flurry, "Doesn't one have the right to withdraw her hand?" and when I insisted, she said, "Is there perhaps a pin hidden in your hand?" To the question, "What makes you suspect me of wanting to stick you?" she would repeat her old statement, "That was an idea that went through my mind," or she would explain, "Sometimes pins are hidden in people's hands." But never would she recognize the idea of sticking as a "memory." (Claparede, 1951, p. 68-69)

Perhaps the most fascinating aspect of amnesia is the fact that under some conditions the profoundly amnesic patient displays evidence of new learning. The often quoted example of Claparede's patient is a striking instance. However, the list of tasks that KD patients perform normally is brief (Table 3.8). The finding that Korsakoff patients have normal immediate memory has already been discussed. Some of the other aspects of memory performance that are normal in KD are reviewed here.

Forgetting rates. The rate at which memories fade from the LTM after a learning episode has been found to be equivalent for Korsakoff and normal patients. KD patients learn more slowly, so they may reach a criterion level after many more learning trials. However, as Huppert and

Piercy (1978) showed, if initial learning performance is equated, forgetting rate is equivalent for KD and control subjects. This result has been replicated by Kopelman (1985). Normal forgetting rates have also been reported for H.M. (Freed, Corkin, & N. J. Cohen, 1984) and for patients with Alzheimer's disease (Kopelman, 1985).

Table 3.8: Memory-related Measures that KD Patients Perform Normally

Task	Representative Studies
Immediate memory	D. N. Brooks & Baddeley, 1976
Forgetting rate after learning to criterion	Huppert & Piercy, 1978; Kopelman, 1985
Repetition priming	Graf et al., 1984; B. E. Longmore & R. G. Knight, 1988
Acquisition of motor and perceptual skills	D. N. Brooks & Baddeley, 1976; N. J. Cohen & Squire, 1980; Martone et al., 1984
Classical conditioning	Weiskrantz & Warrington, 1979.

Motor skill acquisition. The normal performance by amnesics on motor skill learning tasks are in stark contrast to their poor efforts on verbal learning tests. D. N. Brooks and Baddeley (1976) found that amnesics could learn to assemble a 12-piece jigsaw puzzle as rapidly as controls. They also learned a pursuit rotor task at a normal rate. One of the nicest demonstrations of preserved psychomotor learning comes from N. J. Cohen and Squire (1980). They measured speed of acquiring mirror reading skills in a group of KD patients. They asked their subjects to read triads of 8- to 10-letter, low frequency words (e.g., bedraggle-capricious-grandiose) presented in mirror-image form. They read 5 sets of 10 words on 3 successive days and then finally 13 weeks later. Half of the triads were repeated on each occasion, the other half were new, allowing the time taken to read repeated and nonrepeated words to be compared. As the sessions progressed, both the KD subjects and their controls learned to read the mirror-imaged words more quickly. However, the KD patients' performance on the repeated triads did not show the same degree of improvement as the controls. Thus for new words, where only the acquisition of a perceptual skill was tested, KD and control patients performed at an equivalent level. However, when the learning of repeated words was tested, which required memory for specific learning episodes, the patients showed a deficit. So this procedure nicely distinguished between the ability to learn a new skill and the ability to analyze specific repeated items.

It is also interesting to note that KD patients may learn new rules normally. Many of the reports of this preserved ability are informal. For example, Kinsbourne and Wood (1975) taught a group of KD patients a mathematical rule that could be used to predict number sequences. They found evidence that the rules could be applied 12 weeks later even though the patients had no recollection of ever learning the rule. N. J. Cohen and Corkin (1981) reported similar results for H.M.

Semantic priming. As we have already seen, the experiments of Warrington and colleagues suggested that cueing amnesics with 3-letter word stems significantly improved their recall. However, other researchers were unable to replicate these results entirely (e.g., Squire, Wetzel, & Slater, 1978; Wetzel & Squire, 1982). It has now become apparent that it is the way in which amnesics are instructed to perform the recall test that crucially determines how well they will perform.

In 1982, Jacoby and Witherspoon demonstrated normal semantic priming in five KD patients. They were asked a series of orienting questions, designed to prime the *low* frequency meaning of a pair of homophones. Homophones are words that sound the same, but are spelled differently: for example, READ-REED. An orienting question to prime the low frequency word might be, "What is an example of a REED instrument?" After a delay, the subjects were asked to spell a list of words, including the primed homophones, as they were dictated by the experimenter. The KD patients showed a normal tendency for bias toward the low frequency homophone used in the orienting question. Their normal bias is a compelling illustration of preserved semantic priming in KD.

In an important series of experiments, Graf, Squire, and Mandler (1984), were able to tie together the results from Jacoby and Witherspoon's study, and the findings from the 3-letter cuing task Warrington and Weiskrantz (1970) employed. They tested memory performance under three conditions: Free recall, cued recall using 3-letter word stems as cues, and priming using word-completion instructions. The first two conditions were the same as had been used previously in numerous studies. The word-completion instructions were, however, novel. They involved giving subjects an orienting task that made no reference to memory in the recall instructions. One of the orienting tasks Graf et al. (1984) used instructed subjects to rate how much they "liked" words on a scale from 1 (dislike extremely) to 5 (like extremely). Immediately after the subjects had rated the 10 words in the learning list twice, they were asked to recall as many of them as they could (free recall instructions). They were then told that each of the 3-letter cues they were to be given was "the beginning of an English word. Write a few letters to make each into a word. You can write any English word—but write the first word that comes to mind" (p. 168).

The conclusion from Graf et al.'s results was clear. On the cued recall task in which subjects were explicitly asked to remember the words from the learning list, and on the free recall test, the Korsakoffs were grossly impaired. On the word completion task, however, their performance was equivalent to that of the controls. The rate of decay of the priming effect was also normal. These results offered a new understanding of the skills that are preserved in amnesia. When test instructions made no reference to memory or to a previous learning episode, Korsakoff performance was normal. When the instructions focused on overtly remembering a wordlist, the amnesics were obviously deficient. Preserved priming has been shown in a number of other situations (Graf, Shimamura, & Squire, 1985; Schacter, 1985) and appears to be a robust phenomenon.

Conclusions. Korsakoff patients have been shown to learn new motor skills normally and to be unimpaired on semantic priming tasks. These results are important because they provide a theoretical basis for understanding what to expect that they may be able to learn. The tasks that amnesics can and cannot perform normally have to be categorized in a variety of ways. Some of the labels that have been given to the two classes of tasks are presented in Table 3.9. Each of these divisions suggests that memory can be divided into multiple systems that can be damaged independently.

Table 3.9: Labels Used to Describe the Distinction Between Impaired and Unimpaired Memory in Amnesia

| | Amnesic Performance | |
Normal	Abnormal	Reference
procedural	declarative	Squire & N. J. Cohen, 1984
data-driven	conceptually driven	Jacoby, 1983
implicit	explicit	Schacter, 1987
semantic	episodic	Cermak, 1984
incidental	intentional	Jacoby, 1984
indirect tests	direct tests	M. K. Johnson & Hasher, 1987

The distinction between *implicit* and *explicit* memory processes has been particularly influential. Implicit memory "is revealed by a facilitation or change in task performance that is attributable to a previous study episode" (Schacter, 1987, p. 501). In contrast, explicit memory refers to "the conscious recollection of recently presented information, as expressed in traditional tests of free recall, cued recall, and recognition" (Schacter, 1987, p. 501). For an excellent review of the history and substance of this approach, the reader is referred to Schacter (1987). The *indirect-direct* distinction of Hasher and M. K. Johnson (1987) is also useful because it attempts to classify memory measures without reference to the cognitive processes involved. Indirect memory tests are defined as "those tests requiring the subject to engage in some cognitive or motor activity, when the instructions refer only to the task at hand, and do not make reference to prior events" (Richardson-Klavehn & Bjork, 1988, p. 478). Direct tests on the other hand make clear reference to some event in the subject's previous experience.

Of most importance to the clinician is the general finding that KD patients may show they have learned something, provided the demonstration of learning requires no direct or explicit reference to previous learning. Confronted with a puzzle or problem they have seen before, Korsakoffs will show a relatively normal saving in learning. They will, however, almost certainly deny ever having seen the puzzle or problem before. This has interesting ramifications for the understanding of how normal memory works and also some practical implications for the management of amnesic patients. These are introduced at the end of this chapter.

KD and Other Amnesias Compared

Is the pattern of amnesia seen in KD distinct from that seen in other amnesic disorders? There are two reasons why it might be. First, the critical lesions are centered on the midline of the diencephalon, distinguishing them from amnesics with temporal lesions. Second, some KD patients have lesions in other parts of the brain, for instance, the cortex (Victor et al., 1971) and the basal forebrain (T. Arendt et al., 1983). A review of all the issues and research involved in the debate about whether there is more than one type of amnesia is beyond the scope of this chapter. Detailed surveys of the literature are available elsewhere (e.g., N. J. Cohen & Squire, 1984; Parkin, 1984, 1990; Squire, 1986; Weiskrantz, 1985). However, some of the issues involved, as they relate to the deficits of KD, are briefly considered here.

It is obvious from clinical experience and the results reported in the literature that patients described as Korsakoff or amnesic vary considerably in the severity of their anterograde amnesia. They also differ in the extent to which they display dysfunctions associated with memory loss, for example, confabulation or lack of awareness of their deficits. Individual differences in the memory deficits shown by amnesics can possibly be attributed to a number of cognitive factors or to the related variations in the underlying pattern of lesions producing the amnesia. These cognitive factors might include level of concurrent IQ, severity of anterograde amnesia, and/or deterioration in intellect. Lesion-related factors might include the general site of the brain damage (e.g., the diencephalon versus the temporal lobe), the presence of concurrent lesions in other regions (e.g., frontal lobe damage), and/or the extent of the critical amnesia-producing lesions, which may cause damage to fiber tracts projecting to other parts of the brain. As an example of the last possibility, extensive diencephalic lesions may cause amnesia in their own right, as well as disconnecting this part of the brain from the frontal lobes, causing deficits that are normally pathognomic of specific frontal lobe damage (e.g., Graff-Radford, Tranel, Van Hoesen, & Brandt, 1990).

In general, KD patients show a greater range of deficits than do patients with amnesia from other causes. That is, on any memory-related tasks that only some amnesics perform abnormally, KD patients will be more commonly found to show a deficit. Thus KD patients are, for example, more likely to fail to release from PI than other amnesics (e.g., Squire, 1982), less likely to make accurate recency judgments (Squire, 1982), and more often perform abnormally on the WCST (Janowsky, Shimamura, Kritchevsky, & Squire, 1989; Leng & Parkin, 1988). KD patients are also less accurate in their judgments of what they will or will not be able to remember (Shimamura & Squire, 1986a). Confabulation and lack of awareness of deficit is also more common in KD than in other amnesias.

The reason why Korsakoffs show more extensive deficits than some other amnesics are unclear. Any or all of the cognitive and lesion-related factors considered at the beginning of this section could be responsible. Hopefully, continuing systematic evaluations of the performance of amnesics with precisely defined neuroanatomical lesions, using appropriate neuropsychological and experimental tasks will build on our current imprecise understanding of amnesia.

Psychosocial Consequences and Rehabilitation

Close acquaintance with chronic Korsakoff patients also reveals certain marked disturbances of personality. There is often a pronounced degree of apathy and loss of initiative, a bland or even fatuous disposition and a tendency towards self neglect. Lack of insight is usually striking and almost universal; few Korsakoff patients appreciate they are ill, and in those that do the gravity of their defects is minimized or explained away by facile rationalizations. (Lishman, 1978, p. 42)

There are few experimental reports analyzing the personality deficits of Korsakoff patients. This is in contrast to the attention their amnesia has excited. Yet Lishman's description of the personal presentation of the Korsakoff patient draws attention to what is often the central issue in their rehabilitation. The KD patient has, in addition to a profound degree of amnesia, changes in personality and limitations in available psychosocial support that are the consequence of prolonged alcoholism and personal neglect.

Being profoundly amnesic imposes a relationship with the environment that those of us with an intact memory can hardly hope to understand. There is a poignant passage in Milner et al.'s (1968) description of H.M. that provides a sense of the devastation caused by amnesia:

During three of the nights at the Clinical Research Center, the patient rang for the night nurse, asking her, with many apologies, if she would tell him where he was and how he came to be there. He clearly realized that he was in a hospital but seemed unable to reconstruct any of the events of the previous day. On another occasion he remarked "Every day is alone in itself, whatever enjoyment I've had, and whatever sorrow I've had." Our own impression is that many events fade for him long

before the day is over. He often volunteers stereotype descrip-
tions of his own state, by saying that it is "like waking from a
dream." His experience seems to be that of a person who is
just becoming aware of his surroundings without fully compre-
hending the situation, because he does not remember what went
before. (Milner, Corkin, & Teuber, 1968, pp. 216-217)

Chronic KD patients are without the apparent awareness of loss that
H.M. shows. Their presentation is quite lucid, but usually apathetic.

Although it is possible to document amnesic impairments using
neuropsychological tests, for the purpose of rehabilitation it is often more
useful to describe Korsakoff performance of routine tasks in the hospital.
On a scale designed to allow the nursing staff to document practical
memory impairment in chronic amnesic alcoholics, the Inpatient Memory
Impairment Scale (IMIS; Godfrey & R. G. Knight, 1988; R. G. Knight
& Godfrey, 1984b), the restricted abilities of KD can be clearly demonstrated. In Table 3.10 the average IMIS scores of a group of chronic KD
patients who, like Jim, had lived in the same ward for several years are
presented. The IMIS response scale ranges from 5 (all the time) to 0
(not at all). The KD patients are compared with alcoholics (most of
whom had been in the ward for less than 3 months), and long-stay psychiatric patients in another ward.

Memory deficits limit the amount of independence that the KD
patient can enjoy. They learn very slowly about their environment and
routines; any changes are likely to be assimilated gradually. Patients are
usually of average intelligence so they can make full use of salient cues
in the environment.

Another major limiting factor in the rehabilitation of Korsakoff
patients is their lack of both insight and concern about their memory loss.
If left alone, Korsakoff patients are typically apathetic, even though they
may be quite responsive when tested or interviewed. Irritability or
outbursts of emotion or anger do occur, but this is unusual, and a general
blandness of disposition is more typical. Korsakoffs are seldom perturbed
by their failure to perform memory tasks or inability to recall autobiographical details. If asked about their work or ward duties, they can
respond in a general way, but rarely with any specificity. Alcohol abuse
remains a problem in some patients despite their apathy. Talland (1965)
reported that although most of his Korsakoff sample "staunchly denied
ever having drunk excessively or even having cared for alcoholic beverages; several admitted it and also to neglecting their diet" (p. 29). If
allowed downtown unescorted some patients will find a bar. Their tolerance for alcohol is usually very low and they are likely to become offen-

sive or abusive. The Korsakoff patient's ability to manage their money and to care for themselves is also likely to be poor. For these reasons, some degree of long-term supervision is nearly always necessary.

Table 3.10: IMIS Item Means and Standard Deviations for Korsakoff, Alcoholic, and Psychiatric Patients

	Korsakoff Mean (SD)	Alcoholic Mean (SD)	Psychiatric Mean (SD)
Remembers names	2.22 (1.15)	4.23 (0.75)	4.08 (0.91)
Remembers ward routine	2.69 (1.49)	4.42 (0.71)	4.43 (0.75)
Needs reminders of appointments	1.50 (1.42)	3.98 (1.02)	3.83 (1.03)
Recalls recent personal history	2.33 (1.44)	4.12 (0.85)	4.42 (0.71)
Loses things	2.11 (1.25)	4.45 (0.66)	4.25 (0.80)
Recalls events (previous day)	2.08 (1.35)	4.37 (0.74)	4.52 (0.64)
Becomes lost	3.78 (1.57)	4.78 (0.43)	4.97 (0.18)
Remembers directions	2.58 (1.46)	4.73 (0.43)	4.75 (0.58)
Remembers bed or dormitory	4.44 (0.73)	4.93 (0.22)	5.00 (0.00)
Learns new skills slowly	1.42 (1.05)	3.58 (1.10)	3.55 (1.41)

Finally, it is worth stating what will be immediately obvious when confronting the patient with KD—after years of alcohol abuse most have no family and no resources. However, there are exceptions. Some patients drink extremely heavily for only a relatively short period of time before a Wernicke's episode leads to hospitalization. Many of these patients have spouses and children who keep in contact with them. In some instances, Korsakoff patients can be cared for at home by their spouses or other close relatives. Many Korsakoffs, however, have been solitary people who drank heavily, and worked until they could work no more because of their drink-related impairments. Prolonged hospitalization frequently destroys any remaining family or relationship bonds. In general, KD patients requiring care and supervision tend to be older (55-70), to have little or no contact with their relatives, and no financial or other resources left. They are therefore likely to find their way into state-run institutions. It is there that they will be stabilized, treated, assessed, and possibly prepared for release into supervised community-based facilities.

Management of the Korsakoff Patient

Throughout the world, the deinstitutionalization movement has led to a dramatic reduction in the use of psychiatric hospital facilities to care for patients with psychological and neurological handicaps. From the 1960s onward, there has been a greater reliance on halfway houses, hostel care, and community-based services for managing patients with long-term psychiatric disabilities. Despite their obvious personality and cognitive deficits, it is appropriate to consider the placement of Korsakoff patients in facilities outside geriatric or psychiatric wards. For each individual Korsakoff patient, however, the degree of supervision and support required needs careful assessment.

Profound amnesia in itself does not require institutionalization. H.M. and N.A., for example, have lived at home with their parents. Younger KD patients may be able to live in the community in the care of parents or relatives. A few practical adaptations to enhance the probability that patients will remember routines and appointments can easily be contrived. Support for the caregivers will also be important. Older patients are often capable of living in residential care facilities for the elderly, with limited nursing supervision, provided they do not have easy access to alcohol and have good self-care skills. The typical Korsakoff patient's level of competence in dealing with day-to-day activities, work, and routine chores is likely to be better and more stable than that of moderately demented patients with Alzheimer's disease. Self-care skills and money management are likely to require close monitoring. Korsakoff patients will need to be escorted in unfamiliar environments and places where alcohol is available. Otherwise they can often live with a reasonable degree of independence.

The rehabilitation of hospitalized KD patients begins with a comprehensive neuropsychological examination. It is worth bearing in mind that occasionally amnesic patients who are not routinely assessed may be almost "forgotten" by staff in large wards. Sometimes it will be assumed that the patient is still functioning as poorly as they did on admission, when in fact the degree of amnesia may have improved quite substantially. Repeated testing on the Wechsler Memory Scale subtests may reveal a progressive improvement in the patient's cognitive state that may not be noticed because of their apathy.

In addition to the formal neuropsychological assessment, it is often useful to have the patient perform some simple practical memory tests of the kind detailed in Chapter 2. R. G. Knight and Godfrey (1985) used the following two tasks:

> *Route finding.* Select several prominent features within the hospital and ask the patient to describe the route to the designated feature, from their own ward. It is possible to watch the patient actually walking to a particular place and note the route they take and the length of time necessary.

> *Memory for instructions.* This is a simple matter of giving the patient a short list of instructions and seeing how many they manage to execute. These instructions can involve making marks or writing on a piece of paper, or more realistic events like taking a message to a secretary.

Simple maneuvers like the previous two tasks can be adapted to any setting. The patients' response to these practical tasks gives a notion of how well they know their way around their present environment. Given time, they can learn the same skills elsewhere. Individual patient's performance can be contrasted with appropriate age-matched nonamnesic patients in the hospital.

As far as rehabilitation is concerned, the plethora of experimental cognitive studies adds up to specifying some tasks that Korsakoffs can perform normally. Most importantly, amnesic Korsakoffs can learn new perceptual and motor skills at a relatively normal pace. There is an excellent practical demonstration of this described by Charness, Milberg, and Alexander (1988). Over a period of 7 days, they taught G.P., a Korsakoff patient, a method for mentally squaring two-digit numbers. This is a very complex skill, but G.P. was able to learn the procedure as rapidly as a group of age-matched controls. As was found in the N. J. Cohen and Squire (1980) inverted-word reading task, described earlier, G.P. did not show a normal ability to perform more rapidly on repeated specific items. Charness et al. (1988) noted that

> practice with the mental squaring procedure yielded a striking improvement despite the fact that G.P. could not recall anything about the tasks he had performed until the last day. At that time he was able to volunteer that some tasks dealt with numbers. Even with prompting he was unable to note what the procedure was, despite being able to implement it during testing. (p. 269)

In effect, amnesics often know more than they can tell when they are explicitly asked.

Use of mnemonic strategies or other procedures designed to increase memory capacity in amnesia is unlikely to be effective with KD patients (Godfrey & R. G. Knight, 1984). This is due in large part to their lack of awareness or insight and poor knowledge of memory aids. Simply exposing amnesic Korsakoffs to multiple learning experiences, to build up their "mental muscles" has no specific benefits. However, KD patients do profit from an active ward program and are able to engage in a wide range of activities with appropriate encouragement. This helps to build independence. Simple external cues can be extremely valuable: Notebooks/diaries or strategically placed noticeboards in the ward or home can help amnesics to remember, just as they help us all to extend our memory for appointments and daily activities. The more distinctive an environment is, the easier it is to learn routes and the correct location of facilities and resources. Hospital wards are often bland and repetitious environments. Using different colors for doors with different uses and other changes that make the environment more varied and memorable help amnesics greatly. At one hospital, where patients lived in separate villas having 40 or 50 people, the villa where the long-term KD patients lived was painted bright orange: Aesthetically it was horrific, but it was certainly easy to find.

Conclusions

The study of patients with Korsakoff's disease has made an important contribution to the understanding of human memory function. Their profound and relatively circumscribed amnesia has been the subject of numerous investigations. Perhaps the most important outcome of this work has been the appreciation of the fact that amnesic patients do display unimpaired learning under some circumstances. This has led to the dichotomizing of memory skills into those that are lost and those that are preserved in amnesia. This distinction has been represented in a number of ways. Amnesic Korsakoff patients are characterized by failure on direct or explicit memory tests or in any situation where conscious or intentional learning is required; they may, however, perform normally on indirect or implicit memory tests or in situations where incidental learning is assessed. Unlike patients with Alzheimer's disease, who have global dysfunctions that affect semantic memory and language, these functions are typically normal in Korsakoff patients.

Although the amnesia of KD has excited most attention, it is often the changes in personality and loss of initiative that accompany the disorder that provide the major barrier to rehabilitation. Alcoholic Korsakoff patients display a lack of awareness of their deficits, which is a most arresting feature of the disorder. Their return to and management in the community presents many challenges. It is realistic, however, to be optimistic about the ability of KD patients to live beyond the boundaries of the hospital. Some years ago, we (Godfrey & R. G. Knight) reported an attempt to provide cognitive retraining for a group of 12 alcoholic Korsakoff patients. We had little success in extending our patients' memory or learning capacity. But, not long after that, an active policy of providing noncustodial care for KD patients was introduced. As a result, most of the Korsakoffs in the original program were discharged to live in sheltered environments throughout the city. Of the 12 patients in the study, most are no longer in the psychiatric hospital, where it once appeared they would spend the rest of their lives.

Chapter 4

ALZHEIMER'S DISEASE

A former high school mathematics teacher, Ada looks a lot younger than her 72 years. She sits, whitehaired and erect by her husband John. When spoken to, however, it is clear something is very wrong. She responds to questions with a confused half answer that conveys little. Most of the time, her husband John replies for her. He tells how just over three years ago he noticed Ada was having difficulty setting the table before dinner. It was only a trivial incident and he made no comment. But some weeks later Ada herself commented on her forgetfulness. She lost the ability to do even simple arithmetic calculations and her memory loss and disorientation increased. Bothered by her repetitive questioning and tendency to become lost and confused even in familiar surroundings, John consulted his doctor. A diagnosis of Alzheimer's disease was made. Over the past two years Ada has deteriorated still further. Now she cannot remember her husband's name or any of their life together. Despite the fact that she needs almost constant supervision, John has continued to look after her at home. Much of the experience of caring for her he finds rewarding; certainly he does not resent her increasing incapacity and almost complete dependence. Nearly 78 himself, John acknowledges that soon he will have to arrange for her to enter a nursing home. He conveys his sadness that the witty and bright person he knew has now almost completely gone.

Background

Remarkable changes in the neurofibrils appeared. In the interior of a cell that otherwise appeared normal, one or several fibrils stood out due to their extraordinary thickness and impregnability. At a later stage, many fibrils appeared, situated side by side and altered in the same way. Then they emerged into dense bundles and gradually reached the surface of the cell. Finally the nucleus and the cell disintegrated, and only a dense bundle of fibrils indicated the site where a ganglion cell had been (Alzheimer, 1977).

In 1907, Alois Alzheimer published an account of a disease that he regarded as a unique presenile dementia. It was characterized by the occurrence of intraneuronal fibrils (which he called *neurofibrillary tangles*) and senile plaques, located primarily in the neocortex, which could be observed postmortem using microscopy in the brains of demented patients. Of all the neurological disorders that cause dementia, none causes a more tragic and profound disintegration of intellect and personality than Alzheimer's disease.

There are two distinct disease processes that may cause dementia in later life. The first is the result of cerebrovascular changes that cause a reduction or cessation of the blood supply to areas of the brain. The cognitive impairments and behavior changes that occur in this case are referred to as *multi-infarct dementia* (Hachinski, Lassen, & Marshall, 1974) or *vascular dementia* (del Ser, Bermejo, Portera, Arrendondo, Bouras, & Constantinidis, 1990). The second process is the gradual destruction of nervous tissue as a result of pathological changes in the neurons of the neocortex. The most usual cause of this progressive deterioration is the neuropathological changes of a disease referred to as senile *dementia of the Alzheimer's type* (DAT).

DAT is the most common cause of dementia in the elderly (Schoenberg, Kokmen, & Okazaki, 1987). The neuronal changes that characterize Alzheimer's disease can only be identified by histological examination of tissue from affected areas of the brain, therefore the diagnosis can usually only be considered presumptive while the patient is still alive. There are several disorders, such as Pick's disease, that cannot be readily distinguished from AD by their clinical presentation, and because many patients show signs of both Alzheimer and cerebrovascular lesions, the diagnosis of senile dementia of the Alzheimer type is made with caution. This caution is acknowledged here by the use of the term *dementia of the Alzheimer type* (DAT), to describe patients for whom the clinical diagnosis has not been confirmed by histological examination. The term *Alzheimer's disease* is reserved to denote patient samples where the diagnosis has been confirmed postmortem or where the disease is discussed without reference to particular patients.

Before the 1960s, the diagnosis of Alzheimer's disease was reserved for cases of dementia arising without known cause before age 65. The case originally described by Alzheimer was of a women aged 51, who

> *showed jealousy toward her husband as the first noticeable sign of the disease. Soon a rapidly increasing loss of memory could be noticed. She could not find her way around in her own apartment. She carried objects back and forth and hid*

them. At times she would think that someone wanted to kill her and would begin shrieking loudly. (Alzheimer, 1977)

Until the 1960s, Alzheimer's disease referred only to a presenile dementia and it was believed that dementia occurring in an elderly person over the age of 65 was primarily caused by arteriosclerosis and other cerebrovascular changes. However, studies by Tomlinson and colleagues (e.g., Tomlinson, Blessed, & Roth, 1968, 1970) changed this perception. They showed that the characteristic neuronal changes of presenile Alzheimer's disease were present in the brains of many elderly demented patients, who showed no evidence of abnormal arteriosclerotic lesions. Nowadays, the diagnosis of Alzheimer's disease is not usually confined to patients under 65, and is used to describe both senile and presenile cases.

Diagnosis

Although the diagnosis of AD can only be made with certainty after histological examination, a clinical diagnosis can be made with reasonable accuracy while the patient is alive. The *DSM-III-R* describes the major criteria for the diagnosis of primary degenerative dementia of the Alzheimer type as being the presence of dementia, with a gradual deteriorating course and an insidious onset, where all other specific causes of dementia have been excluded. Dementia is described as follows:

The essential feature of Dementia is impairment in short- and long-term memory, associated with impairment in abstract thinking, impaired judgement, other disturbances of higher cortical function, or personality change. The disturbance is severe enough to interfere significantly with work or usual social activities or relationships with others. (p. 103)

More elaborate criteria, suitable for research work, have been established by a number of laboratories. One of the most detailed statements of diagnostic criteria was prepared by a working party from the National Institute of Neurological and Communicative Disorders and Stroke (NINCDS) and the Alzheimer's and Related Disorders Association (ADRDA). The NINCDS-ADRDA work group criteria for the clinical diagnosis of probable Alzheimer's disease have been documented by Tierney et al. (1988). Other groups of researchers have developed similar criteria (e.g., J. C. Morris, McKeel, Fulling, Torack, & Berg, 1988; Wade, Mirsen, Hachinski, Fisman, Lau, & Merskey 1987; Schoenberg et al., 1987). In Table 4.1 the principal diagnostic features of DAT are summarized.

Table 4.1:   Principal Clinical Diagnostic Features of Dementia of the Alzheimer Type (DAT)

Inclusion criteria

Dementia documented by mental status testing and neuropsychological testing demonstrating progressive memory loss and impairment in abstract thinking.

Evidence of cognitive deterioration in areas other than memory including orientation, judgment, language, motor skills, and perception.

Insidious onset.

Gradual deterioration in cognitive and personal functioning.

Duration of 6 or more months.

Impairment of functioning in relationships, the home, hobbies, and other activities of daily living.

Exclusion criteria

Presence of other neurological disorders, including multifarct dementia, Huntington's disease, infection, brain tumor, multiple sclerosis, and stroke.

Evidence of other medical disorders or systemic diseases causing dementia, including overmedication, vitamin or folate-deficiency, diabetes, and renal, cardiac, pulmonary, or hepatic dysfunction.

Abrupt onset and focal neurological symptoms, such as hemiparesis or visual field defects make a diagnosis of DAT less probable.

Evidence that the dementia is a consequence of psychiatric disorder such as alcohol abuse, schizophrenia, or major affective disorder.

The clinical diagnosis of AD is frequently inaccurate, particularly in the early stages where it may be difficult to distinguish mild dementia from normal aging. It is also important to be aware that many patients presenting to geriatric assessment centers with presumed DAT are in fact suffering from potentially reversible disorders (Wolff, 1982). For example, F. R. Feehan and Rudd (1982) found that of 110 elderly patients with signs of dementia, 16 had an underlying disorder that was treatable. The most common causes of what is often termed *pseudodementia* are depression, alcohol problems, hydrocephalus, subdural hematoma, chronic overmedication, hepatic encephalopathy, B12 and folate deficiencies, hypoglycemia, hyperthyroidism, and infections. Where antemortem clinical diagnosis has been compared with postmortem autopsy, concordance is typically high, with agreement of 81% to 88% being found in one recent study of 57 cases (Tierney et al., 1988), and 100% in another study of 26 cases (J. C. Morris et al., 1988). Both studies used carefully specified diagnostic criteria, and their success rates were somewhat greater than had been previously reported (Terry & Katzman, 1983). It is clear that if research diagnostic criteria are strictly applied and complicated or doubtful presentations are excluded, a presumptive diagnosis of Alzheimer's disease can subsequently be confirmed in some 80 to 90% of cases. The accuracy rate for the DAT population as a whole is likely to be somewhat lower.

The symptom patterns of DAT and multi-infarct dementia can be distinguished with some success (Gershon & Herman, 1982; Hachinski et al., 1974; W. G. Rosen, Terry, Fuld, Katzman, & Peck, 1980). A widely used scale to determine vascular dementia is Hachinski et al.'s (1975) Ischemic scale. The scale is reproduced in Table 4.2. Scores of 4 and below are diagnosed as primary degenerative dementia, and 7 or above as multi-infarct dementia. In general, multi-infarct dementia is characterized by abrupt onset, a course in which decline tends to be marked by a series of sudden changes in functioning, and a focal asymmetric pathology that may be evident on a CT scan. On postmortem examination, multi-infarct dementia can be recognized by the localized signs of cortical atrophy and cystic softenings in the grey matter (Tomlinson, 1977).

Epidemiology

How frequently is dementia in the elderly caused by AD? In a review of his work and that of his colleagues (Tomlinson, 1977; Tomlinson et al., 1968, 1970; Tomlinson & Henderson, 1976), Tomlinson concluded that 50% of their sample of 50 dementing patients showed morphological changes associated with AD. In another 12% of cases, dementia was related to changes in the cerebrum caused by arteriosclerosis. A total of 8% of the cases were listed as having both AD and cerebrovascular changes, and another 10% as being of "probably mixed" etiology. The rest were unclassified, or described as "dementia due to other causes." In a recent study of the epidemiology of the dementing illnesses in a well-defined U.S. community—Rochester, Minnesota (Schoenberg et al.,

1987)—the percentage of cases of DAT (with no other diagnosis) amongst 178 cases of dementia was 51.7%, with a further 14.1% having both DAT and some other dementing illness (e.g., dementia from cerebral infarction). About 30% of their sample of patients underwent postmortem microscopic examination of neural tissue, and diagnoses were based on all available clinical, laboratory, and neuropathological data. Multi-infarct dementia was the most common diagnosis (5.1%) and in approximately 10.1% of the cases, dementia was attributable to other neurological disorders, including multiple sclerosis, head trauma, Parkinson's disease, brain tumor, and alcoholism. A total of 19.1% of the cases could not be classified.

Table 4.2:   Ischemic Score (from Hachinski et al., 1975)

Feature	Score
Abrupt onset	2
Stepwise deterioration	1
Fluctuating course	2
Nocturnal confusion	1
Relative preservation of personality	1
Depression	1
Somatic complaints	1
Emotional incontinence	1
History of hypertension	1
History of strokes	2
Evidence of associated atherosclerosis	1
Focal neurological symptoms	2
Focal neurological signs	2

Note. From Cerebral Blood Flow in Dementia by V. C. Hachinski et al., 1975. *Archives of Neurology, 32,* pp. 632-537.   Copyright (c), 1975, American Medical Association. Reprinted by permission.

There have been several studies that have investigated the incidence and prevalence of DAT and dementia in the elderly (e.g., Akesson, 1969; Broe, Akhtar, Andrews, Caird, Gilmore & McLellan, 1976; Kay et al., 1985, Larsson, T. Sjogren, & G. Jacobson, 1963; Molsa, Marttila, & Rinne, 1982; Pfeiffer, 1975; Rocca, Amaducci, & Schoenberg, 1986). Molsa et al. (1982) located 421 patients with moderate to severe dementia in the city of Turku in Finland. Each case was examined by a neurologist, and a total of 51.8% were assigned a diagnosis of degenerative dementia, with a further 36.1% being diagnosed as having a multi-infarct or mixed etiology. The prevalence rate of DAT was 256/100,000 population, or 1961/100,000 population over the age of 65. Age specific prevalence rates (per 100,000) rose sharply with increased age, from 51 at ages 45 to 54, 144 between 55 and 64, 776 between 65 and 74, 3,534 between 75 and 84, and 11,045 above the age of 85. These age-specific figures show clearly that risk increases with age up to a prevalence of 11% and an incidence of 2% over 85 years of age. Incidence rates for the Rochester study (Schoenberg et al., 1987) are presented in Table 4.3. The overall age-adjusted incidence rate per annum for males above the age of 30 was 51.4/100,000 and for females 50.8/100,000. There is no evidence that incidence rates have changed in recent times (Kokmen, Chandra, & Schoenberg, 1988).

Table 4.3: Age-Specific Incidence Rates for Males and Females (Cases/100,000/year) for AD in Rochester, Minnesota

Age Range	Males	Females	Both Sexes
30-59	3.1	5.6	4.4
60-69	152.1	57.5	95.8
70-79	560.5	512.9	530.7
80+	1054.5	1603.8	1431.7

Note. From Alzheimer's Disease and Other Dementing Illnesses in a Defined US Population by B. S. Schoenberg, E. Kokmen, & H. Okazaki 1987. *Annals of Neurology, 22,* pp. 724-729. Copyright (c), 1987, American Neurological Association. Reprinted by permission.

Various predictions of survival post onset have been calculated. Kay (1962), for example, reported an average survival of 2.6 years for demented males, compared to 8.7 for age-matched controls, and 2.3 years for females, compared to an expectation of 10.9 years. Wang and

Whanger (1971) reported that patients with DAT, who had an average age of onset of 74.1 years, lived an average of 5.1 further years, compared to an expected 9.6. Patients with arteriosclerotic dementia, with an average age of onset of 66.8 years, survived an average of 3.8 years, compared to an expected 14 years. Those patients with presenile DAT that commenced before they were 60 survived an average of 7.1 years, despite having an expectation of 23.1 further years. It is evident from these data that both AD and multi-infarct dementia considerably reduced life expectancy.

Course

A series of studies by Reisberg and colleagues have allowed the temporal course of Alzheimer's disease to be documented with some accuracy (e.g., Reisberg, 1982; Reisberg, Ferris, deLeon, & Crook, 1982, 1988; Reisberg, Ferris, deLeon, Kluger, Franssen, Borenstein, & Alba, 1989). Reisberg et al. (1982) reported the development of the Global Deterioration Scale, which comprised a seven-stage scale for rating the elderly subject's cognitive and function abilities. This has subsequently been expanded to allow the specification of the patient's present status on 16 ordinal functional stages. An abbreviated description of each of the functional assessment stages (FAST stages) on Reisberg et al.'s (1989) new scale, together with the estimated duration of each stage in AD is provided in Table 4.4.

Longitudinal studies suggest that memory deficits are the first sign of neuropsychological impairment in DAT (e.g., Grady et al., 1988; Teng, Chui, Schneiner, & Metzger, 1987). Tasks that measure attention or abstract reasoning (such as Raven's Progressive Matrices, the Porteus Maze, and Stroop interference) are typically the next to reveal impairments, and these are followed by dysfunctions on language and visuospatial tests (Grady et al., 1988). The rate of cognitive decline can be measured by changes on dementia rating scales; Katzman et al. (1988) reported a summary of three longitudinal studies in which the decline of clinically diagnosed DAT patients was documented using the information-memory-concentration component of the Blessed Dementia Scale. Subjects ranged in age from 52 to 96 years and the three samples included patients with different degrees of dementia. The maximum number of errors on the Blessed scale is 33; Katzman et al. found that the rate of change in error score per annum was similar when the initial error score lay between 0 and 23. The mean annual rate of error change was 4.4 errors, which was independent of sex, age, and age of onset of the disease. A similar rate of change has been reported by Ortof and Crystal (1989).

Table 4.4:   Functional Assessment Stages in Alzheimer's Disease

Stage	Diagnosis	Characteristics	Estimated Duration[a]
1	Normal adult	No decrement	
2	Normal aged adult	Subjective deficit in word finding	
3	Compatible with incipient AD	Deficits noted in demanding employment	7 years
4	Mild AD	Requires assistance in complex tasks, e.g., handling finances, planning a dinner party	2 years
5	Moderate AD	Requires assistance in choosing attire	18 months
6	Moderately severe AD	a. Requires assistance dressing	5 months
		b. Requires assistance bathing properly	5 months
		c. Requires assistance with mechanics of toileting (e.g., flushing, wiping)	5 months
		d. Urinary incontinence	4 months
		e. Fecal incontinence	10 months
7	Severe AD	a. Speech ability limited to about a half-dozen intelligible words	12 months
		b. Intelligible vocabulary limited to single word	18 months
		c. Ambulatory ability lost	12 months
		d. Ability to sit up lost	12 months
		e. Ability to smile lost	18 months
		f. Ability to hold up head lost	Unknown

Note. From Dementia: A Systematic Approach to Identifying Reversible Causes by B. Reisberg, 1986. *Geriatrics, 41,* pp. 30-46. (c) Modern Medical Publications; Harcourt Brace Jovanovich. Reprinted by permission.

[a] In subjects who survive and progress to the next stage

Biological Basis

Inspection of the brain of patients with DAT reveals a reduction in brain weight and volume, and an increase in the size of the sulci and ventricles. These gross changes are accompanied by the three primary histological signs of AD: The formation of *senile plaques*, the presence, within the neuron cell bodies, of *neurofibrillary tangles*, and signs (primarily in presenile cases) of *granulovacular degeneration*. Senile or neuritic plaques consist of an amyloid center 5-100 micrometers in diameter, surrounded by a zone of degenerated neurites, abnormal fibrillary material, and macrophages containing pigmented lipofuscin and cellular debris. Sometimes the plaques appear spherical in shape, but more often their shape is irregular; under the light microscope they look like small dark stains on the cortical tissue. Alzheimer's neurofibrillary tangles consist of helical, twisted tangles of fibrils, visible within the neuronal cytoplasm. At first, just a single strand may be observed running from the apical dendrite to the base, but gradually a number of strands develop and loop together, until finally the neuron is seen as a degenerated tangle of fibres. Tangles are more prevalent in the anterior frontal and temporal cortex than elsewhere, and the most common sites appear to be neurons of the anteromedial temporal grey matter including the uncus, the hippocampal and parahippocampal gyri, and the amygdaloid nucleus. The post- and pre-central gyri and the parietal and occipital lobes are usually relatively spared.

Alzheimer tangles are also to be found, in far less numbers, in the cortex and hippocampus of many normal brains. Indeed the brains of most people over the age of 90 will show signs of tangles. Alzheimer tangles are also characteristic of the brains of patients with Down's syndrome (Malmud, 1972), boxers who develop dementia (Corsellis, 1978), and patients with postencephalitic Parkinsonism. Granulovacular degeneration is most usually seen in the pyramidal cells of the hippocampus. The cytoplasm of the affected cell is seen to contain one or more bubblelike vacuoles, each containing a granule about 1 micrometre in diameter. As the vacuoles become more numerous in the cell body, the neuron degenerates and dies.

Genetics

Although the changes that occur in the brains of AD patients have been identified, why they should arise in a healthy brain is a mystery. Many investigators have suggested that there is a genetic predisposition for Alzheimer's disease. In some cases there is clear evidence for a familial form of the disease that, like Huntington's disease, is inherited as an autosomal dominant disorder. For example, Goudsmit, B. J. White, Weitkamp, Keats, Morrow, and Gajdusek (1981) found 37 cases of DAT in two families of Jewish ancestry originating from Byelorussia. Examination of the pedigree of these two kindreds suggested the disease was transmitted as a dominant genetic trait. Similarly, Nee, Polinsky, Eldridge, Weingartner, Smallberg, and Ebert (1983) reported a Canadian family where the ancestors were traced through eight generations, and about 50% of the offspring of affected individuals were found to have developed the disease. Genetic markers for AD have been discovered to be located on chromosome 21 for one family (St. George-Hyslop et al., 1987); however, AD is more genetically heterogeneous than HD, which means that diagnostic testing is more complicated and will require the development of probes that are specific to individual families.

Only a small percentage of AD patients, however, come from families where a dominant genetic trait can be identified. Interestingly, the clinical characteristics of the disease in familial cases cannot be distinguished from those of cases of DAT where no genetic component is suspected (Nee et al., 1983). Familial AD does not appear to be a special clinical subtype of the disorder, providing further support for the importance of an inherent or intrinsic biological defect in the development of the disease. There are numerous studies that have found an increased risk for developing AD amongst first-degree relatives of known cases (e.g., Akesson, 1969; Amaducci et al., 1986; Chandra, Philipose, P. A. Bell, Lazaroff, & Schoenberg, 1987; Heston, Mastri, V. E. Anderson, & J. White, 1981; Heyman et al., 1983; Larsson et al., 1963; T. Sjogren, H. Sjogren, & Lindgren, 1952). Heyman et al. found that the culumative incidence of dementia amongst parents of probands was 14.4% and amongst siblings 13.9% at the age of 75. This is a somewhat higher rate of cumulative incidence than in Heston et al.'s study, where 7.7% of siblings and 11.8% of parents were affected by the age of 75. This is much higher than the prevalence rate of about 2% to 5% in the general population. It is important when interpreting these findings to note that the likelihood of a family association emerging may be increased by biased recall by family members of instances of relatives with the disease and the impossibility of determining whether it was actually AD that a relative suffered from, when that person is no longer alive. The size of the increased risk should therefore be interpreted with caution.

It is important to stress also that many cases (at least 50% to 65%; Henderson, 1988) are sporadic and no family history can be established.

Etiology

The nature of the pathogenic process that sets in motion the neuronal degeneration characteristic of AD is, at this time, unknown. However, research into the cause of the disease is proceeding at a rapid pace. Although kinship studies have established that AD is often genetically transmitted, the available data do not make it possible to determine whether the disease is caused by a single gene mutation or by a number of factors, which might include some variable degree of genetic predisposition. The discovery that affected members of one pedigree had a defective gene on chromosome 21 immeasurably strengthened the hope that the genetic basis of the disease could be precisely determined (St. George-Hyslop et al., 1987). The finding was also significant because it was consistent with another clue to the cause of AD, the fact that people with Down's syndrome (Trisomy 21) have an extra copy of chromosome 21 and by middle-age develop the neuronal changes seen in AD. Taken together, these findings suggest that AD might be caused by extra genetic material on chromosome 21. Although patients with AD do not have an extra chromosome 21, it was proposed that they might have an extra copy of a particular gene, and the gene most commonly nominated was that responsible for producing amyloid.

The protein substance amyloid has long been associated with Alzheimer's disease. Since 1920 it has been known that the fibrils associated with the senile plaques and the intracellular filaments characteristic of the neurofibrillary tangles found in both AD and Down's syndrome, were comprised of amyloid. In 1984, Glenner and Wong identified the major protein component of the amyloid fibrils as the ß-protein. Molecular genetic studies allowed the specification of the location of the ß-protein gene on chromosome 21. Research then focused on the proposal that AD may result from the occurrence of an extra copy of this amyloid gene. Unfortunately, however, this was not the case. In familial cases of AD the amyloid gene is not exclusively related to the expression of the dementia, and the excessive genetic material is not present in either patients with Down's syndrome or sporadic AD (Tanzi, Bird, Latt, & Neve, 1987). Defects in the amyloid gene are not responsible for AD and the reason for the presence of abnormal deposits of amyloid in the degenerate neurons of AD will require an alternative explanation. Nevertheless, studies of the control and synthesis of amyloidogenic proteins in AD provide one of the most promising avenues of research currently available (Glenner, 1989).

There are several other etiological hypotheses that have been investigated over the past two decades. One influential proposal arose from the observation that the brains of AD patients show a marked reduction in choline acetyltransferase activity. According to the *cholinergic hypothesis,* AD is a consequence of a reduction in the levels of cholinergic system neurotransmitter acetylcholine (E. K. Perry, R. H. Perry, Blessed, & Tomlinson, 1977). As an extension of this process, it has been found that the nucleus basalis of Meynert, the major source of cholinergic innervation of the neocortex, is selectively destroyed (Whitehouse, Price, Struble, A. W. Clark, & Coyle, 1982). Numerous therapeutic trials using substances that increase acetylcholine levels have been initiated, however, results from such studies have not produced consistent results. In addition, it has become apparent that neurotransmitter depletion in AD is not confined to the cholinergic system. For example, levels of serotonin, GABA, norephinephrine, and glutamate are also reduced. Thus it has not proved possible to relate AD to changes in one particular neurotransmitter system and it appears likely that reduced levels of the various neurotransmitters are a result, and not a cause, of cellular damage (Glenner, 1989).

An exciting line of research (Hefti & Weiner, 1986) that also focuses on the cholinergic system has offered some medium-term hope that neural degeneration in AD can be arrested. For many years it has been known that peripheral nerves contain a protein known as nerve growth factor (NGF), which is important to the growth and maintenance of these nerve cells. NGF has recently been discovered in the human brain, where it acts on the cholinergic neurons. It has subsequently been demonstrated that damage to the cholinergic neurons in rats can be prevented by injecting NGF into their brains. This result suggests that Alzheimer patients, who, as we have seen, have substantial cholinergic system damage, might similarly benefit from NGF injections. There are now plans to test this proposal if trials with aging primates are successful. There are, however, some risks involved in this process, and progress is likely to be made cautiously.

The possibility that AD is the consequence of a virus has also been explored. The discovery of scrapie, an infectious neurodegenerative disease in sheep that produces no fever, inflammation, or immune response symptoms, has stimulated a search for similar infectious agents in human degenerative diseases. It has been shown that a pathogenic protein known as prion is probably responsible for scrapie and for the neurological disorder Jacob-Creutzfeld's disease in humans. However, the protein structure of the degenerate fibrils and processes in AD are different from the structure of prions, and it has not proved possible to transmit AD from human samples to primates. Currently there is no conclusive evidence that Alzheimer's disease results from an infectious agent.

A number of possible cytotoxic substances have been advanced to explain neuronal damage in AD. Aluminium has been the substance most frequently implicated in the etiology of dementia (Birchall & Chappell, 1988). Terry and Pena (1965) showed that neurofibrillary degeneration could be included in laboratory animals by injecting aluminium salts into their cerebrospinal fluid. Increased concentrations of aluminium in Alzheimer patients have been reported (Perl & Brody, 1980), but not consistently (Wisneiwski, Moretz, & Iqbal, 1986). Further evidence for the neurotoxic effects of heavy metals occurring in high concentrations in drinking water have been reported from various areas in the Western Pacific (Kurland, 1988). However, it has not proved possible to establish a definite link between aluminium and the specific neuronal changes in AD. It is possible that the higher concentration of aluminium in AD may be a secondary effect of other metabolic changes. There are other noxious environmental events, such as head trauma, that have been associated with the development of DAT, but not with sufficient consistency to warrant considering them as primary etiological agents (Henderson, 1988).

For the neuropsychologist it is useful to keep in touch with etiological work on AD, because each new theory and discovery brings hope for the victims of the disease and their caregivers. It is important to appreciate that much of this hope will not be realized and a biological treatment for DAT remains a distant prospect; when working with demented elderly it is important to keep hope and reality in perspective. The task of finding the cause or causes of AD is enormously complicated. The research effort at the present time is intense and sophisticated. There is important work continuing into the pathogenesis of amyloid (Glenner, 1989) and into the hypothesis that free oxygen radicals play a fundamental role in neuronal degeneration. However, the turnover of etiological hypotheses is rapid.

Cognitive Deficits

The preceding discussion makes it clear that patients with AD suffer a profound, progressive, and irreversible decline in their cognition. Of all the cognitive changes the clinician encounters, those associated with Alzheimer's disease are perhaps the most disabling and pervasive. Memory and apraxia tests seem to be particularly sensitive indicators. At the time of onset, language skills and the ability to obey simple commands seem to be better preserved. As the disease progresses, however, language function may be severely impaired. Most clinicians would agree that in the end, all aspects of cognition in the senile dement are eventually disturbed to some extent. Although there are considerable individual differences between patients in the relative severity of the various presenting symptoms, in the final stages, very little of the cognitive system is spared.

Intelligence

Early research on intellectual skills in AD showed that the ability to abstract information and use it constructively was a primary defect in presenile AD and senile dementia (Cleveland & Dysinger, 1944; Pinkerton & Kelly, 1952; Rabin, 1945). Subsequently the Wechsler Intelligence scales have been used to document intellectual decline in dementia. The results from these studies are generally clearcut. Performance IQ is usually significantly lower than Verbal IQ (VIQ; Bolton, Britton, & Savage, 1966; Kendrick, Parboosingh, & Post, 1965; Kendrick & Post, 1967; E. Miller, 1977; Weingartner, Kaye, Smallberg, Ebert, Gillin, & Sitaram, 1981). Where VIQ is highest (96 in the Kendrick and Post study; 93 in Kendrick et al., 1965), the discrepancy tends to be greatest. This implies that Performance subtests are the most susceptible to the changes due to dementia, and as the disease progresses, the Verbal subtest scores decline as well.

E. Miller (1977) commented on the reason for the disproportionate deterioration of ability shown on the Performance subtests. The most common explanation has been that slowness of information processing causes the poor results of dementing patients on the Performance subtests because most of the measures are timed. However, as E. Miller noted, even if given as much time as they need on tests like Block Design, the performance of dementing patients does not improve. It is possible, therefore, that dementing patients have a particular difficulty with tasks, like the Performance subtests, that require complex visuospatial manipulation. Alternatively it could be that tests that necessitate adapting to a novel assessment format are especially hard for impaired AD patients. Performance subtests, like Block Design and Picture Arrangement, are usually totally new for the person being tested, unlike the Vocabulary and Arithmetic subtests from the verbal scale, which are similar to academic tests with which most people are familiar. E. Miller noted that Alzheimer patients perform more poorly on Raven's Progressive Matrices than on the usual comparison scale for the Matrices, the Mill Hill Vocabulary Scale. The Matrices test is also an unfamiliar type of assessment for most patients, involving reasoning and visuospatial manipulation, in contrast to the vocabulary scale, which requires the patient to access semantic memory, and makes little, if any, demand on abstracting or reasoning capabilities.

The pattern of Wechsler subtest scores is illustrated in Table 4.5, where detailed results from E. Miller (1977) and Logsdon, Teri, Williams, Vitiello, and Prinz (1989) are presented.

Table 4.5: Wechsler Subtest Scores for Patients with DAT

	Miller (1977) WAIS	Logsdon et al. (1989)[a] WAIS-R	
		Study 1	Study 2
Information	6.4	7.2	8.7
Comprehension	5.8	7.0	9.0
Arithmetic	5.9	7.0	8.4
Similarities	5.3	7.0	8.7
Digit Span	6.2	7.0	9.0
Vocabulary	8.0	8.5	9.5
Digit Symbol	3.3	5.8	8.3
Picture Completion	6.3	7.1	8.3
Block Design	4.2	7.0	8.2
Picture Arrangement	3.0	7.1	9.0
Object Assembly	3.5	6.1	8.3
n	20	67	43

[a] Age-corrected subscale scores

Of the verbal subtests, Vocabulary and Information tend to be higher than the others, which is particularly evident in E. Miller's study because the patients overall deterioration was greatest. Digit Symbol and Picture Arrangement were performed more poorly by the AD patients' tested by E. Miller; the spread of mean subtest scores for the Performance scale was not as great in either of Logsdon et al.'s groups.

One interesting procedure for examining the pattern of subtest performance by AD patients has been advanced by Fuld (1984). She administered seven of the WAIS subtests to 20 students who had been administered 1.0 mg of methoscopalamine an hour previously. Scopalamine is an anticholinergic drug, which can cause an impaired performance on memory and other cognitive abilities in normal subjects. As mentioned earlier, choline depletion is also a characteristic of AD. Fuld was interested in the relationship between choline depletion dementia in normal subjects and the typical deficits of AD. She proposed that there was a pattern of subtest scores that was characteristic of both patients with DAT and subjects taking anticholinergic drugs. The elements of the profile were defined as follows:

A = [Information + Vocabulary] ÷ 2
B = [Similarities + Digit Span] ÷ 2
C = [Digit Symbol + Block Design] ÷ 2
D = Object Assembly

A, B, C, and D were computed from age-corrected subtest scores and the profile was defined as A > B > C ≤ D, A > D. Fuld found that 10 out of 19 (53%) of her scopalamine subjects showed this profile, compared with only 4 of the 22 control subjects. In a second study she found that 44% of the DAT subjects, compared 4% of the demented non-Alzheimer patients, displayed the proposed profile. A number of subsequent studies have shown that the incidence of the Fuld profile is higher in DAT subjects than other demented or patient control groups (Table 3.8). As is apparent in Table 3.8, however, the incidence of the profile is variable, and reached a low of 7% in a group of community-based DAT patients (Study 2, Logsdon et al., 1989).

The significance of this profile as a diagnostic marker for AD is questionable. It is not clear whether the Fuld profile is related to overall IQ scores, although, the greater the VIQ-PIQ difference, the more likely it is that the profile will emerge (Bornstein, Termeer, Longbrake, Heger, & North, 1989). The Logsdon et al. (1989) data, illustrated in Table 4.6, suggest that greater subtest differentiation and hence incidence of the profile, is likely to occur in clinical samples with lower IQ scale scores. Similar conclusions can be drawn from the Filley, Kobayashi, and Heaton study (1987). Although the evidence to date suggests that the Fuld profile is relatively specific to DAT, and not simply a consequence of any type of neurological damage, the overall degree of diagnostic sensitivity is problematic. For example, well over half of all DAT patients do not exhibit the proposed cholinergic profile; hence not having the cholinergic profile does not help exclude DAT as a possible diagnosis. As Bornstein et al. (1989) stated "No responsible clinician would attempt to base the diagnosis of DAT on this profile alone. Without question, a diagnosis of DAT should be made only in the context of a thorough medical and neurological history, careful documentation of the

nature and course of the illness and a complete neurological examination"
(p. 344). Given the poor classification rate in Logsdon et al. (1989)
Study 2, the profile is possibly of least assistance in diagnosis at the
earliest stages of the illness—the point at which it would be most helpful
to have a reliable neuropsychological marker of the disease.

**Table 4.6: Reported Incidence of the Fuld (1984) WAIS
            Cholinergic Profile**

Study	Incidence of Positive Profile (%)	Subject Group
Fuld (1984)	53	Students receiving scopolamine
	44	DAT
	5	Non-DAT dementia
Brinkman & Braun (1984)	56	DAT
	5	Multi-infarct dementia
Filley et al. (1987)	22	DAT
	16	Patient control
	2	Normal controls
Heinrichs & Celinski (1987)	10	Head injured
Tuokko & Crockett (1987)	1	Normal elderly
Satz et al. (1987)	12.8	Patient controls
Logsdon et al. (1989)		
Study 1	22	Clinical group DAT
	13	Nondemented elderly
Study 2	10	Elderly with memory loss
	7	Community group DAT
	7	Depressed elderly
	7	Normal elderly
Bornstein et al. (1989)	16	Depressed
Bornstein & Share (1990)	4	Temporal lobe epilepsy

Memory

Memory impairment is possibly the feature most consistently reported in the early stages of the disease, and the one on which most mental status and neuropsychological testing is focused. Clinically, memory impairment is characterized in the earliest stages of the disease by a simple forgetfulness, indistinguishable from the benign senescence of old age, gradually intensifying, until patients have no recollection of personal information, and show little awareness of the significance of events going on around them. Total amnesia is the endpoint of the disease. The dense amnesia of AD is different in quality from that of patients with Korsakoff's disease. Perhaps because of their concurrent dementia, Alzheimer patients have far less access to previously stored memories from their past lives than Korsakoff patients (Weingartner, Grafman, Boutelle, Kaye, & P. R. Martin, 1983). KD patients are far better able to appreciate and use cues occurring in their environment to supplement their defective learning and recall. As might be expected, Korsakoff patients, despite their profound amnesia, approach new learning situations and memory tests far more intelligently than do patients with DAT. There is an enormous literature on memory defect in Alzheimer's disease; what follows is a selective summary of some of the most significant features of memory loss in DAT. In summarizing this work, the performance of DAT subjects on memory tasks are grouped under general headings that reflect the major research efforts in this area. Experimental analysis of the memory function of DAT patients suggests that they have deficits in each of the following general domains: primary, secondary, semantic, and remote memory.

Primary Memory. In Chapter 3, the distinction between primary and secondary memory was introduced, together with an outline of Baddeley's (1986) influential Working Memory model. The Working Memory model describes a system that involves a Central Executive controlling at least two slave systems: the Articulatory Loop and the Visual-spatial Sketchpad or Scratchpad. Tasks that assess primary memory require the appropriate functioning of this system. Patients with circumscribed amnesia, of whom H.M. is the best example, show no evidence of primary memory deficits; DAT patients, however, have been found to exhibit a reduced capacity to perform STM tasks. Korsakoff patients may occupy an intermediate position—they show a variable degree of primary memory dysfunction.

Studies of primary memory have employed three main tasks: analysis of recency effects in free recall tasks, memory span, and the Peterson-Brown distractor procedure. Results from each of these tasks for KD patients were reviewed in the previous chapter. On free recall tasks, it is assumed that the final three or four items administered remain in primary memory, giving the recency effect, which is a characteristic feature of the serial position curve resulting from such tasks. Korsakoff patients typically show normal recency effects. There is some evidence that DAT patients show impairment on such tasks, although, the deficit is not pronounced (A. Martin, Brouwers, Cox, & Fedio, 1985; E. Miller, 1971). Differences in the strength of the recency effect tend to be the least sensitive of the measures of integrity of primary memory (R. G. Morris & Baddeley, 1988) and may only be apparent in the later stages of the disease (Pepin & Eslinger, 1989). On the Digit Span subtest, which assesses the quantity of information the patient can register and reproduce in correct serial order, dementing patients show some decrements. As is apparent from the data in Table 4.5, this decline in performance is minimal, particularly when compared with the Alzheimer subjects' scores on other WAIS subtests. In several controlled studies significant reductions in the length of digit span in AD patients have been reported (e.g., Kaszniak, Garron, & Fox, 1979; E. Miller, 1973; R. G. Morris, 1984), in others no deficits have been found (A. Martin et al., 1985; Weingartner et al., 1983). Overall, there is general support for the notion that memory span is impaired in AD, although this may not be apparent when patients are in the early stages of the disease.

The most sensitive test of primary memory is the Peterson-Brown distractor technique. As we saw in the previous chapter, on this task Korsakoff patients sometimes show deficits, however, AD patients almost invariably show a reduction in performance. For example, Kopelman (1985) found that although Korsakoff amnesics performed normally on his STM distractor task, the AD patients he tested were severely impaired. Although immediate recall of each three-letter word triad was normal, after only a 5-second delay, the DAT patients were performing at a grossly impaired level. This finding has been confirmed in two other studies (Corkin, 1982; R. G. Morris, 1986). In their review R. G. Morris and Baddeley (1988) concluded that the pattern of performance by DAT patients is readily interpreted by assuming that the three measures of primary memory differ in sensitivity. DAT patients show a minimal reduced recency effect on free recall tasks, and this particular analysis of primary memory seems to be most resistant to the effects of cognitive impairments of any kind. They also display, on average, a moderate but measurable decrement on memory span tests, and almost invariably perform poorly on the Peterson-Brown distractor task. These latter two measures appear to be more sensitive to the consequences of primary memory dysfunction than do recency effect analyses.

There is an emerging consensus that it is disruption to the Central Executive, which controls processing in the Working Memory model, that is responsible for primary memory loss (J. T. Becker, 1988; R. G. Morris & Baddeley, 1988) and primary memory disturbance underlies many of the cognitive features of dementia (Kopelman, 1985; Teng et al., 1989). Teng et al. (1989), for example, concluded that "a fragile working memory that falters or fails when its span is exceeded is a major cause for the poor performance of AD patients on memory tasks" (p. 909). J. T. Becker (1988), however, emphasized the possibility that although many DAT patients have both primary and secondary deficits, it is possible to find patients with a relatively normal secondary memory but clear evidence of primary memory dysfunction and vice versa. In his study, 71 DAT patients and 89 controls were tested on a variety of tasks including Digit Span, Reaction Time, Word Fluency, Story Recall, Rey Figure, and Paired-Associate Learning. A Principal Components analysis grouped together the first three of these tasks, and the second three tasks. He suggested that this analysis dissociated tasks sensitive to Central Executive dysfunction (Digit Span, Reaction Time, and Word Fluency) from tests assessing secondary memory. Becker identified two cases that exemplified the fact that primary memory deficits secondary deficits can be relatively independent:

Patient 213 is a 64-year-old ... with a 3-to-4 year history of progressive intellectual deterioration, and an MMS score of 16 when first evaluated. His performance on tests of memory was quite poor. He did not reach criterion on any of the verbal paired-associates and could recall little of the story or the complex figure. In contrast he could generate 22 words in a minute, and performed the reaction time task well. His digit span forward was 7, which does not differ from the mean of the control group.

Patient 070 had a different pattern of impairment.... . She learned all the face-name pairs, and performed well on the verbal task. Her recall of the story and the figure was amongst the best of the patient group. However, she was virtually unable to perform the word generation task, her reaction times were extremely slow, and digit span forward was 5. (p. 747)

These data support the 2-component model of memory by suggesting that impairments on primary memory tasks may be observed on occasion, in the absence of anterograde amnesia. For clinicians, however, the most important implication of the research covered in this section is the finding that AD almost certainly causes primary memory loss and in more severe cases this deficit will be pronounced. Destruction of the integrity of the Central Executive system appears to be an important determinant of the cognitive failures underlying dementia.

Secondary Memory. There is an abundance of evidence that DAT patients develop a profound anterograde amnesia. For example, on the WMS, Weingartner et al. (1981) found their DAT patients had on average a 24-point IQ-MQ discrepancy. Storandt, Botwinick, Danziger, Berg, and Hughes (1984) tested 42 community-dwelling patients with mild DAT, who showed no signs of depression. These subjects were compared with a group of healthy normal controls. On the Digit Span test, the amount of variance explained by group membership was small, as might be expected from our discussion of primary memory; however, on the other subtests diagnosis accounted for a substantial portion of the variance in scores. The Alzheimer patients showed most dysfunction on the Logical Memory subtest. In our research with a similar group of demented DAT patients (Partridge, R. G. Knight, & M. J. Feehan, 1990) the Logical Memory subtest also clearly discriminated between the two groups (on average 2.43 correct for the DAT patients versus 7.30 for the controls).

On the WMS-R, validity data for various patient groups have been provided in the manual (Wechsler, 1987; Table 19). Included in this table are results from 24 DAT patients with an average age of 67.9. Each of the WMS-R indices has a mean of 100 and a standard deviation of 15. The index scores of the DAT patients are given in Table 4.7, and compared with scores from 8 alcoholic KD patients (average 64.4). The data in Table 4.7 demonstrate that the amnesia characteristic of mild to moderate DAT is comparable to that seen in KD. Both the KD and the DAT patients performed significantly better on the Attention/Concentration index, with the KD patients scoring nearer to the average than the dements.

Experimental studies have confirmed that DAT patients show a progressive, global, and irreversible anterograde amnesia (e.g., J. T. Becker, 1988; Brinkman, Largen, Gerganoff, & Pomara, 1983; P. E. Davis & Mumford, 1984; Ferris, Crook, E. Clark, McCarthy, & Rae, 1980; Inglis, 1957, 1959; Kendrick & Post, 1967; Kopelman, 1985; E. Miller, 1975, 1978; Nebes, D. C. Martin, & Horn, 1984; Tuokko & Crockett, 1989; R. S. Wilson, Kaszniak, Bacon, Fox, & Kelly, 1982). Mildly to moderately impaired DAT patients, like, amnesic KD patients, show some improvement when cued recall procedures are used (P. E. Davis & Mumford, 1984; E. Miller, 1975; R. Morris, Wheatley, & Britton, 1983; Partridge et al., 1990). For example, 3-letter wordstems promote better recall amongst demented patients than free recall, but their level of performance does not, however, reach normal. Improvement as a consequence of cuing is less pronounced in more severely impaired DAT samples and those researchers who have focused on "stage" models of memory processing have generally concluded that AD causes global defects of both encoding and retrieval (P. E. Davis & Mumford, 1984; Tuokko & Crockett, 1989).

Table 4.7: Mean WMS-R Index Scores for DAT and KD Patients

	Alzheimer	Korsakoff
General memory	62.0	67.5
Attention/concentration	81.0	90.8
Verbal memory	68.2	70.0
Visual memory	68.7	77.4
Delayed recall	61.7	57.3

Remote Memory. Although moderately impaired DAT patients often recall autobiographical memories from the past more readily than those from more recent times, when tested for memory of public events across all the decades of their adult life, they show extensive and ungraded impairment. R. S. Wilson, Kaszniak, and Fox (1981), for example, found that on M. S. Albert et al.'s (1979) Famous Faces Test, and on a measure of ability to recall events and people in the news between 1920-1975, demented patients recalled consistently less from each decade than the controls. On average, KD patients tend to show a far more pronounced temporal gradient; the contrasting flat extensive gradient displayed by DAT patients is illustrated in Fig. 4.1.

Semantic Memory. One of the most important outcomes of the experimental investigation of amnesia in neurologically impaired patients is the opportunity to test hypotheses about multiple memory systems. Where amnesic or demented patients can perform one class of tasks, but not another, and the results are not confounded by differences in task difficulty level, evidence for distinct memory systems emerges. Researchers have devised a number of dichotomies to explain how memory operates. The memory systems distinguished in this way by different experimental research groups often have only subtle differences in emphasis and can be difficult for clinicians to apply accurately and consistently. We have already reviewed several of these dichotomies in Chapter 3 (see Table 3.9). One of the oldest distinctions is between long- and short-term memory. The validity of this division, and that between primary and secondary memory, has been supported by the outcome of research with amnesic and KD patients. The normal skill learning of amnesic patients was the basis for Squire's important procedural-declarative learning distinction. More recently, the terms explicit-implicit and direct-indirect have been used to characterize impaired-preserved memory skills in amnesics. At present memory research is in a state of constant change, and the variety of competing models reflects our preliminary understanding of how memory works.

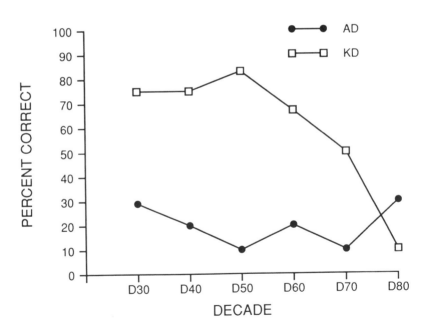

Figure 4.1. Retrograde amnesia in a patient with Alzheimer's disease (AD) and a patient with Korsakoff's disease (KD).

Another influential distinction was proposed by Tulving (1983). He partitioned memory into two aspects: *semantic* and *episodic* memory. Semantic memory involves knowledge about words and the use of symbolic language. The integrity of semantic memory can be tested by assessing such skills as vocabulary or categorical knowledge, use of grammar, and the ability to make use of the semantic associations between words. Semantic memory was not featured in our discussion of KD because these patients show no evidence of having lost these skills. For example, Korsakoff patients are as capable as unimpaired controls in taking advantage of the semantic associations between word pairs in learning tasks. They learn the easy, highly associated word pairs (*gold-silver*) on the WMS more rapidly than the hard associates (*guilty-eagle*). *Episodic memory,* in contrast, is tested by tasks that make overt reference to a subject's previous learning history. Recall or recognition of an event of specific learning episode, with a clear temporal context, provides a test of episodic memory. The terms *episodic, direct, declarative,* and *explicit* have similar connotations. *Semantic memory,* however, has a focus on language skills and the manipulation of concepts that is distinct from terms like *implicit* or *procedural.* For example, it is not easy to see how semantic memory is related to Schacter's implicit-explicit model. Some means of testing semantic memory appear to require explicit retrieval processes as will become apparent in the following discussion; in other cases semantic memory is tested implicitly.

There is a reason for introducing a discussion of semantic memory at this point. DAT patients, unlike amnesics, are impaired on tasks that require access to semantic memory. Many of these deficits might also be classified as some form of dysphasia; anomia, for example, or agrammatism. The next section touches specifically on language problems in dementia; for the present, remember that there is a considerable overlap between semantic failure and aspects of dysphasia in DAT.

One indicator of semantic memory loss, which is often apparent in the speech of Alzheimer patients, is difficulty finding words. The paucity of language in their everyday speech is often a striking early sign of the onset of the disease. Bayles (1982) provided a good example of the "empty" speech that characterizes many demented patients. In response to a request to provide a name for a photograph of a bathtub the patient replied: "Well I see now, yeah, well you can go in the bathtub and you don't have any problems here or there. Funny that you got that over there though on that" (p. 276). Another moderately impaired patient, asked to provide a name for a picture of an orange responded with a series of irrelevant and vacuous phrases: "Same thing, this is, no, no, they may be this here and it didn't get here, but it got there, there, and there" (p. 276). Although the speech of Alzheimer patients may be replete with vague phrases, the syntactic structure of their language production is usually preserved (Hier, Hagenlocker, & Shindler, 1985). Major grammatical errors do not occur until much later in the course of the disease.

Verbal fluency tests are a direct method of testing ability to access lexical-semantic memory. Patients may be asked to generate in 60 seconds as many words as possible starting with a particular letter. Another variation is to ask patients to name as many exemplars from a specified category (four-legged animals) as they can in 60 or 90 seconds. DAT patients perform poorly on this task, even in the early stages of the disorder (e.g., Ober, Dronkers, Koss, Delis, & Friedland, 1986). Partridge et al. (1990) found that in two 60-second periods, mildly impaired DAT patients could name on average only 11.36 words starting with P or S, less than half the number generated by the controls. Object naming is another frequently revealed deficit (e.g., Kirshner, Webb, & Kelly, 1984; Huff, Corkin, & Growdon, 1986). One standard test of confrontation naming is the Boston Naming Test. In this measure, a series of 60 line drawings are exposed to the subject who is asked to name each of the objects depicted. The recognition difficulty of the objects varies (from bed to abacus), and semantic or phonemic cues may be offered if a response given suggests that the object has been misperceived. DAT patients frequently perform poorly on this test (e.g., A. Martin & Fedio, 1983; Williams, Mack, & Henderson, 1989). For example, the range of correct spontaneous responses by the DAT patients in the study of Williams et al. was 16-57 ($M = 37.7$) versus 45-60 ($M = 54.3$) for the elderly controls.

Another word-finding test is naming to definition. An example of this kind of procedure is the situation where the subject is given a sentence to complete ("A piece of furniture on which to sleep is called a _____."). DAT patients typically have problems with this task, especially when they are asked to name the defined referent (Rissenberg & Glanzer, 1987), although they may well be able to recognize the names of defined objects they are unable to recall (Huff, Mack, Mahlmann, & Greenberg, 1988). The basis of this disturbance is unclear. As Nebes (1989) concluded,

> What is uncertain, is whether this problem results from a deficit restricted to lexical access or from a more general semantic impairment. The hypothesis that Alzheimer patients cannot use information about the semantic attributes of a stimulus to determine its identity is an attractive one... . However, even if one accepts the hypothesis that a semantic impairment is a

major, if not the sole, cause of wordfinding deficit in AD, the question still remains as to whether the information is totally lost or merely lost to a direct search. (p. 381)

Loss of the knowledge about the meaning of a concept is another indication that semantic memory is disrupted. Knowledge of a particular concept is presumed to be stored in semantic memory in terms of differentiating and specific attributes (function, form, color, size, etc.) and to be linked together with other concepts that have similar functional or physical features. Failure of semantic memory might result in DAT patients having difficulty spontaneously describing the relevant attributes of objects, or accurately classifying them into appropriate semantic categories. In several studies it has been found that DAT patients do have difficulty recalling the physical or functional aspects of an object (e.g., Flicker, Ferris, Crook, & Bartus, 1987; A. Martin & Fedio, 1983), although they may retain the knowledge of its superordinate semantic category. Hence a hammer may be recognized as a tool, even though its functional significance cannot be described (Warrington, 1975). However, it appears that although DAT patients may not be able to describe the function of an object, they can often correctly indicate they know what objects are used for if they are tested appropriately. Flicker et al. (1987) found that dements could select objects relevant to carrying out a particular task (choose a hammer when asked for a tool to drive in nails), despite being unable to describe the function of the object.

Word association tasks also reveal some interesting deficits in DAT patients. On free association tests, DAT patients are more likely than controls to choose associates that have a sequential relationship to the stimulus words. Such associations are called *syntagmatic* and examples of such responses are *barks* or *plays* to the stimulus *dog*. In contrast, a paradigmatic response to the word dog might be *cat* or *wolf.* Gewirth, Shindler, and Hier (1984) found that DAT patients produced fewer paradigmatic responses than control subjects, and severity of the disease was associated with decline in the number of such responses. On the other hand, the ability to categorize stimuli into semantic classes has generally been found to be intact in mild to moderately impaired patients (A. Martin & Fedio, 1983; Nebes, Boller, & Holland, 1986). Thus, although verbal fluency tests reveal that DAT patients are unable to retrieve exemplars from designated categories with any facility, they can nominate the categories to which such exemplars belong.

The capacity to use the semantic context within which a word appears, both with and without awareness, is another functional indicator of an intact semantic memory. One general paradigm within which the effects of context may be studied is priming. Semantic priming is the situation where a previous event facilitates or inhibits the processing of a subsequent word. For example, the speed with which the word *butter* can be read aloud is faster, if the word preceding it on a list is semantically related, for example, *bread*. There is experimental evidence (Collins & Loftus, 1975) to show that words are stored in semantic memory in such a way that the activation of an individual word spreads to closely related words. The priming effect is therefore the consequence of a spreading activation, which acts to "prepare" related concepts for use. In several studies, Nebes and his colleagues have shown that if speed of a reading-response is used as an indicator, the amount of facilitation afforded by a priming stimulus in DAT patients is relatively normal (Nebes et al., 1984; Nebes et al., 1986; Nebes, Brady, & Huff, 1989).

In contrast to these demonstrations of relatively preserved priming, there are some priming tasks that DAT patients do not perform normally. For example, on the word-stem completion task (Graf et al., 1984) described in Chapter 3, DAT patients show evidence of impairment, unlike both Korsakoff and Huntington's disease patients (Salmon, Shimamura, Butters, & S. Smith, 1988; Shimamura, Salmon, Squire, & Butters, 1987). DAT patients are also less constrained by semantic context in the interpretation of ambiguous words (Cushman & Caine, 1987).

In summary, semantic memory functioning has been shown to be impaired in Alzheimer's disease. It is apparent, however, that the extent to which this deficit is manifest is determined by the nature of the task used to assess performance. Sorting items into categories does not create problems for AD patients, whereas generating items from a specific category is difficult. Under some circumstances, Alzheimer patients can indicate what an object is used for, but not if they are questioned directly. In a thoughtful and comprehensive review of semantic memory and dementia, Nebes (1989) considered a number of explanations for the inconsistent normal and abnormal performance of DAT patients on semantic memory tests. Categorizing performance by demented patients on semantic memory tasks in terms of high or low retrieval demands, explicit or implicit memory functions, or automatic versus effortful processing demands (Jorm, 1986) does not provide a satisfactory explanation for all the available results. Nebes concluded,

At present there is no single explanation for why Alzheimer patients are severely impaired on some tasks but perform quite normally on others. This may be because investigators have not yet discovered the relevant methodological factor differentiating these tasks. Alternatively, the way researchers have partitioned memory into multiple systems may be incorrect. Semantic memory may be composed of a number of different components some of which are impaired in AD while others are not. (p. 392)

Language Disturbance

In his description of a patient with presenile dementia, Alois Alzheimer drew attention to the presence of aphasic symptoms, which coexisted with her memory loss and paranoia. Subsequently, although aphasia features in many accounts of the disease, language impairment has not been accorded a central place either in the clinical diagnostic criteria for DAT or in the experimental study of persons with Alzheimer's disease (Cummings, Benson, Hill, & Read, 1985). Some confusion also exists over whether the term *aphasia* is an appropriate description of language impairment in DAT patients (Critchley, 1964; B. E. Murdoch, Chenery, Wilks, & Boyle, 1987). This is because for many clinicians, aphasia is reserved for cases where language deficits follow a focal brain lesion. Hence, receptive aphasia is a consequence of specific damage to Wernicke's area in the temporal lobe; expressive aphasia results from left frontal damage. Aphasia is regarded as denoting the situation where language loss is circumscribed and other higher cognitive functions appear relatively intact. In DAT, however, language use is often degraded in a gradual and diffuse manner; although focal language deficits with rapid onset are sometimes seen, this is not typical (Hart, 1988). Thus, when clinicians refer to aphasia in DAT, they are using the term in a more general way to describe any language loss following brain injury, without regard to the nature of the lesions.

Although the use of the term *aphasia* does not necessarily imply any assumptions about the neuroanatomical basis of the language impairments under consideration, debate over the appropriate use of the term does reflect some valid concerns about the possibility that different cognitive processes may be involved in producing language loss in different neurological disorders. The heart of the problem, as B. E. Murdoch et al. (1987) noted, is the lack of an adequate theoretical account of language disturbance in DAT. Accordingly, it is not clear whether language disturbance in AD is the product of a globally disorganized cognitive system, that is, a failure of some system like Baddeley's Central Executive, or the result of an accumulation of focal damage to structures important in language use.

Whatever the theoretical basis of language disturbance in DAT, there is general agreement that it is an almost invariable consequence of the disease and becomes more apparent as the disease progresses (Appell, Kertesz, & Fisman, 1982; Bayles, 1982; Hart, 1986). There is some evidence that patients with early onset DAT are more prone to language use abnormalities than those with an onset after 65 (Seltzer & Sherwin, 1983). In addition, language loss, especially when it develops gradually, is often a good indicator of severity (Bayles & Boone, 1982; Skelton-Robinson, & Jones, 1984), and the emergence of language problems has been regarded as a sign that the patient is entering the final stages of the disease (Kaszniak, Fox, Gandell, Garron, Huckman, & Ramsay, 1978).

Most discussions of disturbance of expressive language in DAT highlight the impaired word-naming ability of these patients. Much of this literature was considered in the previous section on semantic memory. Critchley (1964), for example, drew attention to the difficulty demented patients have on word fluency tasks: "Asked to give a list of girl's names, a dement may painfully and slowly produce 2 or 3 examples, which on enquiry, turn out to be the names of some who dwell in close association, such as his wife, or daughter, or granddaughter" (p. 354). As a result, the speech of DAT patients appears telegrammatic and displays a marked poverty of content. As we have seen, on verbal fluency tests, DAT patients usually show impairments (Kirshner et al., 1984; A. Martin & Fedio, 1983) and their word-finding problems and empty speech can often be demonstrated when they are asked to describe some standard visual stimulus. The Cookie Theft picture from the Boston Diagnostic Aphasia Examination is often used to elicit a sample of narrative speech from demented patients, who display increasing difficulty conveying anything meaningful as the disease progresses. Hart (1988) described another interesting means of assessing expressive language, which is based on the Token Test (De Renzi & Faglioni, 1978). This well-known test is used primarily to assess receptive language skills by asking the subject to complete a series of increasingly more complex commands involving the manipulation of tokens of different shapes and colors. In the Reporter's Test (De Renzi & Ferrari, 1978), the patient is asked to describe the manipulation of the tokens carried out by the clinician. Thus, instead of the patients demonstrating their ability to follow instructions, the task requires that they report on the examiner's actions in a systematic way. Hart (1988) found this to be a test that is particularly sensitive to the expressive language deficits of dements.

There has been little interest in the receptive language abilities of DAT patients. On the Token Test, patients with DAT are less capable than healthy controls of executing the various commands. Their impairments appear to be the result of failures to comprehend the more linguistically complex commands and simply a product of reduced memory span or motor problems (Hart, 1988). The ability to read aloud usually remains uncompromised even in moderately impaired DAT patients and this finding has been used to develop measures designed to estimate premorbid IQ such as the National Adult Reading Test.

Several studies have provided quantitative data on language function in DAT patients using comprehensive aphasia batteries. Appell et al. (1982) administered the Western Aphasia Battery to 25 institutionalized DAT patients with an average age of 76. They found that all the patients tested showed signs of language disturbance. They noted,

> A quantitative analysis of the spontaneous speech of these Alzheimer patients reveals a high incidence of semantic jargon. This is characterized by fluent irrelevant speech, with well preserved syntax and words, yet for practical purposes the meaning is lost.... . Nevertheless the sentences are often complete and more or less correct grammatically, without any phonemic disturbances or articulatory problems. (p. 83)

The patients who were less impaired had no problems on measures of language production and articulation, but were impaired on naming and comprehension subtests. Few of their patients exhibited the classic signs of Broca's aphasia. Appell et al. concluded overall that language impairment in DAT is best regarded as "part of a more pervasive cognitive disorganization" (p. 89).

Cummings et al. (1985) found similar results. They likened language problems in dementia to transcortical sensory aphasia. This is an aphasic syndrome in which receptive aphasia occurs in the presence of preserved repetition. Transcortical sensory aphasia is a rare focal disorder presumed to result from the isolation of both Wernicke's and Broca's area from the rest of the brain. Certainly repetition, articulation, and the motor aspects of speech tend to be preserved in DAT. However, the dementing patient does not produce neologisms or paraphasic speech (unintended words or syllables) like the sensory transcortical aphasic. The resemblance of language problems in DAT to transcortical sensory aphasia was also noted by B. E. Murdoch et al. (1987), who tested 18 patients with the Neurosensory Centre Comprehensive Examination of Aphasia. They also found that AD patients' speech was fluent and articulate in character, repetition was preserved, and the incidence of paraphasic speech was low, but auditory and written comprehension was impaired. Their results help clarify the nature of the language tasks in aphasia batteries that DAT patients find most difficult. In essence, they concluded that patients are most impaired on tasks in which language use is dependent on cognition. This underlines the way in which language disturbance in dementia may be distinct in quality from the aphasia resulting from more local lesions seen in other neurological patients. Hence the appropriateness of using terms such as transcortical or Wernicke's aphasia with reference to aphasic patients is questionable, except as preliminary descriptions, and the nature of the relationship between language and cognition impairments in DAT is undoubtedly important and remains to be clarified.

Finally, at a practical level, it is important for clinicians using neuropsychological tests to be aware that language defects may impact on the measurement of other skills. For example, the ability to comprehend instructions may impede the execution of apraxic or sensory tests. Memory tests, that require perception of objects (e.g., Fuld, 1983; Gibson & Kendrick, 1979) may also be affected by linguistic problems.

Cognitive Stimulation Programs

Most institutional care programs for dementing patients involve some systematic attempt to maintain or improve the cognitive functioning and orientation of the patients by creating cognitively stimulating environment. The predominant psychosocial approach to remediating the profound cognitive changes associated with DAT is some form of Reality Orientation Training (ROT; Folsom, 1968). Studies evaluating the outcome of ROT have been reviewed in detail elsewhere (Godfrey & R. G. Knight, 1987; Powell-Proctor & E. Miller, 1982). The aim of ROT is to improve the orientation of dementing patients and to slow the inevitable decline in the cognitive skills of demented patients.

Powell-Proctor and E. Miller (1982) divide ROT into two basic processes: formal class sessions and an informal 24-hour-a-day training process.

> Informal RO is meant to be carried out all the time and during any activity in which the elderly person engages. Care staff are required to remind him continually of who and where he is, what time of day and year it is, what is happening in the environment at the time, and so on. They can often do this by incorporating such information into their ordinary communications with patient. Staff are also encouraged to speak slowly and clearly, to use direct eye contact and touch to maintain the patient's attention, and to make use of aids such as large print calendars, clocks and pictures. (p. 457)

In addition to constant routine prompting from staff, there is a formal class component as well. Small groups of patients meet each day in a special area equipped with calendars, blackboards, clocks, and charts.

Information relevant to current orientation—time, season, place, current event, weather and so on—are rehearsed with the therapist. Topics covered vary with the level of impairment displayed by the patients. This kind of approach has been widely adopted in a variety of institutional settings. There have been a number of evaluations of the effectiveness of ROT (e.g., Brook, Degun, & Mather, 1975; Citrin & Dixon, 1977; Goldstein, Turner, Holzman, Kanagy, Elmore, & Barry, 1982; I. G. Hanley, McGuire, & Boyde, 1981; Harris & Ivory, 1976; M. L. MacDonald & Stettin, 1978; Woods, 1979, 1983). On the whole, it has been found that ROT produces gains in orientation skills relative to no treatment conditions, although this does not occur inevitably (Hogstel, 1979). There are also some results that suggest that ROT works better than nonspecific general activation programs (Brook et al., 1975; Woods, 1979). ROT is limited, however, because no evidence has been found of generalization to aspects of cognition or orientation not included in training (e.g., Goldstein et al. 1982; Woods, 1983). Specific training in mnemonic strategies, such as visual imagery use, appears to have little impact on memory impairment in demented patients (S. H. Zarit, J. M. Zarit, & Reever, 1982). In general, the pattern of results from a number of studies appears to be consistent. Most ROT programs result in a modest improvement in orientation for the information used in training with little generalization of the effect to other measures of orientation or adaptive behavior.

Conclusions

Alzheimer's disease is the most common cause of dementia, affecting as many as 10% of all adults over the age of 65. As the numbers of elderly people in the population increase in the Western world over the next 30 years, so will the prevalence of people with DAT and other forms of dementia. Caring for patients with Alzheimer's disease represents a major challenge to our health care systems both now and in the future.

The magnitude of the problem of caring for so many severely disabled elderly people has stimulated a drive to understand the pathological processes and causes of the disease. Despite the intensity of the research effort, the etiology of Alzheimer's disease remains unclear. This disease causes a profound and irreversible deterioration in the cognition, personality, and behavior of those it afflicts. Neuropsychological research has demonstrated that the disease progresses to compromise all aspects of cognition. Early in the course of the disease, testing reveals memory and intellectual dysfunction. Forgetfulness progresses to a dense and global degree of amnesia. In Korsakoff's disease, anterograde amnesia is not usually complicated by signs of primary memory failure. In contrast, studies of patients with Alzheimer's disease, reveal that secondary memory failure is nearly always accompanied by primary memory loss. Remote memory is also severely affected, with an ungraded impairment over the decades stretching back to childhood being common. DAT is also characterised by impairments in semantic memory and language functioning. Some degree of aphasia is an inevitable consequence of the disease in the later stages. Cognitive stimulation programs have generally been found to have limited effectiveness and there is no evidence that instructing demented patients to rehearse particular skills generalizes to other aspects of adaptive behavior.

In addition to the effects of the disease on the patients themselves, there are millions of people whose lives are affected by the strain of caring for dementing relatives or friends. Caregivers play a vital role in maintaining demented people in the community. However, the burden of caregiving exacts a toll and providing support for those involved in care is an important priority for the clinician. Understanding the stresses that caregivers experience is an important part of planning the management of dementing patients. We look at the psychosocial consequences of caregiving in more detail in Chapter 9.

Chapter 5

MULTIPLE SCLEROSIS

Now aged 34, Peter has been diagnosed as having multiple sclerosis for the past six years. His first symptom was the paralysis of his right arm. Loss of function developed over several days and then slowly improved. A year later both the right arm and leg were severely affected. This time the symptoms persisted and he was left with an ataxic gait and a loss of power in his arm. Shortly afterwards, Peter reported having persistent double vision and although this disappeared, a diagnosis of multiple sclerosis was made. Three years later, both Peter and his wife noticed that he was having difficulties remembering things. His cognitive problems precipitated a referral for neuropsychological testing. On the WAIS, Peter is found to have an IQ of 107 and on the WMS, an MQ of 93. He has noticeable problems with the Paired Associate and Logical Memory subtests.

His most pressing problems, however, are with his marriage. He no longer has a job, and his intense frustration at his physical problems leads to constant arguments with his wife, Christine. He feels that she controls every aspect of his life, treating him more like a child than a partner. Christine maintains that if she did not take charge of things, his poor memory and disinhibited behavior would compromise their personal circumstances further. Both are worried about the future and concerned about whether they should plan to have a family.

Background

Multiple sclerosis (MS), once known as disseminated sclerosis, is the most common nontraumatic neurological disease afflicting young adults in the Occident. For example, in a national survey Baum and Rothschild (1981) estimated that there were some 123,000 persons with MS in the United States on January 1st, 1976; a prevalence rate of 58/100,000 population. This disease, which commonly begins in the third and fourth decades of life, has a course ranging from relatively benign to rapid deterioration. It has the potential to create distressing changes in the lives of MS sufferers and their families.

Jean Cruveillier, professor of Pathological Anatomy at the Faculty of Medicine in Paris during the 1830s is given credit for first describing the clinical features of the disorder (De Jong, 1970). Attribution of the discovery to Cruveillier was made initially by Charcot, who specified 1835 as the year in which the first account of MS was presented. In his *Lectures on Diseases of the Nervous System* Charcot (1877) described some of the critical features of the course of the disease, which he labeled multilocular sclerosis, as follows:

> *Sometimes the drama is begun by cephalic symptoms ... but such is not the most common mode of invasion. Generally, the spinal phenomena first reveal themselves, and so common is this circumstance that during many months—nay even for years—the patients may present no symptoms other than an enfeeblement, a more or less marked paresis of the lower extremities, displaying a tendency to become aggravated in a slowly progressive manner. (p. 210)*

The disease, he noted, had a tendency to episodic remissions, giving rise to hopes of a cure, but was generally characterized in the end

> *by the progressive enfeeblement of the organic functions: inappetency becomes habitual, diarrhoea frequent ... at the same time there ensues an aggravation of all the symptoms proper to this disease, the obnubilation of the intellect proceeds even to dementia... . (p. 213)*

MS is a demyelinating disease. For reasons as yet unknown, the myelin sheath encasing axonal fibres in circumscribed areas of the white matter of the central nervous system (CNS) is progressively destroyed. The conduction ability of the affected neurons is severely compromised, leading to the multiplicity of neurological symptoms found in MS. On autopsy, the brain of the chronic MS patient will reveal numerous grey sclerotic plaques, often triangular in section, and about 5-15 mm across. These plaques are the brain lesions typical of MS. They mark the sites where demyelination has caused the destruction of nervous fibres. The scattered distribution of sclerotic plaques throughout the brain gives the disease its distinctive character—an extremely variable presentation and an unpredictable course, with episodes of remission, progression, and relapse. It is the inconstancy of MS that makes it hard for the clinician to diagnose, manage, and study, and demanding for the person with MS and their families to live with.

Diagnosis

Establishing the diagnosis of MS can be a lengthy and difficult task. In many cases, during the early stages of the disease, MS is a diagnosis that can only be advanced tentatively.

The diagnosis rests largely on the patient's clinical history and pattern of neurological symptoms. In addition, there are various laboratory tests and procedures that may help substantiate the diagnosis. For example, for some time it has been known that disturbances in the immune function may be characteristic of MS (Jersild, Svejgaard, & Fog, 1972). Examination of the CSF for increased production of immunoglobulin is one laboratory test that may provide useful diagnostic information. CT or nuclear magnetic resonance (NMR) scans, neuropsychological tests, and the measurement of visual evoked potentials can also supplement clinical observation and aid in diagnosis. The use of NMR scans to detect MS plaques has been particularly promising (Robertson, Li, Mayo, & Paty, 1984). In the end, however, diagnosis is a clinical decision, principally determined by neurological examination.

In principle, diagnosis of MS depends on detecting clinical evidence for lesions in two or more separate functional systems. One functional system might be the pyramidal motor system, the other the visual system. The lesions should not only be spatially separated in the CNS, but also arise at clearly different times. In 1982, a multidisciplinary group met in Washington to develop diagnostic guidelines for the disease. The subsequent publication of diagnostic criteria for MS by Poser et al. (1983) has been an important step in allowing the consistent use of terminology across different research groups. This is particularly vital for epidemiological work, where international and cross-racial comparisons of prevalence, relapse rates, and prognostic factors may prove to have an important part to play in establishing the etiology of this disease.

The diagnostic criteria of Poser et al. divide persons with MS into two major categories—definite and probable. Each category is further subdivided into clinical or laboratory supported diagnoses. A clinically definite diagnosis of MS requires evidence of two attacks, with each attack being defined as the appearance of neurological symptoms lasting more than 24 hours, caused by two distinct CNS lesions. These two attacks (e.g., one of blurred vision and the other of facial weakness) should be separated by more than one month. A clinically probable diagnosis of MS is defined as the occurrence of two attacks and clinical evidence of a lesion responsible for one (but not both) of the attacks. Similar definitions are provided for the laboratory-supported diagnoses.

Symptoms

It is important to acknowledge at the outset that any account of the signs and symptoms of MS must of necessity be selective. Plaques can and do form anywhere in the CNS and the symptoms of MS are extraordinary in their variability. However, the most common sites for MS plaques are the optic nerves, spinal cord, and the white matter surrounding the ventricular system of both cerebral hemispheres (Brownell & Hughes, 1962). For example, Ikuta and Zimmerman (1976) described a series of 70 autopsies of chronic MS cases, of which 46% had extensive plaques in the optic nerve, 51% in the cerebrum, 19% in the cerebellum, 27% in the midbrain, 39% in the pons, 25% in medulla, and 53% in the spinal cord. Interestingly, some postmortem investigations have revealed the presence of major sclerotic plaques in persons who in their lifetime showed no symptoms and died of other causes (Herndon & Rudnick, 1983). Such cases are presumably at the extreme benign end of the prognostic spectrum.

Numerous studies have reported the incidence of various initial symptoms and signs of MS (e.g., Kurtzke, Beebe, Nagler, Auth, Kurland, & Nefzger, 1968). Many of these reports are based on retrospective patient accounts of unknown reliability, from samples that often do not comprise a representatives series of cases, and therefore are hard to evaluate. In his review, McAlpine (1972) suggested the overall incidence of initial symptoms to be: weakness in one or more limbs (40%), visual disturbance (optic neuritis) (22%), paraesthesiae (21%), diplopia or double vision (12%), vertigo (5%), and disturbance of micturition (5%). As the disease progresses, more and more symptoms emerge. In the advanced stages, most patients show lack of motor control, ataxia, sensory loss, and loss of bladder control. In some cases symptoms may emerge that are rare or not commonly associated with MS. The symptoms may also be constant or paroxysmal. Facial pain (trigeminal neuralgia) is an example of a recurring paroxysmal symptom often seen in MS.

Motor symptoms are the most commonly reported neurological symptoms in the initial stages of MS. A typical initial presenting picture involves the gradual onset of weakness in one limb, most typically one leg, or one arm and one leg. This may be first noticed only on exertion, but as the disease progresses the weakness becomes more pronounced and debilitating. Lesions in the upper motor neuron of the pyramidal tract may result in spasticity (or increased rigidity) or exaggerated tendon or extensor plantar reflexes. The inability to walk unaided or climb stairs is one of the early disabling consequences of the disease. In advanced cases, the lower motor neuron may deteriorate leading to muscle wasting, often most evident in the hands.

Sensory symptoms are also common and frequently subtle. Sensations such as pain or heat may be detected normally by the patient, but discerned as being somehow changed or distorted. Plaques in the posterior columns of the spinal cord typically cause loss of sensation or abnormal feelings such as "tingling," or "pins and needles" in part of the body. Acute vertigo is also sometimes reported, indicating the formation of sclerotic lesions in the vestibular system. Pain is a common and very variable symptom. It may be persistent or paroxysmal, and frequently hard to treat.

The large white fibre tracts of the optic nerves and chiasma are especially susceptible to the deterioration in MS. The result of this damage is frequently optic neuritis, the first signs of which may be blurring of vision. Central scotoma (the loss or deterioration of the center of vision), which may be experienced as a dark patch in the visual fields, may develop. Pain is typically an accompaniment at some stage. This pain may be experienced either in the eye or supraorbital and is often exacerbated by movement.

In addition to the multiplicity of physical symptoms that can occur, the patient with MS may also show changes in cognitive and emotional functioning. These factors are discussed in detail later.

Course and Prognosis

The pathology and symptom pattern of MS is highly variable, thus it should come as no surprise that the course and prognosis for the disease are equally unpredictable. At the time of diagnosis there is little that can be done to counsel patients concerning how their disease will progress. In rare cases, MS may prove fatal within a year; sometimes there may be no progression to disability in 60 years. The outcome is erratic.

Onset of MS is rare before the age of 10, although juvenile cases do occur (Poskanser, Schapira, & H. Miller, 1963). It is, however, primarily a disease with an onset in early or late adulthood. There is a steep increase in the number of new cases after the age of 20, and an equally precipitous decline in the incidence of MS after the age of 40. Nevertheless, there have been autopsy established cases where the first symptoms appear to have occurred after the age of 60. Both prevalence and incidence rate studies show that the disease is more common in women than in men, and may have an earlier age of onset in women. Acheson (1985), in a review of 11 studies of incidence, found male-to-female ratios ranging from 2.5 to 1.8. Most research samples contain more women than men, a factor that needs to be considered in research into psychosocial factors, depression, and adjustment to the disease.

Following the first attack of the disease, relapses may occur that involve either the re-emergence of old symptoms or the appearance of new deficits, or both. Relapses may be characterized by an improvement in and stabilization of the symptoms, without their complete disappearance. It can be difficult to establish criteria for the amount of improvement that constitutes a remission, and to decide when a relapse bout ended, and remission began. Daily fluctuations in symptom severity, which are often a response to fatigue or extra stress, complicate the pattern further.

On average, MS shortens life expectancy. For example, Poskanzer and colleagues (1963) identified 1,156 cases in two English counties and found an estimated reduction in life expectancy of 9.5 years in men and 14.4 in women. The greater reduction for women is explained by their greater average life expectancy. Kurtzke, Beebe, Nagler, Nefzger, Auth, and Kurland (1970) looked at the rate of mortality in their series of 762 men with 90 or more days of military service, who had received a discharge diagnosis of MS in a U.S. Army Hospital during the period 1942-1951. Using life table methods, they calculated that the median survival period for this sample of young men lay between 30 and 35 years following diagnosis, and 35 years after onset. Generalization of these estimates is limited by the absence of women in the sample, and the fact that the age distribution does not include persons with the onset in middle life, where the disease is held to be more likely to be progressive and have a more negative prognosis.

In some cases, where progression to disability does not occur or is very slow, the course of MS is classed as benign. A benign course is not uncommon; for example, in his study of 241 patients, McAlpine (1961) found that 78 were not restricted in everyday life some 10 years later. The definition of benign varies greatly and consequently the rate of benign cases located in any particular series is difficult to compare with that from any other. After 20 years, McAlpine reported that 49 of his 78 benign cases had still not progressed to disablement even although 33 of these had a definite diagnosis of MS. On the negative side, the fact that 19 cases had progressed illustrate the important point that a benign course for 10 years does not guarantee future freedom from progressive deterioration.

It is difficult to predict when any particular person with MS will enter a chronic and disabling stage of the disease. The most consistent predictor of time to disablement is the onset of a progressive phase of the disorder. When symptoms fail to remit and deterioration becomes progressive, severe disability becomes increasingly likely. This may be more likely to occur in patients with a later initial onset (Detels, V. A. Clark, Valdiviezo, Visscher, Malmgren, & Dudley, 1982; A. P. Friedman & Davison, 1945). Kurtzke (1970) summarized the literature on prognosis as follows:

> *To sum up, I think the worst possible prognostic sign for a multiple sclerotic is entry into a chronic progressive stage. This is unlikely without major involvement of pyramidal and cerebellar symptoms—but in our series at least, nearly 9 in 10 multiple sclerotics have such involvement quite early in their illness. Age per se does not appear to me to be a major factor, but chronic progressive illness is more common in older patients. I know no way to determine whether a bout will be "chronic progressive" until time has demonstrated this. It is by no means clear that a benign course for the first five or 10 years means its continuation into the future for an equivalent period. (p. 200)*

Assessment of Disability

Describing the course of the illness requires that the level of disability that the person with MS has can be quantified. This is important not only for research, but also for practice. Planning for rehabilitation or management, as well as monitoring treatment effects, necessitate a reliable measure of disability. Kurtzke (1955) presented a 10-point scale designed to assess level of disability in a standardized fashion. On the Disability Status Scale (DSS) patients are rated primarily in terms of the restrictions imposed by the disease and the focus is on ambulation as the primary indicator of disablement. Scoring of the scale is based on an examination by a neurologist. After its publication, the Kurtzke DSS rapidly became an important tool for research sample description. Examples of the way grades of impairment are formulated are shown in Table 5.1.

**Table 5.1:   Examples of Grades of Impairment from the Kurtzke
Disability Status Scale**

Grade	Description
3	Moderate disability though fully ambulatory, for example, monoparesis, moderate ataxia, or combinations of lesser dysfunctions.
5	Disability severe enough to preclude ability to work a full day without special provisions; maximal motor function: walking unaided no more than several blocks.
7	Restricted to wheelchair but able to wheel self and enter and leave chair alone.
9	Totally helpless bed patients.

The disability rating system evolved further when Kurtzke (1961) provided a system for assessing damage to eight functional systems (pyramidal, cerebellar, brain stem, sensory, bowel, and bladder, visual, cerebral or mental, and other or miscellaneous functions). For example, functioning of the pyramidal system is rated on the following six-point scale:

Pyramidal Functions

    0   Normal
    1   Abnormal signs without disability
    2   Minimal disability
    3   Mild or moderate paraparesis or hemiparesis; or severe
        monoparesis
    4   Marked paraparesis or hemiparesis; moderate quadriparesis;
        or monoplegia
    5   Hemiplegia, paraplegia, or marked quadriparesis
    6   Quadriplegia

The DSS and the Functional Systems (FS) scales were designed to be used together. Kurtzke (1983a) revised the DSS, and this became the Expanded Disability Status Scale (EDSS). The new EDSS is also linked to the FS. The EDSS provides a more fine-grained rating of a patient's current ability. For example, a grade 3 disability has been divided into two parts, each defined in more detail, as follows (FS = Functional System):

3.0 = Moderate disability in one FS (one FS grade 3, others 0 or 1), or mild disability in three or four FS (three/four FS grade 2, others 0 or 1) though fully ambulatory.

3.5 = Fully ambulatory but with moderate disability in one FS (one grade 3) and one or two FS grade 2; or two FS grade 3; or five grade 2 (others 0, 1).

Amato, Fratiglioni, Groppi, Siracusa, and Amaducci (1988) found that the interrater reliability of the EDSS was at best moderate. They recommended that raters be carefully trained in the application of the scale, especially when the data are to be combined in multicenter trials.

Following a meeting of the International Federation of Multiple Sclerosis Societies (Slater, LaRocca, & Scheinberg, 1984) a Minimal Record of Disability (MRD) was prepared. The idea behind the MRD was to provide a comprehensive review of the patient's current adaptive functioning, capable of being used by a variety of professionals. The MRD comprises Kurtzke's FS scale and the DSS. In addition, a more broad-based assessment of disablement is incorporated in the Incapacity Status Scale. This covers not only ambulation but also 15 other factors, such as bathing, dressing, toilet/chair/bed transfer, bladder function, and feeding. The patient's degree of handicap is evaluated using the Environment Status Scale, which measures psychosocial adjustment and rehabilitative needs. Some seven factors are assessed: work status, financial-economic status, personal residence, personal assistance required, transportation, community services required, and social activity. Each factor is rated on a five-point scale. An example of one of the factor scales is given in Table 5.2.

Field testing of the MRD suggests that it can be used reliably and provides useful clinical and research data. The total assessment package provides a comprehensive review of the patient's status. There is some redundancy in the MRD, particularly with respect to the DSS and Incapacity scale. In all, however, the MRD represents a useful step towards standardizing research sample description across different research centers in different countries.

Table 5.2:   **Social Activity Grading Scale. Factor 7 of the Environmental Status Scale (Slater et al., 1984)**

Grade	Description
0	Socially active as before with no changes in social activity and no difficulty in maintaining the pattern.
1	Maintains usual pattern of social activities despite some difficulties.
2	Some restrictions on social activity, such as change in type or frequency of some activities or increased dependence on others.
3	Significant restriction of social activity; largely dependent on actions of others but still able to initiate some activity.
4	Socially inactive except for the initiative of others.
5	No social activity, does not see friends or family; social contact is limited to that provided by community service providers, e.g., visiting nurse.

Epidemiology

The cause of MS is unknown. For the practicing clinician, speculation and debate about the possible etiology of MS is of little practical significance. Nevertheless, the etiological puzzle that the disease presents is too intriguing to ignore completely. Perhaps the most interesting fact about MS is the way in which risk of developing the disease is associated with the latitude of the geographical region in which a person resides. This may eventually provide a clue to the cause of the disorder. Differences in prevalence rates for people living at different altitudes have been well established (R. T. Johnson, 1975; Kinnunen, 1984; Kurtzke, 1983b). In the northern parts of the United States, Northern Europe, and Canada, the prevalence is about 30-80/100,000. This figure drops to about 6-14/100,000 in Southern Europe, and the southern United States (e.g., Kurtzke & Beebe, 1983). However, in some countries where a high prevalence might be expected because of the latitude, racial factors seem to be important. Prevalence rates among Japanese, Chinese, North American Indians, Eskimos, Asian Indians, and Blacks is extremely low even when they reside in areas of high risk (Baum & Rothschild, 1981; Fischman, 1982; Okinawa, McAlpine, Miyagawa, Suwa, Kuroiwa, Shiraki, Araki, & Kurland, 1960).

Another interesting extension of this relationship between incidence of multiple sclerosis and geographical location was reported by Dean (1967). He found that most multiple sclerosis victims in South Africa were immigrants and that whereas the prevalence for white Afrikaan-speaking natives was 3/100,000, and for white English-speaking natives was 11/100,000, the prevalence for immigrants from Europe was 50/100,000. In fact, the prevalence rate for European immigrants was equivalent to that of their country of origin, and far higher than that for white natives of South Africa. Further analysis showed that those immigrants who had left their European homes before the age of 14 had the same rate of incidence of multiple sclerosis as South African-born whites, whereas those who immigrated after the age of 15 had the same rate as the population of their place of birth. This suggested that the years around the age of puberty were somehow significant in determining risk for developing multiple sclerosis. Similar findings, establishing 15 as a critical age, were found in studies of immigrants to Israel (Leibowitz, 1971).

Incidence of multiple sclerosis therefore seems to relate to latitude of residence before the age of 15. The disease itself, however, rarely strikes before the age of 15 or after the age of 50 to 55. The epidemiological evidence has led many researchers to speculate that the disease may have a viral etiology. Another line of investigation has provided additional evidence for the viral hypothesis. Before 1943 the annual incidence of multiple sclerosis amongst Faeroese Islanders who live near Greenland, was practically zero. During World War 2, however, the islands were occupied by over 8,000 British troops and a dramatic upsurge in the number of multiple sclerosis cases amongst the islanders were recorded. Beginning in 1943, 25 cases of multiple sclerosis were reported, no case being younger than 13 or older than 45 in 1942 (Fischman, 1982; Kurtzke, 1983b). This suggested to epidemiologists that viral transmission of the disorder might occur at almost any time in life prior to age 50 (or at any age coinciding with the end of menopause in women), with an abrupt increase of risk after puberty.

It is not known whether multiple sclerosis is transmitted genetically. Some indirect and weak evidence exists to encourage the view that some genetic predisposition may make some individuals more susceptible than others to the disease (Tiwari, Hodge, Terasaki, & Spence, 1980). The incidence of multiple sclerosis is 15 to 20 times higher in the relatives of multiple sclerosis patients than in the general population (McKhanna, 1982). The concordance rates in monozygotic (MZ) twins tend to be higher than in dizygotic (DZ) twins (e.g., Currier & Eldridge, 1982). The precise nature of the genetic basis of multiple sclerosis, if one exists, has yet to be determined.

The indirect evidence presented by the epidemiological studies has led many to propose that multiple sclerosis is transmitted by a viral agent (W. I. McDonald, 1983). Opinion is divided on the strength of the largely circumstantial data presently available. The inflammatory nature of the process that destroys the myelin, the definition of at-risk geographical areas, the age range of onset, and the relapsing course of the disease are all to some degree consistent with a viral aetiology. Probably, however, the event that has most predisposed neurologists to posit that multiple sclerosis is the product of a virus, has been the discovery of the slow viral agents that cause the degenerative neurological conditions of kuru, subacute sclerosing panencephalitis, progressive multifocal leukoencephalopathy, and Jacob-Creutzfeldt's disease. The example of kuru is particularly compelling. Kuru is a disease found to be limited to one of the hill tribes of New Guinea. A major breakthrough in the understanding of the etiology of this disease came when it proved possible to transmit the disease from an infected human brain to the unaffected brain of a non-human primate. It has been proposed that kuru was the result of the transmission of a viral infection because the tribe with the disease practiced cannibalism, which involved consumption of the human brain (Hornabrook & Moir, 1970). Several viral agents produce animal and human diseases with one or more of the features that a multiple sclerosis viral agent would need to have, providing further indirect evidence that it is possible that a virus could be responsible for multiple sclerosis. Viral diseases such as herpes genetalis and herpes zoster in man frequently involve cycles of remission and exacerbation. Other viral agents causing CNS disorders have a long incubation period, for example kuru (4 to 10 years; Hornabrook & Moir, 1970), scrapie in sheep (1 to 4 years), and Jacob-Creutzfeldt's disease. Of the major demyelinating diseases in humans, postinfectious encephalomyelitis, acute necrotizing hemorrhagic leukoencephalitis, and progressive multifocal leukoencephalopathy, are known to be caused by viruses.

Despite the indirect evidence and demonstration of similar viral processes, the direct evidence for a viral etiology is weak. Inoculating material from the brains of multiple sclerosis victims into nonhuman primates has not resulted in the transmission of the disease. No virus has yet been positively identified. When it has been claimed that the crucial virus or viral particle has been discovered, laboratories have not been able to replicate the findings or to have them produced independently (R. T. Johnson, 1975; Kurtzke, 1983b). The etiology of the disease is unknown at the present time, and no curative therapy is available (Waksman, 1983).

Cognitive Deficits

From the time MS was first identified it has been known that some patients progressed to dementia. In recent times the systematic evaluation of the cognitive functioning of MS patients has been the focus of considerable research interest. In interpreting results from these studies it is important to be mindful of the nature of the disease. There are many reasons why persons with MS may perform cognitive tasks poorly, not all of these are a necessary consequence of cerebral damage. Fatigue is one important factor. The host of motor and sensory deficits consequent on the disease is another. Poor vision or weakness in fine-motor coordination are liable to impact on test performance. The level of disease activity, emotional state, and degree of disability may all limit the skill that the patient displays in the execution of a particular task. And so the effects of noncortical lesions, fatigue, and the concurrent level of disease severity all need to be taken into account in the assessment of test data from individual cases.

Nevertheless, there is good reason to suspect that MS patients do show impairments on cognitive neuropsychological tests as a result of their neurological disorder. In several autopsy studies, increased ventricular dilation suggestive of atrophy of the white matter around the ventricles has been reported (e.g., Brownell & Hughes, 1962; A. P. Friedman & Davison, 1945). Some 90% of autopsy cases have plaques in the cerebrum (Lumsden, 1970). Brownell and Hughes (1962) reported that 9% of the plaques located in their autopsy series were to be found in the cerebral gray matter. Thus there is autopsy-based evidence that cortical functioning may be disrupted and this may compromise cognitive processing. However, the amount of damage to the cortical mantle in MS is far less pronounced than in AD and so the incidence and severity of dementia is likely to be less also. This has generally been found to be the case, and the rate of cognitive decline in MS is more gradual and less severe than that seen in Alzheimer's disease (Filley, Heaton, L. M. Nelson, Burks, & Franklin, 1989).

Intelligence

The Wechsler scales have been commonly used to assess intellect in MS patients. In general, results from this measure tend to provide evidence of a mild level of impairment in MS subjects. Jambor (1969) and Reitan, Reed, and Dyken (1971) compared MS performance on the WAIS to that of normal controls and found no significant between-group differences. The MS groups, however, had larger standard deviations and it is likely that these pooled group results disguise individual cases of dementia. Ivnik (1978b) found a decline of three to four IQ scale points in MS subjects over a test-retest interval averaging 3 years, compared to a small improvement in performance by a matched brain damaged comparison group. Fink and Houser (1966) found an increase in VIQ from 106 to 110 over a 1-year retest interval for a group of 44 community-based MS patients. The most marked deterioration was reported by Canter (1951). A group of 47 MS patients and 38 controls were tested using the Wechsler-Bellevue with a 6-month retest interval. The MS patients' VIQ scores decreased from 108.7 to 105, a drop of 3.7 points, whereas the control subjects increased by 7.8 points from an initial score of 109.

The pattern of performance by MS patients on the WAIS can be seen in Table 5.3. The data in this table are a compilation of results from eight studies reporting WAIS subtest scores from groups of MS patients (Canter, 1951; G. Goldstein & Shelley, 1974; Heaton, L. M. Nelson, Thompson, Burks, & Franklin, 1985; Ivnik, 1978a, 1978b; Marsh, 1980; Matthews, Cleeland, & Hooper, 1970; Reitan & Boll, 1971). A mean score was computed for each subtest and IQ scale score, weighted in terms of the number of subjects in each study. A total of 325 MS patients with an average age of 36.7 were tested in the eight studies.

The results in Table 5.3 are informative. The six highest ranked tests are on the Verbal scales. The four subtests on which MS patients perform most poorly are timed and require considerable dexterity—Digit Symbol, Object Assembly, Picture Arrangement, and Block Design. These subtests are likely to be susceptible to the psychomotor problems characteristic of MS. The average scores on the Similarities test, which is one of the Wechsler subtests that requires novel application of knowledge in task solution is comparable with performance on the Vocabulary, Information, and Comprehension subtests, which have a heavy educational component. The better verbal scores of the MS patients is reflected in the positive mean VIQ-PIQ discrepancy of 8.83 (range 7.5 to 14.4).

Table 5.3:   Mean WAIS IQ and Subtest Scores of MS patients in Eight Studies

	Mean Score	Subtest Rank
Full Scale IQ	103.84	
Verbal IQ	108.58	
Performance IQ	99.75	
Information	11.62	3
Comprehension	11.89	1
Arithmetic	10.81	5
Similarities	11.42	4
Digit Span	10.62	6
Vocabulary	11.63	2
Digit Symbol	8.22	11
Picture Completion	10.42	7
Block Design	9.83	8
Picture Arrangement	8.83	10
Object Assembly	9.38	9
Verbal-Performance IQ	8.33	

Heaton et al. (1985) presented separate WAIS scale and subtest scores for relapsing-remitting ($n = 57$) and chronic-progressive ($n = 43$) MS patients. The relapsing-remitting group were defined as "having a clinical course characterized by acute exacerbations that are separated in time by periods of relative disease stability" (p. 104), and had been in remission for at least 1 month. Mean results from the two MS groups and the normal controls are presented in Table 5.4.

The pattern of results in Table 5.4 is consistent with those in Table 5.3; however, it can be seen that the chronic-progressive patients perform more poorly than the relapsing-remitting subjects. The relapsing-remitting group were in a state of remission when tested and about a third of these patients showed no signs of impairment on any of the measures included in the Heaton et al. (1985) battery of tests, including the WAIS. These data suggest that the level of disease activity has an effect on intelligence test scores.

Table 5.4:   Mean WAIS Scale and Subtest Scores

Measure	Normal Control (n = 100)	Relapsing-Remitting (n = 57)	Chronic Progressive (n = 43)
Verbal IQ	114.67	110.70	109.77^a
Performance IQ	113.08	106.21	$98.28^{a,b}$
Information	12.42	12.04	12.05
Comprehension	12.55	12.04	12.05
Arithmetic	12.46	10.84^a	11.14^a
Similarities	12.76	12.33	11.63^a
Digit/Span	11.40	11.23	11.07
Vocabulary	12.32	12.18	11.86
Digit Symbol	11.56	10.32	8.47^a
Picture Completion	11.25	10.75	$9.81^{a,b}$
Block Design	12.09	11.23	$9.30^{a,b}$
Picture Arrangement	10.46	9.96	8.93^a
Object Assembly	11.49	9.98^a	$8.44^{a,b}$

Note. From Neuropsychological Findings in Relapsing-Remitting and Chronic Progressive Multiple Sclerosis by R. K. Heaton et al. 1985. *Journal of Consulting and Clinical Psychology, 53,* pp. 106-107. (c) American Psychological Association. Reprinted by permission.

[a]Significant difference between the MS group and the controls.
[b]Chronic-progressive performed more poorly than relapsing-remitting.

In summary, results from the WAIS suggest that MS patients generally show a minor significant decrement in intelligence. On those subtests where no motor skills are required, and speed is not a factor, MS patients show little disability. This is apparent from the WAIS results in Table 5.4, and from other tests. On both the Shipley-Hartford (Baldwin, 1952), an untimed test measuring vocabulary and reasoning skills, and Raven's Progressive Matrices (Knehr, 1962), MS patients have not been able to be discriminated from normal comparison groups. In contrast, P. A. Beatty and Gagne (1977) found that on the California Short-Form Test of Mental Maturity, MS patients did more poorly than the controls on subtests involving logical reasoning and numerical skills, but not on the test of verbal concepts. It is apparent then that intellectual decline is not pronounced in the majority of MS cases, and where it is manifest, it is most likely to be seen in the progressive or later stages of the disorder. This conclusion, however, should be tempered by noting that in some cases, the early stages of the disease may be characterized by disabling cognitive changes in the absence of significant physical or motor incapacity (Franklin, L. M. Nelson, Filley, & Heaton, 1989).

Memory Deficits

The memory performance of MS patients has been investigated in several studies (for a more detailed consideration see Rao, 1986; Rao, Leo, & St Aubin-Faubert, 1989). Because of the scattered nature of the lesions producing cognitive deficits in MS, this research has contributed little to the literature on the neuroanatomical basis of memory. However, from the clinician's point of view it is worth knowing that memory deficits occur consistently in MS; the degree of amnesia may be quite profound in some advanced cases, but in the early stages, memory impairment tends to be variable and mild in severity, not typically causing incapacity. In a study of 44 chronic progressive patients Rao, Hammeke, McQuillen, Khatri, and Lloyd (1984) found that 36% performed in the same range as the controls, 43% had mild memory problems, and 21% displayed moderate to severe impairment. Similarly, D. Staples and Lincoln (1979) found that 60% of their MS sample showed some degree of memory impairment.

The typical level of memory impairment in MS patients can be illustrated by the WMS performance of the 44 chronic progressive patients described in Rao et al. (1984). The MS subjects were matched for age, years of education, and gender, with a group of patient controls hospitalized while undergoing investigation of their chronic pain problems. The WMS results for the two groups can be seen in Table 5.5. The Logical Memory and Associate-Learning subtests were readministered after a 30-minute delay.

Overall, the patients performed in the normal range, as indicated by a MQ of 100, but their scores tended to be lower than those of age-matched controls. The subtest differences primarily responsible for the lower MQ were the Logical Memory and the Visual Reproduction subtests, even though the latter subtest was scored liberally to take account of the patients' ataxia. A similar pattern of WMS results has been reported by Litvan et al. (1988).

Table 5.5:   Wechsler Memory Scale Scores

	Multiple Sclerosis (*n* = 44)	Patient Controls (*n* = 19)	*p*
Information	5.5	5.8	
Orientation	4.7	5.0	< .05
Mental Control	6.8	8.0	< .01
Digit Span	11.1	11.1	
Logical Memory			
Immediate	7.2	9.6	< .002
Delayed	4.7	8.4	< .001
Visual Reproduction	8.3	11.4	< .001
Associative Learning			
Immediate	13.4	14.5	
Delayed	5.7	7.1	< .02
Memory Quotient	100.5	115.1	< .01

Note. From Memory Disturbance in Chronic Progressive Multiple Sclerosis by S. M. Rao et al. 1984. *Archives of Neurology, 41,* pp. 625-631. Copyright (c), 1984, American Medical Association. Reprinted by permission.

Interestingly, the MS patients' Associate Learning scores in Table 5.5 are comparable with the controls, although differences emerged with the introduction of a delay. Possibly the paired-associates list, which contains a number of highly associated word pairs, is well within the competence of MS patients to learn. On more difficult word lists, rate of learning of MS patients has been found to be substantially reduced relative to normal controls (e.g., P. A. Beatty & Gagne, 1977; I. Grant, W. I. McDonald, Trimble, E. Smith, & Reed, 1984; Heaton et al., 1985; Jambor, 1969; Van den Burg, Van Zomeren, Minderhoud, Prange, & Meijer, 1987). Generally these studies have found a consistent although not marked degree of deficit. For example, using the Bushke and Fuld (1974) selective reminding procedure, Rao et al. (1989) found that the total number of words from a 12-item list, administered 12 times, was significantly less (means of 97.24 versus 115.27, $p < .01$) for the MS patients than for the controls. As with intelligence test scores, however, the variability of patient performance should be stressed. Rao et al. (1984) found that their patients with the most severe cognitive impairments showed almost flat learning gradients on a spatial free recall test.

On the whole, MS patients tend to perform in the normal range on recognition tests (Carroll, Gates, & Roldan, 1984; Rao et al., 1984, Rao et al., 1989). Such tests tend to be easier and less discriminating than recall measures, and only the more severely impaired and advanced patients are likely to perform poorly on recognition tasks. Rate of forgetting over 24 hours tends also to be normal (Rao et al., 1989), a finding that distinguishes MS from AD patients. Finally, it seems unlikely that the differences between MS and normal subjects can be explained by the severity of depression. For example, Rao et al. (1989) found that although their MS subjects were more depressed than the controls, there was no correlation between Zung Depression Scale scores and results on a Verbal Fluency test and several memory and learning tasks. They also reported that there was no correlation between EDSS scores and memory impairment.

MS patients have generally been found to perform normally on immediate span tests (Heaton et al., 1985; Rao et al., 1984). This is in contrast to AD patients who typically show a deterioration in memory span. The only inconsistent result comes from Grant et al. (1984) who found that MS patients were impaired on the Peterson-Brown distractor task. Their 43 MS patients were noticeably impaired when asked to recall consonant trigrams under conditions that prevent rehearsal. However, Rao et al. (1989) were unable to replicate this result using an interference procedure that involved counting backward in threes from a randomly determined starting point. Reconciling these two studies is not possible because Grant et al. did not present sufficient data to allow the assessment of rate of decay in their study. However, it seems reasonable to conclude that MS patients are more likely to show deficits on tasks where memory performance is supraspan than on tasks where the stimuli are within the normal span of apprehension.

Memory deficits in MS patients are common, but certainly not as severe as that observed in Korsakoff or Alzheimer patients. The level of MS memory dysfunction and concurrent impairment is reminiscent of that seen in Parkinson's disease or the early stages of Huntington's disease, although Huntington patients typically show greater impairment on recall tasks than to people with MS.

Conceptual Learning

Several studies have assessed the ability of MS patients to form concepts or infer and learn new rules. One task of this nature that has been employed with MS patients is the Category Test from the Halstead-Reitan Battery. This is a test that involves acquiring new rules. Results have been mixed. In summary, there tend to be no differences in performance between MS and other brain-injured groups (Ivnik, 1978b; G. Goldstein & Shelley, 1974; Ross & Reitan, 1955). However, MS groups perform more poorly than normal controls (Peyser, Edwards, Poser, & Filskov, 1980; Reitan et al. 1971), although this difference may only hold for chronic-progressive patients (Heaton et al. 1985).

Heaton et al. (1985) found that both chronic-progressive and relapsing-remitting MS patients may make more perseverative responses on the Wisconsin Card Sorting Test (WCST) than the matched controls. A more detailed evaluation of WCST performance was reported by Rao, Hammeke, and Speech (1987). Results from their study are reproduced in Table 5.6.

The control group comprised persons undergoing evaluation for chronic pain. As is apparent in Table 5.6, the MS patients exhibited a greater tendency to perseverate and learn fewer categories than the controls. However, the differences were significant only for the chronic-progressive and control group comparisons. The results for the remitting and relapsing patients in this study are inconsistent with those from Heaton et al. (1985). Presumably this is a consequence of using patient rather than normal controls in the Rao et al. study, and the fact that Rao et al.'s relapsing-remitting patients were in an active (exacerbated) stage of the disease. This later methodological difference does not explain why Heaton et al.'s relapsing patients, who were in remission when tested, performed more poorly relative to their controls than Rao's group. It does, however, illustrate an important dilemma in MS research: whether to select patients in remission or exacerbation when testing for cognitive deficits. A similar increase in perseverative response was found in a visual discrimination task requiring subjects to develop appropriate strategies to make correct decisions (Rao & Hammeke, 1984). Rao (1986) noted that the MS patients' inability to shift sets in the WCST and to develop effective rule learning strategies was similar to the deficits seen in patients with frontal lobe tumors.

As with memory and intellectual tasks, conceptual learning is variably affected in MS patients. There is a considerable range of performance and globally impaired and chronic-progressive patients show the most pronounced deterioration. The nature of the deficits, which presumably result from plaque formation in the frontal area, is similar to the impairments seen in prefrontal patients (Stuss & Benson, 1984).

Table 5.6: Mean Summary Scores on the WCST

	Chronic Progressive ($n = 33$)	Patient Controls ($n = 41$)	Remitting-Relapsing ($n = 36$)	Patient Controls ($n = 19$)
Categories achieved	3.67	4.68*	4.75	5.42
Total errors	46.12	39.76	33.39	31.68
Perseverative errors	30.24	20.17*	16.53	14.32
Perseverative responses	36.36	22.95*	18.31	15.74
Nonperseverative errors	15.88	19.59	16.86	17.37
Trials to first category	35.73	23.07	25.61	20.63
Learning to learn	-3.15	-2.58	-2.67	-.36
Failure to maintain set	1.18	.83	.83	.58

Note. From Wisconsin Card Sorting Test Performance in Relapsing-Remitting and Chronic-Progressive Multiple Sclerosis by S. M. Rao et al. 1987. *Journal of Consulting and Clinical Psychology, 55,* pp. 263-265. (c) American Psychological Association. Reprinted by permission.

*Difference between MS and control groups significant, $p < .05$

Other Cognitive Functions

Language deficits have not often been the center of interest in studies of MS patients, suggesting that aphasia is uncommon in the clinical examination of MS patients. As Rao (1986) noted, it is surprising that more disconnection syndromes resulting from disruption to the fibre tracts linking inter- and intra-hemisphere language areas are not reported. Jambor (1969) found a small but significant decrement in the naming and reading but not the spelling or comprehension skills of a group of MS patients. Heaton et al. (1985) found that chronic-progressive, but not relapsing-remitting MS patients performed more poorly on an aphasia screening test than normal controls. Both Heaton et al. (1985) and Rao et al. (1989) found verbal fluency was affected in MS patients. Apart from these few findings, little is known in detail about the incidence or nature of possible language defects in MS.

Although it has been reported that MS patients have slower response latencies and this is related to level of disability (Elsass & Zeeberg, 1983), little else is known about the speed and efficiency of cognitive processing in MS. Focal neurological deficits that may result in apractic or agraphic dysfunctions have been reported in MS, but systematic evaluations of these deficits have not been undertaken.

Cognitive Impairment and Other Factors

Although it is possible that emotional disturbance plays a part in attenuating the cognitive performance in MS patients, it is unlikely that it is solely responsible for the decline in the cognitive functioning of MS patients. Reasoning abilities and depression have been shown to be unrelated in two studies (DePaulo & M. F. Folstein, 1978; Peyser et al., 1980). Several studies have shown that functional disability does not predict cognitive performance (Heaton et al., 1985; D. Staples & Lincoln, 1979).

MS patients are frequently prescribed psychoactive medication. Many neurologists prescribe corticosteroids or adrenocorticotrophic hormone (ACTH), which are anti-inflammatory agents, to hasten remission or immunosuppressants, such as interferon. Muscle spasms may be controlled with benzodiazepines, and tricyclic antidepressants may be used to counter depression. These drugs may all have pronounced side effects. Steroids may cause psychotic symptoms or pseudodementia; cognitive processing speed and memory may be affected by the use of anxiolytics or antidepressants.

Rao et al. (1984) found that 68% of patients with a mild memory impairment were likely to be taking psychoactive medication. This compared with 31% of the patients with no memory deficit and 11% of those classified as having moderate to severe dysmnesia. Heaton et al. (1985) found no difference on the Halstead Impairment Index and other assessments of cognitive and psychomotor function between patients who were or were not medicated. Overall, the data from these two studies suggested that MS may cause some reduction in cognitive performance but this factor alone is not sufficient to explain the deficits seen in MS patients.

Conclusions

Cognitive impairment is a frequent and disabling consequence of MS. In a review of the incidence of cognitive deficits in MS, Franklin et al. (1989) concluded that "using a brief bed-side mental status examination, ... significant cognitive dysfunction may occur soon after onset in 2.0% to 2.9%, or after 17 years in as many as 25% of patients" (p. 165). Peyser, Rao, LaRocca, and Kaplan (1990), who surveyed the results from 8 studies of neuropsychological testing published between 1957 and 1986, found that the prevalence of cognitive deterioration in the MS samples assessed ranged from 54% to 65%. Although the likelihood of cognitive deficits occurring has been well established, little is known about the course of deficits and whether they may show signs of remission and exacerbation like the motor and sensory features of the disorder.

Franklin et al. (1989) noted that the assessment of MS patients frequently focuses on motor and sensory deficits. This is apparent in the way the Kurtzke disability staging scales have been formulated. Franklin et al. presented case histories from 12 MS patients with evidence of marked cognitive deterioration on neuropsychological testing. They found that such impairments were often missed in routine clinical examinations and they were unrelated to either neurological disability or indices of disease severity. They caution clinicians to be aware of the possibility of cognitive disturbance in patients with a chronic progressive disease course, gait disturbances, depression that responds poorly to treatment, complaints of functional cognitive changes, and "moderate to severe periventricular abnormality on MRI scan, even early in the disease course in the absence of progressive neurologic deficit" (p. 167).

In several recent papers, clinical neuropsychologists have offered advice on the constitution of screening and neuropsychological testing battery for use with MS patients. Note that brief mental status screening questionnaires need to be supplemented by other measures in order to reliably detect deficits in many MS patients. For example, on the basis of their experience with the MMSE, W. W. Beatty and Goodkin (1990) suggested that neuropsychological testing should be considered whenever there is clinical or screening test evidence suggestive of cognitive dysfunction. They proposed that the sensitivity of the basic MMSE can be enhanced by concurrent administration of the Boston Naming Test (Kaplan, Goodglass, & Weintraub, 1983), a more demanding verbal recall test (7 items instead of the usual 3), and the Symbol-Digits Modalities Test (A. Smith, 1973). This procedure takes about 15 minutes to administer.

The Neuropsychological Screening Battery of Franklin, Heaton, L. M. Nelson, Filley, and Seibert (1988) provides a more detailed evaluation of the cognitive functioning of the MS patient and takes 30 to 45 minutes to complete. This test battery includes the Symbol-Digits Modalities Test, the Trail Making Test, a Digit Cancellation task, tests of verbal and nonverbal learning and delayed recall, and some language assessment subtests from the Multilingual Aphasia Examination (Benton & Hamsher, 1976) and the Western Aphasia Battery. Peyser, Rao, LaRocca, and Kaplan (1990) published a core set of neuropsychological tests, which they propose should be used to facilitate multicenter comparisons of patient deficits. The individual measures they recommend are presented in Table 5.7. These materials are available at cost through the research and medical programs Department of the National Multiple Sclerosis Society of the United States.

Table 5.7:   **Battery of Tests Recommended for Use with MS Patients (Adapted from Peyser et al., 1990)**

Test	Source
MMSE (dementia screening)	M. F. Folstein et al., 1975
Information, Comprehensive Block Design	WAIS-R
Auditory Letter Detection (Vigilance)*	Lezak, 1983
Paced Auditory Serial Addition Test	Gronwall, 1977
Modified Stroop Test	Stroop, 1955
Logical Memory	WMS-R
California Verbal Learning Test	Delis et al., 1987
7/24 Spatial Recall Test	Barbizet & Cany, 1968
Abbreviated Boston Naming Test	Caine et al., 1986
Verbal Fluency, Abbreviated Token Test	Multilingual Aphasia Examination
Abbreviated Hooper Visual Organizational Test	Hooper, 1958
Wisconsin Card Sorting Test	Heaton, 1981
Raven's Standard Progressive Matrices*	Raven, 1960

*Optional Tests

Psychosocial Consequences

The nature of MS presents the sufferer with profound problems of life-style and emotional adjustment. Research into coping and emotional response to MS is sparse (Devins & Seland, 1987). Some of the issues that patients must work through, however, have been described in several anecdotal accounts (Bauer, 1977; Birrer, 1979; A. Burnfield, 1985; Dowie, Povey, & Whitley, 1981; Forsythe, 1979; Simons, 1984).

Initial Stages

Diagnosis, as we have already seen, can be difficult to establish. The early symptoms are often transient and their significance hard to evaluate. MS can easily be confused with a variety of other neurological disorders; there is no definitive diagnostic test. A definite diagnosis requires at least two attacks separated in time and caused by distinct lesions: Almost invariably this imposes a delay in establishing with certainty the diagnosis of MS. This can be a frustrating time for both the patient and the clinician. Where MS is suspected but not certain, the physician or neurologist has to consider how much of this concern to share with the patient. Completely evading the issue can create mistrust. Frequently, patients will have their own suspicions about the meaning of a particular symptom, based on their reading or contact with people in their social experience who have the disease. They may not be able or may not be given the opportunity to share their fears with their doctor. Sometimes patients learn of their physician's diagnosis of suspected MS indirectly from reading a referral letter, from another consultant, or from another family member. The period of time during which patients must live with the threat of a diagnosis of MS is stressful not only for themselves but also for their families.

Adjusting to the Diagnosis

For some people a definite diagnosis is a relief. For others, the news is devastating and produces either a catastrophic reaction or pathological denial. Whatever the initial response, confirmation of the diagnosis brings new problems. There is a considerable negative publicity about MS; many patients and their families automatically assume a gloomy course for the disease, with total disability occurring in short order. The patient naturally has many questions about their prognosis. Many of these are unanswerable with any certainty. Coming to terms with having a chronic and disabling illness is compounded by not knowing how it may progress. Periods of optimism come with the times of remission.

There is resignation and despair with the onset of new problems or the return of the old. For many patients in their young adulthood there is the prospect of a life of prolonged restriction, ending in severe disability. There will be decisions to be made about work, career, or family commitments.

Often in the initial stages of the illness the symptoms are not obvious to others. The fatigue that many MS patients suffer, problems in vision or balance, can be debilitating, but invisible to family and friends. Living with a person who is constantly tired and unable to participate fully in domestic and family life, yet shows no overt signs of illness, can be demanding. Coming to terms with the uncertain future of the person with MS is a considerable task for the patient's family.

It is imperative that those responsible for the care of MS persons are given hope and a positive description of the possibilities of prognosis. Alexander Burnfield (1985), a psychiatrist with MS, in his personal account of the disease, has this to say:

> *In my experience, the vast majority of people with MS have wanted to know the nature of their disease as early as possible. They have been keen to discover all that they could about MS to enable them to make their own decisions about their future. Many have felt that they had a right to know about their own illness and to control their own treatment.*
>
> *A moral question for the doctor is whether to do what he or she thinks is right when this differs from the patient's wishes. It is difficult to be sure that he or she accurately knows what the patient really wants... . He or she must be prepared to consider what the truth could mean for particular patients, and it is surely right to respect a person's need to make his or her own decisions. The doctor's prime task must be to serve the patient and the patient's family and to provide them with the information and support they require to adapt to the demands of an uncertain future. (p. 65)*

Elizabeth Forsythe, another physician with MS, concluded that when telling the family and the patient about the disease: "Honesty is paramount but optimism comes a close second. Multiple sclerosis is not a death sentence; rather it is a diagnosis that needs some thought and considerable adaptation of life style" (p. 86)

Living with MS

Adjusting to a life with MS is a gradual and demanding process. In the end every case is a unique conjunction of circumstances. The course of the illness brings individuals their own experiences of triumph, misery, acceptance, and failure. Acknowledging the presence of the disease is an important first step. Building an understanding about what is going on for patients and their family or psychosocial network is an important task for the physician or counsellor. Developing good communication with a physician or neurologist is particularly significant for the person with MS. Involvement with an MS society or self-help group can provide an important source of information and support for persons with MS and their caregivers.

Few studies of adaptation to MS have been reported. Researchers have not systematically reviewed the process of coping with MS and most information available comes from anecdotal accounts of personal experience. Maybury and Brewin (1984) assessed several factors thought to be related to social adjustment in 36 MS patients at age 42. Seven were in an acute or progressive phase and 29 were in a stable stage; their level of disability on the DSS ranged from grade 1 to grade 8. The authors assessed patients' knowledge of the disorder and level of adjustment, and administered the General Health Questionnaire (GHQ) and Rosenberg Self-Esteem Scale (SES). The patients' knowledge of the disease varied considerably, but was not related to GHQ or SES scores. The main finding was that those patients who had greater contact with able-bodied people tended to have more self-esteem and fewer emotional difficulties. Level of adjustment was unrelated to level of disability and amount of contact with other disabled people.

N. A. Brooks and Matson (1982) reported a detailed longitudinal study of adjustment. They conducted a postal survey of a Kansas chapter of the National Multiple Sclerosis Society of the U.S. in 1974 and 1981. The return rate was about 60%. The major variable of interest was self-concept, assessed using a 30-item semantic differential scale. Changes in scores from the first to the second assessment were correlated with a variety of disease-related factors. At the time of the first assessment the average disease duration was 10.6 years; at the second it was 17.6 years. The resulting mean self-concept score of the 103 respondents to the survey was only marginally (even if significantly) lower (5.6 versus 5.2) than the comparison sample mean. The most important predictor of level and decrease in self-concept at the second assessment was the number of episodes or relapses in the past seven years. Decline in self-concept was predicted by the occurrence of symptoms that impacted on the patient's life-style, reduced physical mobility, and the degree to which the patient felt able to control the course of the disease.

Fatigue and Depression

Two features of the disease that do not figure prominently in neurology texts are mood changes and fatigue. This is undoubtedly because neither have definite biological determinants, and both tend to be relatively nonspecific secondary effects of this and many other diseases. The fatigue MS patients describe is similar to that seen in many postviral conditions. It is not simply a matter of muscle weakness or depression, although these factors may play a part on occasion. For some MS patients, even the simplest activity requires an extra effort, and by the end of the day a prolonged period of rest may be needed. Adjusting to a reduced level of activity can be exceptionally difficult for people who have led complex and busy lives:

> *Now ... I get less tired, but I am sure this is because I have become more used to doing less. Sometimes I feel well and forget for a while, work harder, and then find myself so utterly exhausted that I get depressed at my stupidity. It is a sense of failure and inadequacy that I can manage little. (Forsythe, 1979, p. 42)*

A measure of fatigue in chronic diseases, including MS, has been constructed by Krupp, LaRocca, Muir-Nash, and Steinberg (1989). The Fatigue Severity Scale is nine-item self-report scale that instructs patients to rate fatigue and its affect on their lives (e.g., "Fatigue interferes with my work, family, or social life"). They found this to be a reliable measure, and that fatigue scores were independent of depression in MS patients.

There is an increased incidence of depression in MS (Dalos, Rabins, B. R. Brooks, & O'Donnell, 1983; J. Gould, 1982; Schiffer & Babigian, 1984). There have been some studies of depression in MS, far fewer, however, than is the case for Parkinson's disease. Early reports of the disease, including Charcot's initial descriptions, included euphoria or emotional blunting as typical signs of the mental changes seen in MS. At their most extreme, in the later stages of the disease, these mood changes may be characterized by involuntary laughing or weeping. This is a symptom occasionally seen in patients with forebrain lesions resulting from stroke, trauma, or multiple sclerosis, where the motor systems involved in the inhibition of emotional expression become compromised. Minden and Schiffer (1990) described pathological laughing and weeping as involving "the display of emotions and not the subjective emotional state experienced by the patient. Patients may laugh or weep with slight provocation, regardless of their underlying mood, as if a disconnection had arisen between neuronal centers involved in perceived emotion and those involved in displayed emotion" (pp. 99-100). They speculated that this may be a consequence of "disconnection between diencephalic or brainstem centers from right hemisphere or frontal control" (p. 100). Schiffer, Herndon, and Rudnick (1985) found that these symptoms can be controlled in many cases by low doses of the tricyclic antidepressant, amitriptyline. Although euphoric or disinhibited behavior is seen in MS patients, this is more common in the later or progressive stages of the disease, and has been found to be associated with intellectual decline (Surridge, 1969). Compensatory overactivity and denial during the early stages of adjustment to the illness may be mistaken for a euphoric mood disturbance or pathological indifference.

Surridge (1969) found that some 27% of 108 MS patients he surveyed showed evidence of depression, compared to only 13% of a group of 39 muscular dystrophy cases. Not surprisingly, severity of depression has been found to be greater during exacerbations or relapses than during periods of remission. Dalos et al. (1983) administered the GHQ, a broad-based measure of emotional status, to 64 MS clinic attenders and 45 spinal cord injury patients. The MS patients were substantially older (40.4 versus 29.0 years) than the spinal cord subjects. The average GHQ score of the MS patients in an active or exacerbated stage of their disease was 15.7, compared to 4.4 for subjects with MS in remission, and 2.7 for the spinal injury patients. The prevalence of emotional disorder was 90% for the exacerbation group, and 39% for those MS patients in remission. Although the Depression subtest scores were elevated for both the exacerbation and the remission MS groups, the Somatic Dysfunction, Anxiety, and Social Dysfunction scores were almost twice as high as the Depression scores. This may indicate that MS causes a negative affective response and this is not primarily depressive in quality.

McIvor, Riklan, and Reznikoff (1984) administered the BDI to 120 MS outpatients with spinal rather than cerebral symptoms and found that patients with a chronic progressive disorder were more depressed than those with a relapsing/remitting disorder. Older patients were more depressed than younger, and elevated scores on the Kurtzke DSS predicted higher levels of depression. The more depressed patients were, the more likely they were to perceive that they were not receiving adequate support from their family and friends.

These studies and others (Devins & Seland, 1987) suggest that, as might be expected, disease activity and disability tend to be related to depression levels. Greater disablement promotes emotional distress and chronic-progressive patients and MS patients in the midst of a relapse tend to report higher levels of negative mood. It is important to note that estimation of depression in MS (and in other similar neurologic diseases) may be inflated by the nature of the measures used. Many of the somatic symptoms measured by items of self-report depression scales such as the BDI and the Depression Scale of the MMPI, may also result from the disease process, introducing a potentially misleading inflation of the score.

Whether or not depression in MS is the result of neurological damage, or a reactive consequence of the disease itself, has not been resolved. Several researchers have suggested the depression in patients with MS has a biological basis (Frances & Yudofsky, 1985; Whitlock & Siskind, 1980). Schiffer, Caine, Bamford, and Levy (1983) compared 15 MS patients whose lesions were primarily cerebral, with 15 patients whose lesions were confined to the spinal cord or cerebellum. There were no differences between the groups on the BDI or on a series of neuropsychological screening tests. The cerebral MS group had a greater incidence of past episodes of depression. This suggests that either awareness of cerebral deficits is more likely to produce depression or MS patients with predominantly cerebral plaques are more likely to have lesions that cause depression, indirect evidence for a biological basis for the affective state. Both Joffe, Lippert, Gray, Sawa, and Hovarth (1987) and Schiffer, Wineman, and Weitkamp (1986) found an increased incidence of bipolar affective disorder in patients with MS, and concluded that the two disorders might be related. Methodological inadequacies, such as failure to use blind raters in the assessment of psychiatric disorders and the use of retrospective accounts from MS patients, renders the research in this area, at best, equivocal.

There is evidence that psychological interventions can assist depressed MS persons. Larcombe and P. H. Wilson (1984) randomly assigned 20 MS patients with scores above 20 on the BDI and a history of depression greater than 12 months to either a waiting list control or a cognitive-behavioral therapy group. On both the BDI and Hamilton Rating Scale, the treated group showed a significant improvement relative to the controls, which was maintained at the 1-month follow-up. The results suggested that psychological therapy procedures successful with other groups are also likely to be efficacious with MS patients.

Stress, Personality, and MS

One of the issues with the longest research history in multiple sclerosis is the relationship between personal factors, stress, and the occurrence or exacerbation of MS (Trimble & I. Grant, 1982; VanderPlate, 1984). As noted earlier, depression or euphoria are frequently associated with MS, particularly in the later stages. Charcot noted, "Nor is it rare, amid this state of mental depression, to find psychic disorders to arise which assume one or other of the classic forms of mental alienation." Subsequent studies have confirmed a higher incidence of emotional disturbance in MS than in normal controls (Pratt, 1951; Surridge, 1969; Whitlock & Siskind, 1980). The incidence of psychosis appears not to be elevated in MS (Surridge, 1969).

A major focus of research in the first half of the century was on the identification of an MS prone personality. In general, the search for a set of psychosomatic factors responsible for MS has not been successful (LaRocca, 1984; VanderPlate, 1984). In recent times, however, the proposal that stress or personal style might exacerbate, initiate, or hasten the progression of the disease has been the subject of renewed interest. This follows the discovery of a relationship between psychological, neurological, and immunological factors in a variety of chronic diseases (Ader, 1981). Changes in immune functioning have long been associated with MS. Some studies have found results suggestive of the possibility that MS patients have more stressful events in their lives prior to disease onset than do normal comparison subjects (e.g., Philippopoulous, Wittkower, & Cousineau, 1958; S. Warren, Greenhill & K. G. Warren, 1982). On the whole, however, results from these studies, although tantalizing, are not conclusive. The methodological difficulties associated with obtaining retrospective reports on stress-related events and disease activity, from known cases, undermine the validity of the results. Methods used to measure stress have typically been weak, and other relevant factors, such as coping, adaptation, and perception of events, have been almost totally neglected (LaRocca, 1984). The low incidence of MS makes prospective studies impracticable, but longitudinal designs could be employed to study the ongoing relationship between disease activity, the incidence of exacerbations, and stress. Of particular interest in this regard would be studies of the relationship between immune system function and stress levels.

One study has been reported in which psychological interventions were implemented to reduce stress in MS. This is a significant piece of research because it establishes a methodology and rationale for treatment, which might profitably be extended to other groups of neurologically impaired patients and their families. Foley, Bedell, LaRocca, Scheinberg, and Reznikoff (1987) initiated a stress inoculation training program with a series of 36 outpatients with MS. The group sessions focussed on teaching active coping skills, such as relaxation, and on the identification of potential stressors. Subjects were randomly assigned to either the stress-inoculation group or to a current available care condition. After the treatment, the stress inoculation group subjects were less anxious, less depressed on the BDI, and reported fewer hassles (on the Hassles Scale of Kanner, Coyne, Schaefer, & Lazarus, 1981). They were also more likely to use problem-focused coping strategies than the controls. Data were available for some of the subjects at follow-up and indicated continued improvement. These results suggest that counsellors and psychologists may have an important role in the development of adaptive strategies for people learning to cope with chronic neurological diseases.

Marital and Sexual Difficulties

Changes in marital and sexual functioning are likely to follow the onset of MS. The response of couples to the news that one partner has a chronic disease is likely to depend on a number of factors. Much of the evidence of how couples cope with the disease is anecdotal (e.g., A. Burnfield & P. Burnfield, 1982; Forsythe, 1979; J. Gould, 1982). Some couples are mutually supportive, in other cases partners drift apart and there may be considerable denial of the impact of the disease. When MS is diagnosed after marriage, both partners have to adapt to the unpredictable nature of the disease and its disabling or disfiguring consequences. There are social consequences that follow because the MS patient fatigues easily (Birrer, 1979). The spouse of a MS person may have to cope with depression, grief, anxiety, and euphoria in their partner, and to add nursing and physical support to the other roles implicit in an intimate relationship.

Sexual responsiveness is frequently affected directly or indirectly by multiple sclerosis. Szasz, Paty, and Maurice (1984) reported that the incidence of sexual dysfunction in MS, as in many chronic diseases is elevated. Lilius, Valtonen, and Wikstrom (1976), for example, found that 80% of the men with MS he surveyed reported some degree of erectile dysfunction, and 33% of the women reported being no longer orgasmic. This group of patients had a median disease duration of 10 years. Sexual dysfunctions in MS may have a physical basis, for example, loss of sensation in the vagina and clitoris. In some cases, the sexual dysfunction predates the onset of MS; the incidence of erectile or orgasmic dysfunction is of course relatively high in the normal population.

Psychological factors may also contribute. These include anxiety and fear of the disease or its specific effects. Changes in bodily functioning and physical competence change the patient's self-image and their partner's perception of desirability. False assumptions, misinformation, anxiety, and poor communication can all exacerbate or initiate any sexual problem. The ability to discuss problems openly and constructively is possibly the most important factor in successful adjustment, as Birrer (1979) concluded:

> *The partners must make as many opportunities as they need to discuss with each other their feelings. Talking about things, laughing about them, however wryly, helps to relieve tension and keep problems well in perspective. Putting those very personal feelings into words and deeds helps a couple to understand and appreciate each other, to grow as individuals, and the marriage to develop into something deep and lasting. Conversely if they are not dealt with, frustrated feelings can lead to hostility and ultimately, a complete breakdown of the relationship. The saddest event in the life of any multiple sclerotic is the loss of a spouse through the inept handling of the strains and stresses caused by the state of being multiple sclerotic. (p. 238)*

Conclusions

The occurrence of a relapsing-remitting course for many patients and the multifocal nature of the lesions underlying the disorder distinguish MS from other diseases reviewed in this book. The pattern of symptoms and the course of the disease vary greatly from one person to the next. Although a viral etiology is often assumed, the agent causing the disease is unknown.

The diversity of possible lesions makes group studies of cognitive dysfunction hard to interpret. Consequently, such studies have made little contribution to our understanding of brain-behavior relations. Studies of individual cases with magnetic resonance imaging (MRI) determined lesions, particularly where these involve evidence of a disconnection syndrome, may be more productive.

Experimental neuropsychological studies have, however, drawn attention to the high prevalence rates for cognitive dysfunction in MS. The clinical neuropsychologist has a significant role in documenting the extent of cognitive changes. Little is known about the course of cognitive impairment in relapsing-remitting patients. This is a possibly fruitful area for longitudinal research. Guidelines for appropriate testing strategies have been provided by Franklin et al. (1988) and Peyser et al. (1990).

An equally important task for the neuropsychologist working with MS clients is the identification of the psychological effects of the disease. Active support may be necessary for the client and family during the process of initial adjustment to the disease onset and subsequent deterioration. There is good evidence that MS patients are at risk for depression. Self-help support groups involving persons with MS and their families have an important part to play in the long-term process of adjustment. Teaching active coping skills to clients has also been found to be useful (Foley et al., 1987). The further investigation of coping and adjustment, and the implementation and evaluation of interventions aimed at mobilizing the personal and external resources of people with MS are important future research and clinical priorities.

Chapter 6

PARKINSONS DISEASE

*Louis is a 66 year old architect. Some 6 years ago he first
noticed he had occasional difficulty with "tightness" in his arm
muscles. Two years later he developed a tremor in his left hand
when it was at rest. At this time he was told he had Parkinson's disease. The tremor has gradually become more pronounced and affects his right hand as well. He can still do
most things he could do before, although he finds walking
increasingly difficult. "It seems," he says, "as if the muscles
just seize up if I go too far." The change has been gradual and
it is only looking back on things he could do a year ago, but
cannot do now, that makes him realise the disease is progressing.*

*Asked about changes in his mental abilities, Louis reports that
his memory is not as good as it was, and he finds it hard
sometimes to find a word that he needs. His reaction to the
disease is stoical. He describes himself as less outgoing than
he used to be, but he "is determined to keep busy and not to
give up."*

Background

In his classic "An Essay on the Shaking Palsy" (1817), James Parkinson
opened his account of the disease he labeled *Paralysis Agitans* with the
following summary: "Involuntary tremulous motion, with lessened
muscular power, in parts not in action and even when supported; with a
propensity to bend the trunk forward, and to pass from a walking to a
running pace: the senses and intellects being uninjured" (Parkinson,
1955, p. 153).

His description was based on six cases, one of whom was observed
only casually ("the lamented subject of which was only seen at a dis-
tance") but he captured the essence of the disease and its manifestations.
The progress of the disease, barely perceptible at first, proceeds until
"the hand failing to answer with exactness to the dictates of the will.
Walking becomes a task which cannot be performed without considerable
attention ... care is necessary to prevent frequent falls." (p. 154)

Since Parkinson's time, the neuropathological basis of the disease and its course have been defined with greater accuracy and there have been remarkable developments in the treatment and management of patients with Parkinson's disease (PD). The usual form of the disease is termed *idiopathic*, that is, of unknown cause. Idiopathic PD has been found to result from the development of intraneuronal intrusions known as Lewy bodies located primarily in the dopaminergic nigrostriatal system. It is the consequent damage to the basal ganglia that causes the characteristic involuntary movements and motor disorders of PD. In addition to the motor disorders, a number of Parkinson patients eventually develop signs of an organic dementia. Whether or not there are changes in cognition that are the inevitable consequence of the disease remains unclear. James Parkinson's initial assertion that the disease does not itself cause injury to the senses or intellect has been a matter of debate, and is considered in more detail later in this chapter.

Symptoms

The clinical presentation of the patient with PD is dominated by motor symptoms. The four primary symptoms of PD are *tremor, akinesia, rigidity,* and *loss of postural reflexes.* Tremor is usually the earliest sign of the disease, although it is not invariably present. The Parkinsonian patient has signs of tremor at rest, and typically the degree of tremor is abated by purposeful movement. Tremor is the abnormal and involuntary rhythmic contraction of the muscles at any joint, and when sitting still or standing, may be seen in one of the limbs, the jaw, or fingers. Akinesia (loss of spontaneous movement) or bradykinesia (slowness of voluntary movement), are also commonly seen in PD. These signs are evident from observation of Parkinsonian patients. They walk with short, shuffling steps and without any swinging of the arms; the movements associated with walking tend to be lost. Turning is often effected in a series of short steps, with the patient looking ahead, rather than in the direction of the turn.

Rigidity is seen in the way in which the patient has an increased resistance to passive movement. If the arm of a person with PD is moved about by the clinician, then there is an abnormal degree of resistance throughout the range of motion, which is either consistent (*leadpipe rigidity*), or inconsistent, such that the arm movement feels jerky (hence the name *cogwheel rigidity*). Muscular rigidity accounts for the bowed posture of the Parkinson patient and the immobility of the face muscles gives a masklike appearance. A fixed expression and a stare uninterrupted by blinking are often characteristic. Poor balance is another feature of the disease, which tends to become apparent at a later stage than the other symptoms. Failure of the postural reflexes can be demonstrated by threatening the balance of the patient. A light push in the chest will cause the patient to stagger backward or even to fall if unsupported. This inability to maintain their balance can be a major problem for patients in the advanced stages of the disease.

Hoehn and Yahr (1967) found that the most common initial symptom in their 183 cases of idiopathic Parkinsonism was tremor (70.5%). A similar result was reported by DuPont (1976), who listed tremor (69.8%), rigidity (9.5%), gait disturbance (7.3%), muscle pains (4.8%), and akinesia or bradykinesia (3.5%) as the most common initial symptoms. The most usual initial site of the tremor is the arm, with tremor in the leg (8.7% of cases) or head (.7%) being less common. Tremor and rigidity tend to be the most common symptoms in Parkinson patients with only 10% being free of tremor, and 10% free of rigidity in Hoehn and Yahr's sample.

Course

The severity and progression of PD varies considerably. Rate of progression does not appear to relate to sex of the patient, age at onset, or to the presence of the disease in other family members. Hoehn and Yahr (1967) found that in patients with tremor as the initial symptom the disease progressed more slowly. The most common method of describing disease severity in PD is by means of Hoehn and Yahr's 5-stage scale. They based their staging system on results from 672 patients with primary Parkinson's disease and an average age of 55.3 years. The main elements of Hoehn and Yahr scale are presented in Table 6.1. There is evidence that PD shortens life expectancy, particularly in patients untreated by levodopa (e.g., Marttila, Rinne, Siirtota, & Sonninen, 1977; Rajput, Offord, Beard, & Kurland, 1984).

Forms of Parkinsonism

The Parkinsonian syndrome can be divided into idiopathic Parkinson's disease and symptomatic Parkinsonism. The idiopathic form of the disease is characterized by degeneration resulting from Lewy body intrusions and is by far the most common form of the disease. In over 80% of new cases, there is no known etiology. The most common cause of symptomatic Parkinsonism is arteriosclerotic changes in the basal ganglia. Arteriosclerotic Parkinsonism is often difficult to distinguish from idiopathic PD, and diagnosis is usually made on the basis of a sudden onset in an elderly patient with a history of hypertension or heart disease. In the recent past, encephalitis was the most common cause of symptomatic Parkinsonism. During the decade 1916-1926, an epidemic of encephalitis lethargica swept the world and many of the survivors were left with neurological symptoms including Parkinsonism (Ziegler, 1928).

Table 6.1   The Stages of Idiopathic Parkinson's Disease, Hoehn and Yahr (1967)

Stage	Clinical Presentation
1	Unilateral tremor or rigidity. Little functional impairment.
2	Bilateral or midline involvement. No loss of postural reflexes.
3	Evidence of unsteadiness. Employment functioning impaired, however, physical independence is maintained. Disability is mild to moderate.
4	Fully developed, severely disabling disease. Patient still able to walk and stand unassisted, but has a marked physical incapacity.
5	Confinement to bed or wheelchair.

From descriptions of the postencephalitic form of the disease in the 1920s, it is apparent that the constellation of symptoms differed from those seen in idiopathic PD. Focal neurological symptoms, including cranial nerve paralyses, aphasia, abnormal eye movements, and tics, were more common, as were psychiatric or behavioral problems. The age of onset was often much earlier than is seen in idiopathic PD, which is usually a disease of later life. Hoehn and Yahr (1967) reported that postencephalitic Parkinson patients seen in their New York clinic were less likely to report tremor as the initial symptom of the disease (52.3% versus 70.0% in idiopathic cases). They found that the other common initial symptoms in postencephalitic cases were speech problems (27.3%), gait disturbance (18.2%), rigidity (15.9%), fatigue and weakness (13.6%), slowness (13.6%), and psychiatric symptoms (11.4%). There has been a progressive decline in the number of cases seen with an encephalitic etiology, and new cases are less common than arteriosclerotic Parkinsonism.

There are some other rare causes of PD such as trauma of the kind sustained by boxers, and the toxic effects of heavy metals or other chemical substances. Parkinsonian symptoms can also be observed in up to 60.0% of psychiatric patients treated with phenothiazines. Neuroleptic drugs deplete dopamine and often cause a degree of tremor, rigidity, and slowing of movements indistinguishable from idiopathic forms of the disease. In an epidemiological study, Rajput et al. (1984) found that drug-induced Parkinsonism, which had persisted for more than 12 months and was characterized by the cardinal features of idiopathic PD, accounted for 7.0% of their cases, the second most common cause of Parkinsonian symptoms in their survey. A total of 85.5% of their cases were classified as idiopathic, and 1.4% as arteriosclerotic.

Epidemiology

Rajput et al. (1984) found an average annual incidence of Parkinsonism in a United States sample of 20.5/100,000. The incidence rate was 18.2/100,000 when drug-induced cases were excluded. Various prevalence rates have been published. In a Finnish study, Martilla and Rinne (1976) found a prevalence estimate of 120.1/100,000. In the United States, Kurland (1988) estimated the prevalence rate as being 157/100,000. A British study (Sutcliffe, Prior, Mawby, & McQuillan, 1985) estimated the prevalence of idiopathic PD as 108.4/100,000. Overall, prevalence estimates range from about 60/100,000 (e.g., Broman, 1963; Garland, 1952) to 170/100,000 (Gudmundsson, 1967). The likelihood of males and females developing the disorder is usually about equal (Martilla & Rinne, 1976; Rajput et al., 1984). The peak age of onset is in the sixth decade. In general, data from epidemiological surveys have revealed no geographical anomalies in the occurrence of the disease nor any racial group that appear to be immune to it.

Biological Basis

Knowledge of the physical basis of the symptoms seen in PD disease has advanced considerably in the past two decades. Nevertheless much remains to be determined, particularly the precise mechanisms that produce the characteristic involuntary movements, rigidity, and slowness of PD. At a microscopic level, the presence of Lewy bodies is as pathognomonic of Parkinson's disease as neurofibrillary tangles are of Alzheimer's disease. The dopaminergic neurons of the substantia nigra are especially susceptible to these cytoplasmic intrusions and on histological examination the loss of the pigmented cells of the zona compacta of the substantia nigra are clearly evident. Indeed, to the unaided eye, the substantia nigra of the Parkinson patient seen postmortem will appear to have faded to a far grayer color than normal. Lewy bodies are to be found in other pigmented nuclei of the brainstem and also in nonpigmented serotonergic nuclei such as the dorsal raphe nuclei (Alvord, 1971; Forno, 1982). The distribution of these intrusions appears to be systematic, however, the reason why some nuclei are affected while others are spared is unknown.

Parkinson's disease is regarded primarily as a consequence of degenerative lesions in the basal ganglia and related structures. The basal ganglia are a collection of forebrain nuclei regarded as being part of the motor system, although they have no connection with the spinal cord and are not directly linked to the pyramidal motor system. A simplified diagram outlining the relationship between the basal ganglia (neostriatum, globus pallidus), the substantia nigra, thalamus, the cortex, and the subthalamic nuclei, is presented in Fig. 6.1. The basic structure of the diagram is a circuit, with projections that arise in all parts of the cortex and pass through the basal ganglia, thalamus, and substantia nigra to return to the motor cortex. It is this circuit that is damaged in PD.

The loss of the nigrostriatal tract, a reciprocal pathway linking the putamen and the substantial nigra, as we have already observed, is one important element of the basal ganglia system that is disrupted. In addition, pathological changes are also seen in other parts of this circuit, including the globus pallidus, the neostriatum, the subthalamic nuclei, and the ventral and medial nuclei of the thalamus. This damage may be a consequence of the disease process or it may be a secondary effect of the degeneration of substantia nigra.

Abnormal cell loss is also seen in other parts of the brain of patients with idiopathic PD. Selective cell loss in the nucleus basalis of Meynert (e.g., T. Arendt et al., 1983) and another dopaminergic system, the mesolimbic system (Bogerts, Hantsch, & Herzer, 1983) have also been reported, and linked to the occurrence of dementia in PD (Whitehouse, Hedreen, C. L. White, & Price, 1983). Neurons with signs of Lewy body degeneration are also found in the cerebral cortex, but not usually in substantial numbers. In postencephalitic cases the pattern of damage is distinctly different. The characteristic tangles of AD are likely to be found in subcortical and cortical structures, and damage in the brainstem and the reticular formation is more common. Degeneration of the cortical mantle is likely to be more noticeable in postencephalitic cases than in those with the idiopathic form of the disease. Alzheimer tangles are also plentiful in the brains of patients with idiopathic PD (Boller, Mizutani, Roessmans, & Gambetti, 1980). There does not, however, appear to be a greater than chance association between the occurrence of tangles and Lewy bodies, but the additive effect of the combined pathology may play a part in the occurrence of dementia in PD patients (Gibb, 1989; Gibb, Mountjoy, Mann, & Lees, 1989).

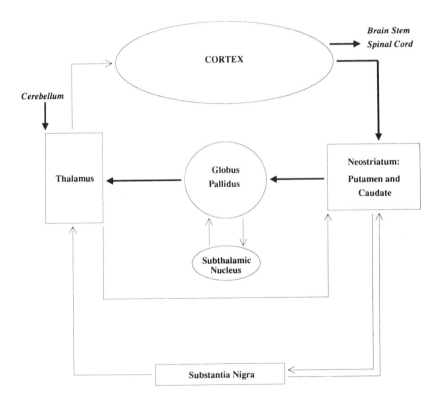

Figure 6.1. Schematic representation of the relationship between the cortex and the subcortical structures involved in Parkinson's and Huntington's diseases.

The principal biochemical change in idiopathic PD is dopamine depletion, which is a result of the destruction of the nigrostriatal fibers that contain the highest concentrations of dopamine in the brain. As is apparent from Figure 6.1, if this system is compromised, then its controlling effect on tracts linking the neostriatum, palladium, and thalamus will be lost. Uncontrolled or involuntary movements may be a result of overactivity of these parts of the basal ganglia. It might therefore be supposed that anything that inhibited the action of the neostriatal-thalamic circuit would reduce the incidence of symptoms such as tremor, whereas excitation would accentuate their occurrence. There are some clinical findings that support this view.

In 1952, it was discovered by chance in the course of a neurosurgical operation that a lesion in the medial globus pallidus and adjacent parts of the ventrolateral thalamus gave relief from tremor and rigidity in patients with postencephalitic PD. The infarction in those areas was caused by accidental damage to the anterior choroidal artery during a surgical procedure designed to lesion the left peduncle. Subsequent experience with surgical intervention suggested that a lesion in the ventrolateral thalamic region provided the most satisfactory means of reducing tremor. Looking at Figure 6.1, we can see that such an operation would have the effect of disrupting the striatal-thalamic circuit and compensating for the imbalance caused by the loss of the nigrostriatal system.

In addition, any drug that increases the concentration of acetylcholine makes the symptoms of PD worse. The highest concentration of acetylcholine and cholinesterase is to be found in the caudate nucleus, part of the neostriatum. Conversely, anticholinergic drugs, which reduce the concentration of acetylcholine can relieve symptoms of PD. The cholinergic neurons in the basal ganglia presumably play an important part in the production of the unwanted movements in PD.

The foregoing discussion provides the rationale for the pharmacological and surgical treatment of Parkinson's disease. In the 1940s and 1950s, surgical procedures, focusing on the globus pallidus and the ventrolateral thalamus were used to relieve the incapacitating tremor. However, the introduction of pharmacological treatments has led physicians to abandon these procedures. In the late 1960s it was shown that high doses of L-dopa administered over an extended period of time produced relief from tremor and rigidity. Another drug with a therapeutic action similar to L-dopa, but somewhat less effective, is amantadine. The other class of drugs commonly employed are the anticholinergics, such as benzhexol and procyclidine. These drugs are often used in combination with L-dopa and are usually only effective when used with patients who have mild symptoms. Rajput et al. (1984) found that L-dopa was used with some 50% of the patients in their sample, either alone or in combination with amantadine and/or an anticholinergic agent. Amantadine was administered either alone or together with an anticholinergic to 10% of the patients, anticholinergics were administered alone to 17%, and 23% received no treatment.

L-dopa presumably asserts it effect by enhancing the ability of the remaining dopaminergic neurons to synthesize dopamine. Its effectiveness, however, decreases over time. Moreover, the response to the drug begins to fluctuate as the disease progresses, which results in the so-called "on-off" phenomenon (Lees, 1989). Patients begin to experience diurnal variations in the degree of control they have over their symptoms, possibly as a result of the chronic administration of L-dopa. This has led to the search for more effective pharmacological treatments designed to prolong the efficacy of L-dopa (e.g., Lieberman et al., 1985). Another more radical approach is the experimental use of transplants of dopamine-producing cells from the adrenal gland, and more recently, from the brain of aborted fetuses (Lindvall et al., 1990). It is apparent that such transplants can be made successfully, that the grafted tissue produces dopamine, and this can provide relief of symptoms in the recipient. The production of dopamine is likely to be more consistent and the "on-off" phenomenon diminished. Results from larger trials will no doubt appear in the future. The use of fetal transplant does, however, raise numerous ethical issues. Although fetal tissue is available as a by-product from terminations of pregancy that take place legally at the present time, the prospect has been raised that fetuses may be conceived and aborted specifically for use in the treatment of degenerative diseases (Turney, 1990).

Etiology

The cause of idiopathic PD is, of course, undetermined. There are some reports of familial forms of PD (e.g., Bell & A. J. Clark, 1926; Spellman, 1962) with an autosomal dominant mode of inheritance. However, it is generally agreed that such cases are rare and there is no strong evidence for a genetic predisposition (Duvoisin, Gearing, Schweitzer, & Yahr, 1969; Gibb, 1989; W. E. Martin, Young, & V. E. Anderson, 1973). The search for a viral agent, stimulated by the obvious example of postencephalitic Parkinsonism, has proved fruitless.

A number of researchers have speculated that Parkinsonism is the consequence of the natural process of neuronal degeneration, following findings that the neuronal population of substantia nigra declines with age (Hirai, 1968). It is possible that the accumulation of oxyradicals or neuromelanin, or some other by-products of dopamine metabolism, might cause long-term neuronal degeneration. Such an explanation is consistent with the decline in nigrostriatal neurons, but does not explain the abnormal destruction of cells in PD. Or, it is possible that some environmental toxin or other insult is a necessary precursor of the accelerated aging process (Langston, 1989). Or perhaps exposure to an environmental toxin alone is sufficient for the later onset of the disease. The discovery by Langston, Ballard, Tetrud, and Irwin (1983) of MTPT, a synthetic pethidine analog that caused severe and specific Parkinsonism in a 23-year-old drug addict, has provided support for this view. The uncovering of this neurotoxin with specific Parkinsonian effects has prompted the search for naturally occurring compounds that might have a similar long-latency neurotoxic effect. To date, however, this has not been successful.

Motor Disorder

The predominant disability that PD patients must come to terms with is the motor dysfunction caused by the destruction of fiber systems in the basal ganglia. The basic circuitry of the basal ganglia, and their connections with the cortex, cerebellum, and brain stem suggest that they are involved in the modulation of cortical motor systems. There is, however, still much to learn about the functioning of the basal ganglia; the study of patients with PD continues to contribute to our understanding. Much of such research with PD patients has focused on motor activity. Tasks used to define the motor disabilities of PD can be divided into those that measure speed of initiation of movement (or Reaction Time, RT), and those concerned with the speed or accuracy of movements, including tests of ballistic aiming movements, automatic responses, and continuous tracking. Studies of the movement pathology of PD are reviewed in this section.

Reaction Time

In the Croonian lectures of 1925, Kinnier Wilson stated: "That the Parkinsonian is 'slow off the mark' is a matter of common observation. Recent measurements with special apparatus for muscular response to a single visual stimulus have given the figures of 0.24 seconds for normal individuals and .36 seconds for the subjects of paralysis agitans" (p. 7). This slowness in response can be shown to be reflected in a slowness of the muscles to begin contracting when a movement is required. A further observation from Wilson illustrated this:

In the movement of raising the shoulders from the supine position ... the normal individual contracts both recti femoris simultaneously and within a very brief period after the shortening of
the recti abdominis. In unilateral cases delay in the contraction
of the rectus femoris on the affected side has been constantly
found. (p. 54)

The difficulty that PD patients have in initiating movements has
been confirmed in several studies of simple RT (e.g. Barbeau, 1966;
Brumlik & Boshes, 1966; Cassell, Shaw, & G. Stern, 1973; Evarts,
Teravainen, & Calne, 1981; Heilman, Bowers, Watson, & Greer, 1976;
Sanes, 1985; Talland, 1963). Brumlik and Boshes selected 30 patients
with PD, excluding those with severe tremor or clinical evidence of an
organic brain syndrome, and a normal control group of equal size. They
employed a visual RT task that required subjects to hold down a switch
with a finger of their dominant hand and then to move the hand so as to
depress a second switch following a visual signal. This procedure allowed the measurement of the time from the visual signal to the initiation
of action potentials in the forearm, movement initiation time (time to
release the first switch), and movement time (MT) between the two
switches. Results were presented in terms of number of Parkinsonian
patients who substantially exceeded the normal range on each measure.
Over 80% of the patients had abnormal mean total RT scores, and over
65% of patients had either initiation or movement times beyond the
normal limits. It was more usual for PD patients to have both initiation
and movement times significantly elevated, but in some cases, only MT,
or only RT was abnormal. Heilman et al. (1976) compared 10 hypokinetic PD patients with 10 age- and sex-matched normals on a visual RT
task, with and without a warning signal cuing the time of onset of the
visual signal. They found that the hypokinetic patients performed more
poorly on the RT task in all conditions, relative to the controls, but
performance on the warning signal absent condition was not specifically
worse for the PD patients. They concluded that slowness to initiate a
response is not a simple consequence of reduced arousal or awareness of
external cues.
   One of the most systematic evaluations of RT in PD patients was
reported by Evarts et al. (1981). They compared 29 Parkinson patients
(median age 61 years) with 21 somewhat older control subjects (median
age 70 years). The PD patients were part of a study comparing the treatment effects of levodopa and bromocryptine. Evarts et al. measured
simple and two-choice RT, and MT, using a task requiring subjects to
turn a handle 45° to the left or right in response to a visual or kinesthetic
signal. In the simple RT condition, the direction the handle was to be

turned was specified at the same time as the warning signal light came on, allowing the subjects 2 to 4 seconds to prepare to move the handle before the signal to initiate the movement was presented. In the two-choice RT condition, no cue was given about which way the handle was to be turned before the response initiation signal occurred. This signal instructed subjects to turn the handle to either the left or right. The visual signal was a colored light, and the kinesthetic signal was a slight handle displacement to left or right produced by a torque motor. RT was defined as the time taken for the handle to be moved from its initial vertical placement to a point 5° from vertical, and MT was the time taken to complete the response by moving 45° from the original vertical position of the handle. No statistical analyses were reported, but raw data from each of the subjects were presented. On average, PD patients had slower RT and MT values. Despite instances of dissociation between these two measures, MT and RT tended to be as highly correlated for the PD subjects as they were for the control group. Of note also was the finding that PD patients were not selectively impaired by the choice RT or kinesthetic conditions. Although the PD patients' RT and MT data in these conditions were slower than the control group, the degree of impairment was constant relative to their simple RT results.

Movement Time

On tasks measuring speed or accuracy of movements, as was apparent in two of the studies already cited (Brumlik & Boshes, 1966; Evarts et al., 1981), movement time is slowed in PD. In both studies, the authors noted that MT was a more pronounced and consistent deficit in PD patients than simple RT. On clinical examination, it is often obvious that PD sufferers have difficulty making rapid ballistic movements. S.A.K. Wilson (1925) displayed the dynamometer records of a patient with unilateral PD making five rapid voluntary contractions of the quadriceps muscles. The recordings showed the consistent and regular response of the muscle on the unaffected side, while the execution of movements on the affected side was slow and irregular.

Flowers (1975, 1976) provided some of the best descriptions of the inability of patients with PD to make fast ballistic movements. Flowers (1976) monitored the performance of PD patients on an aiming task in which subjects were required to align a response marker with a target moving randomly to different positions on an oscilloscope screen. Subjects tracked the circular target with a dot on the screen, controlled by a joystick, and were instructed to put the dot inside the circle as quickly as possible when it moved to a new location. Six levodopa-treated outpatients with a history of PD of more than 2 years, were tested, and their results compared with those of seven age-matched paid volunteers. The PD group were found to have slow and more deliberate movement patterns than the controls, and when they attempted rapid ballistic movements, their responses were erratic and inaccurate. Flowers concluded that PD particularly impairs the ability to make accurately the kind of ballistic movements required in simple aiming tasks, where the action required is normally preprogrammed and requires no continuous sensory feedback for successful execution. Flowers (1978a) expanded this conclusion and proposed that:

> the Parkinsonian deficit may be described as a loss of skill, especially of the "programs" of movement learnt in the course of normal perceptual motor development. (These programs allow quick and efficient movement on the basis of a predictive selection of actions which are known to be more or less appropriate to the particular conditions of the task in hand). (p. 19)

PD patients, therefore, may lose the ability to make accurate preprogrammed movements, and consequently perform tracking tasks hesitantly, using a series of slow, jerky, and self-corrected movements. This does not occur simply because the pattern of muscle activity in the PD patient when making a movement is disturbed. S. A. K. Wilson (1925) stated emphatically: "My definite conclusion is, that these movements are executed normally by Parkinsonians—that is to say, the movements follow the normal physiological lines and are neither lost or perverted.... . I have not seen a single instance either of failure to perform the movement..., or of interference with normal physiological order" (p. 53). It appeared to Wilson that failed or erratic movement in Parkinsonism was a result of the weak action of one or more of the muscle groups involved. These views have been confirmed by Hallett and Khoshbin (1980) and Hallet, Shahani, and Young (1977) in their studies of the ballistic flexions of the elbow in PD and control subjects. Normal subjects are able to make such movements in one cycle of agonist-antagonist-agonist muscular activity. Parkinson patients show the same pattern of muscle activity, but in order to achieve complete flexion, must initiate additional cycles of this triphasic pattern of muscle action. They concluded, therefore, that bradykinesia in this circumstance is the result to some extent of the fact that the initial burst of activity is insufficient to allow one triphasic cycle to execute the movement required.

PD patients typically have considerable difficulty with repetitive movements and this can be readily demonstrated on clinical examination of the patient. These deficits have been shown on the tapping test of the Halstead-Reitan battery (Matthews & Haaland, 1979; Reitan & Boll,

1971) and on similar measures of tapping speed (Schwab, Chafetz, & S. Walker, 1954). In a study of the effects of unilateral thalamotomoty on PD motor symptoms, Perret, Eggenberger, and Siegfried (1970) measured rate of simple and complex finger movements in a group of 36 right-handed PD patients prior to surgery. The patients' performance was compared with that of 22 control subjects (who were considerably younger than the PD group). In both the simple and repeated fixed sequence (complex) finger movements, rate of repetition was markedly higher in the normal sample. Similarly, Cassell et al. (1973) measured the number of times patients and controls depressed a switch and found that the average performance by the PD patients was considerably poorer than the controls.

Parkinson patients do not appear deficient on tasks where the movement of the target is regular and slow. On copying tasks patients perform normally, indicating that their visual processing of these tasks is not defective. However, on tasks where the tracking movements required are regular, and rapid, their deficits become more apparent. Flowers (1978a) assessed the performance of 15 PD outpatients, all being treated with levodopa, on a task where subjects tracked the movement of a circular target across the face of an oscilloscope, using a joystick control. The target movements were either regular, sinusoidal, or unpredictable, and varied systematically in the speed and amplitude of movement required. The results from the continuous tracking of the sine waves were interesting. Regardless of the speed or amplitude of the pursuit tracking required, Parkinsonian patients were markedly deficient in the way they generated these easy and predictable movements relative to the age-matched controls. Practice had little effect on their performance. Flowers (1978a) concluded that these results indicated that PD patients were unable to form an accurate internal model of these movements that could be used subsequently to perform and control regular motor actions.

He tested this proposal in a further study (Flowers, 1978b). In three experiments, PD patients were instructed to follow a target moving continuously across a screen in a predictable manner. At random intervals the target disappeared for a short period of time and the subjects' response to these data gaps was observed. On the three tasks Flowers devised, 10 nondeteriorated PD patients performed differently from the controls, showing an abnormal tendency to respond to the sensory data provided rather than learning to anticipate the movement of the target. PD patients showed less ability than control subjects to use prediction to regulate movement, thereby inhibiting the development of smooth automatic motor movements. Similar results have been reported by Mayeux, Stern, and colleagues (Y. Stern, Mayeux, & J. Rosen, 1984; Y. Stern,

Mayeux, J. Rosen, & Ilson, 1983), and these data seem to implicate higher order motor control deficits in PD. Supporting the conclusions of Flowers (1978b), Stern et al. (1984) concluded that "poor performance in filling in missing segments of paths could be considered a deficit in sequential and predictive movement. Patients either could not generate a proper motor plan to guide the movement, or could not carry out that plan" (pp. 987-988).

Before proceeding further, it is important to elaborate on this concept of a *motor plan*. The term refers to the higher-order conceptual schema required to generate the sequence of motor programs necessary to effect some action. Thus the motor plan is a higher-order control mechanism that oversees the proper operation of motor programs. These motor programs are the simple sequences of muscle action needed to carry out a total movement. For example, to sign one's name, the motor plan will be the conception of the written form the author wishes to achieve and subsets of motor programs will need to be initiated to achieve this. Different motor programs would be needed if the signature were written with the left rather than the right hand, but the same motor plan would be used in each instance. Evidence for the difficulty PD patients have in effecting a motor plan, comes from a variety of sources. One is the failure of PD patients to learn to execute accurately predictable movement sequences (Flowers, 1978b; Y. Stern et al., 1984). Marsden (1982) also reported unpublished data that support this conclusion. Unlike controls, PD patients were unable to adopt predictive control of their motor movements after being informed of the regularity of movement of the apparently random target they were tracking.

Another interesting deficit in PD patients is their inability to carry out two concurrent voluntary motor actions. Schwab, Chafetz, and S. Walker (1954) demonstrated this deficit by instructing Parkinson patients to squeeze an ergographic bulb, while at the same time copying a drawing of a triangle containing three perpendicular lines. The commencement of the drawing task had the effect of producing an erratic ergographic response pattern for the PD group. They assessed over 150 PD patients and also a total of 80 controls, ranging in age from 10 to 80. The PD patients were clearly worse than control subjects in this situation, but it was also apparent that controls over the age of about 70 began to show the same kind of impaired functioning on these combined tasks that PD patients showed at a much earlier age. Talland and Schwab (1964) investigated this impairment further in a group of 50 PD patients and 50 matched control subjects. In a situation where subjects were instructed to manipulate small beads with a tweezer while pressing a tally counter with their nondominant hand, the deficit PD patients have in simultaneously performing two separate tasks bimanually was shown. In a second experimental situation, they demonstrated that although PD patients could perform normally on a letter cancellation task, when they were asked to alternate rapidly between that task and another, their performance deteriorated rapidly relative to that of a control group.

A study by Bowen, Hoehn, and Yahr (1972b) raised some intriguing questions about differences in motor performance between patients with motor symptoms lateralized predominantly in the right versus those with symptoms on the left side of the body. Two motor tasks were used: repetitive tapping, and tracking a randomly moving light on a glass screen. A total of 89 patients were divided into three groups, with either bilateral, left-sided, or right-sided symptoms, and their performance compared with those from 39 age-matched normal control subjects. As has been found in previous studies, both tracking and repetitive movements were made more slowly and erratically by PD patients. Handedness was an important factor on the repetition movement task, with normal subjects tending to tap faster with their dominant hand. However, those patients with right-sided symptoms (presumably resulting from left-hemisphere lesions) had a reduced tapping rate in both hands, whereas those who had left-sided symptoms (presumed right hemisphere lesions) had a reduced tapping rate for the hand contralateral to their inferred dysfunctional hemisphere. For those patients whose lesions could not be lateralized, there was also a bimanual reduction of tapping rate, but the dominant hand-tapping rate tended to be superior. On the tracking task, handedness was not a factor, and the control group performed equally well with either hand. Analysis of the PD group performance on the tracking task showed that patients with a left-sided (right hemisphere lesion) dysfunction were more impaired than patients with predominantly right-sided symptoms. This implies that the right hemisphere plays a significant role in visual motor tasks, and suggests that the laterality of symptoms may be an important variable to consider when documenting deficits consequent to PD.

Conclusions

Studies of voluntary movement performance have shown that speed of initiation (RT) and movement time are indeed impaired in many PD patients. Parkinson patients make rapid ballistic movements more slowly and less accurately than controls. They have difficulty anticipating the movement of targets in tracking tasks and have considerable difficulty effecting a series of repetitive movements. Many of the defects point toward a higher-order dysfunction in the ability to organize a series of complex motor programs. Marsden (1982) proposed that the basal ganglia play an important part in the automatic assembly and execution of sequences of motor programs, that is, in the discharging of a motor plan. He suggested that it is an impairment in motor planning that underlies the deficits in voluntary movement seen in PD patients. For the clinician testing patients it is important to be alert to the motor disabilities of Parkinson patients. The execution of the motor components of any task will take longer and require more processing effort in these patients. This may have an impact on the apparent ability of the patient to perform many primarily cognitive tasks, such as the Performance subtests of the WAIS-R.

There are two additional issues that might be considered under the heading of motor disorders. One is motor skill learning and retention, the other is whether or not PD patients have bradyphrenia—that is, a slowness of thinking. However, because they are both closely linked to failures of cognition rather than the execution of movements, they are considered in the next section.

Cognitive Disorders

Intelligence

The prevalence of Alzheimer tangles and the reported degeneration of nuclei outside the basal ganglia in patients with idiopathic PD suggest that the motor symptoms in PD are likely to be accompanied by changes in cognition and the occurrence of dementia. In fact, numerous epidemiological studies have found a high incidence of dementia in PD. Some of these findings are reviewed first before progressing to look more closely at neuropsychological test results.

Dementia. Failure of intellect in PD is of interest not only from a theoretical point of view, with current interest centering on the possibility of a subcortical-based dementia, but also with respect to advising families about prognosis (R. G. Brown & Marsden, 1984). Epidemiological surveys using mental status examinations and clinical interview to determine the presence of dementia have provided widely varying estimates of the presence of dementia in PD. Prevalence rates vary from a high of 81.0% (W. E. Martin, Loewenson, Resch, & Baker, 1973) to 14.0% (Girotti, Soliveri, Carella, Piccolo, Caffarra, Musicco, & Caraceni, 1988; Hoehn & Yahr, 1967). Reviewing the research over the 60 years prior to 1984, R. G. Brown and Marsden (1984) found that the average published prevalence rate was 35.1%. Variations in reported rates can be attributable to differences in the sampling method used and the procedures used to establish the presence of dementia.

In their survey, R. G. Brown and Marsden examined the prevalence figures in detail to determine prevalence of dementia in primary idiopathic PD and adjusted these figures to take account of age-related cognitive changes on measures like the MMSE.   They proposed that a more precise estimate of the rate of dementia in PD was in the range of 15% to 20%, a risk some 10% to 15% higher than the expected risk of dementia in the general population. This is a far more optimistic appraisal than the usual prognostic expectation that dementia will afflict a third of PD patients.

It is possible that the basal ganglia damage of PD causes the changes in cognition and this accounts for the increased risk of dementia. Quinn, Rossor, and Marsden (1986), however, argued it is the interaction between Parkinson's disease and pathological changes responsible for other disorders that produce the excess risk of dementia. For example, subclinical or clinical AD might summate with clinical or subclinical Parkinsonism to produce coincident dementia and motor disability. In addition to the possible expression of subclinical forms of the disease that might otherwise not be symptomatic, lesions in the cortical cholinergic system and elsewhere in the cortex, as a function of Lewy body pathology, may also result in dementia. They argued, therefore, that destruction of the basal ganglia does not need to be invoked to explain dementia in idiopathic PD. Rather, "changes common to the two diseases may quantitatively summate to cross the threshold" (Quinn et al., 1986, p. 88) for the expression of dementia.

Wechsler Scale Scores. A detailed account of the WAIS performance of PD patients is presented in R. G. Knight, Godfrey, and Shelton (1988). Parkinson patients, on average, have lower IQ scale scores than matched control subjects. Results from six studies that report WAIS IQ scores for PD patients untreated by L-dopa are presented in Table 6.2.

Results from the studies surveyed (Asso, 1969; Donnelly & Chase, 1973; Lees & E. Smith, 1983; Loranger, Goddell, McDowell, Lee, & Sweet, 1972; Matthews & Haaland, 1979; Reitan & Boll, 1971; Riklan, Whelihan, & Cullinan, 1976) were combined such that the IQ score averages were weighted for the number of subjects tested. Four studies reported subtest scores for the WAIS results (Asso, 1969; Loranger et al., 1972; Pirozzolo, Hansch, Mortimer, Webster, & Kuskowski, 1982; Reitan & Boll, 1971). Weighted averages of the subtest scores from the 209 Parkinson subjects tested are also detailed in Table 6.2. It is noticeable that the three subtests that require the most manual dexterity have the lowest mean scores. Overall, the average reduction in WAIS Performance subtest scores is probably largely attributable to problems in motor performance rather than changes in cognition. Groups of Parkinson patients in the early stages of the disease, who do not display clinical evidence of dementia, typically do not perform more poorly than controls on the WAIS (Lees & E. Smith, 1983). Greater deficits are seen in patients with longer disease durations (Matthews & Haaland, 1979).

Table 6.2: Weighted Average WAIS Scores for Parkinson and Matched Control Subjects

	Controls	Parkinson Patients
WAIS IQ Scale[a]		
Verbal IQ	112.36	109.00
Performance IQ	111.55	98.73
Full Scale IQ	114.21	104.26

WAIS Subtest Scores[b]

Vocabulary	10.82	Block Design	8.63
Information	10.81	Picture Completion	8.51
Comprehension	10.78	Object Assembly	7.57
Similarities	10.52	Picture Arrangement	7.49
Digit Span	10.12	Digit Symbol	7.26
Arithmetic	9.23		

[a]Results from 6 studies
[b]Results from 4 studies, PD subjects only

Conclusions. About 15% to 20% of PD patients begin to dement as the disease progresses (R. G. Brown & Marsden, 1984). The higher risk of dementia in Parkinsonism is probably attributable to Lewy body damage in the cortex or cholinergic forebrain nuclei, or to concurrent Alzheimer neuropathology. On the Wechsler scales and other measures of intelligence (Horn, 1974), PD patients show evidence of intellectual decline. Much of the difference in scores between matched PD and control subject is attributable to motor dysfunction—many of the Performance subtests of the WAIS require considerable manual dexterity. Decline in IQ performance tends to be nil to mild in most cases without clinical signs of dementia, and the results are similar to those seen in patients with MPTP-induced Parkinsonism (Y. Stern & Langston, 1985).

Duration of illness has been correlated with WAIS scores (Matthews & Haaland, 1979) but not degree of dementia (e.g., Mayeux, Y. Stern, J. Rosen, & Leventhal, 1981). Severity of particular motor symptoms has been found to predict intellectual decline, but these results have not been consistent. Rigidity has been occasionally found to predict level of impairment, and both positive and negative correlations have been found between impairment and rate of tremor. Bradykinesia is the only symptom that has been consistently correlated with cognitive impairment. Although the relationship between factors such as disease duration and onset, patient's age, and dementia is complex, dementing patients have usually been found to be older and to have a later onset of the disease.

Bradyphrenia

In the experiment described in the previous section, Evarts et al. (1981) failed to find evidence that PD patients are specifically impaired on a choice RT task. This is interesting because it is relevant to the debate about whether Parkinsonism results in a slowness of information processing, often called *bradyphrenia* (Rogers, 1986). Naville (1922) used this term to describe the chronic loss of initiative and intellectual activity that followed the acute stages of encephalitis lethargica. His observation was echoed by several of his contemporaries (e.g., Aubrun, 1937; Steck, 1931). From early on there was debate about the validity of bradyphrenia as a particular manifestation of Parkinson's disease. Some authors have attributed the apparent slowing of intellectual ability to the patient's loss of confidence or to attributions made about cognition on the basis of the clinical presentation in which slowness of movement and impassive facial features predominated. That is, because patients look "slowed up" and have lost their physical agility, observers may be tempted to generalize from the motor disabilities to cognition, and describe this as slowed, laborious, and inflexible.

There has been a great deal of recent interest in bradyphrenia and Parkinsonism, prompted by the designation of slowing in thinking as one of the characteristics of subcortical dementia and by the discovery of lesions in the dopaminergic mesocortical-limbic system (e.g., Javoy-Agid & Agid, 1980) that might provide a physiological basis for the dysfunction. Chapter 8 looks more closely at subcortical dementia. A variety of experimental procedures have been used to test for bradyphrenia. Such tasks rely on increasing the amount of *cognitive* processing required, while holding the *motor* component of the task constant, and looking to see if speed of processing disproportionately increases in the patient group. An example of this approach is provided by an unpublished experiment conducted in our laboratory. It is well known that it takes longer to decide whether a letter is correctly oriented when it has been rotated. For example, in order to determine whether a letter is in its correct orientation or is a mirror-image, it is necessary to rotate the letter "mentally" in some way. This is a purely cognitive operation and the greater the degree of rotation, the longer it takes. We tested the speed of rotation of a group of PD and control subjects (Davidson & R. G. Knight, 1991), and found that increases in the length of processing time caused by the rotation were the same for both groups (Fig. 6.2). On this task, and in other similar experiments, we have not been able to find evidence of bradyphrenia in nondementing PD patients.

This result is generally in accord with the literature. A number of studies have been reported that show PD patients do not have a specific disability in the processing of increased cognitive loads and therefore no evidence of bradyphrenia. (R. G. Brown & Marsden, 1986; Hines & Volpe, 1985; Rogers, Lees, E. Smith, Trimble, & Y. Stern, 1987; A. E. Taylor, Saint-Cyr, & Lang, 1987; A. E. Taylor, Saint-Cyr, Lang, & Kenny, 1986). One result supporting bradyphrenia comes from R. S. Wilson, Kaszniak, Klawans, and Garron (1980), who reported limited evidence for slowed processing. They found that as the number of elements to be processed on a memory scanning task increased, the performance of their PD sample declined disproportionately, relative to the controls. This deficit was, however, only shown by the older (mean age 69) patients in the sample. Rafal, Posner, J. A. Walker, and Frie drich (1984) looked at the relationship between the occurrence of brady kinesia and bradyphrenia using three tasks measuring memory scanning, attention shifting, and preparation for hand movements. They found no evidence of disproportionate cognitive slowing in their PD patients, and that bradykinesia did not predict speed of information processing. Overall, there is little in the way of evidence linking bradyphrenia with PD. Although older and demented patients may show abnormal slowing relative to controls, there is nothing to suggest that bradyphrenia is an inevitable consequence of damage to the dopamine systems of the basal ganglia.

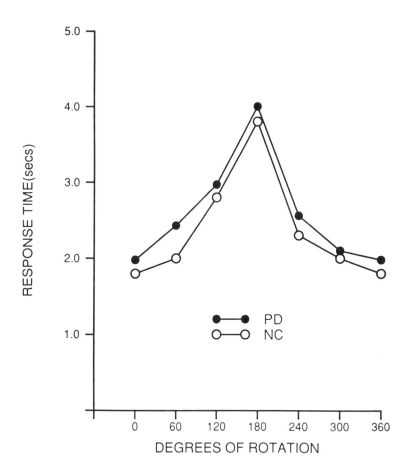

Figure 6.2. Performance of a group of Parkinson's disease (PD) patients and normal controls (NC) on a mental rotation task measuring speed of information processing.

Memory

Several studies investigating the short- and long-term memory functions of Parkinson patients have been reported, following early reports suggesting that amnesia was seen in dementing PD patients (Bebb, 1925; Critchley, 1929; Mjones, 1949).

Talland (1962) investigated PD patients' recall of a list of 10 nonsense trigrams after 0-, 280-, 360-, 540-, and 720-second delays. On this task, no difference was found between the 45 PD patients and an age-matched control group of 40 subjects. However, when the same groups of subjects were asked to recall the text of two paragraphs read to them an hour before, the control subjects reproduced significantly more of the verbal passages than the PD patients. The finding that the two groups did not differ on immediate recall of the paragraphs suggested that rate of forgetting was greater in PD patients. Warburton (1967b) compared a sample of 140 PD patients with 140 patients suffering from medical disorders with no CNS involvement on a 24-item personal information questionnaire. The PD patients showed a greater range of scores and were more frequently in the lowest score range of the test than the controls. Impairment on this measure was also associated with patients' age and disease duration.

A more detailed evaluation of the recall and recognition capacity of PD patients was provided by Tweedy, Langer, and McDowell (1982). Several memory tasks were administered to 35 PD outpatients (mean age 69.2 years), 23 right-hemisphere stroke patients in an inpatient rehabilitation facility (mean age 65.4 years), and 21 neurologically normal elderly adults (mean age 66.5 years), spouses of the PD sample. There were no differences between these groups in education, age, and WAIS vocabulary score. In one experiment, each subject was read a 16-word list, comprising four randomly ordered items from four different semantic categories. In phase 1, subjects were asked to recall as many of the items as possible without cues from the experimenter. In phase 2, the subjects were given the category labels to assist recall, and in phase 3, a two-choice recognition procedure was used. The proportion of words recalled in each phase was least for the PD patients, and their deficit was most marked during the initial free recall phase. In a second experiment, with essentially the same groups, subjects were asked to detect repetitions or synonyms of previously presented stimuli in a sequence of unrelated words. The PD group subjects recognized significantly fewer repetitions and synonyms.

Results from two further studies have suggested that when retention is tested using recognition rather than free recall, PD patients perform at an equivalent level to controls. Lees and E. Smith (1983) assessed a sample of 30 mildly disabled, untreated PD patients, with no intellectual deficits, and found no differences between these patients and a NC group on a two-choice recognition task. Similarly, Flowers, I. Pearce, and J. M. S. Pearce (1984) tested a sample of 50 PD patients on four visual recognition tasks and found neither immediate or delayed recognition was impaired by the disease. Weingartner, Burns, Diebel, and LeWitt (1984) studied six untreated and mildly impaired PD patients, who showed no decrement in performance on tasks that measured word fluency and other automatic memory processes, but were unable to learn 12 unrelated concrete nouns as rapidly as a group of controls. They concluded that memory impairment may be characteristic of PD but only demonstrable with more difficult or effortful tasks. Similar findings of relatively intact recognition performance, but impairment on recall tasks, have been reported in other studies (El-Awar, Becker, Hammond, Nebes, & Boller, 1987; Mohr, Juncos, Cox, Litvan, Fedio, & Chase, 1990; A. E. Taylor, Saint-Cyr, & Lang, 1987).

Freedman, Rivoira, Butters, Sax, and Feldman (1984) tested the remote memory of demented and nondemented PD patients and found the performance of the demented group was similar to that seen in patients with DAT. Impairment was equal across the time tested. The nondemented subjects' performance was equivalent to that of normal controls. Remote memory impairments in PD have also been reported by Sagar, N. J. Cohen, Sullivan, Corkin, and Growdon (1988). They compared DAT and PD patient with normal controls on tests assessing recall and recognition of public events, and autobiographical memory. The PD patients displayed deficits on the remote memory tests that were similar to those of DAT patients, but with a more pronounced temporal gradient on the recall tests of memory for public events.

In summary, there is evidence that persons with Parkinson's disease have memory impairment and their performance becomes more markedly deficient in cases where the disease becomes more advanced and the patients are older (e.g., Scholz & Shastry, 1985). As with the intellectual deficits reported previously, memory performance seems to be only mildly impaired, and deficits are only apparent on effortful free-recall tasks.

Motor Skill and Procedural Learning

Chapter 3 discussed how Korsakoff patients show a normal ability to learn new motor or perceptual skill tasks, despite their almost total failure of declarative or explicit memory. Mishkin, Malamut, and Bachevalier (1984) suggested that a distinction can be made between the outcome of procedural learning, which they term a *habit*, and declarative learning, which usually results in the storage of memories. It has been proposed that the basal ganglia, particularly the caudate nucleus, might form part of a system responsible for laying down new habits, just as Mishkin's proposed limbo-diencephalic-cortical circuit consolidates new memories.

There seems to be good evidence that the rate of learning a new motor skill is slower in PD patients than controls. For example, on a target tracking task, Frith, Bloxham, and Carpenter (1986) found that although PD patients showed evidence of learning the task, and retained the new skill over a 10-minute rest period, their rate of task acquisition was much slower. Similarly, Harrington, Haaland, Yeo, and Marder (1990) found that PD subjects learned a pursuit rotor task more slowly than controls over a 3-day period. In contrast, Heindel, Salmon, Shults, Walicke, and Butters (1989) found pursuit rotor learning was normal in a group of nondemented Parkinson patients.

On tasks of procedural learning that do not involve motor skills there is evidence that although PD subjects perform more poorly overall, their actual *rate* of learning is not reduced. Harrington et al. (1990) found that although PD patients performed more poorly on the mirror reversal reading task reviewed in Chapter 3, there was no difference in rate of learning. A similar result was reported by Saint-Cyr, A. E. Taylor, and Lang (1988). They found that PD patients learning of a puzzle (a variant of the Tower of Hanoi problem) was less efficient than a group of controls, however, there was no evidence that rate of learning was different. Performance on the first trial of the test distinguished the two groups and this difference remained consistent with repeated testing.

Thus, there is some evidence that damage to the basal ganglia results in slowing of the learning of new motor skills. It is possible that such deficits are only seen in groups containing some demented patients. It is likely that motor skills, once acquired, are retained and are not abnormally forgotten. Although PD patients perform more poorly on visuoperceptual learning tasks, there is no evidence that rate of learning is affected. At this time the evidence that the basal ganglia subserve habit formation in the manner envisaged by Mishkin and his colleagues is inconclusive.

Language

Many Parkinson patients have obvious impairments in the motor production of speech. They speak more slowly and quietly, with numerous lengthy hesitations and inappropriate silences. They are often slow to respond to questions (Boshes, Wachs, Brumlik, Mier, & Petrovik, 1960; Darley, J. R. Brown, & Swenson, 1975). Deficits in language use and comprehension have been reported in a few studies. Matison, Mayeux, J. Rosen, and Fahn (1982) found that PD patients performed more poorly on a test of confrontation naming. Verbal fluency, often taken as a measure of language production, has also been found to be impaired in some studies (e.g., Gurd & Ward, 1989). The next section looks more closely at research with fluency tasks. S. Scott, Caird, and Williams (1984) found that PD patients had more difficulty appreciating the intonation and prosodic contrasts of spoken speech. Syntax comprehension deficits have been reported by P. Lieberman, J. Friedman, and Feldman (1990). In all these studies, however, it is apparent that language changes are associated with disease duration or a mild degree of dementia. It is likely that linguistic behavior in PD declines in concert with other cognitive changes.

Frontal Lobe Deficits

Most neuropsychological impairments are described in terms of specific functions; for example, memory, language, or spatial skills. There are, however, a number of impairments that are described as "frontal" on the basis of their association with frontal or prefrontal lobe damage. The tasks included under this heading are heterogeneous, but there are three general classes of test purported to reveal frontal lobe impairments that have been used with Parkinson patients: Tests of "set shifting," fluency, and temporal sequencing. Another deficit that is also often ascribed to frontal damage, bradyphrenia, has already been discussed.

Explanations for the occurrence of frontal deficits in PD have cited the close anatomical connections between the neostriatum and the frontal cortex (Gotham, R. G. Brown, & Marsden, 1988; A. E. Taylor, Saint-Cyr, & Lang, 1986). The frontal area is known to be connected to the basal ganglia structures by a series of complex circuits involving the caudate, thalamus, substantia nigra, and the globus pallidus, structures known to degenerate in PD. It has been proposed that a reduction in dopamine, particularly in the caudate, possibly combined with dopamine depletion in the mesocortical limbic system, produces the frontal deficits seen in PD. A detailed review of the "frontal caudate loop" explanation is provided elsewhere (R. G. Brown & Marsden, 1990; Gotham et al., 1988).

Set shifting. The most frequently used test of set shifting is the Wisconsin Card Sorting Testing (WCST). This test measures not only the ability to learn a rule, but also the ease with which a new rule can be acquired when conditions change. Deficits on the WCST have been reported in several studies involving Parkinson patients (e.g.,

W. W. Beatty, Staton, Weir, Monson, & Whitaker, 1989; Bowen, Kamienny, Burns, & Yahr, 1975; R. G. Brown & Marsden, 1988a; Gotham et al., 1988; Lees & E. Smith, 1983; Lichter et al., 1988; Starkstein, Leiguarda, Gershanik, & Berthier, 1987; A. E. Taylor et al., 1986). These studies show that Parkinson patients learn fewer categories than controls regardless of whether or not they are being administered L-dopa (Bowen et al., 1975), are in an "on" or "off" phase (Gotham et al., 1980), or have clinical signs of dementia (e.g., W. W. Beatty et al., 1989; Lees & E. Smith, 1983; Taylor et al., 1986). Several studies have found that PD patients make more perseverative errors (Bowen et al., 1975; R. G. Brown & Marsden, 1988a; Gotham et al., 1987; Lees & E. Smith, 1983); but not all (e.g., Starkstein et al., 1987). Of note is the often-reported result that PD patients actually take longer to learn the first rule than do healthy controls (e.g., W. W. Beatty et al., 1989). This particular finding, that rule-learning is slowed by PD, has also been reported using other procedures (Matthews & Haaland, 1979; Talland, 1962), and could account, in part, for the reduction in the number of WCST categories PD patients learn.

Further evidence for set-shifting deficits in Parkinson's disease was provided by Flowers and Robertson (1985). Their Odd-Man-Out test required subjects to indicate which of a set of three or four elements was different from the others. Two or more rules of classification, for example, size or shape, were available to the subjects. Two distinct decks of cards were used on alternate trials. On the first trial, subjects were free to choose whatever rule they liked, but were required to use the same rule for the remainder of the trials, until the deck had been completed. With the second deck of cards, in Trial 2, they were asked to change the rule and apply the new rule consistently to the series of cards in the second deck. On Trial 1, there was no between group difference, suggesting that the patient's ability to apply a rule consistently was normal. On subsequent trials, however, alternation impaired the performance of the PD subjects. They showed an inability to maintain the correct set once they had been exposed to more than one response strategy.

A similar finding was reported by Cools, Bercken, Horstink, Spaendonck, and Berger (1984). They found that a group of PD patients performed more poorly than normals on a word fluency task, were slower in detecting a shift in criterion on a rule learning task, and showed an inability to alternate normally between two sequences of motor actions (involving the generation of a series of finger movements). Cools et al. (1984) explicitly linked the failure to execute alternating motor sequences exhibited by PD patients with their inability to adapt to new mental sets. They proposed that Parkinsonism is characterized by a generalized failure of shifting aptitude, a deficit they attributed to dysfunctional basal ganglia operation. Motor set in Parkinson's disease was investigated further by Robertson and Flowers (1990). They taught subjects complex sequences of button-pushing, and then instructed them to alternate between different sequences. They found that although the PD patients learned new sequences normally, they experienced difficulty when asked to shift spontaneously between sequences. This finding served to confirm that Parkinsonism involved impairments in shifting both motor and mental sets.

R. G. Brown and Marsden (1988a) reported an interesting dissociation between those tasks that do and those that do not show "switching" deficits. They compared performance on the WCST with ability to complete a set-shifting RT task, which involved making left-right discriminations under two perspectives. On each trial, subjects saw an arrow that pointed either upward or downward and a square that was placed either to the left or right of the arrow. The subjects were told to imagine they were facing the same way as the arrow and to decide whether the square would be to their left or right. Subjects responded by pressing one of two buttons designated either "left" or "right." Thus, when the arrow was pointing up, and the target was on the left, the "left" button was the correct response. On the other hand, when the arrow was pointing down, and the target was to the left, the "right" button was correct. The experiment was arranged with alternate blocks of 10 trials with the arrow facing up, followed by 10 trials with the arrow down. There were six such alternations. According to the experimental hypothesis, changes from up to down, and vice versa, would result in disproportionately slower RTs for the Parkinson patients at the point of change over. This did not happen. The overall pattern of responding was the same for both groups, suggesting that on this task, there was no deficit in set switching. This was in contrast to results from the WCST, where clear evidence of impairment in the PD group was found. The validity of the task comparison here depends on the equivalence of the two tasks, and on the validity of the RT task as a measure of frontal lobe impairment. R. G. Brown and Marsden did not present evidence that this experimental task is sensitive to putative frontal lobe damage causing set-switching deficits. However, the results are preliminary evidence contradicting the notion that set-shifting impairment is a generalized deficit in PD.

Verbal fluency. When asked to generate spontaneously as many instances of a specific taxonomic category (animals) or words beginning with a particular letter, nondemented PD subjects have been shown to display either mild or inconsistent deficits (e.g., W. W. Beatty et al., 1989;

Cools et al., 1984; DuBois, Pillon, Legault, Agid, & Lhermitte, 1988; Gurd & Ward, 1989; Lees & E. Smith, 1983; A. E. Taylor et al., 1986) or no deficits (Mohr et al., 1990; Weingartner et al., 1984). A study by J. R. Hanley, Dewick, Davies, Playfer, and Turnbull (1990) helped to clarify some of the inconsistencies in the results from the studies surveyed. They initially found a significant group difference for PD and control subjects matched for age and IQ on letter and category fluency tests. However, when age and vocabulary scores were taken into account using analysis of covariance, these effects disappeared. They concluded that differences in verbal fluency between PD and healthy controls may be largely attributable to differences in current verbal functioning.

Temporal sequencing. The ability to recall data in its correct temporal sequence on memory-related tasks has been shown to be impaired under some circumstances in PD. Perhaps the best demonstrations of these deficits are provided by studies carried out by Sagar and his colleagues (e.g., Sagar, N. J. Cohen, Sullivan, Corkin & Growdon, 1988; Sagar, Sullivan, Gabrieli, Corkin, & Growdon, 1988; Sullivan, Sagar, Gabrieli, Corkin, & Growdon, 1985). Sullivan et al. (1985) found that PD patients had particular sequencing problems on the Picture Arrangement subtest of the WAIS. Sagar et al. (1988) subsequently found that on measures of remote memory, PD patients had a specific difficulty dating or correctly sequencing past events relative to their ability to remember them.

Sagar et al. (1988) pursued this evidence of dating failure in Parkinsonism by examining the patient's ability to make recency discriminations. In this study, they used a task in which a sequence of 493 words were presented to subjects every 2 seconds. From time to time content recognition was tested by presenting a word that had appeared previously with one that had not, and asking subjects to identify which of the words had been exposed before. Recency discrimination was tested by exposing two words that had already appeared in the list and then asking which had been presented more recently. PD patients were found to differ in accuracy from the controls on the recency discrimination test but not content recognition. Alzheimer patients were impaired on both tasks. A similar outcome, using nonverbal stimuli, was reported by Sullivan and Sagar (1989). Finally, it is of note that Sagar, Gabrieli, Sullivan, and Corkin (1990) showed that H.M. does not have any signs of specific recency discrimination problems. This supports the view that this defect may be characteristic of amnesia involving the frontal lobes, and is not seen after temporal damage.

Conclusions. Tasks designed to measure frontal damage have been shown to be sensitive in revealing deficits in PD patients. Lesions in tracts linking the prefrontal cortex with the basal ganglia, the caudate nucleus in particular, have been cited as providing the biological basis for these deficits. Results on "frontal" tasks have, however, not always been consistent. In part this is a consequence of the uncertain validity of some of the tests, the complexity of the functions ascribed to the frontal cortex, and the differential psychometric properties of contrasted tasks. The latter point needs some explanation. Where results from two or more tasks are compared, it is important that the difficulty level of the tasks used is generally equivalent. Unless this is attempted, then explanations for differential results based on the content or procedures employed in the contrasted tasks, are likely to be invalid. As an example, the experiments of Sagar and colleagues comparing content recognition and recency discrimination are contaminated by differences in task difficulty level. The recency task was found to be more difficult than the recognition procedure by all groups of subjects. Hence the failure by the PD patients at the more difficult levels of the recency task might be attributed to the discriminatory power of sections of this test rather than to a specific problem that Parkinson patients have in making recency judgments.

The fact that there are differences in the difficulty levels of contrasted tasks has been recognized implicitly in some of the explanations offered to describe the pattern of deficits seen in PD. For example, Weingartner et al. (1984) made use of the distinction between effortful and automatic processing, which we reviewed in Chapter 4, and suggested that persons with PD are differentially impaired on tests requiring effortful processing. This proposal predicts a linear increase in the "amount" of deficit displayed by Parkinson patients as a function of increases in effort. R. G. Brown and Marsden (1988b, 1990) elaborated this theory by incorporating Baddeley's Working Memory model and arguing that persons with PD will only show specific processing deficits when attentional capacity is exceeded. They proposed, "Provided attentional resources are not overstretched, performance will be maintained despite increases in task demands" (p. 344). Once the threshold has been exceeded, however, further increases in effort will cause a differentially poorer performance by the Parkinson patients.

R. G. Brown and Marsden (1988b) supported their position by results from an experiment using a modification of the well-known Stroop effect. The primary focus was on external and internal control of attention. Following A. E. Taylor et al.'s (1986) proposal that PD patients have particular problems with "self-directed task specific planning," they adapted the Stroop test to allow internal and external cuing to be compared. Subjects were presented with a sequence of stimuli consisting of either the word *red* written in green, or *green* written in red. The task was to respond to the meaning of the word for 10 trials, and then to switch to the color of the word for 10 trials, and so on, alternating between the two attributes for 12 blocks of 10 trials. In the *external* condition an explicit cue was given to remind the subject if the meaning or the color was the relevant attribute. In the internal condition no such cue was provided. They found a differential effect of cuing on RT that was only apparent in the PD group. These results suggest that increasing attentional demands, as in the internal condition, resulted in the attentional capacity of the PD patients, but not the controls, being exceeded. R. G. Brown and Marsden's (1989) theory proposes that the critical factor is the attentional resources, and on any task where these are exceeded, PD patients performance will decline. Their resources are more limited, so deterioration will occur at an earlier level on any task in a Parkinsonian group than in healthy controls. Tasks that require internal self-control will be particularly susceptible to these effects. Hence set shifting is a problem for PD patients on tasks like the WCST because they are required to formulate the rules themselves. This approach explains many of the inconsistencies in the data, and as such, is likely to be influential in future research into the cognition of Parkinson patients.

Visual-Spatial Defects

The interconnections between the cortex and the basal ganglia, and the interdependence of spatial and motor skills suggests that one of the early symptoms of PD might be visuospatial impairments. In general, spatial function involves "(1) the appreciation of the relative positions of stimulus-objects in space, (2) the integration of those objects into a coherent spatial framework, (3) the execution of mental operations involving spatial concepts" (R. G. Brown & Marsden, 1986, p. 987). The visuospatial abilities of PD patients have been tested in a number of different ways.

Early research confirmed that subtle impairments in visual vertical and personal orientation can be found in some PD patients (e.g., Bowen, Hoehn, & Yahr, 1972b; Danta & Hilton, 1975; Proctor, Riklan, S. T. Cooper, & Teuber, 1964). More recently Hovestadt, de Jong, and Meerwaldt (1987) found that untreated PD patients had considerable difficulty setting two rods to the equivalent orientation of the two rods on an experimenter's model. Mohr et al. (1990), in their study of PD subjects of intellectual distinction, detected impairments in the identification of complex visual patterns. Other tests of visuospatial abilities have not produced evidence of impairment. Boller, Passafiume, Keefe,

Rogers, Morrow, and Kim (1984) found impairments in an unselected group of patients on an angle-matching task, but not on measures of visual organization, spatial localization, spatial orientation, and mental rotation. R. G. Brown and Marsden (1986) found no evidence that PD patients had difficulties with the spatial component of a left-right discrimination task. Della Salla, DiLorenzo, Giordana, and Spinnler (1986) found that ability to judge directions and point of intersection of lines was not impaired by Parkinson's disease.

There is no compelling evidence for a general deficit in the spatial abilities of Parkinson patients. Where impairments have been detected, explanations for their occurrence that do not depend on spatial impairments have been proposed. For example, as R. G. Brown and Marsden noted, results from Bowen et al. (1972b) can be explained in terms of set-shifting difficulties. On tasks involving spatial cognition (e.g., mental rotation) there is no evidence that nondemented persons with PD display deficits. Where the task has some perceptual-motor components, deficits are more likely to occur, however, these findings may be compromised by the presence of demented patients in the samples tested.

Conclusions

Although PD causes many cognitive impairments, perhaps those deficits attributed to damage to circuits involving the frontal area of the brain are most interesting. From a variety of lines of research there is an emerging consensus that one critical deficit is the "inability to keep apart two plans of action, especially where these overlap and have the potential to interfere with each other. Thus in situations where alternatives are available patients experience difficulties with controlling the independent generation of motor sequences which they previously learnt" (Robertson & Flowers, 1990, p. 591). This difficulty in changing set manifests itself on simple motor tasks, the WCST, and on tests measuring Stroop performance.

Another important conclusion was formulated on the basis of a variety of experimental results; Parkinson patients have special problems with tasks that necessitate formulation of internal rules of action or the initiation of self-directed behavior. However, given external cues to control action, the nondemented Parkinson patient's performance is often normal. This emphasis on the failure of self-initiation of action as being characteristic of Parkinsonism has been shown on a range of cognitive tasks (e.g., A. E. Taylor et al., 1986). Drawing on the ideas advanced by Weingartner and others about reduced attentional capacity in PD, and Baddeley's Working Memory model, R. G. Brown and Marsden (1988b) advanced the idea that Parkinson patients have a primary and specific deficiency in available attentional resources. This deficit becomes obvious when the demands of a task (or combination of subtasks) exceed the resources available to complete it. Tasks that require internal control, make powerful demands on processing capacity and are therefore particularly vulnerable to dysfunction.

From recent advances in the understanding of higher-level motor and cognitive impairments in PD, and a better understanding of the functional relationships between the basal ganglia and the frontal lobes, a more complete appreciation of the role of the basal ganglia is emerging.

Adaptation to Parkinson's Disease

Coming to terms with the diagnosis and reality of Parkinsonism is a challenge to both the patient and their families. Like the person with MS, the Parkinson patient has to cope with a disease of unpredictable course and a fluctuating symptom pattern. Although medication helps patients lead more active lives for longer than was possible in the past, some deterioration is inevitable. Patients have to accept that treatment for the disease will be necessary for the rest of their time. In addition, as we have seen, L-dopa loses much of its effectiveness as the disease progresses, and fluctuations in symptom severity, the "on-off" phenomenon, become more pronounced. For a significant percentage of patients dementia will be a further complication at some stage in the illness. Often people with Parkinsonism are very aware of their gradual cognitive decline; their families and caregivers will be faced with caring for some one with a profound cognitive impairment complicated by disabling physical symptoms. In short, Parkinson patients and their families are required to adapt to a variable, physically disabling and chronic disease, and in many cases, coping with severe mental deterioration.

Little is known about the process of adapting to Parkinsonism. There have been few studies of psychosocial response to the disease, a dearth of interest in the problems of caregivers, and "virtually no data on how the very substantial proportion of Parkinson patients who do not have any psychological disorders live with the disease or how it affects their lives" (Dakof & Mendelsohn, 1986, p. 384). Studies of the psychological aspects of Parkinsonism have mainly focused on the incidence of depression, which has largely been explored in a biomedical context, rather than as a sign of distress as the disease process unfolds. We look first at depression and PD, and then turn our attention to other aspects of adaptation.

Depression

There is a general acceptance that Parkinsonism leads to an increased risk of depression. The nature of the samples of patients assessed, methods of diagnosis, criteria for depression, and a host of other methodological factors make comparisons of incidence rates problematic. However, the average rate of depression in Parkinson patients has been variously estimated as about 30% to 50% (e.g., Gotham, R. G. Brown, & Marsden, 1986; Lieberman et al., 1979; Mayeux, Y. Stern, J. Rosen, & Leventhal, 1981). Some researchers have linked depression in PD with the organic or biochemical changes associated with Parkinsonism. This view has been prompted by some studies that have shown that depression occurs more often in Parkinsonism than in some other chronic diseases (although this finding is not universal). An alternative view holds that depression is a psychological reaction, a sign of an inability to cope with the disablement of the disease. It is also possible that both positions are tenable.

There is one methodological problem with determining the incidence of depression : some of the symptoms of Parkinsonism are similar to the somatic signs of depression. The primary pathology of Parkinsonism causes tiredness and sleep problems. It is not surprising that Parkinson patients tend to be preoccupied about their health (one of the items of the BDI) or to find work an effort. This alone may serve to inflate the scores of PD patients on standard depression inventories such as the BDI. In this respect, it is interesting to examine the depressive symptoms that distinguish PD patients from other subjects. Results from two recent studies (Gotham et al., 1986; Huber, Friedenberg, Paulson, Shuttleworth, & Christy, 1990) in which items on the BDI that distinguish Parkinson patients from normal controls are outlined in Table 6.3. Seven BDI items were found to be characteristic of PD in both studies. Of these, suicidal cognition, and discouragement about the future, are clearly depressive in quality, and indicate a realistic concern about the future. At the other end of the scale, guilt and lack of esteem were not associated with PD. Such depressive symptoms are usually seen in cases of depression of psychotic depth; PD patients do not have a sense of personal failure, punishment, or self-depreciation as significant features of their disease. This argues for the occurrence of reactive depression in PD, an understandable response to the onset of the disease.

It has been asserted that PD patients are more likely than other persons with chronic disorders to be depressed. Horn (1974) found that PD patients were more depressed than a group of paraplegics, and Robins (1976) and Warburton (1967a) found a higher rate of depression in PD than in mixed groups of patients with chronic medical conditions.

Table 6.3: **Significant Differences Between PD and Control Groups on the items of the BDI ($1 = p < .01; 0 = p > .01$)**

	Gotham et al. (1986)	Huber et al. (1990)
Patient age (years)	65	65
Duration of disease (years)	12.5	7
BDI mean	15.1	7.7[a]
m : f	51:49	65:38
Discouraged about future	1	1
Dissatisfied, bored	1	1
Suicidal thoughts	1	1
Decision making	1	1
Work effort	1	1
Tiredness	1	1
Worry about health	1	1
Feeling sad	1	0
Crying	1	0
Irritability	1	0
Physical appearance	1	0
Sleep disturbance	1	0
Appetite	1	0
Interest in sex	1	0
Interest in others	0	1
Weight loss	0	1
Sense of failure	0	0
Guilt	0	0
Sense of being punished	0	0
Self-hate	0	0
Self-blame	0	0

[a] Weighted average of males (7.2) and females (8.6)

However, as Dakof and Mendelsohn (1986) noted, PD has a number of unique features that render such comparisons difficult. The disease is progressive, typically has an insidious and late onset, and an uncertain course. The symptoms are both physical and cognitive. Possibly the most appropriate medical comparison group is patients with rheumatoid arthritis. This is a disease causing pain and physical disability in later life, usually with a gradual onset and a variable progression. In their study, Gotham et al. (1986) compared 57 arthritic patients with 187 Parkinson subjects. Although both groups differed from healthy controls on the BDI, the Beck Hopelessness Scale, and the STAI, the arthritic and Parkinson patients could not be distinguished.

It might be argued that if depression in PD is a result of the disease, then severity and duration should predict the occurrence and depth of depression. Duration of the disease and mood levels have generally been found to be unrelated (e.g., Gotham et al., 1986; Mayeux et al., 1981; Warburton, 1967a). However, there is no real reason to expect a linear relationship between depression and time since onset, because adaption is likely to be a dynamic process. The peak time of psychological distress may vary for different individuals. For some, accepting the diagnosis will cause the most distress; others may become depressed as their disabilities become more manifest. In addition, it is not necessarily the objective severity of the disease that predicts burden, but rather the *perceived* level of disability. This may help to explain the significant but relatively low (e.g., Hoehn, Crowley, & Rutledge, 1976; Gotham et al., 1986) or insignificant (e.g., Mayeux et al., 1981) correlations between clinical ratings of disease severity and depression in PD. Gender does not consistently predict depression in PD (Dakof & Mendelsohn, 1986) and depression and age seem to be independent (e.g., Celesia & Wanamaker, 1972).

At this time, there is no conclusive answer to questions about the origin of depression in PD. Most of the research that bears directly on this issue is equivocal. For example, L-dopa seems to improve motor disability but has no effect on mood, suggesting that mood level is not a psychological reaction to disease activity. However, as we have already seen, it is perception of disability not the objective level that predicts distress. Alternatively, it might be equally plausibly argued that if depression is a consequence of the biochemical changes of PD, then increases in dopamine should serve to alleviate depression. This does not happen however, so perhaps the depression is not connected with the biological basis of the disease. A counter to that argument is the possibility that depression is the consequence of reduced levels of neurotransmitters other than dopamine (such as serotonin) and that the depressed Parkinson patient represents a subtype of idiopathic Parkinson's disease with a different pathological basis. Support for a reactive-psychological basis for the depression seen in PD comes from the patterns of depressive symptoms previously described, and evidence that the cognitive changes seen in depressed PD patients are consistent with reactive rather than endogenous depression (e.g., A. E. Taylor et al. 1986). The picture, however, is not clear, and it may be that both biological and psychological factors interact to produce depression in Parkinsonism.

It is undisputed, however, that there is a scarcity of data about the pattern of depression and the psychosocial stressors in lives of PD patients. How does the temporal course affect the mood levels? Are there premorbid factors or coping mechanisms that play a part? How important are the attributions patients make about the disease to their response to disability? What part is played by social support? Regardless of the etiology of the depressive symptoms, an understanding of the individual differences in response to the disease is likely to be useful in developing appropriate case management strategies.

Cognition and Depression

Depression has been found to have some impact on the cognitive performance of patients with PD. For example, Mayeux et al. (1981) found that cognitive impairment and depression were positively related. Data from a study by Starkstein, Prezios, Berthier, Bolduc, Mayberg, and Robinson (1989) also illustrated this. They found that Parkinson patients diagnosed as having a major depression performed more poorly on a neuropsychological test battery. A causal relationship in this instance is, however, difficult to determine. In a follow-up study (Starkstein, Bolduc, Mayberg, Preziosi, & Robinson, 1990), those patients who were depressed at the time of initial testing were more cognitively impaired 3 or 4 years later than those who were not, even though the initial depression was no longer apparent. It is not clear, therefore, whether depressed PD patients show a reduction in cognitive capacity because of their mood problems, or whether greater cognitive impairment causes a higher risk for depression. However the relationship between these variables operates, it is important to be aware that depression may be a factor in the poor neuropsychological test performance of some PD patients.

Coping with Parkinsonism

The studies initiated at the New York Center for Policy Research by Eleanor Singer (1973, 1974a, 1974b, 1976), designed to assess the social impact of L-dopa therapy, are amongst the handful of research reports available on the social consequences of PD. Singer likened the effects of PD on the social life of sufferers to a "premature social aging." That is, the activity levels and pursuits of people with the disease were similar to those of people chronologically much older. She found that although PD patients had the same living standards and family circumstances as same-aged controls, their current role performance differed substantially. Parkinson patients were less likely to be working than people of the same age and to have fewer close friends. Their involvement in household management had also declined. Singer also asked the Parkinson patients about the leisure activities that they had engaged in on the day prior to the interview. Significantly more PD patients reported watching TV or reading than a general population sample to which they were compared. However, it was in the category of idleness and napping that the figures were most discriminating. A total of 85% of the Parkinson sample reported spending part of the day in idleness and napping, and the figure was 75% for patients under 65 years. In contrast, among the oldest general population sample (80+ years) only 73% reported spending part of their day in this manner; among the general population group in the age range 65-69 years, the rate was 49%.

Singer (1974b) also found that PD patients were less likely to perceive themselves as adequate in fulfilling a parental role. Furthermore, it was striking that PD patients were more likely to rate themselves as bored or lonely than the general population control group. On an index of stigmatization, the younger PD patients also reported that they felt socially unacceptable because of the disablement caused by the disease. This raises the possibility that younger PD sufferers are likely to disengage themselves from social interaction and activities, even when they are not forced to do so because of their disabilities. Singer highlighted the special problems of those people who develop the disease before the age of 65 and might have expected many further productive years: "These findings, taken together, document the relatively greater handicap of younger Parkinson patients, the greater social costs incurred by such patients, and therefore also the greater potential benefit of therapy to them" (Singer, 1973, p. 254).

A further investigation of the psychosocial consequences of Parkinsonism has been reported (MacCarthy & R. G. Brown, 1989). In this study, an attempt was made to identify the important variables mediating between objective disability and psychological function. They obtained data from 136 PD patients (mean age 64.5; disease duration 9.4 years), using a postal questionnaire to assess the significance of four possible mediating variables: self-esteem, coping, social support, and cognitions relating to the illness. The latter factor focused on internal and external attributions about the initial onset and exacerbations of the illness. Social support was assessed by asking patients about the frequency of receiving *instrumental* or *emotional* support. Coping was evaluated by the Ways of Coping Checklist (Folkman & Lazarus, 1985) and items were divided into those involving a maladaptive response and those indicating positive attempts to cope. The outcome measures used to provide an indication of psychological adjustment, were the BDI, a rating of wellbeing, and a scale assessing Acceptance of Illness (Felton & Revenson, 1984), which measured adjustment to the chronic illness. The patient's physical status was assessed using an Activities of Daily Living Schedule, which focused on performance of instrumental skills, and ratings on the Hoehn and Yahr Staging Scale.

A regression analysis revealed that, as with Haley's studies of care-givers, different outcomes had different predictors. Progression of the disease did not predict depression; Instrumental disabilities in everyday living, combined with low self-esteem, and poor coping skills had some predictive power. Disease severity, however, had some impact on acceptance of the illness, when linked with functional disability, and poor coping style. The only outcome with a positive valence, wellbeing, was directly associated with positive factors such as degree of instrumental support, self-esteem, and positive coping skills. Severity and progression of the disease had no impact on subjective happiness. In addition, cognitive attributions about the cause and nature of the disease seemed to have little relevance. In addition, time was an important factor. MacCarthy and R. G. Brown concluded:

> Patients are unlikely to complete the process of coming to terms with this kind of chronic illness at the onset. Since our sample had been ill for a minimum of two and a half years, we could not examine the process of adjustment immediately after diagnosis, when important changes are likely to occur. In the present sample, however, unlike other chronic conditions..., adaptation and resignation do not seem inevitably to improve with increasing chronicity. Progressive disability appears to present a continual challenge to the patient's ability to adapt to an incurable illness, and may be best understood as an evolving process which has no finite successful outcome. (p. 48)

The implications of this study provide an appropriate and significant conclusion to this chapter. The authors underscore the way in which it can be misleading to focus solely on depression as an outcome variable and on medical factors in predicting the impact the disease has on the lives of Parkinson patients. As they noted:

The results suggest that the clinical management of PD patients should take account of a wider field of relationships other than that between disability and depression.... . Those patients whose feeling of self-worth is low may be particularly vulnerable to psychological distress and may therefore need more intensive support. Maladaptive coping behavior is also associated with poor adjustment, and may in the long term further reduce the patient's ability to function independently. Interventions which modify coping behavior may therefore benefit both mental and physical health. Finally, since levels of positive well-being appear to be relatively independent of physical disability, interventions which aim to enhance well-being may be able to improve quality of life, regardless of the patient's disabilities. (p. 51)

Chapter 7

HUNTINGTON'S DISEASE

Graham is a 47-year old accountant. Two months ago he was diagnosed as having Huntington's disease. Sitting and talking with him, the casual observer might notice nothing unusual in Graham's presentation. It is only in the light of his diagnosis that his behavior and symptoms take on any significance. The involuntary choreic movements that characterize the disease are barely perceptible. He appears restless when seated with his legs constantly changing position, and his thumbs moving rhythmically even when his hands are clasped. More apparent are his chewing jaw movements, which he reports have increased in frequency in the last few months. Graham also believes that his coordination is not as good as it ought to be and that he can feel a "tremble" in his upper body. There are signs of dysfluency in his speech. He has difficulty finding and pronouncing words, and he reports that he has problems modulating the volume and tone of his voice. All these symptoms are unobtrusive and might easily be mistaken for signs of general nervousness.

It is the cognitive changes that Graham finds most noticeable. He reports that he first observed these changes nearly three years previously. A broad range of abilities have been affected. He states that he has difficulty with short-term memory, rapidly forgetting telephone numbers after he has consulted a directory and names of people to whom he has just been introduced. He finds it difficult to concentrate and tends to lose track of conversations and to forget what has just been said. He also reports having problems with language. He notes that often he "jumbles" the words in a sentence and has difficulty finding the most appropriate words to express what he wants to say. He is not overtly depressed or emotionally distressed. He reports feeling apathetic and unmotivated and remarks how this contrasts sharply with his early life, when he was busy, active, and well-organized.

Background

In what proved to be his only significant contribution to the medical literature, George Sumner Huntington (1973) provided the classic description of an hereditary chorea in a paper read before the Meigs and Mason Academy of Medicine in 1872. As Bruyn (1968) has detailed, Huntington was not the first to give an account of the disorder. Some 30 years previously, Waters had described an hereditary disorder with a characteristic convulsive presentation known as "the magrums," prevalent amongst the Dutch settlers in the southeast of New York state. In 1859, the Norwegian physician Lund (Bruyn, 1968) described a choreiform disorder in a family in Saetesdal, Norway. But it was Huntington's clear, concise, and accessible report that was to become the standard description of the disease, and it is with his name that the chorea has been associated.

George Huntington's identification of the disease was in part made possible by the observations of his grandfather and father who had practiced in the same area of Eastern Long Island since 1797. George later recalled seeing his first cases of the chorea as a boy while accompanying his father on his rounds.

Driving with my father through a wooded road leading from East Hampton to Amagansett, we suddenly came upon two women, mother and daughter, both tall, thin, almost cadaverous, both twisting, bowing, and grimacing. I stood in wonderment, almost in fear. What could it mean? My father paused to speak with them and we passed on. (Vessie, 1932, p. 564)

The families of the cases Huntington observed came originally from the village of Bures in Suffolk, England, on the *John Winthrop* fleet of 1630. Vessie (1932) examined the public records of the colonial settlements in Massachusetts and Connecticut and uncovered a history of social maladjustment and behavioral problems amongst the forebears of Huntington's choreics. As Vessie noted, in some cases the symptoms of chorea were interpreted as signs of demonic possession and several of the women were persecuted as witches:

In European history this possession of a demon, manifested by personal peculiarities, denoted to horrified observers, that the victim had been changed to a Werewolf. The distinguishing feature of a transformation into an animal was the involuntary character of behavior, the victim having no control over the animal familiarity. It is possible that the awkward efforts, the jerking movements, the uncertain and dance-like gait, may have lent special significance to the belief that the choreric, like the Werewolf, was a "turn-coat." (p. 561)

Symptoms

Huntington's report was followed by numerous others establishing the disease as a widespread hereditary disorder marked by both psychiatric and physical changes occurring in later life. Typically, the most prominent signs of Huntington's disease (HD) are the choreic movements. In Greek, *chorea* means "dance" and this term is most evocative of the way such patients present. The stereotyped patterns of continuous involuntary movement resemble the undulating and rhythmic features of dance. As Huntington noted, the disease begins as any other chorea, with the "irregular and spasmodic action of certain muscles as of the face, arms, etc." The initial stages may be easily mistaken for a tic and the involuntary nature of the movements masked by an intentional movement. Thus an uncontrolled movement of the fingers or arms may become a sweeping gesture to brush back the hair. As the disease progresses, more muscle groups become involved and the patient's movements become less precise and more laborious.

Bruyn (1968) provided an excellent account of the range of stereotypical movements that may emerge. Each patient tends to develop a relatively distinct and idiosyncratic pattern of movement. Often the pattern involves a slow swaying of the trunk or a repetitive grimacing of the face with a circular twisting of the head. While standing, the patient appears to be posturing and writhing in a strange and peculiar manner. Flexion and extension of the fingers, reminiscent of the movements made by a concert pianist preparing to perform, is also a common behavior. The patient's gait may become uncoordinated, broad-based, and lurching, accompanied by uncontrollable choreic hand movements. Speech may become dysarthric and communication frustrating. The clinician can impede the involuntary movements readily, without causing distress; when the patient is resting the force of the movements diminishes, and they disappear completely during sleep. Although not typically aphasic or agnosic, HD patients tend to perform apraxic tests poorly and with considerable difficulty (Paulson, 1979).

Chorea, although the most compelling symptom of HD, is not the only motor deficit. The rigidity and slowness of movement (bradykinesia) more characteristic of Parkinson's disease, are also found in HD. Frequently, where there is some relief from HD using neuroleptics, the bradykinesia becomes more evident. Parkinsonian symptoms are also more pronounced in the later stages of the disease. For some patients, notably those with either the juvenile form of HD, or the Westphal variant, rigidity and akinesia may present without any signs of chorea. Westphal (Bruyn, 1968) originally regarded the hypokinetic rigid form of HD as a distinct disease, which he termed *pseudo-sclerosis*. However, greater awareness amongst clinicians of HD, and the hereditary background of Westphal's patients, led to the reclassification of pseudo-sclerosis as an instance of Huntington's disease. These findings serve to highlight the variability of the clinical picture in Huntington's disease. There are also differences in the course of the disease. Some patients have a slow progression and never show any indications of mental impairment. Others develop signs of dementia soon after onset. Onset may occur as early as 4 or 5, or may be delayed until as late as 60 or 70. About 10% of all cases occur before age 20, and juvenile HD is regarded as a homogeneous variant, with dementia, rigidity, bradykinesia, and seizures being more common than in the adult-onset form of the disease.

Huntington also remarked on "a tendency to that insanity that leads to suicide" as one of the prime features of the disease. Subsequently, several studies have commented on the high rate of suicide or suicide attempts by patients with the disease. The insight that patients have at the time of onset and their expectations of how the disorder will progress is likely to promote despair. In many cases, newly diagnosed patients have seen the course of the affliction in one of their parents. Severe depression often occurs (M. F. Folstein, S. E. Folstein, & McHugh, 1979). No doubt this is the consequence of not only a knowledge of the outcome of the disease, but also of the resulting incapacity. The inability to remain employed, the dysarthria that makes communication a tribulation, and the insidious and degrading loss of motor control, all combine to assault the sufferers' self-esteem and dignity.

Many patients also develop schizophreniform psychotic features. Delusions of grandeur, suspiciousness, and exitability predominate; hallucinations or illusions are rarely seen. Some data regarding the prevalence of psychiatric symptoms come from Lieberman et al. (1979). They undertook a clinical evaluation of 50 patients with HD, and a series of 520 patients with Parkinson's disease. All patients were evaluated on a series of mental status tests to determine the presence of dementia, and were questioned by a psychiatrist about the occurrence of such symptoms as delusions, depression, and alterations in perception. On the basis of this, patients were divided into three syndromes: affective, schizophreniform, or personality disorder. The results reveal some clear differences between the two diseases. The rate of dementia was 32% in Parkinson's disease, but 90% in HD. Of the 45 HD patients who were demented, 12 had shown signs of dementia at the time of onset, and on average the difference between disease onset and dementia onset was 3.5 years. In contrast, the duration of the disease to dementia in the demented PD patients was 6.2 years. Of those patients with dementia, 25% of the Parkinson's disease and 80% of the HD patients were diagnosed as having a concurrent psychiatric syndrome. In Parkinson's disease, 90% of the diagnoses were affective, versus 53% in HD. The remaining HD patients with psychiatric symptoms were equally likely to be classified as being schizophreniform (25%) or personality disordered (22%). This study confirmed clinical reports that dementia and psychosis were more common in Huntington's than Parkinson's disease.

Epidemiological Studies

Numerous studies reporting prevalence or incidence rates for HD have been published. One such recent detailed survey from Norway is typical. Saugstad and Odegård (1986) reviewed the National Register of patients admitted to psychiatric hospital with a diagnosis of Lund-Huntington's chorea (the name honoring Lund's contribution to the recognition of the disease). Their data suggested a prevalence rate of 6 to 7 per 100,00 population during the years 1930 to 1950. It is of interest to note that on first admission to hospital, only 60% of patients were diagnosed as having HD, with the major alternative diagnoses being schizophrenia or paranoid psychosis. This illustrates how frequently functional psychoses occur in the early stages of the illness. There were no sex differences in the prevalence of the disease, and the average rate of marriage and reproduction amongst HD patients was comparable to that of the Norweigan population. The social adjustment of patients prior to the onset of the disease seemed unexceptional. The average reduction of life expectancy was estimated as 20 years, with the mean disease duration being 13.4 years.

Huntington's disease is genetically transmitted, so cases tend to cluster in circumscribed geographical areas. Therefore, studies of high prevalence areas do not readily provide information about the general distribution of HD in a particular population. In turn, population-based incidence figures may disguise the uneven geographical distribution of the disease. One method of determining general levels of incidence is to examine annual death rates from the disease. In a review of a number of studies where this method has been used, Kurtzke (1979) concluded that the white population of Western Europe (and areas colonized by Europeans such as the United States and Australia), have an average annual mortality rate from HD of 1.6 per million. If the further 0.8 per million persons whose death certificates list HD as a contributory factor are added to this figure, an incidence rate of about 2.4 per million results. Probably the death rate statistics underestimate incidence and Kurtzke suggested that estimates based on prevalence data (averaging 48 per million) imply that the incidence rate of occidental whites is about 3.4 per million. Age-specific incidence data set the peak age of onset at between 30 and 40 (e.g., Brothers, 1964), although the median age of onset appears to be in the mid-40s. Newcombe (1981) constructed a life table for the onset of HD and found that 50% of cases had been diagnosed by about age 47, with 75% by age 55-60, and 25% by age 37-40. Kurtzke's review of estimated prevalence rates shows clear racial differences. White populations have prevalence rates varying between 30 and 70 per million. Japan, however, has a prevalence rate of 4 per million (Kishimoto, Nakamura, & Sotokawa, 1957) and for U.S. Blacks the rate is 15 per million. Hayden and Leighton (1982) found that the prevalence rate for Blacks in South Africa was less than a quarter that of whites. These figures add up to the conclusion that HD has its origins in Western Europe.

Genetic Factors

HD is transmitted as an autosomal dominant gene with complete penetrance. This means, as Huntington noted over a century ago, that when "either or both parents have shown manifestations of the disease, one or more of the offspring invariably suffer from the disease. It never skips a generation to manifest itself in another. Once having yielded its claims, it never regains them" (Huntington, 1973, p. 319). Approximately 50% of those with an affected parent develop the disorder. Epidemiological studies have repeatedly shown that HD is not sex-linked. The only unusual feature of the hereditary aspect of the disease is that cases that occur before age 10 are inherited more commonly from the father (Bird, 1978).

Until recently this was the extent of knowledge about the genetic basis of HD. An important breakthrough, however, came in 1983. In that year, Gusella et al. (1983) reported in *Science* that the HD gene could be localized to a polymorphic DNA marker, G8, on the distal arm of chromosome 4. This result was the culmination of a genetic linkage analysis using material collected in part from a large family living near Lake Maracaibo, Venezuela, all of whom appear to have inherited the disease from a common ancestor, a Spanish sailor who lived in the area in the 1860s. This large and well-described pedigree was critical to the success of the project. The implications of this discovery were profound for the detection and clinical care of HD patients. It opened up the possibility of presymptomatic testing, which has now become a reality. We return to this issue again when we review the psychosocial consequences of the disease.

Biological Basis

The most prominent postmortem abnormality in the central nervous system (CNS) of HD patients is atrophy of the striatum (Vonsattel, Myers, Stevens, Ferrante, Bird, & Richardson, 1985), particularly the head of the caudate, the anterior putamen, and the globus pallidus. However, the brain of HD patients also shows generalized cortical atrophy, particularly of the frontal and occipital lobes. At death, the basal ganglia are found to weigh about 50% of normal and total brain weight is reduced by about 20% (Bird, 1978). The cortex is reduced in thickness and atrophy is particularly evident in layers 3, 5, and 6. Histological examination of the striatal neurons affected by HD give no clues as to the reason for their death (Kowall, Ferrante, & J. B. Martin, 1987), although some neuron types are more vulnerable than others. The spiny projecting neurons that make up some 80% of all the striatal neurons in humans, are particularly predisposed to degenerate in HD. The network of these neurons play an important role in striatal activity, being the primary endpoint of cortical input to the striatum, and the major source of striatal output projections (Kowall et al., 1987).

The underlying reasons for the destruction of neurons in the striatum has been explored in numerous biochemical studies. One abnormality that has been uncovered is a decrease in gamma aminobutyric acid activity in the basal ganglia (Bird & Iversen, 1974). Other neurochemicals that show an abnormal decrease include choline acetyltransferase (ChAT), substance P, encephalin, and angiotensin converting enzyme. Other substances that are found primarily in striatal inputs, especially dopamine (DA), norepinephrine, and serotonin are either unaffected or somewhat increased in HD (Spokes, 1981).

Models of the direct cause of neuronal degeneration in HD invoke the idea of an excitatory neurotoxin. This proposal has been strengthened by the finding that the pattern of neuronal degeneration seen in HD can be induced in experimental animals by introducing kainic acid into the striatum. Kainic acid has strong neuroexcitatory effects and produces neuronal depletion in the striatum by means of overstimulation of the glutamate receptors. Although this animal model does not fit perfectly with what is known about HD, these results, and those of Kowall et al. (1987) using another excitotoxic substance, quinolic acid, do suggest a possible explanation for the biochemical abnormalities in HD. In this view, the pathological mechanism in HD would be overactivity in the glutaminergic corticostriatal pathway. The result of the excessive excitation is the destruction of the GABAinergic and cholinergic striatal neurons. As a consequence, activity of such systems as the dopaminergic nigrostriatal fibres will be uninhibited, resulting in elevated DA levels, and possibly causing the characteristic involuntary movements.

How the structures of the basal ganglia work to prevent involuntary movements is generally unknown. Recently, P. D. Thompson et al. (1988) proposed that the subthalamus may have an important part to play in the production of chorea. Penney and Young (1986) hypothesized that inhibition of wanted movement is accomplished in part by a cortico-striato-pallido-subthalamo-pallidal pathway. This circuitry was introduced in the previous chapter and illustrated in Fig. 6.1. The subthalamus is regarded as having an excitatory effect on the globus pallidus, which acts in turn to suppress involuntary movements. As is evident in Fig. 6.1, destruction of the striatal neurons would leave projections *to* the subthalamus to act without inhibition, presumably suppressing output *from* the subthalamus. This might mean that the connections between the globus pallidus and the thalamus were not modulated by input from the subthalamus. As a result, choreiform movements would emerge.

The overactivity of DA system has prompted parallels with the dopamine-linked theories of the biochemical basis of schizophrenia. For example, this finding may explain the increased incidence of psychotic features in HD. Excessive DA has also provided the rationale for treatment of HD patients with drugs such as chloropromazine, which inhibit DA. However, chemotherapy has met with minimal success. HD involves the destruction of a variety of cell groups, so there is little cause to the optimistic that a replacement regime might be found. To date, attempts to manipulate either the cholinergic or GABAinergic systems have not been successful.

Cognitive Deficits

Intelligence

Studies in which intelligence scales have been administered to HD patients confirm clinical reports—on average, such patients show considerable deterioration in general cognitive abilities. Intellectual decline appears soon after onset (Caine, Hunt, Weingartner, & Ebert, 1978), but is most obvious as the disease inexorably advances. Results from studies in which Wechsler Intelligence (and Memory) scale scores have been detailed, are provided in Table 7.1. The general trend in this table is for mean IQ to be below 100, and for deficits to be more marked on the Performance IQ score. Butters, Sax, Montgomery, and Tarlow (1978), who compared recently diagnosed HD (diagnosis less than 12 months), with advanced HD patients (average disease duration 5.5 years), found significant differences between the advanced and recent groups on all three Wechsler IQ scale scores. The recent HD patients differed significantly from the matched controls on both FSIQ and PIQ, although their scores remained in the same range as the control sample. There is clear evidence from this research that there is a progressive decline in intellect in HD as the disease progresses.

Table 7.1:   Wechsler Adult Intelligence Scale (WAIS) IQ and Wechsler Memory Scale Scores for HD Patients

Study		VIQ	PIQ	FSIQ	MQ
Fedio et al. (1979		101	91	97	84
Butters et al. (1978)	Advanced HD	91	81	86	78
	Recent HD	102	97	100	87
M. S. Albert et al. (1981a)		91	-	-	84
Biber et al. (1981)		95	86	-	82
Strauss and Brandt (1986)		93	84	89	80
R. S. Wilson et al. (1987)		-	-	-	82
W. W. Beatty and Butters (1986)		-	-	86[a]	82

[a]WAIS-R IQ estimates

Subtest scores from two studies that report Wechsler IQ scores in detail appear in Table 7.2. Fedio, Cox, Neophytides, Canel-Frederick and Chase (1979) tested 10 HD patients with an average age of 40.8 who displayed "mild motor and/or mental symptoms." Strauss and Brandt (1986) tested 44 HD patients with a mean age of 44.5 years ($SD = 13.2$) and an average disease duration of 5.1 years ($SD = 4.2$). Performance decline is most obvious on subtests requiring motor skills (Digit Symbol and Object Assembly). Measures of knowledge acquired prior to illness onset (Vocabulary or Information) are far better preserved. This pattern is typical of the performance of demented patients on WAIS subtests. A decline in IQ is frequently seen as an early sign of HD, thus the possibility that preclinical WAIS scores might identify those at-risk patients who will eventually develop the disease has been advanced. Lyle and Gottesmann (1979) tested a group of at-risk subjects and followed them up some 15 to 20 years later. Those who eventually developed the disease had lower Wechsler IQ and Shipley-Hartford scores than those who did not develop the disease. However, the predictive utility of these results was not examined. Strauss and Brandt (1986), using both discriminant function analysis and hierarchial clustering, were unable to develop a statistical procedure that classified prospectively at-risk subjects accurately on the basis of their WAIS subtest patterns. The development of genetic presymptomatic tests has rendered obsolete attempts using neuropsychological tests to identify individuals vulnerable to HD.

Table 7.2: WAIS Subtest Scores for Two Groups of HD Patients

Tests	Fedio et al. (1979)[a]	Strauss & Brandt (1986)
Information	10.2	9.5
Comprehension	11.0	7.9
Arithmetic	9.2	7.6
Similarities	10.8	10.4
Digit Span	8.1	8.3
Vocabulary	11.2	9.3
Digit Symbol	<7.0	6.6
Picture Completion	9.0	7.7
Block Design	8.0	8.0
Picture Arrangement	7.5	7.3
Object Assembly	7.5	6.4

[a] Subtest results estimated from graphical presentation.

Memory

Numerous studies have documented the presence of amnestic symptoms in HD patients (e.g., Caine, Ebert, & Weingartner, 1977; Weingartner, Caine, & Ebert, 1979; R. S. Wilson, Commo, Garron, H. L. Klawans, Barr, & D. Klawans, 1987). A detailed breakdown of WMS scores was provided by Butters et al. (1978) in their comparison of advanced and recent cases of HD. They found that MQ scores declined sharply in HD and the average MQ of 78 scored by the advanced group was comparable to that of moderately deteriorated Alzheimer or Alcoholic Korsakoff patients. Decrements were most evident on subtests such as Associative Learning, Logical Memory, and Visual Reproduction. Patients in the later stages of HD are markedly amnesic.

On the WMS-R, HD patients perform at a level of deficit comparable to Alzheimer patients and other amnesics. Butters et al. (1988) tested 24 patients with HD and contrasted these results with data from other patient groups. They found that Alzheimer and global amnesic patients forgot material from the Logical Memory and Verbal Reproduction tests more rapidly than the HD patients. Scores on the WMS indices from Butters et al. (1988) and the WMS-R manual are presented in Table 7.3.

Table 7.3:   WMS-R Results for HD Patients.

	Butters et al. (1988)	Manual WMS-R (Table 19)
Attention-Concentration	67.3	68.2
Verbal Memory	68.0	69.5
Visual Memory	62.1	59.5
General Memory	60.9	60.4
Delayed Memory	63.7	66.6

The comparability, in terms of absolute level, of organic amnesics and HD patients is evident in a study by Butters, Wolfe, Martone, Granholm, and Cermak (1985). They compared nine (six Korsakoff) amnesics with an MQ of 80.11 with 10 HD patients (MQ = 83) on the Rey Auditory Verbal Learning Test. Although the HD patients learned the words significantly more rapidly than the amnesic group, and recalled more words after a delay, overall level of performance was similar. On a yes/no recognition test, again using verbal stimuli, the performance of the HD patients was clearly superior to that of the amnesics. The difference between recall and recognition performance was probably a function of the differential discriminatory power of the two tasks: Recall performance tends to be less sensitive to individual differences amongst amnesics because of floor effects. Recognition is an easier task and results in a greater range of performance. Overall, Butters et al.'s (1985) results show that the degree of amnesia seen in HD is not as great as may be seen in Korsakoff patients, but there is likely to be considerable overlap in memory test scores between these two disorders. Amnesia in HD is more severe than in either multiple sclerosis or Parkinson's Disease.

Butters and his colleagues (Butters, 1984) focused on identifying specific patterns of memory loss in HD patients that might distinguish such patients from other amnesics. In doing so, they have produced some intriguing results. Some of the comparative studies of amnesics, which involve HD groups, are reviewed here.

Short-term Memory. In several studies employing the Peterson-Brown distractor procedure, Korsakoff and HD patients have been found to show a similar rate of rapid decay from STM (Butters & Grady, 1977; Butters, Tarlow, Cermak, & Sax, 1976; Meudell, Butters, & Montgomery, 1978). Although recall tends to decline equivalently in Korsakoff and HD subjects, some interesting qualitative differences have emerged. Butters and Grady (1977) found that increasing the predistractor delay (the interval between stimulus presentation and the beginning of the distraction condition), and thereby increasing the opportunity for rehearsal, substantially improved the Korsakoff patients' performance. This was not the case for HD patients. Moreover, in an analysis of the errors made by subjects, Meudell et al. found that HD patients tend to make considerably more intrusions of items from prior presentations. Finally, Butters et al. (1976) found that reducing the level of proactive interference in an STM task facilitated Korsakoff performance but not that of HD patients.

These results provide some preliminary evidence for differences between demented and amnesic HD patients, and the more specifically memory-impaired Korsakoff patients. Taken together, these data suggest that HD patients are less able to consolidate new input in STM or primary memory tasks, even under favorable conditions. This provides support for contentions by Kopelman (1985) and others that poor performance on primary memory tasks, like the Peterson-Brown procedure, is primarily a consequence of dementia. Dementing patients may forget more rapidly (that is, make more omission errors) and are generally less capable of compensating for their deficits.

Remote Memory Tests. Unlike Korsakoff patients, HD patients have been found to have flat temporal gradients (M. S. Albert, Butters, & Brandt, 1981a, 1981b) generally. M. S. Albert et al. (1981a) found that normal control subjects recalled 83% of items from the 1930s and 80% from the 1970s. In contrast the Korsakoffs scored 62% and 20% on these two subtests; HD patients 49% and 50%. Both recent and advanced cases of HD showed extensive ungraded remote memory loss

(M. S. Albert et al., 1981b), although the decline was greater for the advanced HD patients. The implication of these results is clear. One consequence of HD, which separates this disorder from other disorders with amnesic features, is a retrograde amnesia with a flat temporal gradient. Retrieval of previously acquired information is more pronounced and undifferentiated in HD than Korsakoff's syndrome, and reminscent of the performance of Alzheimer patients.

Effect of Verbal Mediation. In several studies, some of which have already been reviewed, HD patients were found to be less able to make use of experimental manipulations that normally enhance short-term memory performance. For example, the recall of HD patients on such tasks did not improve with longer predistractor intervals, less proactive interference, and the use of intertrial rest intervals (Butters, 1984). Similarly, Biber et al. (1981) found that HD patients did not show normal improvement on a face recognition under global orientation conditions. In this study, memory for faces was tested after asking subjects either to judge an isolated facial feature, or to rate the general likability of the face. Typically, the more global orientation task promotes better memory performance than requesting only a specific feature to be considered. Although this manipulation helped the Korsakoff group to do better, it had no effect on the recognition memory of the HD patients.

One explanation for the aforementioned finding is that dementia prevents HD patients with amnesia from adopting compensatory strategies. Their deficits on the short-term memory tasks and their more pronounced retrograde amnesia may be attributable to nonspecific intellectual decline. However, Butters and his colleagues found one situation where HD patients can make use of extra information whereas Korsakoff's disease patients cannot. They were primarily interested in the effect of verbal mediators on picture recognition. There were two conditions. In the no story condition, subjects were shown a background picture (for example, a living room), on which were located three animal or human figures. The patients were instructed to look at six such scenes and remember the identity and location of the figures. They were then given a two-choice recognition test to assess their memory for the figures, and then, 10 minutes later, a further recognition test. The second test (picture-context) required subjects to select the 18 target figures and locate them on the correct background. In the story condition, this procedure was repeated, with a different set of backgrounds and target figures. This time, however, as the subjects were studying each set of background and figures, they were read a story describing what was happening in the scene. There were no differences between grounds on the initial two-choice recognition test. On the picture-context test, however, both the control and the HD patients clearly showed the benefit of the story condition. In contrast, providing verbal mediation by means of a story linking the characters and the scene, had no effect on the performance of either the Alzheimer's or Korsakoff's disease patients. These results could have been attributable to the superior performance of the HD patients in the no story condition. This was found to be untrue. When scores in the no story condition were treated as a covariate in the analysis of the story condition data, the HD patients still performed significantly better than the Korsakoff patients. Butters concluded that this result completed a double dissociation between HD and Korsakoff patients. HD patients perform poorly on short-term memory tasks, but are able to make better use of verbal mediators than Korsakoff patients.

What is to be made of this dissociation? There are several possible explanations of these findings. Butter's first proposed, following the defective performance of HD patients on the Peterson-Brown distractor task, that HD patients had a fundamental and specific problem with encoding or storage (Butters & Grady, 1977; Butters et al., 1976). However, doubt was cast on the encoding deficit theory when it was found that HD patients showed a normal release from proactive interference. W. W. Beatty and Butters (1986) found that HD patients showed a normal release from proactive interference when tested using the Wickens (1970) technique. This result has been partly confirmed and extended by Huber and Paulson (1987). They found normal release from PI in a group of HD patients with mild disability, but a poorer rate of recall from Trial 1 onward, and a failure to release after taxonomic shift in a group of moderately disabled patients. These results imply that as the disease progresses, memory processes qualitatively alter. Encoding and storage defects may become more pronounced as patients become more disabled. Unfortunately, because no standard measures or memory performance, such as the WMS, were used with Huber and Paulson's patients, direct comparisons with W. W. Beatty and Butter's (1986) results are not possible. For example, it is not clear whether Huber and Paulson's mildly disabled patients showed clinical evidence of amnesia or dementia. Once again, this illustrates the hazards of making comparisons between results from different laboratories using samples of HD patients in differing stages of their disease.

A more plausible explanation of the difference between Korsakoff and HD patients might be that Huntington's disease patients specifically benefit when memory is tested using recognition procedures. The Peterson-Brown distractor task requires free recall, using self-generated retrieval strategies. Butters, M. S. Albert, Sax, Miliotis, Nagode, and Sterste (1983) employed a recognition procedure in their picture-context test. Several other studies have been reported in which HD patients, but not amnesic patients, show improvement when recognition procedures are used. This difference is most clearly seen in the Butters et al. (1985) study discussed previously. Amnesic patients and HD patients performed equivalently on the recall version of the Rey Auditory Learning Test: On a recognition test, however, the two patients groups were clearly distinguished. Butters et al.'s (1985) argument that this supports the notion of a general retrieval defect is supported by the results from the remote memory tests discussed previously. The undifferentiated temporal gradients that M. S. Albert et al. (1981a) found, which were quite different to the graded performance of a group of KD patients, suggest problems in retrieving even long-term, well-consolidated material.

The qualitative differences between Korsakoff and HD patients matched in memory performance on verbal learning tasks on standard tests of memory like the WMS are compelling, even if difficult to explain in an entirely convincing fashion. Butters et al. (1985) concluded that "amnesic patients are probably impaired in actual storage of new information, whereas HD patients seem deficient in their search for information stored in long term memory," which provides a reasonable working hypothesis for the present time. Why this should be is not clear. There is neither a strong cognitive nor neuroanatomical reason for drawing a distinction between recall and recognition performance. This is not, however, the case for the skill learning deficits that HD patients display.

Skill Learning. When Korsakoff's disease was reviewed it was apparent that on several memory-related tasks, amnesics tend to perform normally. These tasks include perceptual motor skill learning and semantic priming. In effect, amnesic performance on tasks that measure memory indirectly or implicitly, tends to be unimpaired. The role of the basal ganglia in skill learning is virtually unknown. As discussed in the previous chapter, it has been proposed, however, that they are intimately involved in motor skill or habit acquisition (e.g., Mishkin et al., 1984). Results from HD patients on motor skill learning tasks are therefore of interest in establishing a role for the basal ganglia in skill acquisition.

Martone, Butters, Payne, Becker, and Sax (1984) conducted an informative investigation of skill, or to use Squire's (1986) term, *procedural learning*, in HD patients. They made use of N. J. Cohen and Squire's (1980) mirror-reading technique. In this task, subjects are asked to read work triads that appear as mirror images. Half the words in each testing session were novel and half are repeated. Cohen and Squire found that Korsakoff patients acquired the skill of reading the unique words as efficiently as did the controls, but did not show the normal benefit of repeated exposure to the other half of the word triads. The Korsakoff amnesics had learned a new skill but did not behave as if they recognized the previously presented words. Martone et al. compared the mirror reading performance of HD patients with that of a group of Korsakoff's. Korsakoff and control subjects shared equivalent skill learning (speed of reading unique words), and Korsakoff patients were significantly slower on the repeated items, thus replicating N. J. Cohen and Squire's (1980) findings. The HD patients actually showed a *normal* rate of learning for the repeated items, but an *abnormal* rate for the unique items. This result is important. It demonstrates an interesting double dissociation between HD and Korsakoff groups, one that might be interpretable in terms of the different neurological damage sustained by the two groups. This finding also identifies a group of patients with defective skill or procedural learning, thereby strengthening the distinction Squire and others make between procedural and declarative memory systems.

Implicit Memory. In several studies it has been shown that HD patients show normal semantic (Butters, Heindel, & Salmon, 1990; Heindel et al. 1989; Salmon et al. 1988) and picture-fragment priming (Butters et al., 1990; Heindel, Salmon, & Butters, 1990). Heindel et al. (1990) found that although HD patients were defective on a cued-recall task using a fragmented picture procedure, their priming was intact. A group of DAT patients, matched for level of dementia with Huntington's subjects, were impaired on both tasks. Of interest also is the finding that HD patients perform skill learning tasks abnormally slowly even though their semantic priming ability is unimpaired. DAT patients in contrast perform pursuit rotor skill learning tasks normally, but are impaired on semantic and pictorial priming tasks (Heindel et al., 1989). These data provide evidence for a distinction between motor skill procedural learning (which may depend on a cortico-striatal system) and verbal priming, which is more dependent on the integrity of the neocortical structures.

Other Cognitive Deficits

Although memory has received the most extensive study of all the cognitive processes in HD, other major impairments have been identified. Spatial defects have received particular attention. Fedio et al. (1979) investigated the spatial abilities of 10 HD patients on the Money Road Map test. This measure requires subjects to orient themselves on a simulated city street map as they move along a designated route. The map is kept in a constant orientation as subjects make 32 right-left judgments at intersections, half of which occur as the route moves away from the subject and half as the designated route returns toward the subject. This requires mental rotation of the route to maintain personal orientation. HD patients made significantly more errors than controls. This study was followed by a report from Brouwers, Cox, A. Martin, Chase, and Fedio (1984), who compared the spatial performance of Alzheimer and HD patients. They found an interesting double dissociation. On the Mosaic Comparison's test, a visual matching task in which subjects compare two 3 x 3 matrices and identify by letter the column that differs between the two matrix configurations, HD patients performed normally. The Alzheimer patients were, however, significantly impaired. On the Money Road Map test, the HD patients were impaired; the Alzheimer patients performed normally. This implies that HD patients have special difficulties on a task requiring egocentric orientation. Alzheimer patients, on the other hand, have a marked problem with visual discrimination or to Bouwer et al.'s term, extrapersonal perception.

The problem HD patients have with egocentric orientation had been noted previously by Potegal (1971). He hypothesized that because caudate lesions in the rat resulted in poor performance on a test of egocentric spatial orientation, the same kind of deficits should be observed in HD patients, who have pronounced caudate lesions. Portegal instructed his subjects to observe the whereabouts of a target dot, and mark its location after they had been blindfolded and moved sideways. Seven HD patients were found to be more impaired on this task than normal controls. These results, and those of Fedio and his colleagues implicated the caudate damage of Huntington's patients in the production of spatial disabilities that emerge primarily when patients are tested for their skill in locating themselves relative to a constant environment.

HD patients have also been found to perform more poorly on tasks that require spontaneous self-directed behaviour, mental flexibility, or alternation between mental sets. On a verbal fluency task, in which patients generate spontaneously as many words as they can starting with a particular letter, both Caine et al. (1978), and Fedio et al. (1979) found that HD patients produced fewer words than controls. Josiassen, Curry, and Mancall (1983) found that HD patients showed a significant impairment in flexibility and a tendency to perseverate on the Wisconsin Card Sorting Test. These deficits were more apparent in patients in the later stages of the disease than in those recently diagnosed HD patients, suggesting these spatial disturbances may be an important early sign of the onset of Huntington's disease. These findings support the importance of basal ganglia lesions in producing spatial impairments and suggest that it is only with progressive cortical atrophy that the intellectual deficits and frontal lobe signs emerge.

Psychosocial Consequences

The diagnosis of HD has profound personal and social consequences. For those at risk, there are decisions to be made about presymptomatic testing, commitment to relationships and children, and how to live a life that may be foreshortened by a lengthy and burdensome illness. The genetic transmission of this disease and the recent availability of a test to predict its adult onset, make HD distinctive amongst the degenerative disorders. Much of the psychological burden of the disease for families springs from its genetic basis.

As with DAT, the progressive decline of the afflicted person is a distressing experience for all those associated with the sufferer. For families there may be the burden of caring for demented and disabled relatives and the additional psychological stress of living with others who are at risk. Individuals at risk have to learn to cope with their risk status. They have not only their own fears to contend with, but also the concerns of those around them that simple failings, the occasional clumsiness, are the first signs of the disease. They have pressures and fears to face when it comes to making decisions about predictive testing.

When the disease is first diagnosed, whether by clinical means or DNA testing, the clinician has an important role in providing supportive genetic counseling. This is an issue likely to be of special concern to the physician responsible for establishing the diagnosis. Nevertheless everyone concerned with care of persons with HD will need to be aware of how well the patient understands the disease, particularly in the early stages of the illness, when the patient is grappling with the implications of the onset of the symptoms. Shoulson and Fahn (1979) advised that counseling begin by determining what the patient knows about the illness. Some patients will have an extensive and very personal knowledge of the disease. Others may have denied the possibility of the disease and will require support as they come to acknowledge the reality and consequences of the diagnosis. The clinical symptoms, the progression and variability of the disease, and its organic basis need to be discussed. Talking about the genetic aspects of the disease provides a natural context within which to discuss the risk status of any children and related matters. Genetic counseling of persons with HD and their partners is a crucial task that needs to be initiated once diagnosis is established. At the end of the information exchange, the clinician should evaluate the impact of the counseling on the patient and others involved. It is important that any misperceptions be corrected. It is imperative also that discussion is initiated about support for the patient and for their caregivers. These are considerations that are likely to be dealt with over a lengthy period of time. Shoulson and Fahn (1979) counseled that it is important to distinguish "between a cure for the disease, which is unavailable, and medical assistance, which is always available" (p. 2).

Presymptomatic Testing

The discovery of a genetic marker for HD changed the lives of families with the disease in a significant way. This advance offered the possibility that at-risk individuals could determine whether they inherited the disease before any clinical symptoms appeared. In addition to testing adults, prenatal testing was also possible. The prospect of a predictive test has now become a reality, and legal and ethical issues that were first debated hypothetically, are now discussed in the context of actual cases. HD was the first of the human genetic disorders where the chromosome location was identified using linkage analysis. The experience of developing a testing process has provided lessons for genetic counseling with other diseases.

At the outset it is important to be aware that the gene responsible for HD has not been located. All that is available are DNA markers that are predictive of the disease. These markers may differ in each family tested, so accurate predictive estimates necessitate obtaining DNA samples from a number of affected and unaffected family members. Without the cooperation of several family members, testing is impossible. Furthermore, the test is not absolutely accurate. An informative test can, however, provide a positive risk estimate of up to 96% accuracy.

Presymptomatic testing has created an important counseling role for clinicians and brought to light many clinical and ethical dilemmas for both clinicians and families with Huntington's disease. For at-risk individuals, the decision to undertake testing needs to be carefully considered. An informative test means that uncertainty about whether the disease will occur is ended. For those that test positive for HD, there is a life to be carried on knowing that the symptoms of an incurable and disabling disease will inevitably appear. The response may be depression, guilt, anger, and anxiety on the part of the patient and the possibility of discrimination from employers and others who know of their disease. Wexler (1989) raised the issue of how the presymptomatic individual will respond: "Will a young person, age 21, with a 96% probability of carrying the gene, be willing to expend the time, money, and energy on developing a career? ... Will physicians, parents, friends, and relatives discourage them from pursuing careers they could not sustain once they become ill? Will universities and employers refuse to accept the presymptomatic individual if this status is known?" (p. 433). Those who receive a negative result, however, have the knowledge that they can plan their lives without the threat of the disease hanging over themselves and their children.

Surveys conducted prior to the availability of the test, but with the knowledge that such a test would become available, found that the majority of those at risk (63% to 70%) would choose to be tested. Mastromauro, Myers, and Berkman (1987) surveyed 131 at-risk subjects and found that 66% of the respondents would want to be tested, 12% would not, and 22% were unsure. Fewer married than unmarried people wanted to be tested, and the most frequent reason for choosing to be tested was the desire to end uncertainty. These surveys also highlighted the risk of suicide. Kessler, Field, Worth, and Mosbarger (1987) found that 11% of the at-risk individuals they questioned stated they would consider or plan suicide, and about 5% said they would end their lives. Similarly, Mastromauro et al. (1987) found that as many as 15% of their sample felt they would be suicidal if they tested positive. HD patients appear to be at particular risk for affective disorders (Mindham, Steele, M. Folstein, & Lucas, 1985).

Looking back, one of the interesting outcomes of these surveys conducted on persons at risk for HD, is the discrepancy between the percentage of people who expressed the desire to be tested before the test was available and the number who actually now present for testing. Centers offering predictive testing have been surprised by the small number of people who elected to be tested. As Wexler (1989) stated "The reality of the test, particularly a linkage test that involves other family members and is not entirely accurate, is less appealing that the prospect" (p. 342).

Process of Predictive Testing. The predictive testing of people at risk for HD using linkage analysis of DNA samples passes through a number of stages. A number of centers offering DNA tests have now reported on their testing and counseling procedures (e.g., Brandt et al., 1989; Hayden et al., 1988; Meissen et al., 1988). The successful completion of the testing of an at-risk individual involves a series of important steps.

Pretest Counseling. Candidates for testing are initially provided with a detailed outline of the test process and the need for involvement of a number of family members. Motivation for testing may be explored, and the issues associated with testing, including the possible outcomes and the impact of these on their lives are discussed with the program participants. A supportive confidant, who can be present on occasion during counseling and at the time of the disclosure of the test result may be identified at this time (Brandt et al., 1989).

Pedigree Determination. Another initial task is drawing up a pedigree of the family of the candidate. This is an important part of the process of confirming the at-risk status of the candidate and determining the availability of relatives for testing. Relevant medical history is obtained from affected relatives or their medical records. In some cases the DNA testing can make use of stored brain samples from deceased relatives.

Exclusion Criteria. After initial counseling and history taking, it is necessary to consider the appropriateness of testing the candidate. Various grounds for exclusion have been proposed. Criteria for Hayden et al.'s (1988) program at the University of British Columbia "include being at least 18 years old and having either a parent affected with documented HD or a grandparent affected with HD." Applicants need to be able "to participate in the three pretest—and seven post test—assessment counseling sessions over 2 years" (p. 690). Psychiatric symptoms may also lead to exclusion. The criteria devised by Meissen et al. (1988) to exclude personally disturbed or depressed persons "were a diagnosis of schizophrenia or unipolar or bipolar depression, a suicide attempt within the previous 10 years, an intent to commit suicide if the Huntington's disease test was positive, serious depression, or drug or alcohol use" (p. 536). Anyone who was currently under stress, who had contemplated suicide in the event of a positive result, was moderately depressed, or had made a suicide attempt more than 10 years ago, was referred for a more detailed psychiatric evaluation.

Informed Consent. All participants in testing, including family members donating samples, are required to give full informed consent. It is necessary to obtain blood or tissue samples for DNA testing from at least three family members, one of whom must have a clinical diagnosis of HD. The more members of the affected family that can be tested, the greater the precision of the risk estimation.

Laboratory Analysis. Procedures for the completion of the DNA testing and risk estimation are described in detail elsewhere (e.g., Brandt et al., 1989). Often the results of testing are uninformative. This may be in part a consequence of the limited number of family members that can be tested; later testing may be possible when samples from other relatives become available. However, this sometimes has to wait until their disease status is known. As more markers of HD are identified, the number of uninformative tests is likely to decline (Hayden et al., 1988).

Disclosure. The results of testing are disclosed to the at-risk individual, who may be accompanied by the confidant if this has been arranged in the early stages of counseling. Questions about the test results are discussed fully and follow-up sessions, which may extend over several years, are arranged.

Response to Testing. As we have already seen, several research centers offering DNA testing for at-risk individuals have reported on their experience. Brandt et al. (1989) described the outcome of 55 tests, 12 of which were positive, 30 negative, and 13 uninformative. They found no significant pretest difference between the positive and negative test subjects in terms of psychiatric history, neurological testing, or depressive features. In general, their subjects coped "well with the news at least over the short term." As might be expected, "Initial reactions have ranged from extreme joy and relief to disappointment, sadness, and demoralization. Thus far, there have been no severe depressive reactions" (p. 3112). Similar results have been reported by Meissen et al. (1988). However, they found that some of their subjects with positive results were markedly depressed 3 months after disclosure; by 9 to 12 months after disclosure, however, these emotional upsets had diminished in intensity. No formal psychiatric care was necessary. It was also their experience that about a third of those people entering the testing program dropped out voluntarily before receiving the test results. This emphasizes the importance of pretest counseling and the provision of sufficient time to at-risk applicants for consideration of all the issues involved.

Prenatal Testing. It is possible to obtain genetic material from a fetus of a parent at risk for HD or with a confirmed diagnosis. A recent report describes the options for prenatal testing available to HD families (Fahy, Robbins, Bloch, Turnell, & Hayden, 1989). One possible scenario is where an at-risk parent has been found in a predictive testing program to be positive for HD or where a clinical diagnosis of HD in one parent has already been made. Here it is possible to complete *definitive* testing and determine the child's inherited risk of the disease. Another situation arises where an at risk parent does not want to know their own risk status via a DNA test, but would like to learn whether the risk to the fetus is low (around 4%) or the same as their own (50%). Fahy et al. referred to this as prenatal *exclusion* testing. It allows the parent to learn whether the child is likely to be disease free. If the test is not negative and the child has inherited a 50% risk, one option is for the parent to then undergo predictive testing. It would then be possible to determine the risk factor for parent and child more precisely. This avoids the difficulty of deciding whether or not to terminate the pregnancy, when the risk factor is only 50%. Fahy et al. presented the case of one young woman at risk "who would, if at all possible, ideally prefer not to learn of her status, but would request information about her own risk rather than terminate a 50% fetus risk" (p. 356). In this case, exclusion testing was followed by definitive testing. Working with parents before prenatal testing is likely to present the counselor with a number of ethical and practical issues and dilemmas.

Ethical Dilemmas. In the past, eradication of HD was dependent on at-risk individuals avoiding reproduction. Availability of a presymptomatic test offers the prospect of improved genetic counseling for at-risk parents and the opportunity for prenatal testing. However, although testing brings benefits, it also has costs. As a consequence, "Despite years of careful planning predictive testing for HD is turning out to be more complex and challenging than ever expected" (Bloch & Hayden, 1990, p. 4).

The fact that predictive DNA testing for HD would pose ethical and legal dilemmas was recognized as soon as the genetic marker was located. Procedures for caring for the best interests of the at-risk applicant for testing have been initiated in all the research reported in the literature. These guidelines for administering the tests have been developed on the basis of three widely accepted principles of clinical practice: respect for autonomy, beneficence, and confidentiality (Huggins et al., 1990).

In this situation, autonomy refers to the right of individuals to decide for themselves to take the test, to be free from any coercion, and to be fully informed of all information relevant to their choice. For this reason, minor children under the age of 18 are not tested, for example, at the request of their parents. Bloch and Hayden (1990) concluded, "The self-esteem and sense of worth of a developing child may be profoundly and negatively affected. The attitude of society and its agencies toward high-risk individuals has not yet been clarified. Since no treatment is available and there is a possibility of harm, we oppose the testing of children" (p. 2). Where the testing of children is requested, testing centers have regarded the best interests of the child as guiding their decision. A positive test is likely to lead to stigma or discrimination, thus the testing of children is seldom justified.

Beneficence refers to the obligation to do no harm. It is important that test results are not given to people who are not emotionally capable of dealing with the outcome. It is for this reason that the risk of suicide is carefully assessed. Also, it behoves those administering testing programs to monitor the response of the people they test so that any harmful effects of testing can be known. Finally, confidentiality is another cardinal principle. It is important that the results of the tests are not directly or inadvertently available to anyone other than the at-risk individual, including other family members and employers. The absolute right to privacy presents numerous ethical dilemmas but should be maintained unless there is a clear reason (such as the prevention of harm) to override confidentiality. Problems arise particularly in circumstances where testing is requested independently by two or more members of the same family (Huggins et al., 1990).

Summary

Issues relating to predictive testing dominate any discussion of the special psychosocial stressors of HD. Many of the ethical dilemmas that present to the clinician are not unique to this disease; there are, for example, similar issues to be faced with HIV testing of presymptomatic persons at risk for AIDS. Predictive testing for HD provides an important opportunity to research the impact of testing on at risk individuals and their families. Undoubtedly other predictive DNA tests for adult disorders will be developed in the future and the experience with HD will be invaluable. Perhaps before leaving this topic one final caution is in order:

> The day may be close when individuals can request a personalized genetic "map" with all of their health "landmines" demarcated. Geneticists may replace astrologers in predicting strengths, weaknesses, predilections, and predispositions. They can know our future by reviewing our past inheritance. But we must determine if this new knowledge is to be life enriching or destructive. (Wexler, 1985, p. 302)

Conclusions

The genetic transmission and the onset in middle life are perhaps the factors that most impact on the lives of families with Huntington's disease. It is from these features of the disorder that much of the stress and tragedy of the disease emanate. For the at-risk individual there is the fear that a sudden forgetfulness, a slight clumsiness or stumble, or a feeling of fatigue may signal the start of the inevitable changes that are to come. Small failures mobilize the concern of relatives; there is a sense of watching and waiting. The importance of the role of the psychological or the medical counselor in providing support and understanding for patients with HD and their families cannot be overemphasized.

The development of presymptomatic testing has raised a host of ethical and professional issues. It creates dilemmas for those at risk. On the one hand, for those identified as having the disease there may be an end to uncertainty or denial, but also a premature beginning to living with the disease. On the other hand, for those whose tests are negative, there is joy at the lifting of omnipresent threat. It is important to remember that it is families that must make the decision about testing, because chromosomal material from a number of affected and unaffected family members must be collected if test accuracy is to reach an acceptable level. For couples, where one spouse may be affected, there are decisions to be made about whether to have children and/or test fetal material for transmission of the defective genetic attributes. Each case and each family will present its own unique combination of worries and decisions.

For those who are diagnosed as having HD, there are immediate problems of adjustment. Reactions range from relief and calm to depression or despair. There is an increased risk of suicide. The patient's concerns about their children and their own future care and support need to be considered. For the unaffected spouse, there is the personal and economic burden of caring for a chronic invalid, increasing loneliness, and fear for the future of the children with which to cope. Children will have a constant remainder of their own possible fate as they watch the life of their affected parent change and will need to come to terms with the possible early loss of one parent. All these needs and pressures must be accepted and worked through.

Initially the choreic movements and deterioration of motor skills are the most pronounced and disabling features of the disease. The majority of HD sufferers also report changes in cognition. Reasoning, judgment, and problem-solving abilities may noticeably decline. Failures of memory are common. Communication becomes severely affected as the motor symptoms become more advanced. Many patients report difficulties planning, organizing, and executing complex activities such as preparing a meal or even getting dressed. Neuropsychological testing tends to substantiate the presence of these impairments in intellect, memory, and behavioral sequencing. Many, but by no means all, HD patients show a marked degree of deterioration on standard measures of IQ. Amnesia is often apparent on tests such as the Wechsler Memory Scale and in the advanced states of the disease, memory decline may be profound.

Neuropsychological studies have found a number of interesting double dissociations between HD and other chronic neurological conditions. Some of these may ultimately serve to shed light on the functions of the basal ganglia and related structures. Huntington's disease patients appear to have more difficulty acquiring new skills, particularly in the perceptual-motor domain, than do Korsakoff patients. This is a significant finding, suggesting that the basal ganglia may play a crucial role in habit or procedural learning. It also appears likely that HD patients have particular problems on tasks requiring personal or egocentric spatial orientation. In this respect they differ from Alzheimer patients who perform normally on such tasks, but have problems with visuospatial discrimination.

There are many challenges for the clinician and researchers working with HD patients. The psychosocial consequences of the disease and the fact that the total family is involved in these consequences have important implications for clinicians. Working with patients and families affords the opportunity to learn more about adjustment to chronic disease and coping with being at risk. The nature of the cognitive deficits associated with the disorder and how they relate to structural changes in the brain also requires further clarification. In this respect, comparative neuropsychological studies have been both informative and heuristic and are likely to yield further insights into the disease in the future.

Chapter 8

PROGRESSIVE SUPRANUCLEAR PALSY, SUBCORTICAL DEMENTIA, AND OTHER DEGENERATIVE DISEASES

The first change that Marie noticed in her husband William's behavior that gave her cause for concern was his uncharacteristic impulsiveness and occasional rudeness to other people. Some 5 months after this apparent alteration in his personality, William found that he was having difficulty running or walking. He sometimes felt unsteady and dizzy on his feet and had the occasional fall when he moved too quickly. At about the same time, Marie noticed that his memory was beginning to deteriorate. William could remember things that had happened in the past, but his recall of events or conversations in his every day life was unreliable. He also developed a slight tremor in his right hand.

A year later, his symptoms have progressed. His gait is clumsy and unsteady, and he looks stiff and uncertain as he walks into the room. He has trouble moving his eyes in the lateral plane, and is unable to move them upwards at all, even when following the physician's finger. His WAIS-R FSIQ is 85, however, his vocabulary skills and education suggest he was once functioning well above average. On the Rey Auditory Verbal Learning Test he learns 7 words after 5 trials. Neuropsychological testing provides clear evidence of cognitive dysfunction amounting to a mild dementia. The neurologist confirms that William has progressive supranuclear palsy.

The neurological conditions that have been reviewed so far are those disorders that have been most subjected to neuropsychological or psychosocial investigations. There are, however, a number of other degenerative diseases that have received less attention in this literature, some of which are introduced in this chapter. The first of these is progressive supranuclear palsy (PSP). There is neuropsychological research interest in this disorder because it is often regarded as the best instance of subcortical dementia. Consequently a number of studies have focused on the cognitive deficits of PSP. Before introducing the distinction between cortical and subcortical dementia, however, the features of PSP are reviewed.

Progressive Supranuclear Palsy

This rare condition of later life was first identified as a distinct clinical syndrome by Steele, Richardson, and Olszewski (1964). The initial presentation of the disease is sometimes mistaken for Parkinson's disease, because of the early signs of rigidity in the PSP patient. However, the appearance of neurological deficits consequent on progressive damage to upper brainstem nuclei differentiates PSP from Parkinsonism.

There are four distinctive features of PSP: Supranuclear ophthalmoplegia, rigidity of the neck and upper trunk, pseudobulbar palsy, and a mild, slowly progressing dementia. The ophthalmoplegia, or paralysis of eye movements, is typically manifest as an inability to move the eyes in the vertical plane. Downward gaze is most affected. Initially the failure is seen only on command, but as the disease progresses, the patient is unable to move the eyes vertically when following the movement of the clinician's hand. The effects of this are clumsiness, and difficulty reading, eating, and dressing. Visual activity is usually normal, but visual accommodation to an approaching target is generally impaired.

Pseudobulbar palsy is another typical symptom of the disorder resulting from the progressive damage to the brainstem nuclei. This results in a rigidity of the facial muscles, giving a mask-like appearance to the face, slurred speech, and a difficulty with swallowing. Balance is also often affected. The rigidity of the neck and upper trunk gives the PSP patient an unusual appearance of erectness, which contrasts to the bowed posture of the PD patient. When dementia occurs, it is usually mild, and progresses slowly. The severity and manifestations of cognitive deficit vary greatly; the intellectual impairments are discussed in more detail later. In general, the early symptoms of PSP tend to involve problems of unsteadiness, visual problems, or perceived changes in cognition or personality (Kristensen, 1985).

Postmortem examination of the brain reveals little evidence of cortical atrophy. However, degeneration of subcortical and midbrain structures is more evident. The subthalamic nuclei, globus pallidus, superior colliculus, substantia nigra and red nuclei, locus coeruleus, tegmentum, and the grey matter around the aqueduct and fourth ventricles are typically affected. Perhaps the most significant point about the lesions from the perspective of neuropsychological experimentation is that their distribution does not overlap with that seen in Alzheimer's disease. On microscopic examination, many of the degenerating cells are found to contain neurofibrillary tangles, many with straight filaments that can be distinguished from the twisted filaments characteristic of AD.

PSP is an uncommon disorder with a prevalence estimated at about 4/100,000. In a review of cases in the literature, Kristensen (1985) calculated a median age of onset of 60 (range 12-80), and a median survival time of 5 years. There are no known environmental or hereditary factors involved in the incidence of the disease; the etiology is unknown. The course is progressive, with extreme motor incapacity leading to the patient becoming bedridden and unable to communicate.

Subcortical Dementia

The term *subcortical dementia* dates back at least to the work of Kinnier Wilson in 1912. In his account of hepatolenticular degeneration, a disorder resulting from an inborn error of copper metabolism (now often known as Wilson's disease), he contrasted the cognitive failures seen in senile dementia with those in patients with subcortical lesions. Wilson's disease causes damage to the basal ganglia, leaving the cortex intact. Wilson observed that patients with subcortical damage, although showing signs of mental deterioration, did not exhibit the amnesia, apraxia, or agnosia typical of senile dementia.

Interest in subcortical dementia was stimulated in the 1970s by two reports, one detailing the cognitive changes seen in PSP (M. L. Albert, Feldman, & Willis, 1974), the other focusing on similar changes in HD (McHugh & M. F. Folstein, 1975). In both studies the cognitive dysfunction of the subcortical patients was contrasted with the dementia seen in Alzheimer's disease. M. L. Albert et al. (1974) described five cases of PSP in detail and reviewed a further 46 cases that had appeared in the literature. They concluded that "a characteristic pattern of dementia, 'subcortical dementia', may be contrasted sharply with that of the cortical dementias" (p.129). They went on to speculate that:

> *Although the specific subcortical structures involved may differ, the fact that lesions in these areas produce a common symptomatology suggests that a common pathophysiological mechanism may be present. We propose as a tentative hypothesis that the common mechanisms underlying the subcortical dementias are those of impaired timing and activation. Impaired functioning of the reticular activating systems from thalamic and subthalamic nuclei may result in a slowing down of normal intellectual processes. (p. 129)*

They identified a reduction in arousal as the intrinsic deficit underlying subcortical dementia, and the resulting slowness of cognition as a cardinal element of the pattern of impairment. This slowing process is often known as bradyphrenia, an effect often attributed to the lesions caused by PD, as discussed in Chapter 6.

Table 8.1 lists the distinguishing features of the cortical and subcortical dementia. M. L. Albert et al. (1974) identified four primary signs of subcortical dementia: forgetfulness, slowed cognition, personality change, and poor calculating and abstracting ability. These characteristic changes have been widely accepted in subsequent reviews and research. M. L. Albert et al. drew particular attention to the slowness of thinking in PSP; they observed that often, if the patient was given enough time, they could respond correctly, demonstrating that elementary verbal and perceptual capabilities were untouched by the disease. The diseases most strongly identified with subcortical dementia are PSP, HD, and PD, as well as a number of rarer conditions such as Wilson's disease, and spinocerebellar degeneration. Cortical dementia has been studied almost exclusively in patients with DAT.

Table 8.1: **Characteristic Features of Cortical and Subcortical Dementias**

Subcortical	Cortical
Mild to moderate severity during the course of the disease; slow progression	Constant progression to severe degree of dementia.
Slowness in cognition	Speed of cognition normal
Forgetfulness	Moderate to severe amnesia from an early stage
Language and perception generally unimpaired	Impairments of language and perception
Personality change, particularly apathy and depression	Affective disturbance uncommon

There is no doubt that the brain lesions resulting from diseases like PSP on the one hand and DAT on the other are distinctive, and cause different clinical syndromes. It is also in accord with clinical experience that the severity and quality of the cortical and subcortical dementias differ. However, whether the dementia seen in patients with primary subcortical damage is a result of subcortical lesions, or whether it is a consequence of adjunctive cortical changes, is a matter of debate. The validity of the concept of subcortical dementia is discussed at the conclusion of this section. First, however, the neuropsychosocial changes associated with PSP are considered.

Neuropsychology of PSP

Mild memory impairments, amounting to "forgetfulness" have been found in some studies with PSP patients. Litvan, Grafman, Gomez, and Chase (1989) found an average MQ of 96 in a group of 12 PSP patients. Although this score was significantly different from the average MQ of the normal comparison subjects, an MQ of 96 is much higher than would be expected from a group of DAT patients. Similar mild memory deficits on the WMS were reported in PSP patients by Dubois, Pillon, Legault, Agid, and Lhermitte (1988) and on Warrington's RMT by Maher, E. Smith and Lees (1985). Milberg and M. S. Albert (1989), however, found no significant difference between PSP and normal subjects on the Logical Memory or Verbal Reproduction subtests of the WMS, although group differences approached significance on the nonverbal test. These studies suggest where sensitive measures of memory are used, a mild degree of memory loss is seen in PSP patients. However, these changes are minimal when compared to the amnesia seen in DAT.

Dubois et al. (1988) provided good evidence for slowed thinking in PSP. They investigated bradyphrenia in groups of PSP, PD, and healthy volunteers using a reaction time task that allowed the speed of execution of the procedure to be divided into motor and cognitive components. The PD patients and controls showed similar rates of cognitive processing, a finding consistent with our review of bradyphrenia and PD in Chapter 6. In contrast, the PSP patients did show a slowed rate of information processing. The authors concluded that bradyphrenia may be related to degree of frontal impairment: The performance of the PSP patients on tests sensitive to frontal deficits was impaired relative to the PD patients (who occupied an intermediate position between the PSP patients and the controls).

M. S. Albert et al. (1974) found that of the 46 cases they identified in the literature, personality change was mentioned as a significant symptom in 22 cases. Inappropriate mood disturbances were reported in

14 cases. The most commonly reported affective changes were apathy and depression, followed by irritability and euphoria. The high incidence of affective changes has been confirmed by Maher et al. (1985) and Dubois et al. (1988). The average clinician-ratings of depression in PD and PSP patients in the Dubois et al. study were equivalent, and both groups had scores elevated relative to the normal controls. It seems that PSP is characterized by similar emotional changes to those seen in PD.

Impairment on the WAIS has been consistently demonstrated in PSP patients (Kristensen, 1985), however, these results must be tempered by consideration of the patients' concurrent visual scanning and motor deficits (Kimura, Barnett, & Burkhart, 1981). For example, Fisk, Goodale, Burkhart, and Barnett (1982) found that degree of ophthalmoplegia predicted degree of intellectual impairment. However, even when account is taken of visuomotor defects, some evidence of intellectual deterioration remains. Both Dubois et al. (1988) and Pillon, Dubois, Lhermitte, and Agid (1986) found a significant reduction in VIQ scores in their PSP patients. Nevertheless, it is apparent that the severity of intellectual decline in PSP patients is mild and progresses slowly. The level of intellectual dysfunction in a group of PSP patients is comparable, or marginally more pronounced, than that seen in a matched group of PD patients (Fisk et al., 1982; Pillon et al., 1986).

In many ways, the pattern of performance displayed by PSP patients on neuropsychological tests is similar to that of Parkinson patients. An illustration of this is provided by Pillon et al. (1986). They found that overall, PSP patients performed more poorly on tests of frontal lobe integrity, such as the WCST, and were also rated as showing more behavioral signs of frontal lobe damage (e.g., inertia, stereotype, indifference, and disinterest) than DAT patients. On the other hand, DAT patients were considerably more impaired on subtests of the WMS. Parkinson patients tended to show more signs of frontal impairment than the DAT patients and more memory impairment than the PSP subjects. Depression was more common amongst PSP and PD patients than the DAT patients. Milberg and M. S. Albert (1989) similarly found that whereas confrontation naming and memory were affected by DAT relative to the effects of PSP, Alzheimer patients were more successful on the Verbal Fluency test than the PSP patients. Results from these studies suggest a double dissociation for PSP and SDAT patients between memory and language tests that are abnormal in DAT, but relatively unimpaired in PSP, and "frontal lobe" tests that are more severely affected in PSP than in DAT. Persons with Parkinsonism appear to have both cortical and subcortical-frontal lobe impairments.

Psychosocial Consequences

There have been few investigations of the psychosocial aspects of PSP. The feature of the disease that perhaps causes the most distress is the progressive physical disability. The final stages of the disease, as described by Kristensen (1985), leave the patient "anarthric, bedridden and akinetic, lying opisthotonus and in double hemiplegic posture, nourished by a gastric tube and unable to communicate with his surroundings. Even at this stage, dementia is possibly only moderate and the patient is painfully aware of the situation" (p. 182).

The early stages of the disease are marked by a paralysis of gaze making everyday activities like eating, reading, and writing difficult. Gradually, more functional motor systems are compromised and there is a steady loss of independence. Adjusting to dependence on other people creates problems for many of the disabled. Physical failure, combined with a loss of the ability to communicate, reduces the possibility of social activities. The resulting social isolation may be compounded by the need to give up work and loss of leisure time skills. The family and caregivers have the stress of caring with an increasingly disabled person. Those who care for patients with PSP must deal not only with physical disablement, but also with the patient's deteriorating personality and the appearance of negative emotions, such as anger and depression.

Validity of Subcortical Dementia

Although the division of the dementias into cortical and subcortical has been widely accepted, the distinction has not been without its critics (e.g., Mayeux, Y. Stern, J. Rosen, & Benson, 1983). Determining the validity of subcortical dementia is problematic for two reasons. First, there are difficulties caused by comparing and contrasting cognitive deficits in two or more groups that are not matched for severity of dementia. It is possible that if groups were matched for severity then both quantitative and qualitative differences on multicomponent tests like the MMSE or the WAIS-R might disappear. There are many methodological hazards involved in comparing groups with different average ages, rate of disease progression, and clinical severity of dementia. In addition to these measurement problems, the neurological damage resulting from various diseases is seldom exclusively either cortical or subcortical; for example, subcortical lesions are seen in DAT (Whitehouse et al., 1982).

There are, however, some important reasons for persisting with the notion of subcortical dementia. The lesions caused by PSP and AD are quite distinctive and the resultant clinical syndromes are seldom, if ever, confused. Furthermore, some of the quantitative features of the dementia associated with PSP offer the prospect of a better understanding of the role of subcortical structures in cognition (Cummings, 1986; Cummings & Benson, 1984; Huber & Paulson, 1985). Some interesting dissociations between the cognitive deficits in DAT and PSP (and other primarily subcortical diseases) have emerged.

One useful characterization of the distinctive qualities of subcortical dementia has been provided by Cummings (1986). He observed that subcortical structures have an important part to play in cortical arousal, and in the analysis and integration of motor and sensory information. Consequently, damage to these structures causes deficits in arousal, response speed, attention, activation, motivation, and mood. Cummings labeled the diffuse processes disrupted by subcortical lesions *fundamental functions*, because of the way they underpin cortical processing. He proposed that "fundamental functions are crucial to survival and emerge early in phylogenetic and ontogenic development. Dysfunction of the fundamental abilities produces the cardinal features of subcortical dementia including slow information processing, dilapidation of memory and cognition, and disturbances of mood and motivation" (p. 692). Measuring these primary deficits is difficult and often their presence can only be inferred from the way in which a patient fails a test (for example, because of slowness rather than lack of knowledge), rather than from the failure itself. Measures of generalized arousal and attention are poorly developed in neuropsychology.

In contrast, cortical dementia is the result of loss of what Cummings terms *instrumental functions*. These include language, memory, perceptual, and constructional abilities. Such functions are more specific and are relatively well-localized in the cortex. Neuropsychological test development has been primarily focused on measures of instrumental functioning.

Conclusions. The distinction between instrumental and fundamental (arousal) processes is a useful way of considering the differential effects of the dementing disorders. This proposal suggests that cortical dementias like AD or Pick's disease will be characterized by amnesia, agnosias, and aphasia. Diseases like PSP, Parkinsonism, and HD will cause changes in arousal and motivation because of damage to interconnected subcortical and frontal lobe structures (Filley et al., 1989). It may be appropriate, in view of the predominance of frontal lobe dysfunctions in PSP and Parkinson's disease (Pillon et al., 1986), to elaborate the term *subcortical.* Cummings (1986) suggested that "terms such as 'frontal systems disorder' ... are acceptable alternatives to 'subcortical dementia' and might more accurately reflect the realm of anatomic, metabolic, and neurochemical dysfunctions found in this group of conditions" (p. 692).

Amyotrophic Lateral Sclerosis

There are a heterogeneous group of degenerative diseases that involve destruction of the large motor neurons of the brain. Amyotrophic lateral sclerosis (ALS) is one. The motor effects of this disease can be devastating. The usual course is a progression to death within 3 to 4 years. In the United Kingdom, ALS is often known as *motor neuron disease.*

ALS results in progressive damage to the pyramidal motor system. There is a degeneration of both the upper and lower motor neurons leading to muscle weakness, atrophy, and losts of function. In most cases there is no loss of sensation, and intellect and sphincter control are preserved. The damage is typically bilateral, and although usually rapid in progression, the disease may on occasion proceed slowly, or stabilize after a period of progression. The reported incidence is about 0.4 to 1.8/100,000 (Tandan & Bradley, 1986) and prevalence estimates range from 4 to 7/100,000. The mean age of onset lies between 55 and 60 and the disease is more common in males than females (2:1; Hudson, 1981). Death is usually preceded by progressive respiratory failure.

The cause of ALS is unknown. In about 5% to 10% of cases the disease is familial; in most of these cases the mode of inheritance is autosomal dominant. The disease also occurs amongst the Chamorros on the island of Guam at a much higher rate than elsewhere, suggesting an environmental toxin can cause the disease (Rowland, 1987). However, the majority of cases arise sporadically.

Cognitive Deficits

Clinicians working with ALS patients generally conclude that the disease does not cause dementia. Although there are cases of ALS where dementia does present, this can be attributed to the concurrent effects of DAT (Caroscio, 1986). Testing ALS patients with intellectual scales has produced mixed results. Poloni, Capitani, Mazzini, and Ceroni (1986) found no difference on the WAIS between 21 ALS subjects and 21 comparison subjects with nondementing neurological conditions. In two other studies (Gallassi, Montagna, Ciardulli, Lorusso, Mussuto, & Stracciari, 1985; Iwaski, Kinoshita, Ikeda, Takamiya, & Shiojima, 1990) intellectual deterioration in ALS patients was found when the test results were compared to those of healthy controls. It remains to be determined whether these cognitive changes occurred as a result of ALS, or whether the differences were due to the nonspecific effects of hospitalization and treatment. ALS is not generally regarded as a dementing disorder.

Psychosocial Consequences

The individual with ALS faces major problems in communication because of dysarthria, a reduction in mobility, pain from muscle atrophy, and the knowledge that the disease will progress to incapacity and death. Motor dysfunctions occur in the absence of cognitive decline and so patients retain the capacity for awareness of their disabilities.

The nature of the disorder is likely to provoke an emotional response. The onset of the disease provides an illustration of the working of psychosocial stress model outlined in the next chapter. Although ALS patients confront the disorder with courage (B. S. Gould, 1980), the debilitation caused by the disease challenges the capacity to adjust in even the most resolute individual. Luloff (1986) describes the demands and emotional sequelae of the disease as follows:

> *Loss of resources—physical, psychological, social, and economic—evokes grief and depression. As the patient anticipates experiences or experiences failures in mastering problems and challenges of everyday life, he develops feelings of helplessness... . Helplessness and failure, real or anticipated, lead to decrease of self-esteem, sense of worth, dignity and confidence. Anger becomes mixed with fear and accentuated by limitations in ability to master everyday problems, in achieving relief from tension, and in providing oneself with gratifying experiences. Anger is often directed against oneself for being damaged, helpless, and worthless, and a failure... . Anger is also directed against other persons, and at natural processes which appear to be increasingly harsh and threatening as the individual becomes progressively impaired and weaker. (p. 268)*

Although anecdotal reports of depressive and emotional reactions are common in the literature, few studies have examined emotionality in ALS systematically. Houpt, B. S. Gould, and Norris (1977) found that the incidence of depression in ALS was comparable to that in cancer patients. About 65% of the ALS patients scored in the nil-mild range on the BDI, 32.5% were moderately depressed, and 2.5% were severely depressed. Other reactions to ALS have been cited in clinical reports including denial (Tandan & Bradley, 1985), guilt (Luloff, 1986), and diminished self-esteem (Ringel, 1987). Emotional lability and inappropriateness have also been reported on occasion (Gallagher, 1989). These symptoms have been attributed to damage to brainstem nuclei. Controlled investigations of psychiatric symptoms suggest these are not a consequence of ALS (Houpt et al., 1977; Peters, Wedell, & Mulder, 1977).

Families and caregivers are likely also to feel distressed by the onset and progress of the disease. The physical deficits reduce the patient's mobility and communication, leading to greater dependence on the family for emotional and functional support. The demands involved in caring for the ALS sufferer at home can result in the caregiver feeling alone, housebound, and unappreciated. Financial concerns and preexisting family conflict may accentuate these problems (Ringel, 1987). For spousal caregivers there are many changes in role to be contemplated.

Finally it is important to recognise that many people with ALS adapt to their illness in a creative, positive, and stoical manner. In an insightful commentary, B. S. Gould (1980) described how many ALS patients project a positive aspect to the people around them. Although this may mask a deeper and realistic concern or fear, the use of some degree of denial may represent an adaptive response to the disease. In his view, the role of the counselor may be to provide a supportive environment in which this despair may be acknowledged:

> *The ALS patients in our series frequently maintained a strategy of partial denial throughout their illness, but in a most healthy fashion. Reality was not denied as much as redefined; the most distressing immutable aspects of the disease were not part of ordinary conscious functioning, and hope was maintained. Under safe conditions that allowed reflection and ventilation, however, the second-order denial was easily overridden; distressing awareness was allowed to enter the consciousness in a controlled fashion, and considerable dysphoric tension was discharged.*

Conclusions. ALS is a crippling degenerative disease resulting in profound physical disablement and minimal evidence of cognitive impairment. The psychosocial consequences stem from the loss of voluntary motor systems causing speech problems, reduced mobility, and eventually, respiratory distress. There have been few neuropsychological or psychosocial studies of ALS patients. Most of the data available on adaption to the disease are anecdotal.

Other Degenerative Diseases

Wilson's Disease

This rare disorder was introduced in an earlier section on subcortical dementia. Wilson's disease is an autosomal recessively transmitted disease, which causes brain and liver degeneration because of abnormalities of copper metabolism, and was identified by Wilson in 1912. The main neurological damage is to the basal ganglia. If untreated, Wilson's disease can cause cognitive changes consistent with subcortical dementia. The disease may appear in late childhood or early adolescence and onset is heralded by spasticity, rigidity, dysarthria, and difficulty swallowing. A chronic form, appearing in late adulthood, has also been described.

Unlike other diseases reviewed in this book the dementia of Wilson's disease may be reversed to some extent following treatment with a copper chelant (Lang, 1989). M. Rosselli, Lorenzana, A. Rosselli, and Vergara (1987) reported a case in which improvements in memory test and Wechsler Performance IQ scores followed treatment. Neuropsychological investigations of this disorder have been confined to assessments of treatment outcome.

Jakob-Creutzfeldt's Disease (JCD)

This disease is frequently classified as a degenerative disorder although the etiology is now attributed to an as yet unknown infectious agent. This followed demonstrations of successful transmission of the disease to a variety of animal species (Gibbs et al., 1968). The agent is assumed to be a slow virus, although the nature of this virus is yet to be determined. The disease is rare with an annual incidence rate of 0.5-1.0 cases per million. The disease appears to have a long latency period with the mean age of onset being about 60.

Richard Knight (1989) divided cases of JCD into three categories: Subacute, chronic, and amyotrophic. About 85% of cases fall into the subacute classification. In this instance a prodromal period characterized by vague neurological symptoms is followed by a rapidly progressive neurological collapse. Dementia is an invariable and early symptom. Speech is lost early, motor disturbances are profound, and progressive visual disturbance may result in cortical blindness. The median duration of the disease is about 4 months from the onset of dementia. The chronic form runs its course over about a 2-year period and comprises some 8% of cases (P. Brown, Rodgers-Johnston, Cathala, Gibbs, & Gajdusek, 1984). The amyotrophic form accounts for 5% of cases and presents as similar to ALS but with clear evidence of dementia.

Atrophy is usually most pronounced in the frontal and occipital cortex of the cerebrum, the brain stem, and the grey matter of the cerebellum. The pattern of dementia is similar to that seen in AD. Formal cognitive assessments have not been reported. The psychosocial implications of the disease are determined largely by its rapid progression and severe disability. Management is limited to nursing care, with precautions to prevent accidental transmission of the disease being important.

Pick's Disease

First described in 1892 by Arnold Pick, this rare degenerative disorder of unknown etiology is classed as a cortical dementia. It is characterized by gross atrophy, usually regarded as relatively circumscribed, of the grey matter of the frontal and temporal lobes. In practice, this disorder is difficult to distinguish from Alzheimer's disease and the presence of the disease can usually only be established by postmortem examination. One clinical feature of the disease that may distinguish it from Alzheimer's disease is the early development of Kluver-Bucy syndrome. This syndrome was first described in monkeys who evidence gross behavioral changes after surgical ablation of the temporal lobes. In patients with Pick's disease, profound damage to the temporal lobes results in hyperorality (a propensity to put into the mouth inappropriate objects such as flowers, fabrics, burning matches, etc), hypersexuality, and emotional changes, in particular, uncharacteristic placidity. On histological examination degenerate neurons are observed containing large dense inclusions known as Pick's bodies. The course and staging of the disease, and consequent neuropsychological changes and psychosocial consequences are similar to those seen in AD.

Conclusions

In this chapter, a number of degenerative diseases have been surveyed that have a relatively low incidence and have not been investigated extensively by neuropsychologists. Studies with people who have progressive supranuclear palsy have given rise to one major issue that has been discussed in the literature of the past 15 years: the possibility of a distinction between cortical and subcortical dementia. Cummings's (1986) division of cognitive processes into two classes, *instrumental* (impaired in cortical dementias) and *fundamental* (compromised in subcortical dementia), provides a useful way of organizing much of the research in this area. Comparisons between patient samples with cortical and subcortical dementia have also served to highlight some of the difficulties inherent in comparing groups with different disease on neuropsychological tests. It

is perhaps useful to end this chapter by drawing attention to the formida-
ble methodological obstacles involved in making valid comparisons of the
performance of different patient groups.

The primary problem is in matching groups on all the variables that
are not the primary target of the investigation. As we have seen in the
preceding chapters, different degenerative diseases have different patterns of onset, progression, and symptom expression. Unselected groups
of patients are likely to be unmatched on variables such as age, length of
disease, and psychiatric comorbidity (e.g., Filley et al., 1989). On the
other hand, matching groups for these variables is likely to lead to an
unrepresentative or restricted range of subjects. Matching groups for
severity of impairment on extraneous neuropsychological or cognitive
variables can also present problems. For example, comparing two
groups of Parkinson's and Alzheimer's disease patients on a measure
such as speed of information processing, necessitates some account being
taken of severity of dementia. Given that dementia is less severe and less
prevalent in PD than in DAT, matching samples for the extent of their
intellect decline is something of a challenge. This may result in the
selection of patients who are older, more physically impaired, and unrepresentative of PD patients as a whole. Making statistical adjustments
using covariance and related procedures to allow for differences between
groups on extraneous variables is seldom satisfactory, particularly when
sample sizes are relatively small.

These concluding comments are not intended to diminish the importance of comparative neuropsychological studies with patients who have
degenerative brain diseases. This work has an important place in the
development of an understanding of specific deficits arising from particular disorders. Nevertheless, constituting valid samples for comparison is
a difficult business, usually involving some methodological compromises,
and the conclusions from such studies need to be treated circumspectly.

PART 3

PSYCHOSOCIAL ASPECTS

Chapter 9

CAREGIVER BURDEN

*Few other disorders place so much stress on families as demen-
tia. Caregivers routinely report stress-related symptoms such
as anxiety, depression, or feelings of fatigue. They are often
angry and resentful, feel guilty about not doing enough, even
though they may spend 24 hours a day with the patient. The
stresses they experience have many sources. Often they must
take over tasks that the patient can no longer do, such as
housekeeping or dressing the patient. They must keep vigilant
watch over the patient; and often they must cope with the patient's specific behavioral disturbances, such as wandering
around or not sleeping at night. Moreover caregivers often
experience a great sense of personal and psychological loss as
they see their relative gradually decline. Often the care they
must provide demands all their time. (S. H. Zarit, Orr, &
J. M. Zarit, 1985, p. 69)*

There can be few more demanding occupations than caring for a
person with dementia; indeed S. H. Zarit et al. (1985) called the families
of patients with dementing disorders the "hidden victims" of the disease.
Estimates of the prevalence of DAT amongst people over the age of 65
ranges from about 2 to 6 cases per 100 population. Because prevalence
increases with age, the number of cases is steadily increasing as the
proportion of people in developed countries surviving to later life increases. It has been estimated that the number of people in the United
States over the age of 65 will double between 1985 and 2020. Based on
current prevalence estimates there were perhaps 1.35 million persons
with Alzheimer's disease in the United States in 1985; to this could be
added the significant percentage of people with other dementing illnesses,
particularly vascular dementia. The number of cases of dementia can be
expected to at least double by the year 2020. For each of these people
there will need to be institutional support and informal family care. It is
little wonder that AD has been described as the coming silent epidemic
(e.g., Henderson, 1983). In addition to the problem of the increasing
number of elderly people and cases of dementia, demographic trends
predict that there will be proportionately fewer younger productive
workers supporting elders in retirement. This factor will also create the

need for significant social readjustment. One of the major implications of all these population trends has to be the increased pressure of the formal and informal services caring for the demented.

In the United States in 1990 the number of persons over the age of 65 was approximately 30 million. Aging cohorts from the postwar baby boom mean that the numbers of the elderly will continue to expand. Amongst that 30 million, the prevalence of some form of dementia could be estimated to be about 1.5 to 2.1 million (5%-7%; S. H. Zarit et al., 1985). Each of these people is likely to have two or three family members involved at some level in their care and support. Thus the lives of about 5 to 8 million Americans are currently affected one way or another by dementia.

Who Are the Caregivers?

Cantor (1983) conducted a survey in New York of 111 people caring for the "marginal income frail elderly" in the community. Some 50% of the care-receivers lived alone, a further third lived with a spouse, and 14% with a relative or friend; all were rated as suffering from some degree of impairment. A third of the caregivers were spouses, 36% were children, 19% other relatives, and 12% were friends or neighbors. Most of the spouses were also elderly, at least half over the age of 75, and 84% rated their own health as impaired. Half of the spouses were male and half female. A total of 75% of the children caregivers were married daughters (60% of whom were in paid employment). Although their income was generally higher than that of spouse caregivers, 75% of the children reported financial stress as a consequence of caring for their own families as well as their parents. The other relatives involved in care were mostly elderly and resembled the demographic profile of the spouses. The 13 friends and neighbors involved in care were predominantly women (92.3%) living near the care-receiver, and their ages ranged from 20 to 75.

In the Cantor survey, about 70% of all caregivers reported getting along well with their care-receivers. However, on a day-to-day basis, closeness was inversely related to satisfaction with the relationship: Over 90% of the neighbors reported getting on well with the care-receiver, as opposed to 60% of the spouses and 53% of the children. The children in particular felt alienated from their frail parents. Only 48% reported that they understood their impaired parent well, and only 28% felt they were understood by their parents. The results also suggested that caregivers were required to make substantial changes to their lives to accommodate the disabilities of the person for which they were caring. The greatest impact was on the spouses, who lived at home with their impaired partner. Many of the husbands, for example, were involved in housework, nursing care, and shopping for the first time in their lives. Caregiver children were the next most affected. They reported that caregiving reduced free time and vacations, and opportunities to socialize with friends. Overall, the emotional stress of constant care was regarded by caregivers as more burdening than the financial strain; in general, the closer the bond between the caregiver and the recipient, the greater the stress.

Similar results were found with a larger and more representative sample of 1924 caregivers (Stone, Cafferata, & Sangl, 1987). Stone et al. (1987) found that the majority of informal caregivers were women and 35% of the total caregiver sample were themselves over the age of 65. They drew attention to the demands placed on caregivers and the implication of this for future trends in employment patterns:

> *A substantial proportion of caregivers were juggling familial and employment responsibilities, which placed competing demands on them. These role conflicts may represent an even greater challenge to future cohorts of caregivers. Due to longer life expectancy and delayed childbearing, an increasing proportion of women will be in the position of providing care to both children under the age of 18 as well as elderly parents. These social trends, coupled with the projected increase in labor force participation rates among older women, imply that work and family obligations may conflict with care giving responsibilities to a greater extent than they do today. (p. 625)*

From both these surveys it is clear that without informal care, a greater reliance on costly institutional services would be necessary. Appropriate support for spouse and child caregivers serves to increase the likelihood that this care can continue. Cantor has some excellent suggestions about how support might be provided at a community level. Providing minimal financial support for inhouse or respite services is one solution. Another is to recognize that flexible job schedules would greatly help employed children caregivers. Just as employers can make allowance for childcare demands, so they could make workplace adjustments to help caregivers of the elderly. Demand for this is likely to increase in the future. Rationalising the bureaucratic systems involved in obtaining help and providing education in the availability of resources for caregivers would also help. Support and education for male spouses thrust into a primary caregiving role for the first time could be of value. Within the community, voluntary agencies, church groups, and other neighborhood support organizations can be encouraged to provide time-limited practical assistance and respite services for individual cases. The surveys of caregivers, however, stress that each caregiver-recipient dyad has particular needs, strengths, and weaknesses. Assessments need to take account of this, and management programs need to be constructed to mobilize to meet particular needs.

Symptoms as Stressors for Caregivers

Much of the discussion in the previous section focused on the impaired elderly, not all of whom are dementing. Nevertheless, the profile of people caring for AD sufferers is likely to be the same as for any other group of impaired elderly. The care of AD patients does, however, present some particular stressors. Although the central feature of AD is cognitive incapacity and memory problems, there are also a variety of behavioral, emotional, and social changes that the dementing Alzheimer patient displays that are at least as, if not more, distressing for caregivers (Diemling & Bass, 1986; Petry, Cummings, Hill & Shapira, 1988; Rabins, Mace, & Lucas, 1982; Swearer et al., 1988). Rabins et al. (1982) surveyed the primary caregivers of 55 persons with irreversible dementia, 60% of whom had clinical diagnoses of AD. The percentage of caregivers reporting individual behaviors to be a problem is listed in Table 9.1. This table gives a perspective on the incidence of the various problems AD caregivers confront. The authors also asked families to nominate the most serious problem they faced. The rank order that emerged from this exercise was somewhat different to that listed in Table 9.1. The most serious problems, expressed as a percentage of the number of times the problems were actually reported as occurring were, in rank order: physical violence, memory disturbance, catastrophic reactions, hitting, making accusations, and suspiciousness. Thus, although "hitting" was reported by only 33% of the respondents, it was rated by 50% of these as a serious problem.

A similar picture of the problems of caring for AD patient was described by Chenoweth and Spencer (1986). Members of the Minnesota Chapter of ADRDA were asked to respond to the question "What are the major problems you and your family face in caring for your relative?" The fact that the patient required total physical care and/or constant supervision was the most common problem mentioned. The other problems mentioned were, in rank order: strain on the physical or emotional health of the caregiver, caregiver unable to get away from home, concern about financial costs of care, patient wandering, patient incontinent, feeding or eating difficulties, patient's driving unsafe, patient's mood swings, and patient being unsafe when alone. M. P. Quayhagen and M. Quayhagen (1988) found repetitive questions, "embarrassing things,"

difficulty bathing, and difficulty handling money were particularly stressful by the caregivers. Inappropriate sexual behavior was a problem for
more caregivers in this study than in the survey reported by Rabins et al.
(1982).

Table 9.1:   Behavior Problems of Patients Cited by Families

Behavior	Occurrence (%)	Problem (%)
Memory disturbance	100	93
Catastrophic emotional reactions	87	89
Demanding or critical behavior	71	73
Night waking	69	59
Hiding things	69	71
Communication problems	68	74
Suspiciousness	63	79
Making accusations	60	82
Meals	60	55
Daytime wandering	59	70
Bathing	53	74
Hallucinations	49	42
Delusions	47	83
Physical violence	47	94
Incontinence	47	86
Cooking	33	44
Hitting	32	81
Driving	20	8
Smoking	11	4
Inappropriate sexual behavior	2	0

Note. From The Impact of Dementia on the Family by P. V. Rabins et al.,
1982. *JAMA, 248,* pp. 333-335. Copyright (c), 1982, American Medical
Association. Reprinted by permission.

There is also evidence that some behavioral disturbances increase in
likelihood as the disease progresses, whereas others are relatively stable.
Teri, Larson, and Reifler (1988) related occurrence of behavioral problems to scores on the MMSE and the Blessed Dementia Rating Scale.

They found that incontinence, hygiene problems, agitation, and wandering increased in frequency of occurrence as dementia became more profound. The incidence of hallucinations, falling, suspiciousness, and restlessness remained independent of the disease severity. They suggested that problems not associated with severity need not be routinely incorporated into intervention programs.

Another difficulty that caregivers often face is lack of information about Alzheimer's disease, especially at the time when the disease is first diagnosed. Admittedly, this can be a time of stress and the information physicians give may not be recalled or appreciated later. However, in the Chenoweth and Spencer (1986) study, replying to a question concerning what the family were told initially about the disease, the response was "nothing can be done, hopeless" in 54% of the cases, a factual adequate explanation of AD of 28% of the cases, no information or explanation, 20%, and advice for coping with behavior problems or stress, in 16% of the cases. Chenoweth and Spencer noted that caregivers often had difficulty in communicating with their physicians: "What they (the caregivers) did report was difficulty articulating subtle changes ... so that in many families, dementia was undetected for several years. Moreover, some families had a problem convincing the physician that something was wrong even when they were certain that the changes were serious" (p. 269).

The Consequences of Caregiving

The outcome of the behavioral and cognitive changes in the AD patient can be a sense of burden, depression, and reduced wellbeing in caregivers. The sheer pressure of the demands made on a caregiver can lead to physical illhealth, emotional distress, and social isolation. The consequences of being a caregiver for a demented patient have been documented in several studies. Rabins et al. (1982) found that the most common problems amongst their group of 55 caregivers were chronic fatigue, anger, and depression. A total of 87% of the respondents reported these effects as the consequence of the responsibility of care. Family conflict (56%), loss of friends and hobbies, no time for self (55%), worry that caregiver would become ill (31%), difficulty assuming new roles and responsibilities (29%), and guilt (25%) were the other major difficulties reported. The finding that caregiving places strains on the caregivers' own intimate relationships has been shown in other studies. For example, Creasey, Myers, Epperson, and J. Taylor (1990) found that wives with an Alzheimer parent perceived themselves as having a more negative relationship with their husbands than did wives with healthy parents.

The best known measure of subjective burden is S. H. Zarit, Reever, and Bach-Peterson's (1980) Burden Interview. A 22-item version of this scale is reproduced in S. H. Zarit et al. (1985). Some representative items are listed in Table 9.2; each item is rated on a 5-point scale from 0 (never) to 4 (nearly always). The Caregiver Strain Index (Robinson, 1983) is a similar measure that consists of 13 items to which the respondent answers yes or no. The 13 domains assessed provide a good summary of the stressors resulting from involvement in care (Table 9.3).

Table 9.2:   Sample Items from the Burden Interview
(S. H. Zarit et al., 1985)

---

1. Do you feel that your relative asks for more help than she/he needs?

4. Do you ever feel embarrassed over your relative's behavior?

8. Do you feel your relative is dependent on you?

12. Do you feel your social life has suffered because you are caring for relative?

15. Do you feel that you don't have enough money to care for your relative, in addition to all your other expenses?

20. Do you feel you should be doing more for your relative?

Depression is another consequence of strain on caregivers (Haley, E. G. Levine, S. L. Brown, & Bartolucci, 1987). Sometimes the degree of depression is such that the caregiver requires hospitalization:

A 73 year old homemaker had experienced extreme initial insomnia and a 20 lb weight loss since her family physician informed her that her husband had Alzheimer's disease several months earlier. She berated herself for not having the energy or "drive" to take better care of her husband, and she claimed there were no other family members to help her. She was quite hesitant to follow recommendation for both antidepressants and psychotherapy, and four months later she was hospitalized. (L. S. Goldman & Luchins, 1984)

Two studies have shown that depression levels in AD caregivers are predicted by whether caregivers feel the patients' behaviors are controllable, and whether they attribute upsetting events to internal or external causes. The tendency to have self-blaming, or internal attributions has been shown to be associated with higher levels of depression (Coppel, Burton, Becker, & Fiore, 1987; Pagel, Becker, & Coppel, 1985). This implies that counseling work with caregivers can usefully focus on education about appropriate external casual attributions for the behaviors of people with AD and that fostering a sense of control will reduce the possibility of depression.

Table 9.3:   The Caregiver Strain Index : List of Stressors and Consequences Involved in Caring for an AD Relative (Robinson, 1983)

Sleep disturbance	Emotional adjustments
Inconvenience	Patient's upsetting behavior
Physical and mental strain	Distressing changes in patient's
Problems of family adjustment	behavior
Changes in personal plans	Work-related adjustments
Life confined and restricted	Financial strain
	Feeling overwhelmed

Another personal response to caregiving is a sense of frustration or anger. Anthony-Bergstone, S. H. Zarit, and Gatz (1988) administered the Brief Symptom Inventory to 184 caregivers of demented patients. This measure includes nine subscales assessing a variety of emotional re sponses: Somatization, Obsessive-Compulsive, Interpersonal Sensitivity, Depression, Paranoid Ideation, Psychoticism, Hostility, Anxiety, and Phobic Anxiety. Compared to the scale norms, it was on the Hostility subscale that caregivers showed the highest and most consistent elevations. The women in the sample were also prone to significantly raised anxiety, hostility, and obsessive-compulsive scores. It was the Anxiety and Hostility Scale scores that were found to be most highly correlated with scores on the Zarit Burden Interview. A sense of hostility and resentment may be an important feature of the caregiver's response, and one not often considered by researchers as an important personal consequence of burden.

Although the dimensions of burden amongst caregivers of DAT patients have been extensively researched, there has been little interest in the burden experienced by caregivers of other groups of patients. One exception is a study (Dura, Haywood-Niler, & Kiecolt-Glaser, 1990) in which spousal caregivers of demented Alzheimer and Parkinson patients were compared. The two groups were comparable with respect to length of time they had been providing assistance, however the DAT caregivers were providing far more daily hours of assistance than the PD carers. It was apparent that the degree of dementia and consequent disability was far greater in the DAT group than the Parkinson patient. However, despite this, the DAT and PD dementia caregivers did not differ on measures of personal distress, although both groups were more distressed than a matched control group. Once again "level of spouses' impairment and extent of problem behaviours had negligible effects on caregiver distress, even though PD with dementia victims likely had much more limited mobility" (p. 336). The findings from the Dura et al. (1990) study suggest that results concerning DAT caregivers can be generalized to PD caregivers who have a moderate degree of dementia. Little is known about burden amongst caregivers of those Parkinson patients who have no overt signs of dementia.

A Model of Stress in Caregivers

S. H. Zarit et al. (1980) were amongst the first to note with some surprise that the level of perceived burden in caregivers was not correlated with the severity of the behavior problems presented by the demented person. In fact, it was the reduced amount of support (the number of visitors to the house) that was most strongly related to burden. These results, which have been confirmed in other studies, provide clear evidence for the fact that burden level is not simply a matter of the severity of a stressor; the effect is moderated by the individual characteristics of the caregiver. This is not to deny, however, that burden and depression may be predicted to some extent by disease severity. Pruchno and Resch (1989b) found that there is a relationship between caregiver burden and the frequency of an impaired spouse's amnesic, asocial, and disoriented behavior. They found a linear relationship between the stress experienced by the caregiver and the frequency of asocial or disoriented behaviors, and a *nonlinear* relationship between occurrence of forgetfulness and caregiver stress. Pruchno and Resch argued that:

Forgetful behaviors increase linearly as Alzheimer's disease
progresses. Cognitive symptoms develop as the illness
progresses. Mild and moderate levels of forgetful behavior are
especially burdensome for caregivers who must adapt to the
changes in their spouses... . When forgetful behaviors become
more severe, the tasks of caregiving are much different... . As
the patient becomes more and more forgetful, eventually becom-
ing vegetative, the role of the caregiver becomes one of tending
to basic needs. (p. S181)

Pruchno and Resch's (1989b) results suggest that stressors can change over time and a linear increase in severity of symptoms does not necessarily result in a matching increase in burden. The possibility that different stressors emerge at different stages of the disease was investigated by Haley and Pardo (1989). They found that higher-level instrumental skills are affected early in the disease, and basic adaptive functioning skills did not cause problems until the disease progressed. Some stressors actually declined in frequency, for example, potentially dangerous behavior declined in incidence as time passed and the dementia became more pronounced. In the discussions that follow it is important to remain aware that stressor severity fluctuates considerably as the disease develops.

Many of the possible stressors for caregivers have already been reviewed. In essence, they comprise the severe cognitive impairments, behavioral changes, and reduced adaptive functioning displayed by the dementing patient. The caregiver's response to these stressors will vary depending on how much of a strain they perceive them to be, how well they can cope with them, and the amount of external social support they receive. Another important factor may be the quality of the premorbid relationship between the caregiver and the care-receiver (L. W. Morris, R. G. Morris, & Britton, 1988). It is important to take account not only of the objective severity of stressors, but also to ask caregivers to provide their subjective appraisal of particular stressors. From the time of the earliest research into life-change stress it has been apparent that there are individual differences in the appreciation of stress. Divorce can be a negative experience for some people and the beginning of a new and better future for others. In their study, Haley et al. (1987) asked caregivers to rate each potential stressor both for degree of stress it provoked and for the confidence they felt in handling it (a measure of perceived self-efficacy).

The adequacy of caregivers' coping response is important in predicting outcome (M. P. Quayhagen & M. Quayhagen, 1988). It is possible that caregivers' ability to cope with problems increases as they become more experienced in handling the problems that arise. S. H. Zarit, Todd, and J. Zarit (1986) found that over a 2-year follow-up period caregivers' tolerance of problems improved and caregivers stated "that they had learned to manage problems more effectively or simply did not let problems bother them any more" (p. 265). S. H. Zarit et al. discovered that "many of those providing home care in this sample genuinely seemed to have established a daily routine that while not without its stresses, also was not excessively demanding or burdensome" (p. 265). There are a variety of ways of assessing caregiver coping. A list of possible coping responses is provided by the Health and Daily Living Form (Billings & Moos, 1984). This provides a list of possible problem-solving strategies and asks subjects to describe how frequently they use each one. Sample items include "Tried to find out more about the situation" and "Made a plan of action and tried to stick to it." The use of this measure is illustrated by Haley et al. (1987).

Social support has been shown to be an important factor in buffering caregivers against the effects of stress in a variety of situations (e.g., Aronson, G. Levin, & Lipkowitz, 1984; Heller, Swindle, & Dusenbury, 1986; Lehman, Ellard, & Wortman, 1986). In the present context, social support refers to external coping assistance (Thoits, 1986). In S. H. Zarit et al.'s (1980) study, the factor that was most predictive of burden was the number of family visits the caregiver received. This correlated -.48 with burden, and the magnitude of this association stands in contrast to the other possible predictors assessed: Duration of illness ($r = -.06$), mental status ($r = .02$), memory problems ($r = .14$), behavior problems ($r = -.07$), physical adaptive functioning, for example, dressing and walking ($r = -.06$), and instrumental adaptive functioning ($r = -.20$). Zarit et al. concluded:

> *Clearly, such things as severe memory loss and the problems associated with it are distressing to family members, but the ability of caregivers to cope with the situation may depend on the other supports available to them. No information was elicited on what visitors were doing or the quality of the visits, which undoubtedly affect the degree of relief caregivers receive. Nonetheless, the sheer quantity of visits from other family members was important. (p. 653)*

The finding that the quantity of relationships is predictive of health and wellbeing has been reported by numerous researchers, dating back to Durkheim's (1951) observation that married people were less likely to commit suicide. For example, Berkman and Syme (1982) found that people with few close relationships are at a greater risk of mortality from all causes. Social network measures typically focus on the social relationships found to be most important for health-related outcomes—marital status, number and frequency of contacts with friends and relatives, church attendance, and participation in other social or voluntary group activities (House, Robbins, & Metzner, 1982). Assessing the social network of elderly caregivers is an important aspect of the full assessment of burden. Haley et al. (1987), for example, recorded the number of friends each caregiver had, and how many people they knew who could be called on in times of need. The number of times the caregiver has been out to make visits or take part in social, church, or family activities also gives an idea of the caregiver's degree of social isolation.

However, it is important to do more than rely simply on the number of social contacts caregivers have as an indication of degree of social support: It may be far more important to know how satisfied the caregiver is with the support available (Heller, 1979). Several researchers have reported that it is the extent to which need for support is perceived to be met that is most important in reducing morbidity (e.g., Procidano & Heller, 1979). This process requires further investigation, particularly with respect to determining the kind of social assistance caregivers of dementia patients find useful. For example, Gottleib (1978) looked at particular ways in which single mothers had found other people to be supportive. He found that various behaviors not usually identified as supportive by researchers, such as being accompanied when facing a stressful situation or modeling appropriate childcare skills, were regarded as especially helpful by the women. It would be useful to know what kind of helping makes a difference before building programs to support caregivers.

The importance of perception of social support is illustrated by a study carried out by George and Gwyther (1986). They assessed wellbeing in terms of physical and mental health, financial resources, and social participation in 510 caregivers of dementing patients involved in the Duke University Family Support Program. Compared to data from relevant normative samples, the caregiver group showed a reduced level of wellbeing on most of the indicators used. Most striking was the greater number of stress symptoms amongst the caregiver group and the fact that they spent less time relaxing or involved in hobbies. George and Gwyther also asked the caregivers whether or not they felt a need for more social support. When the respondents were divided into those who responded yes (59%) and those who responded no (41%) to this question, it was clear that perception of social support was closely related to wellbeing. For example, there were significant differences between the two groups on the mental health measures used; those people who felt they needed more social support were more depressed, stressed, and dissatisfied with their lives, and more likely to be prescribed psychoactive medication. Those people who did not feel the need for more support had a greater involvement in social activities, made more visits, and spent more time in church, hobby, and club activities or just relaxing. Social networks and community involvement are obvious buffers against burden and feelings of isolation.

In Fig. 9.1 a simple model of stress based on the work of Lazarus and Folkman (1984) is presented to help clarify the relationship between stressor and caregiver burden. This stress model implies that there will be individual differences in the response to stress that are not predicted by the actual severity of the stressors. S. H. Zarit et al's. (1980) finding that level of dementia does not predict subjective burden amongst caregivers has been replicated in several studies (Fitting, Rabins, Lucas, & Eastham, 1986; Gilhooly, 1984; Novak & Guest, 1989; S. H. Zarit, Todd, & Zarit, 1986). One illustration of the subjective effects of stressors is that wives involved in primary caregiving usually report higher

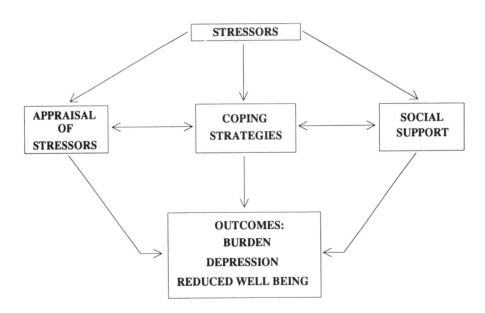

Figure 9.1. A model of stress response in the caregivers of demented patients.

mean levels of burden than do husbands (Fitting et al., 1986; S. H. Zarit et al., 1986). This is particularly true during the early stages of the disease process (S. H. Zarit et al., 1986). This seems paradoxical because studies of women suggest that they are more likely to develop close relationships with other people in their social network and therefore might be expected to have available stronger social support than men. Similarly, women put more value on relationships and have been, rightly or wrongly, traditionally more deeply involved in caregiving than men. It is apparent, for example, that it is more common to find middle-aged women caring for a dementing parent.

These factors suggest that women should do better than men when it comes to coping with the demands of caregiving. And yet it is women who more commonly experience the negative effects of the stresses involved. Fitting et al. (1986) found that wives who were caregiving were more likely to be depressed than husbands, and the men were more likely to report that their relationship with their partner had actually improved after they became responsible for the care of their wives. Part of the reason for this may be that many women look forward to relief from the role of caring in their middle and late age years. They may feel that their life has been devoted to providing care and feel a sense of resentment at not being able to escape. In contrast, Pruchno and Resch (1989a) found, for example, that husbands often expressed a positive attitude toward caregiving:

> *Informal comments expressed by respondents may help to explain these results. Husbands, more than wives, were likely to utter comments such as, "She took care of me when I was ill—now it's my turn to take care of her," or, "She did everything for our family, now it's my turn to help." Husbands expressed a greater sense than did wife caregivers that the care they were currently providing to their spouses was due to them. (p. 163)*

Haley et al. (1987) tested the significance of the components of the model of stress represented in Fig. 9.1 with a sample of 54 caregivers. They were interested in the prediction of caregiver outcome, measured in terms of depression, life satisfaction, and self-reported health. The objective level of the stressor (the severity of the care-receiver's dementia) was found to have no direct impact on the caregiver's wellbeing. Caregivers' appraisal of the stressors, however, was predictive of depression; those caregivers who rated more likely to report being depressed. Overall life satisfaction was predicted by subjective appraisal of stressors (as with depression) and also by amount of social support and activity. Coping responses and social support levels were the best predictors of self-rated health problems. Thus, the regression analyses Haley et al. computed showed that different outcomes were predicted by different factors. Appraisal was related to depression; social support and appraisal predicted life satisfaction; and coping and social support predicted health ratings. This study provides important support for a multivariate approach to understanding the effects and outcomes of stressors. In particular this model provides an impetus for designing broad-based interventions for caregivers. If burden and stress outcomes are largely determined by levels of support, coping mechanisms, and appraisal, then management techniques that focus on strengthening and developing caregivers' skills, resources, and confidence are likely to be beneficial. This proposition is explored in the next section.

Interventions for Caregivers

Institutional treatment of the impaired elderly is enormously expensive for both the taxpayer and the families involved. The quality of stimulation provided for nursing home residents can also vary in quality. Feier and Leight (1981) discussed the way that the elderly in residential homes can lapse into social isolation and may lose their ability to communicate both with the staff and each other. It can happen that residents gradually withdraw and become increasingly less involved and communicative. Weinstock and Bennett (1971) found that after the initial stimulation provided by arriving in a new environment, interest and motivation decline markedly, resulting in a concurrent reduction in cognitive performance. Staff have to make a conscious effort to plan activities for residents that involve them in constructive and meaningful programs that will serve to extend and develop their residual capabilities. Often, however, residents receive little more than custodial care. It is therefore in everyone's interests, including the patients themselves, that the impaired and demented elderly are maintained in their home environment, and have the stimulation of life in the community, for as long as feasible.

One of the most important implications of the preceding section is rooted in the fact that caregiver burden is largely independent of the recipient's objective level of disturbance. This means that an important target of service programs aimed at keeping the patient out of the nursing home must be on the caregiver. This conclusion is reinforced by a study by L. J. Brown, Potter, and Foster (1990). They analysed data from 109 people assessed at a geriatric assessment center at the University of Nebraska, to determine the factors most predictive of entry to nursing home care. Although their focus was not only on DAT patients, the average MMSE score of their sample was about 20. In a series of regression analyses, they found that burden, as measured by Zarit's Burden Interview, was strongly associated with the decision to make a nursing home placement. MMSE scores and behavior problems on the other hand were not associated with the decision. Residential placement is therefore not a simple consequence of the patient's disablement, but is more likely to reflect the family's success at coping. This in turn means that the orientation of formal services in the community toward providing interventions that reduce caregiver burden are likely to reduce dependence on expensive institutional care.

As S. H. Zarit (1989) asserted, the fact that caregiving is stressful is beyond doubt. Research emphasis is now turning toward testing stress-reducing interventions. Although a precise model of how various factors interact to produce stress awaits large-scale multivariate longitudinal research, enough evidence has now accumulated to justify such interventions. There is an expanding literature providing accounts of the implementation of such programs and more recently, some controlled trials of their efficiency. Some of this work is described later.

Content of Caregiver Programs

The content of supportive programs for caregivers varies greatly. Some interventions provide little more than written educational material; others extend to organized peer support within the group to help caregivers work through their feelings of inadequacy, isolation, and guilt. Listed in Table 9.4 are some of the common elements of various intervention programs aimed at enhancing caregiver wellbeing.

Education. Most support groups organized by professionals or organizations such as ADRDA emphasise the importance of understanding as much as possible about the disease and its effects. One of the earliest programs for families with demented relatives was set up at the Isabella Geriatric Centre in New York City. This project was described by Safford (1980). The Isabella program involved six 2-hour sessions in which education was combined with an opportunity for individual participants to discuss their personal care-related problems. The education component comprised description of the physical causes of dementia and their behavioral consequences. Participants were also educated in practical solutions to some of the problems confronting caregivers. For those families with relatives in nursing homes, education about the nature of institutions and to relating constructively to staff was an important focus.

Table 9.4: **Content and Processes Involved in Intervention Programs Designed to Reduce Caregiver Burden**

Strategy	Representative Studies
Education in the nature of the disease, practical approaches to care, and the meaning of symptoms	N. M. Clark & Rakowski, 1983; Haley et al., 1987; Kahan et al., 1985; Mohide et al., 1990; Safford, 1980; Winogrond et al., 1987; S. H. Zarit et al., 1985
Coping with declining family organization	Aronson et al., 1984
Constructing nonfamilial support networks	Aronson et al., 1984; Goodman & Pynoos, 1988; Kahan et al., 1985
Emotional support; expression of feelings	N. M. Clark & Rakowski, 1983; Lazarus et al., 1981; Winogrond et al. 1987; S. H. Zarit et al., 1985
Teaching and discussing practical management procedures	Aronson et al., 1984; Chiverton & Caine, 1989; Kahan et al., 1985
Teaching problem-solving skills	Haley et al., 1987; N. B. Levine et al., 1983; S. H. Zarit et al., 1985
Assertiveness training	N. B. Levine et al., 1983
Cognitive restructuring; coping self-statements	N. B. Levine et al., 1983
Stress reduction/inoculation, relaxation	Kahan et al., 1985; N. B. Levine et al., 1983
Dealing with institutions and making visits constructive	Chiverton & Caine, 1989; Safford, 1980
Respite services	Lawton et al., 1989; Mohide et al., 1990

Subsequent interventions involving education for caregivers have adopted a similar approach. Formal lecture/discussion sessions are often supplemented with reading material Caregivers are often given Mace and Rabins's (1981) book *The 36 Hour Day* to read at home. Education programs typically provide information about the cognitive and behavioral symptoms of the disease, the stages of deterioration, and the physical brain changes associated with dementia. Caregivers often find it reassuring to learn that there is a physical basis to the disease and the behavioral and personality changes they are seeing are not just the product of the patient's willfulness.

S. H. Zarit et al. (1985) emphasized the importance of educating families about the reasons why symptoms occur. Many of the consequences of a profound dementia result in behaviors that are irritating and difficult to deal with. A good example is repetitive questioning. Some dementing patients will ask the same question over and over and over again. It is easy to misinterpret this as attention-seeking behavior or a deliberate attempt to be provocative. Learning that the repetition is a consequence of the patient's memory loss and beyond their control can lead to a more constructive response on the part of the caregiver. Similarly it can help to know that denial of cognitive deficits is common. Some demented people literally cannot remember that they cannot remember; denial is not simply a defence against facing up to the truth. Fluctuations in the ability to remember seem to occur naturally in amnesics; these day-to-day changes in memory performance are not a sign that patients remember only those things they want to. Disinhibition can also create problems for caregivers. People who were formerly controlled and refined sometimes become gross and inappropriate in their behavior. This is a common feature of any form of brain injury, and is not something the patient does maliciously to provoke embarrassment. Paranoid accusations are sometimes a consequence of amnesia. S. H. Zarit et al. (1985) described a case of a man whose wife repetitively asked him about a bank account, which had been closed several years previously. When she continually appeared to ignore his answer, and repeated the questions, he became upset at her implied accusations. When the husband realized that her repetitive questions were a consequence of her sense of insecurity, which in turn resulted from her amnesia, it allowed him to respond more directly to her questions. Reassuring her that they had enough money reduced the wife's anxiety; understanding the nature of her problems alleviated his distress.

Stress Inoculation. One of the best-known cognitive-behavioral approaches to handling anticipated stress and anxiety is stress inoculation. Some of the elements of this procedure have been used to help caregivers deal with the unexpected stresses that arise when providing care. Stress inoculation is designed to help people deal with stressful situations by enhancing their self-control skills. The technique has three important components. First, there is the education of the client in the idea that cognitive self-statements have a role in creating tension. The emphasis is on teaching clients that these self-statements can be modified and the result is a reduction in feelings of stress and anxiety. The second involves the teaching of a relaxation coping response and practicing the skill of creating appropriate coping self-statements. This latter process requires the patient to rehearse coping self-statements that are relevant to overcoming panic, anxiety, or the sense of being out of control. Such self-statements might be: "Just think about what you can do about it. That's better than getting anxious" when anticipating a stressor, or "One step at a time: You can handle this" when confronted with the stress provoking situation. The third component involves presenting actual stressful situations either in imagination or *in vivo* and encouraging clients to practice applying the procedures they have acquired.

Stress inoculation and related procedures are most likely to be helpful with caregivers who have strong emotional reactions to stressful situations or who have difficulty handling aggression, feelings of anger, or social embarrassment. The use of stress management and self-talk (or cognitive restructuring) procedures with caregivers is described in two reports by Levine, Gendron, and colleagues (Gendron et al., 1986; N. B. Levine, Dastoor, & Gendron, 1983) in which they outline a program they labeled Supporter Endurance Training. Gendron et al. illustrated the use of self-statements with reference to handling an unexpected episode of incontinence. Negative and angry self-statements such as "I knew this would happen just before the visitors arrived" might be replaced by a more constructive thought: "So what if everything isn't ready. It'll just make things a little more informal and relaxed." N. B. Levine et al. (1983) found that positive coping skills contributed to a greater tolerance of patient behavior problems and it was feasible to train caregivers in these procedures.

Problem-Solving. Teaching clients to apply a consistent and rational problem-solving strategy to the difficulties encountered in everyday living is one of the most useful therapy techniques available to clinicians. S. H. Zarit et al. (1985) applied this process, which is based on the work of D'Zurilla and Goldfried (1971), as a method of teaching caregivers to find solutions to their own needs or to controlling the excessive or deficient behaviors of their dementing patients. The process of teaching problem-solving skills in this context is described in detail by S. H. Zarit et al. (1985). There are five basic steps:

1. *Identification of the Problem.* The problem needs to be clearly defined in terms of the demented persons behavior, the caregivers reaction, and the consequences. In terms of the example used in the aforementioned section, the problem might be unexpected fecal incontinence. The caregivers reaction is to feel frustrated and angry; the consequences might be to cancel an activity or to express anger to the patient.

2. *Generation of Alternatives.* The next step is to develop as many solutions to the problem as possible. It is often helpful to have group insights and input at this stage: Generating alternatives requires creativity and imagination.

3. *Choosing a Solution.* Once solutions have been listed systematically, the caregiver needs to review them and decide on the best approach to adopt.

4. *Cognitive Rehearsal.* Mentally reviewing the rehearsing the solution and the actions required is the next step. This allows checking for possible problems implementing the solution chosen and to rehearse any skilled behaviors that might be necessary.

5. *Carrying Out the Plan.* If necessary the strategy may need to be modified or adapted.

Teaching problem-solving skills is really part of an overall stress-management approach. The idea is not to solve specific problems for caregivers but rather to leave them with an active coping skill that they can use whenever they are faced with a problem with no immediate obvious solution. The technique can be applied not only to dealing with the problems arising from the patient's behavior, but also to difficulties in finding resources or developing support networks.

Supportive Group Therapy. Much of the useful work that can be transacted in group sessions amounts to sharing experiences and providing a supportive environment within which caregivers can come to terms with their feelings and discuss the dilemma or choices they are facing. Aronson et al. (1984) outlined a program that contains many of these elements. They worked with family caregiver groups to help develop the potential of group members and to encourage them to assume as much responsibility as they are capable of managing. This emphasis can be important, particularly where some role reversal is required. A wife may have to take more control of financial matters, a husband may be required to undertake personal nursing care or domestic tasks that he has not been involved in previously.

Another function of the Aronson et al. groups was to allow the expression of anger and frustration. As we have already observed, many caregivers feel guilty or resentful; they need the opportunity to ventilate these feelings and to learn that they are natural responses to the strain they are experiencing. Group members can often provide practical solutions to caregiving problems from their own experience. Advice from people who are undergoing the same demanding experiences can be more motivating and compelling than similar advice from a professional. The group can also serve as a support system that lies beyond the immediate boundaries of the family. Linking families with common problems as an informal network of support is an effective ingredient in a comprehensive approach to enhancing coping skills amongst caregivers. Aronson et al. (1984) also observed that:

> *The mutually supportive atmosphere of the family group encourages new adaptions through specific educational means, such as discussion of new research findings, experimental therapies, public policy issues, and service needs, and through development of insight. Perhaps the most difficult adaptation crisis for the family caregiver occurs in making a decision regarding placement of the patient in an institution. Confronting this issue necessitates the breakdown of denial, the reassessment of changing relationships, and making changes in lifestyle for both the well and ill family members. Caregivers are urged to maintain their group attendance after placement has been made. (p. 341)*

Assertiveness Training. A number of caregiver interventions involve a component that is labeled assertiveness training (N. B. Levine et al., 1983) or communication skills (Chiverton & Caine, 1989; Haley, S. L. Brown, & E. G. Levine, 1987). There are a number of reasons why these techniques might be of value to caregivers. One is in dealing with institutions, bureaucracy, and resource services. Many people have difficulty accessing services simply because they are uneasy about asking for help. They may have problems consulting services in the first instance, or in clarifying misunderstandings when they arise. Part of the education process for caregivers ought to involve a description of the services available, however, this needs to be supplemented in some cases by positive assistance in the use of these resources.

Assertion can also be important in approaching other relatives or friends for assistance or support. Assertiveness skills strengthen coping and personal resolve, giving caregivers the power to deal with interpersonal situations they may find daunting. This might include asking an old friend of the patient to visit from time to time, or approach°ing other relatives to provide respite assistance from time to time.

Respite Services. The use of in-home or institutional respite care to relieve the strain of caregiving has commonly been employed (e.g., Burdz, Eaton, & Bond, 1988; Lawton et al., 1989), sometimes as a part of a broaderbased intervention (Mohide et al., 1990). Initial evaluations of this procedure have indicated that caregiver burden is not greatly influenced by respite, although users express a high level of satisfaction with such services. In a controlled study in which respite services were available to one group but not another, a small gain in length of community residence (22 days) prior to nursing home placement, was achieved for the respite group (Lawton et al., 1989). However, the researchers concluded:

> *Most of those who wished for respite services used them and most of those who used them were extremely satisfied with them. Although there is clearly a need to explore further the limits of the effects of more intensive respite on caregivers with the highest need, the conclusion that ordinary respite care is a mild intervention with moderate effects seems inescapable. (p. 15)*

Concluding Comments. Throughout the various reviews and studies of caregiver burden that have been considered thusfar in this chapter, there are numerous descriptions of practical interventions for dealing with specific patient problems. It is beyond the scope of the present review to detail all of these. Each individual caregiver-recipient dyad presents with unique circumstances and problems, and clinical experience and initiative will be needed to solve the many specific clinical problems that present. For example, S. H. Zarit et al. (1985) detailed many practical and useful interventions with individual clients designed to help deal with memory-related problems and other behavioral difficulties. N. B. Levine et al. (1983) successfully employed many of the well-tested interventions in behavioral psychology with caregivers, including stress inoculation, assertiveness training, and roleplay-communication exercises. Haley (1983) described three cases where behavioral procedures were applied with success to ameliorating problems with elderly clients. There is considerable anecdotal and case evidence to suggest that caregivers can be counseled successfully. In the next section, we review formal attempts to assess the impact of caregiver intervention on burden.

Evaluation of Caregiver Programs

Uncontrolled reports on caregiver interventions generally indicate that such strategies are useful (e.g., Aronson et al., 1984; N. M. Clark & Rakowski, 1983; Goodman & Pynoos, 1988; Kane et al., 1983; L. W. Lazarus, Stafford, Cooper, Cohler, & Dysken, 1981). Until recently, there have been few randomized and controlled trials of such interventions; however, some are now beginning to appear.

Chiverton and Caine (1989) divided 40 spouses caring for AD patients into either a control or an education-oriented group. The primary outcome measure was an index of the family's ability to cope with actual and potential physical and psychosocial problems. They found that spouses in the education group felt a greater degree of competence in dealing with the problems caused by the disease. Interestingly, Chiverton and Caine (1989) expressed some caution in their discussion about the possible negative effects of education. The timing of such an intervention seems critical. Some caregivers felt overwhelmed by the input, and one, whose husband had only recently been diagnosed, reacted with considerable distress as she began to appreciate the nature of his prognosis. Constituting groups with members of comparable experience in caregiving would seem to be advisable.

An experimental investigation by Haley, S. L. Brown, and E. G. Levine (1987), found that more broad-based interventions for caregivers had little impact. In this study, three groups of caregivers were randomly constituted. By the end of treatment there were 9 in the waiting list condition, 14 in the support only group, and 17 in the support plus skills training group. The support activities involved 10 sessions and comprised education about a variety of relevant issues and informal discussion of the practical problems faced by caregivers. The additional skill component incorporated problem-solving, cognitive restructuring, and other behavioral interventions. There were no differences between groups on measures of depression, coping, life-satisfaction, or degree of social support. The outcome of a similar but larger study by S. H. Zarit, Anthony, and Boutselis (1987) was equally disappointing. They randomly assigned 184 primary caregivers of demented patients to one of three conditions: individual and family counseling group, support group; and waiting-list control. The therapy for the two intervention groups was similar and based on the procedures outlined in S. H. Zarit et al. (1985):

problem-solving, stress-management, and supportive strategies. The family and individual counseling therapy was aimed at the caregiver family or networks of individual dementia patients; the support group work was done with groups of caregivers. There were no significant group differences. The wait list controls did as well as subjects in the two interventions. As S. H. Zarit et al. (1987) concluded: "These results do not confirm the enthusiastic reports that have been frequently made about support groups, nor do they verify clinical impressions of gains made by clients in the IFC (Individual and Family Counselor) program" (p. 230). The authors went on to note that these results should be treated cautiously. It is possible that a 7-week intervention was too short or the results were affected by the high group drop-out rate (37%).

In the most recent report, Mohide et al. (1990) instituted a random trial of support for caregivers of dementia patients in an urban region in Ontario. There were 30 caregivers assigned to the experimental intervention, which involved education, help with problem-solving, use of inhome respite services, and peer-oriented self-help support groups. A further 30 caregivers were assigned to a control group, which received conventional community nursing care. The trial lasted for a 6-month period. The experimental group showed no improvement on measures of depression and anxiety, which remained abnormally elevated. There was a trend toward an improvement on a measure of quality of life, which the authors felt indicated a useful clinical gain. On the whole, however, the impact on caregiver distress was minimal.

The outcome literature, therefore, suggests that changing subjective burden in caregivers may be difficult. It should be noted that the magnitude of the problems caregivers face make it difficult to effect substantial changes. In addition, relatively small group sizes and group heterogeneity make the demonstration of any improvements problematic. Haley et al. noted, however, that group members do report finding the groups useful and this provides an important justification for continued development of programs in this area:

> *Caregivers' responses to the participant checklist provided important information about caregivers' perceptions of the important components of successful group intervention. Supported by these results was the suggestion ... that information, problem-solving, and emotional support are essential components of such intervention. In particular, caregivers valued specific information about community resources and dementia and its effects on the brain and behavior. The importance of emotional support was most apparent in caregivers' ratings of the importance of identifying with other group members, be-*

longing to a cohesive group, learning from others in the group, and support for increasing attention to their own needs. Assistance with problem-solving appeared to be important to caregivers, as indicated on several items having to do with encouragement to experiment with new approaches, direct advice, and modeling from other group participants. These ratings revealed that caregivers valued a number of outcomes not assessed in this project, including increases in knowledge about dementia and about coping skills which might help them to face the progression of dementia expected. Clinically, many caregivers also seemed more concerned with the goal of improving their effectiveness as caregivers than with decreasing their current levels of distress. (p. 381)

Chapter 10

CONCLUSIONS: A NEUROPSYCHOSOCIAL MODEL

Although all the diseases introduced and described in the preceding chapters have their own pattern of symptoms and prognostic character, they each present for the person with the disease a crisis of adaptation. This process of adjustment affects not only the patient, but also those who live in their personal psychosocial community. The assaults that such diseases make on the minds and bodies of those who are afflicted are profound and distressing. Much of what is written about the consequences of the diseases focuses on deficits and disabilities, and on the negative impact on caregivers and families. Yet despite the stress of coping with progressive incapacity, many caregivers and persons with the disease respond to the challenges and restructure their lives in a host of resourceful ways. In this final chapter, the focus is on the process of adaptation.

A key to the understanding of the effects of a neurological disease for any individual person, is recognition that this necessitates consideration of the unique circumstances that apply to that person. These circumstances include the particular constellation of symptoms and other clinical features of the disease seen not only from the clinician's perspective, but also from the viewpoint of the patient. Understanding patients' views of their disease, however, involves making explicit the meaning they ascribe to their symptoms and their personal response to the consequences and prognosis of their disorder. Furthermore, every person who contracts a chronic disease has their own set of competencies, weaknesses, resources, and coping skills. These premorbid factors will help determine response to the onset and progress of the disease on the part of both patients and caregivers. Taking account of the way in which each patient has their own unique psychosocial environment is also important. They have a life beyond the clinic that moderates the malignancies of the disease in a variety of relevant ways. The process of adaptation will be facilitated by support from the patient's and caregiver's network. Finally, it is important to remember that the disease process is rarely static. Adaptative tasks differ as the disease progresses.

A large portion of the published research on degenerative diseases is concerned with biomedical aspects of the disease process. There has also been a considerable emphasis on the study of brain-behavior relationships. The comparative study of the effects on cognition of various neurological conditions has an important part to play in helping to build up a picture of the nervous system structures involved in information processing. For the clinician, the ability to assess both qualitatively and quantitatively degree of cognitive dysfunction is of value in assessing a patient's present abilities. Traditional psychometric measures of neuropsychological functioning, such as the Wechsler scales, need to be supplemented by measures that systematically review an individual's functional abilities in an ecologically valid manner. This need is being met by an increasing trend in the literature toward the development of practically oriented methods of testing cognition and other adaptive skills. For example, in Chapter 2 the Rivermead Battery for assessing practical memory skills was introduced. There are numerous scales available for evaluating caregiver burden, functional skills, and cognitive disabilities appearing in the literature. Although many of these procedures have been developed for use with DAT patients, they can be readily adapted for use with other groups of clients.

In contrast to the biomedical and neuropsychological research effort, there is a scarcity of reported studies on the psychosocial and adaptive changes consequent on degenerative brain diseases. Although the study of stress and coping has been a major focus of experimental psychological research, this has had little impact on the study of neurological diseases. There are signs that this is changing however. For the social psychologist, learning how patients adjust to progressive neurological conditions adds a significant dimension to the study of psychological adaptation. For the clinician, this research promises to provide a wider and more valid conceptualization of the factors of relevance to successful coping.

To reflect the full range of disruption that brain disease visits on a patient, the model outlined in Fig. 10.1 has been labeled *neuropsychosocial*. This blending of *neuropsychological* and *psychosocial* is intended to reflect the fact that brain injury causes a complex of biological, psychological, and social-interpersonal changes. Figure 10.1 is an attempt to make explicit the processes involved in dealing with a chronic brain disease for both patient and their caregivers. In essence this schema is an attempt to explain the factors that moderate adjustment outcome and is based on the conceptualization of stress advanced by Lazarus (Lazarus & Folkman, 1984) and others. The basic ingredients of this approach were outlined in the previous chapter where research on caregiver burden was considered.

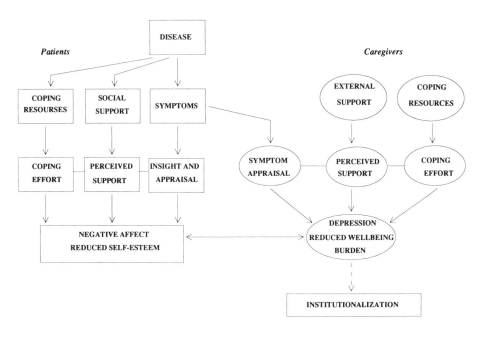

Figure 10.1. A model of the effects of degenerative diseases on caregivers and patients.

The effects of the disease on both patients and caregivers is represented in the same model, recognizing that the adjustment of all involved is interdependent. Poor coping on the part of the caregiver will have negative consequences for the adaptation of the person with the disease. Ultimately, decisions about care may depend more on the caregiver's response to the disease, than on a clinician's appreciation of the severity of symptoms. In addition, the predictive elements of the model are divided into those that can be assessed in some objective manner, and those that represent the subjective responses of the individuals involved. As we have already observed in Chapter 9, subjective appraisal of disease severity is more closely associated with burden and stress response than the objective level of incapacity caused by the disease. The markers of the failure of adaptation are outcome variables such as depression, feelings of burden, low self-esteem, and reduced life-satisfaction. The various parts of the model are considered in more detail here.

Symptoms. In the neuropsychosocial model, it is the changes caused by the degenerative disease that initiate the need for adaptation. The nature and significance of the clinical symptoms of the disease are central to an understanding of the effects of the disorder. Anyone who has been exposed to a range of patients with a specific disorder cannot help but be impressed with the sheer variety of symptoms and patterns of disability that present. As we have seen, the degenerative brain diseases cause a diversity of behavioral, emotional, and motor changes. These symptoms vary in their intensity, frequency, predictability and duration, and consequently in their potential to disrupt the routines of daily living.

In any understanding of the impact of symptoms on a patient's or caregiver's wellbeing, time is an important factor. Some symptoms tend to emerge later in the disorder and require different coping mechanisms than those that emerge at the onset. Moreover, the progress of the disease varies dramatically from person to person. For example, MS can be characterized by unpredictable episodes of remission and exacerbation. In Alzheimer's disease, the progression from initial symptoms to a severe dementia may take place in a matter of months or may stretch over many years. A slower progression of any disease allows a more measured approach to personal adjustment. A rapid onset can overwhelm caregivers and patients. Periods of stability and remission result in a more positive approach to the disease; an exacerbation of symptoms may lead to disappointment, hopelessness, and disengagement.

Many of the assessment procedures surveyed in Part 1 provide clinical assessments of symptom severity and functional incapacity. Appraisal of symptomatology and disability by clinicians is, however, likely to differ from that of the patients themselves or their caregivers. This is in part a consequence of the difference in experience that clinicians, patients, and caregivers bring to the appraisal context. For the clinician, severity is defined with reference to their knowledge of a range of patients with the disease; their background allows a normative comparison of a particular patient with the disability of others. In addition, the clinician typically receives reports about the patient's daily functioning in their home environment, and can only appreciate the disruption created by the symptoms at secondhand. In contrast, the caregivers and patients, particularly in the early stages of the disease, may have only their own experiences of the dysfunctions resulting from the disease on which to base a judgment of severity. Their appreciation of the effects of the disease is likely to be determined by internal factors and by the psychosocial consequences of the disease for them personally. Thus clinician ratings of severity are not necessarily going to be congruent with the appraisal of caregivers and patients.

Subjective Appraisal of Symptoms. Initial research on stress using the life events scales pioneered by Holmes and Rahe (1967) identified changes as the crucial factor in producing stress-related illnesses. Implicit in these early models of the stress response was the notion that life change challenged the ability to cope, and if the change was great enough, the individual would not be able to handle the consequences and so become vulnerable to physical or psychological illness. It soon became apparent, however, that it was not change itself that was important, but rather the undesirability of the change that provoked a stress response. In general, research on the impact of life events suggests that it is the number of undesirable changes that occur, rather the total number of changes aggregated regardless of their desirability, that is predictive of psychological stress (e.g., Thoits, 1983).

The changes associated with progressive brain conditions can usually be described with certainty as aversive and undesirable. Nonetheless, there are exceptions. On occasion, a patient who suffers neurological damage may lose a lifelong propensity for aggressiveness or obsessionality, and actually becomes easier to live with. Such occurrences are unusual, however. In addition to undesirability, there are several other factors that make symptoms and behavior changes stressful. Controllability, unexpectedness, and the presence of other stressors are all important determinants of subjective appreciation of symptom severity.

Controllability is a central feature of helplessness models of depression (e.g., Abramson, Seligman, & Teasdale, 1978). Life changes that are uncontrollable are more likely to evoke a sense of hopelessness or withdrawal than those that are not. Controllability can be seen as an aspect of clinical symptoms, some of which, like tremor in a Parkinson patient, may be beyond physical or medical control. Other symptoms, however, can be ignored, ameliorated, or construed more positively, given appropriate coping skills. There is also an element of expectation of coping effectiveness implicit in the notion of controllability. Attributions or expectations about the disease process can be an important determinant of the amount of coping effort engaged. Assessment of such expectations can be of value as they are frequently amenable to change via some educative process.

The unexpectedness of undesirable changes is also of significance in causing stress. Sudden loss, for example, of a job or a spouse, is often associated with a reactive depression (e.g., G. W. Brown & Harris, 1978). Under some circumstances the diagnosis of a disease can be unexpected event. The initial acknowledgment of a diagnosis is likely to be determined to some extent by its unexpectedness. Some people who are told of a diagnosis of Parkinson's disease may have had previous experience with the disease, having seen it in friends or relatives. For them, the neurologist's diagnosis may be a confirmation of something they have suspected from the time when they first noticed, for example, a tremor in one hand. Others receive the news that the development of a minor tremor is probably Parkinson's disease with a sense of shock. They may know nothing about the disease and the meaning of the diagnosis may take some time to assimilate.

An important factor that influences the extent to which a particular disability or symptom is regarded as stressful is the presence of coexisting symptoms or stressors. People with more symptoms or stressors may not necessarily feel more stress than those with fewer, but a variety of dysfunctions in different domains may, under some circumstances, interact to multiply the impact of individual symptoms. Coping with Parkinsonism, for either patients or caregivers, is compounded by the need to cope with other systemic or neurological diseases. Many elderly people have pre-existing medical conditions such as coronary disease, diabetes, or arthritis, that add to the burden of coping with a neurological condition. Some patients or caregivers have a history of depression, alcoholism, or other psychiatric disorder; the behaviors associated with these problems may interact with the ongoing symptoms of neurological disease.

Finally, in any discussion of the appraisal of symptoms the problems of insight in dementing patients should be noted. In Chapter 4, the frequent absence of awareness of the limitations imposed by their cognitive failures in amnesic or dementing patients, or their apparent indifference to their disabilities, has already been mentioned. In these circumstances, the self-reported appraisal of level of severity or the impact of behaviors or symptoms on others, is likely to be misleading.

External Support. The ability to handle stress depends in a large part on the availability of external support. In Fig. 10.1 a somewhat arbitrary distinction is made between the external and internal resources available to support the coping of both patients and caregivers. Internal (or coping) resources are the experiences, attitudes, knowledge, and skills that a person brings to a stressful situation. These are reviewed briefly in the next section. External resources are usually seen to comprise the community of support that a person has available to meet crisis situations. The objective availability of such support, however, does not mean that self-perceived need for support is being met. A resource is only a resource if it is regarded as such by the potential recipient.

The objective quantification of amount of social support has typically involved measuring a person's social support network. Networks can be characterized in terms of their size, availability, density (number of contacts between members without the index person being present), and reciprocity of contact or support. Incorporated into networks may be a variety of associations made through religious or sporting affiliations, work, and other interests. A key support person in anyone's life is a spouse or partner.

Social networks provide a supportive series of reciprocal obligations that bolster coping in times of need. Most people respond to personal crises by turning to their informal network of support, and access professional assistance only when this fails. However, institutions, self-help support groups, and health professionals from a variety of disciplines constitute an important external support system for patients. The roles served by networks include providing supportive advice, giving feedback on plans and ideas, assisting with problem-solving, and rendering instrumental assistance, for example, running errands and providing help with housekeeping chores.

There are a number of external factors that can be negative in their effect that also need to be acknowledged. The stress of caregiving may be increased by the presence of other pressures such as child rearing, marital or family conflict, or work-related problems. Finance is another important consideration. Concern about financial resources, or inadequate health insurance or pensions, can have a significant negative effect on coping.

Perceived Support. Availability of resources is only a positive strength if needs are being met. The fit between a person and their psychosocial support environment is of considerable significance. If there is conflict in the family or a spouse is unhelpful, then a potential source of assistance may be effectively negated. Evaluating satisfaction with support is an important factor in obtaining an understanding of how patients and caregivers are living with the disease.

One of the practical implications of the recognition of the significant role that support networks play in enhancing coping is the development of a variety of community- and hospital-based support groups for persons with particular diseases and their carers. We reviewed support groups in relation to the caregivers of demented patients in Chapter 9. Support groups of families with other degenerative brain diseases have been set up in many towns and cities. The groups provide a source of mutual support, social contact, and education for patients and caregivers.

Coping Resources. The personal beliefs, attitudes, and competencies that a person has available to them, help alleviate the effects of many stressors and crises. Although many of the stressors involved in coping with a chronic neurological illness are likely to be unique in their nature and intensity, successful mastery of problems in the past will predispose toward successful coping in the present.

Negative personality attributes of relevance include oversensitivity to stress, low self-esteem, and a predisposition to negative emotional response to stress, a positive self-concept, and a belief that personal responsibility determines successful health care are likely to adapt more rapidly to the effects of illness. Competencies are also important. These include problem-solving skills, communication abilities, self-management skills, and ability to seek out external assistance. Being comfortable in asking for help is also important. Many people find the experience of needing aid and the implied loss of autonomy extremely aversive. Others are simply not skilled in making their needs clear to the agents of complex bureaucracies. All these factors are important in handling day-to-day stresses successfully.

Coping Efforts. Overcoming the stressors and mastering the disabilities associated with progressive neurological disease involves making a substantial coping effort. This effort begins with having adequate coping resources and a belief that mastery is possible. In Chapter 9 many of the skills or coping procedures that can be taught to clients were introduced. Most of the methods that psychologists have used for dealing with stress can usefully be taught to clients under the appropriate circumstances. A list of stress-reduction and coping strategies include:

Goal setting and developing appropriate expectations
Problem solving skills
Cognitive restructuring and reinterpretation of stressful events
Relaxation training and stress inoculation training
Communication skills
Assertiveness training
Use of positive self-statements
Skills in accessing external resources and seeking information

The clinician's task is to assess clients with a view to identifying needs, deficits, and level of stress-management competencies, to provide training that remedies deficiencies, and to reinforce the use of new skills and competencies.

Adjustment and Outcomes. The psychosocial stress model in Fig. 10.1 implies that the failure to adjust to neurological disability at a psychological level will predispose the individual to stress. Failure to adapt underlies distress in patients and burden in caregivers. The success of the adjustment process (and of procedures designed to help strengthen adaptive coping) can be gauged from the level of distress. The personal responses most likely to reflect failure to adjust include: depression and negative affect, reduced self-esteem, a sense of stigmatization, feelings of isolation, loss of a sense of belonging, a reduced interest in daily activities and events, and loss of energy. Symptoms of psychological distress should not simply be regarded as a natural consequence of the disease, but as a signal that adaptation is currently less than adequate.

Conclusions

Degenerative brain diseases cause profound and largely irreversible changes in the neurobiological function of the individual with the disease. The biochemical changes and neuroanatomical legions set in motion the physical, mental, and emotional changes that typify the particular disease. The onset of the initial symptoms does more than simply signal the presence of these neurological changes: It initiates a complex process of readjustment in the patients psychosocial environment.

In this final chapter we pick up a theme that runs through all preceding chapters; understanding the consequences of a neurological disease for lives of the individuals who are affected requires an ecological approach. The changes that occur as a result of the disease need to be evaluated in terms of the manner in which they interact with and disturb an individual's personal environment. This is the essence of the neuropsychosocial model outlined in Fig. 10.1. This model implies that appropriate assessment of people who develop degenerative brain disease involves not only medical and neuropsychological investigations, but also the evaluation of a range of psychosocial factors. This in turn reinforces the need for the refinement, implementation, and evaluation of treatment modalities that effectively enhance natural coping skills and augment primary medical care.

REFERENCES

Abramson, L. Y., Seligman, M. E. P., & Teasdale, J. P. (1978). Learned helplessness in humans: Critique and reformulation. *Journal of Abnormal Psychology, 87,* 49-74.

Acheson, E. D. (1985). The epidemiology of multiple sclerosis. In W. D. Mathews, E. D. Acheson, J. R. Bachelor, & R. O. Weller (Eds.), *McAlpine's multiple sclerosis* (pp. 3-48). Edinburgh, Scotland: Churchill Livingstone.

Ader, R. (Ed.). (1981). *Psychoneuroimmunology.* New York: Academic Press.

Aggleton, J. P., & Mishkin, M. (1983). Memory impairments following restricted medial thalamic lesions in monkeys. *Experimental Brain Research, 52,* 199-209.

Akesson, H. O. (1969). A population study of senile and arteriosclerotic psychoses. *Human Heredity, 19,* 546-566.

Albert, M. L., Feldman, R. G., & Willis, A. L. (1974). The subcortical dementia of progressive supranuclear palsy. *Journal of Neurology, Neurosurgery, and Psychiatry, 37,* 121-130.

Albert, M. S., Butters, N., & Brandt, J. (1980). Memory for remote events in chronic alcoholics. *Journal of Studies on Alcohol, 41,* 1071-1081.

Albert, M. S., Butters, N., & Brandt, J. (1981a). Development of remote memory loss in patients with Huntington's disease. *Journal of Clinical Neuropsychology, 3,* 1-12.

Albert, M. S., Butters, N., & Brandt, J. (1981b). Patterns of remote memory in amnesic and demented patients. *Archives of Neurology, 38,* 495-500.

Albert, M. S., Butters, N., & Levin, J. (1979). Temporal gradients in the retrograde amnesia of patients with alcoholic Korsakoff's disease. *Archives of Neurology, 36,* 211-216.

Alexander, M. P., & Freedman, M. (1984). Amnesia after anterior communicating artery aneurysm rupture. *Neurology, 34,* 752-757.

Alvord, E. C. (1971). The pathology of Parkinsonism: Part II. An interpretation with special reference to other changes in the aging brain. In F. H. McDowell, & C. H. Markham (Eds.), *Recent advances in Parkinson's disease* (pp. 131-162). Philadelphia: Davis.

Alzheimer, A. (1977). A unique illness involving the cerebral cortex: A case report from the mental institution in Frankfurt am Main. Translated in D. A. Rottenberg & F. H. Hochberg (Eds.), *Neurological classics in modern translation* (pp. 41-44). New York: Hafner. (Original work published 1907)

Amaducci, L. A., Fratiglioni, L., Rocca, W. A., Fieschi, C., Livrea, P., Pedone, D., Bracco, L., Lippa, A., Gandolfo, C., Bino, G., Prencipe, M., Bonatti, M. L., Girotti, F., Carella, F., Tavolato, B., Ferla, S., Lenzi, S., Lenzi, G., Carolei, A., Gambi, A., Grigoletto, F., & Schoenberg, B. S. (1986). Risk factors for clinically diagnosed Alzheimer's disease: A case-control study of an Italian population. *Neurology, 36,* 922-931.

Amato, M. P., Fratiglioni, L., Groppi, C., Siracusa, G., & Amaducci, L. (1988). Inter-rater reliability in assessing functional systems and disability on the Kurtzke scale in multiple sclerosis. *Archives of Neurology, 45,* 746-748.

American Psychiatric Association (1987). *Diagnostic and statistical manual of mental disorders* (3rd ed., rev.). Washington, DC: Author.

Anthony, J. C., Le Resche, L., Niaz, U., Van Korff, M. R., & Folstein, M. F. (1982). Limits of the Mini-Mental State as a screening test for dementia and delerium among hospital patients. *Psychological Medicine, 12,* 397-408.

Anthony-Bergstone, C. R., Zarit, S. H., & Gatz, M. (1988). Symptoms of psychological distress among caregivers of dementia patients. *Psychology and Aging, 3,* 245-248.

Appell, J., Kertesz, A., & Fisman, M. (1982). A study of language functioning in Alzheimer patients. *Brain & Language, 17,* 73-91.

Arendt, T., Bigl, V., Arendt, A., & Tennstedt, A. (1983). Loss of neurons in the nucleus basalis of Meynert in Alzheimer's disease, paralysis agitans, and Korsakoff's disease. *Acta Neuropathologica, 61,* 101-108.

Aronson, M. K., Levin, G., & Lipkowitz, R. (1984). A community-based family/patient group program for Alzheimer's disease. *Gerontologist, 24,* 339-342.

Asso, D. (1969). WAIS scores in a group of Parkinson patients. *British Journal of Psychiatry, 115,* 554-556.

Atkinson, L. (1991). Concurrent use of the Wechsler Memory Scale-Revised and the WAIS-R. *British Journal of Clinical Psychology, 30,* 87-90.

Aubrun, W. (1937). Responses aux emotions-chocs chez les parkinsoniens [Response to emotional shock in Parkinson patients]. *Annee Psychologique, 37,* 140-171.

el-Awar, M., Becker, J. T., Hammond, K. M., Nebes, R. D., & Boller, F. (1987). Learning deficit in Parkinson's disease: Comparison with Alzheimer's disease and normal aging. *Archives of Neurology, 44,* 180-184.

Bachevalier, J., & Mishkin, M. (1986). Visual recognition impairment follows ventromedial but not dorsolateral prefrontal lesions in monkeys. *Behavioural Brain Research, 20,* 249-261.

Baddeley, A. D. (1986). *Working memory.* Oxford: Oxford University Press.

Baddeley, A. D., & Hitch, G. J. (1974). Working memory. In G. H. Bower (Ed.), *The psychology of learning and motivation* (Vol. 8, pp. 47-88). New York: Academic Press.

Baddeley, A. D., & Warrington, E. K. (1970). Amnesia and the distinction between long- and short-term memory. *Journal of Verbal Learning and Verbal Behavior, 9,* 176-189.

Baddeley, A. D., & Warrington, E. K. (1973). Memory coding and amnesia. *Neuropsychologia, 11,* 159-165.

Baldwin, M. V. (1952). A clinico-experimental investigation into the psychological aspects of multiple sclerosis. *Journal of Nervous and Mental Disease, 115,* 299-343.

Barbeau, A. (1966). The problem of measurement in akinesia. *Journal of Neurosurgery, 24,* 331-336.

Barbizet, J., & Cany, E. (1968). Clinical and psychometrical study of a patient with memory disturbances. *International Journal of Neurology, 7,* 44-54.

Barona, A., Reynolds, C. R., & Chastian, R. (1984). A demographically based index of premorbid intelligence for the WAIS-R. *Journal of Consulting and Clinical Psychology, 52,* 885-887.

Bauer, H. J. (1977). *A manual on multiple sclerosis.* Vienna, Austria: International Federation of Multiple Sclerosis Societies.

Baum, H. M., & Rothschild, B. B. (1981). The incidence and prevalence of reported multiple sclerosis. *Annals of Neurology, 10,* 420-428.

Baumgarten, M., Becker, R., & Gauthier, S. (1990). Validity and reliability of the Dementia Behavior Disturbance Scale. *Journal of the American Geriatrics Society, 38,* 221-226.

Bayles, K. A. (1982). Language function in senile dementia. *Brain & Language, 16,* 265-280.

Bayles, K. A., & Boone, D. R. (1982). The potential of language tasks for identifying senile dementia. *Journal of Speech and Hearing Disorders, 47,* 210-217.

Beatty, P. A., & Gagne, J. J. (1977). Neuropsychological aspects of multiple sclerosis. *Journal of Nervous and Mental Disease, 164,* 42-50.

Beatty, W. W., & Butters, N. (1986). Further analysis of encoding in patients with Huntington's disease. *Brain & Cognition, 5,* 387-398.

Beatty, W. W., & Goodkin, D. E. (1990). Screening for cognitive impairment in multiple sclerosis. *Archives of Neurology, 47,* 297-301.

Beatty, W. W., Staton, R. D., Weir, W. S., Monson, N., & Whitaker, H. A. (1989). Cognitive disturbance in Parkinson's disease. *Journal of Geriatric Psychiatry and Neurology, 2,* 22-33.

Bebb, G. L. (1925). A study of memory deterioration in encephalitis lethargica. *Journal of Nervous and Mental Disease, 61,* 356-365.

Beck, A. T., Ward, C. H., Mendelson, M., Mock, J., & Erbaugh, J. K. (1961). An inventory for measuring depression. *Archives of General Psychiatry, 4,* 561-571.

Beck, N. C., Horwitz, E., Seidenberg, M., Parker, J., & Frank, R. (1985). WAIS-R factor structure in psychiatric and general patients. *Journal of Consulting and Clinical Psychology, 53,* 402-405.

Becker, J. T. (1988). Working memory and secondary memory deficits in Alzheimer's disease. *Journal of Clinical and Experimental Neuropsychology, 10,* 739-753.

Bell, J., & Clark, A. J. (1926). A pedigree of paralysis agitans. *Annals of Eugenics, 1,* 445-462.

Bennett-Levy, J., & Powell, G. E. (1980). The Subjective Memory Questionnaire (SMQ): An investigation into the self-reporting of "real life" memory skills. *British Journal of Clinical Psychology, 19,* 177-188.

Benton, A. L. (1974). *The Revised Visual Retention Test* (4th ed.). New York: Psychological Corporation.

Benton, A. L., & Hamsher, K. de S. (1976) *Multilingual aphasia examination.* Iowa City, IA: Department of Neurology, University Hospitals.

Berg, L. (1984). Clinical dementia rating [Letter]. *British Journal of Psychiatry, 145,* 339.

Berg, L. (1988). Clinical Dementia Rating (CDR). *Psychopharmacology Bulletin, 24,* 637-639.

Berg, L., Hughes, C. P., Coben, L. A., Danziger, W. L., Martin, R. L., & Knesevich, J. (1982). Mild senile dementia of Alzheimer type: Research diagnostic criteria, recruitment, and the description of a study population. *Journal of Neurology, Neurosurgery, and Psychiatry, 45,* 962-968.

Berkman, L. S., & Syme, S. L. (1979). Special networks, host resistance, and mortality: A 9-year follow-up of Alameda County residents. *American Journal of Epidemiology, 109,* 186-204.

Biber, C., Butters, N., Rosen, J., Gerstman, L., & Mattis, S. (1981). Encoding strategies and recognition of faces by alcoholic Korsakoff and other brain-damaged patients. *Journal of Clinical Neuropsychology, 3,* 315-330.

Billings, A. G., & Moos, R. (1984). Coping, stress, and social resources among adults with unipolar depression. *Journal of Personality and Social Psychology, 46,* 877-891.

Birchall, J. D., & Chappel, J. S. (1988). Aluminium, chemical physiology, and Alzheimer's disease. *Lancet, 2,* 1008-1010.

286

Bird, E. D. (1978). The brain in Huntington's chorea. *Psychological Medicine, 8,* 357-360.

Bird, E. D., & Iverson, L. L. (1976). Neurochemical findings in Huntington's chorea. In M.B.H. Youdin, W. Lovenberg, D. F. Sharman, & J. R. Lagnado (Eds.), *Essays in neurochemistry and neuropharmacology* (pp. 177-195). London: Wiley.

Birrer, C. (1979). *Multiple sclerosis: A personal view.* Springfield, IL: Charles C Thomas.

Blessed, G., Tomlinson, B. E., & Roth, M. (1968). The association between quantitative measures of dementia and of senile changes in the cerebral gray matter of elderly subjects. *British Journal of Psychiatry, 114,* 797-811.

Bloch, M., & Hayden, M. R. (1990). Opinion: Predictive testing for Huntington disease in childhood: Challenges and implications. *American Journal of Human Genetics, 46,* 1-4.

Bogerts, B., Hantsch, J., & Herzer, M. (1983). A morphometric study of the dopamine containing cell groups in the mesencephalon of normals, Parkinson patients, and schizophrenics. *Biological Psychiatry, 18,* 951-969.

Boller, F., Mizutani, T., Roessmann, U., & Gambetti, P. (1980). Parkinson disease, dementia, and Alzheimer disease: Clinicopathological correlations. *Annals of Neurology, 7,* 329-335.

Boller, F., Passafiume, D., Keefe, N. C., Rogers, K., Morrow, L., & Kim, Y. (1984). Visuospatial impairment in Parkinson's disease: Role of perceptual and motor factors and of disease stage. *Archives of Neurology, 41,* 485-490.

Bolton, N., Britton, P. G., & Savage, R. D. (1966). Some normative data on the WAIS and its indices in an aged population. *Journal of Clinical Psychology, 22,* 184-188.

Bornstein, R. A., & Share, D. (1990). WAIS-R cholinergic deficit profile in temporal lobe epilepsy. *Journal of Clinical and Experimental Neuropsychology, 12,* 265-269.

Bornstein, R. A., Termeer, J., Longbrake, K., Heger, M., & North, R. (1989). WAIS-R cholinergic deficit profile in depression. *Psychological Assessment: A Journal of Consulting and Clinical Psychology, 1,* 342-344.

Boshes, B., Wachs, H., Brumlik, J., Mier, M., & Petrovick, M. (1960). Studies of tone, tremor and speech in normal persons and Parkinsonian patients. *Neurology, 10,* 805-813.

Bowen, F. P., Hoehn, M. M., & Yahr, M. D. (1972a). Cerebral dominance in relation to tracking and tapping performance in patients with Parkinsonism. *Neurology, 22,* 32-39.

Bowen, F. P., Hoehn, M. M., & Yahr, M. D. (1972b). Parkinsonism: Alterations in spatial orientation as determined by a route walking test. *Neuropsychologia, 10,* 355-361.

Bowen, F. P., Kamienny, R. S., Burns, M. M., & Yahr, M. D. (1975). Parkinsonism: Effects of levodopa treatment on concept formation. *Neurology, 25,* 701-708.

Bowman, K. M., Goodhart, R., & Jolliffe, N. (1939). Observations on the role of Vitamin B1 in the etiology and treatment of Korsakoff psychosis. *Journal of Nervous and Mental Disease, 90,* 569-575.

Brandt, J., Quaid, K. A., Folstein, S. E., Garber, P., Maestri, N. E., Abbott, M. H., Salveney, P. R., Franz, M. L., Kasch, L., & Kazazian, H. H. (1989). Presymptomatic diagnosis of delayed-onset disease with linked DNA markers. *Journal of the American Medical Association, 261,* 3108-3114.

Brinkman, S. D., & Braun, P. (1984). Classification of dementia patients by a WAIS profile related to central cholinergic deficiencies. *Journal of Clinical Neuropsychology, 6,* 393-400.

Brinkman, S. D., Largen, J. W., Gerganoff, S., & Pomara, N. (1983). Russell's revised Wechsler Memory Scale in the evaluation of dementia. *Journal of Clinical Psychology, 39,* 989-993.

Broadbent, D. (1958). *Perception and communication.* New York: Pergamon Press.

Broadbent, D. E., Cooper, P. F., Fitzgerald, P., & Parkes, K. R. (1982). The Cognitive Failures Questionnaire (CFQ) and its correlates. *British Journal of Clinical Psychology, 21,* 1-16.

Broe, G. A., Akhtar, A. J., Andrews, G. R., Caird, F. I., Gilmore, A. J. J., & McLellan, W. J. (1976). Neurological disorders in the elderly at home. *Journal of Neurology, Neurosurgery, and Psychiatry, 39,* 362-366.

Broman, T. (1963). Parkinson's syndrome prevalence and incidence in Goteborg. *Acta Neurologica Scandinavica, 39*(Suppl. 4), 95.

Brook, P., Degun, G., & Mather, M. (1975). Reality orientation, a therapy for psychogeriatric patients: A controlled study. *British Journal of Psychiatry, 127,* 42-45.

Brooks, D. N., & Baddeley, A. D. (1976). What can amnesic patients learn? *Neuropsychologia, 14,* 111-123.

Brooks, N. A., & Matson, R. R. (1982). Social-psychological adjustment to multiple sclerosis: A longitudinal study. *Social Science and Medicine, 16,* 2129-2135.

Brophy, A. L. (1986). Confidence intervals for true scores and retest scores on clinical tests. *Journal of Clinical Psychology, 42,* 989-991.

Brothers, C. R. D. (1964). Huntington's chorea in Victoria and Tasmania. *Journal of Neurological Science, 1,* 405-420.

Brouwers, P., Cox, C., Martin, A., Chase, T. N., & Fedio, P. (1984). Differential perceptual-spatial impairment in Huntington's and Alzheimer's dementias. *Archives of Neurology, 41,* 1073-1076.

Brown, G. W., & Harris, T. (1978). *Social origins of depression: A study of psychiatric disorder in women.* New York: The Free Press.

Brown, J. A. (1958). Some tests of the decay theory of immediate memory. *Quarterly Journal of Experimental Psychology, 10,* 12-21.

Brown, L. J., Potter, J. F., & Foster, B. G. (1990). Caregiver burden should be evaluated during geriatric assessment. *Journal of the American Geriatrics Society, 38,* 455-460.

Brown, P., Rodgers-Johnson, P., Cathala, F., Gibbs, C., & Gajdusek, D. (1984). Creutzfeldt-Jakob disease of long duration: Clinicopathological characteristics, transmissibility, and differential diagnosis. *Annals of Neurology, 16,* 295-304.

Brown, R. G., & Marsden, C. D. (1984). How common is dementia in Parkinson's disease? *Lancet, 2,* 1262-1265.

Brown, R. G., & Marsden, C. D. (1986). Visuospatial function in Parkinson's disease. *Brain, 109,* 987-1002.

Brown, R. G., & Marsden, C. D. (1988a). An investigation of the phenomenon of "set" in Parkinson's disease. *Movement Disorders, 3,* 152-161.

Brown, R. G., & Marsden, C. D. (1988b). Internal versus external cues and the control of attention in Parkinson's disease. *Brain, 111,* 323-345.

Brown, R. G., & Marsden, C. D. (1990). Cognitive function in Parkinson's disease: From description to theory. *Trends in the Neurosciences, 13,* 21-29.

288

Brownell, B., & Hughes, J. F. (1962). The distribution of plaques in the cerebrum in multiple sclerosis. *Journal of Neurology, Neurosurgery, and Psychiatry, 25,* 315-320.

Brumlik, J., & Boshes, B. (1966). The mechanism of bradykinesia in Parkinsonism. *Neurology, 16,* 337-344.

Bruyn, G. W. (1968). Huntington's chorea. In P. J. Vinken & G. W. Bruyn (Eds), *Handbook of clinical neurology* (Vol. 6, pp. 298-378). Amsterdam: Elsevier North Holland.

Burdz, M. P., Eaton, W. O., & Bond, J. B. (1988). Effects of respite care on dementia and nondementia patients and their caregivers. *Psychology and Aging, 3,* 38-42.

Burnfield, A. (1985). *Multiple sclerosis: A personal exploration.* London, England: Souvenir.

Burnfield, A., & Burnfield, P. (1982). Psychosocial aspects of multiple sclerosis. *Physiotherapy, 68,* 149-150.

Buschke, H. (1973). Selective reminding for analysis of memory and learning. *Journal of Verbal Learning and Verbal Behavior, 12,* 543-550.

Buschke, H., & Fuld, P. A. (1974). Evaluating storage, retention, and retrieval in disordered memory and learning. *Neurology, 11,* 1019-1025.

Butters, N. (1984). The clinical aspects of memory disorders: Contributions from experimental studies of amnesia and dementia. *Journal of Clinical Neuropsychology, 6,* 17-36.

Butters, N. (1985). Alcoholic Korsakoff's syndrome: Some unresolved issues concerning etiology, neuropathology, and cognitive deficits. *Journal of Clinical and Experimental Neuropsychology, 7,* 181-210.

Butters, N., Albert, M. S., Sax, D. S., Miliotis, P., Nagode, J., & Sterste, A. (1983). The effect of verbal elaborators on the pictorial memory of brain-damaged patients. *Neuropsychologia, 21,* 307-323.

Butters, N., & Brandt, J. (1984). The continuity hypothesis: The relationship of long-term alcoholism to the Wernicke-Korsakoff syndrome. In M. Galanter (Ed.), *Recent developments in alcoholism* (Vol. 3, pp. 207-229). New York: Plenum.

Butters, N., & Cermak, L. S. (1974). Some comments on Warrington's and Baddeley's report of normal short-term memory in amnesic patients. *Neuropsychologia, 12,* 283-285.

Butters, N., & Grady, M. (1977). Effect of predistractor delay on the short-term memory performance of patients with Korsakoff's and Huntington's disease. *Neuropsychologia, 13,* 701-705.

Butters, N., Heindel, W. C., & Salmon, D. P. (1990). Dissociation of implicit memory in dementia: Neurological implications. *Bulletin of the Psychonomic Society, 28,* 359-366.

Butters, N., Salmon, D. P., Cullum, C. M., Cairns, P., Troster, A. I., Jacobs, D., Moss, M., & Cermak, L. S. (1988). Differentiation of amnesic and demented patients with the Wechsler Memory Scale-Revised. *Clinical Neuropsychologist, 2,* 133-148.

Butters, N., Sax, D., Montgomery, K., & Tarlow, S. (1978). Comparison of the neuropsychological deficits associated with early and advanced Huntington's disease. *Archives of Neurology, 35,* 585-589.

Butters, N., Tarlow, S., Cermak, L. S., & Sax, D. (1976). A comparison of the information processing deficits of patients with Huntington's chorea and Korsakoff's syndrome. *Cortex, 12,* 134-144.

Butters, N., Wolfe, J., Martone, M., Granholm, E., & Cermak, L. S. (1985). Memory disorders associated with Huntington's disease: Verbal recall, verbal recognition, and procedural memory. *Neuropsychologia, 23,* 729-743.

Caine, E. D., Bamford, K. A., Schiffer, R. B., Shoulson, I., & Levy, S. (1986). A controlled neuropsychological comparison of Huntington's disease and multiple sclerosis. *Archives of Neurology, 43,* 249-255.

Caine, E. D., Ebert, M. H., & Weingartner, H. (1977). An outline for the analysis of dementia: The memory disorder of Huntington's disease. *Neurology, 27,* 1087-1093.

Caine, E. D., Hunt, R., Weingartner, H., & Ebert, M. (1978). Huntington's dementia: Clinical and neuropsychological features. *Archives of General Psychiatry, 35,* 377-384.

Canter, A. H. (1951). Direct and indirect measures of psychological deficit in multiple sclerosis. *Journal of General Psychology, 44,* 3-50.

Cantor, M. (1983). Strain among caregivers: A study of experience in the United States. *Gerontologist, 23,* 597-604.

Carmichael, E. A., & Stern, R. D. (1931). Korsakov's syndrome: Its histopathology. *Brain, 54,* 189-213.

Caroscio, J. (Ed.). (1986). *Amyotrophic lateral sclerosis: A guide to patient care.* New York: Thieme.

Carroll, M., Gates, R., & Roldan, F. (1984). Memory impairment in multiple sclerosis. *Neuropsychologia, 22,* 297-302.

Cassell, K., Shaw, K., & Stern, G. (1973). A computerized tracking technique for the assessment of Parkinsonian motor disorders. *Brain, 96,* 815-826.

Celesia, G. G., & Wanamaker, W. M. (1972). Psychiatric disturbances in Parkinson's disease. *Diseases of the Nervous System, 33,* 577-583.

Cermak, L. S. (1976). The encoding capacity of a patient with amnesia due to encephalitis. *Neuropsychologia, 14,* 311-326.

Cermak, L. S. (1982). *Human memory and amnesia.* Hillsdale, NJ: Lawrence Erlbaum Associates.

Cermak, L. S. (1984). The episodic-semantic distinction in amnesia. In L. R. Squire & N. Butters (Eds.), *Neuropsychology of memory* (pp. 55-62). New York: Guilford Press.

Cermak, L. S., Butters, N., & Goodglass, H. (1971). The extent of memory loss in Korsakoff patients. *Neuropsychologia, 9,* 307-315.

Cermak, L. S., Butters, N., & Moreines, J. (1974). Some analyses of the verbal encoding deficit of alcoholic Korsakoff patients. *Brain & Language, 1,* 141-150.

Cermak, L. S., & Reale, L. (1978). Depth of processing and retention of words by alcoholic Korsakoff patients. *Journal of Experimental Psychology: Human Learning and Memory, 4,* 165-174.

Chandra, V., Philipose, V., Bell, P. A., Lazaroff, A., & Schoenberg, B. S. (1987). Case control study of late-onset "probable Alzheimer's disease." *Neurology, 37,* 1295-1300.

Charcot, J. M. (1877). *Lectures on the diseases of the nervous system delivered at La Salpetriere* (G. Sigerson, Trans.). London: New Sydenham Society.

Charness, N., Milberg, W., & Alexander, M. P. (1988). Teaching an amnesic a complex cognitive skill. *Brain & Cognition, 8,* 253-272.

Chenoweth, B., & Spencer, B. (1986). Dementia: The experience of family caregivers. *Gerontologist, 25,* 267-272.

Chiverton, P., & Caine, E. D. (1989). Education to assist spouses in coping with Alzheimer's disease: A controlled trial. *Journal of the American Geriatrics Society, 37,* 593-598.

Citrin, R. S., & Dixon, D. N. (1977). Reality orientation: A milieu therapy used in an institution for the aged. *Gerontologist, 17,* 39-43.

Claparede, E. (1951). Recognition and "me-ness." In D. Rapaport (Ed. & Trans.), *Organization and pathology of thought,* (pp. 58-75). New York: Columbia University Press. (Original work published 1991)

Clark, N. M., & Rakowski, W. (1983). Family caregivers of older adults: Improving helping skills. *Gerontologist, 23,* 637-642.

Cleveland, S., & Dysinger, D. (1944). Mental deterioration in senile psychosis. *Journal of Abnormal and Social Psychology, 39,* 368-372.

Coblentz, J. M., Mattis, S., Zingesser, L. H., Kasoff, S. S., Wisniewski, H. M., & Katzman, R. (1973). Presenile dementia: Clinical aspects and evaluation of cerebrospinal fluid dynamics. *Archives of Neurology, 29,* 299-308.

Cohen, J. (1952). Factor-analytically based rationale for the Wechsler-Bellevue. *Journal of Consulting Psychology, 16,* 272-277.

Cohen, N. J., & Corkin, S. (1981). The amnesic patient H.M.: Learning and retention of a cognitive skill. *Society for Neuroscience Abstracts, 7,* 235.

Cohen, N. J., & Squire, L. R. (1980). Preserved learning and retention of pattern analyzing skill in amnesia: Dissociation of knowing how and knowing that. *Science, 210,* 207-209.

Cole, M. G. (1989). Inter-rater reliability of the Crichton Geriatric Behavioral Rating Scale. *Age and Aging, 18,* 57-60.

Collins, A. M., & Loftus, E. F. (1975). A spreading-activation theory of semantic processing. *Psychological Review, 82,* 407-428.

Cools, A. R., Bercken, J. H. L., Horstink, M. W. I., Spaendonck, K. P., & Berger, H. J. (1984). Cognitive and motor shifting aptitude disorder in Parkinson's disease. *Journal of Neurology, Neurosurgery, and Psychiatry, 47,* 443-453.

Copeland, J. R. M., Kelleher, M. J., Kellett, J. M., Gourlay, A. J., Gurland, B. J., Fleiss, J. L., & Sharpe, L. (1976). A semi-structured clinical interview for the assessment of diagnosis and mental state in the elderly: The Geriatric Mental State Schedule. *Psychological Medicine, 6,* 439-449.

Coppel, D. B., Burton, C., Becker, J., & Fiore, J. (1985). Relationships of cognitions associated with coping reactions to depression in spousal caregivers of Alzheimer's disease patients. *Cognitive Therapy and Research, 9,* 253-266.

Corkin, S. (1982). Some relations between global amnesias and the memory impairments in Alzheimer's disease. In K. L. Davis, J. H. Growden, E. Usdin, & R. J. Wurtman (Eds.), *Alzheimer's disease: A report of progress in research* (pp. 149-164). New York: Raven.

Corsellis, J. (1978). Post-traumatic dementia. In R. Katzman, R. Terry, & K. L. Bick (Eds.), *Alzheimer's disease: Senile dementia and related disorders* (pp. 125-133). New York: Raven.

Craik, F. I. M., & Lockhart, R. S. (1972). Levels of processing: A framework for memory research. *Journal of Verbal Learning and Verbal Behavior, 11,* 671-684.

Crawford, J. R., Parker, D. M., Stewart, L. E., Besson, J. A. O., & De Lacy, G. (1989). Prediction of WAIS IQ with the National Adult Reading Test: Cross-validation and extension. *British Journal of Clinical Psychology, 28,* 267-273.

Crawford, J. R., Stewart, L. E., Cochrane, R. H. B., Foulds, J. A., Besson, J. A. O., & Parker, D. M. (1989). Estimating premorbid IQ from demographic variables: Regression equations derived from a UK sample. *British Journal of Clinical Psychology, 28,* 275-278.

Crawford, J. R., Stewart, L. E., & Moore, J. W. (1989). Demonstration of savings on the AVLT and development of a parallel form. *Journal of Clinical and Experimental Neuropsychology, 11,* 975-981.

Creasey, G. L., Myers, B. J., Epperson, M. J., & Taylor, J. (1990). Couples with an elderly parent with Alzheimer's disease: Perceptions of familial relationships. *Psychiatry, 53,* 44-51.

Critchley, M. (1929). Arterio-sclerotic Parkinsonism. *Brain, 52,* 23-83.

Critchley, M. (1964). The neurology of psychotic speech. *British Journal of Psychiatry, 110,* 353-364.

Crook, T., Ferris, S., McCarthy, M., & Rae, D. (1980). Utility of digit recall tasks for assessing memory in aged. *Journal of Consulting and Clinical Psychology, 48,* 228-233.

Crook, T., Gilbert, J. G., & Ferris, S. H. (1980). Operationalizing memory impairment in elderly persons: The Guild Memory Test. *Psychological Reports, 47,* 1315-1318.

Crook, T. H., & Larrabee, G. J. (1988). Interrelationships among everyday memory tests: Stability of factor structure with age. *Neuropsychology, 2,* 1-12.

Crook, T. H., & Larrabee, G. J. (1990). A self-rating scale for evaluating memory in everyday life. *Psychology and Aging, 5,* 48-57.

Crook, T. H., Youngjohn, J. R., & Larrabee, G. J. (1990a). The Misplaced Objects Test: A measure of everyday visual memory. *Journal of Clinical and Experimental Neuropsychology, 12,* 808-812.

Crook, T. H., Youngjohn, J. R., & Larrabee, G. J. (1990b). TV News Test: A new measure of everyday memory for prose. *Neuropsychology, 4,* 135-146.

Crowder, R. G. (1982). The demise of short-term memory. *Acta Psychologica, 50,* 291-323.

Cummings, J. L. (1986). Subcortical dementia. *British Journal of Psychiatry, 149,* 682-697.

Cummings, J. L., & Benson, D. F. (1984). Subcortical dementia: A review of an emerging concept. *Archives of Neurology, 41,* 974-879.

Cummings, J. L., Benson, D. F., Hill, M. A., & Read, S. (1985). Aphasia in dementia of the Alzheimer type. *Neurology, 35,* 394-397.

Currier, R. D., & Eldridge, R. (1982). Possible risk factors in multiple sclerosis as found in a national twin study. *Archives of Neurology, 39,* 140-144.

Cushman, L. A., & Caine, E. D. (1987). A controlled study of processing of semantic and syntactic information in Alzheimer's disease. *Archives of Clinical Neuropsychology, 2,* 283-292.

Cutting, J. (1978). The relationship between Korsakov's syndrome and alcoholic dementia. *British Journal of Psychiatry, 132,* 240-251.

Cyr, J. J., & Brooker, B. H. (1984). Use of appropriate formulas for selecting WAIS-R short forms. *Journal of Consulting and Clinical Psychology, 52,* 903-905.

Dakof, G. A., & Mendelsohn, G. A. (1986). Parkinson's disease: The psychological aspects of a chronic illness. *Psychological Bulletin, 99,* 375-387.

Dalos, N. P., Rabins, P. V., Brooks, B. R., & O'Donnell, P. (1983). Disease activity and emotional state in multiple sclerosis. *Annals of Neurology, 13,* 573-577.

292

Danta, G., & Hilton, C. R. (1975). Judgement of the visual vertical and horizontal in patients with Parkinsonism. *Neurology, 25,* 44-47.

Darley, F. L., Brown, J. R., & Swenson, M. (1975). Language changes after neurosurgery for Parkinsonism. *Brain & Language, 2,* 65-69.

Davidson, O. R., & Knight, R. G. (1991). *Bradyphrenia in Parkinson's disease.* (Unpublished manuscript)

Davis, P. B., Morris, J. C., & Grant, E. (1990). Brief screening tests versus clinical staging in senile dementia of the Alzheimer type. *Journal of the American Geriatrics Society, 38,* 129-135.

Davis, P. E., & Mumford, S. J. (1984). Cued recall and the nature of the memory disorder in dementia. *British Journal of Psychiatry, 144,* 383-386.

De Jong, R. N. (1970). Multiple sclerosis: History, definition, and general considerations. In P. J. Vinken & G. W. Bruyn (Eds.), *Handbook of clinical neurology* (Vol. 9, pp. 45-62). Amsterdam: Elsevier North Holland.

Dean, G. (1967). Annual incidence, prevalence, and mortality of multiple sclerosis in white South-African-born and white immigrants to South Africa. *British Medical Journal, 2,* 724-730.

del Ser, T., Bermejo, F., Portera, A., Arredondo, J. M., Bouras, C., & Constantinidis, J. (1990). Vascular dementia. *Journal of the Neurological Sciences, 96,* 1-17.

D'Elia, L., Satz, P., & Schretlen, D. (1989). Wechsler Memory Scale: A critical appraisal of the normative studies. *Journal of Clinical and Experimental Neuropsychology, 11,* 551-568.

Delis, D. C., Freeland, J., Kramer, J. H., & Kaplan, E. (1988). Integrating clinical assessment with cognitive neuroscience: Construct.validation of the California Verbal Learning Test. *Journal of Consulting and Clinical Psychology, 56,* 123-130.

Delis, D. C., Kramer, J. H., Kaplan, E., & Ober, B. A. (1987). *California Verbal Learning Test, research edition: Manual.* New York: Psychological Corporation.

Della Sala, S., Di Lorenzo, G., Giordano, A., & Spinnler, H. (1986). Is there a specific visuo-spatial impairment in Parkinsonian's? *Journal of Neurology, Neurosurgery, and Psychiatry, 49,* 1258-1265.

Deluca, D., Cermak, L.S., & Butters, N. (1976). The differential effects of semantic, acoustic and nonverbal distraction on Korsakoff patients' verbal retention performance. *International Journal of Neuroscience, 6,* 279-284.

DePaulo, J. R., & Folstein, M. F. (1978). Psychiatric disturbances in neurological patients: Detection, recognition, and hospital course. *Annals of Neurology, 4,* 225-228.

De Renzi, E., & Faglioni, P. (1978). Normative data and screening power of a shortened version of the Token Text. *Cortex, 14,* 41-49.

De Renzi, E., & Ferrari, C. (1978). The Reporter's Test: A sensitive test to detect expressive disturbances in aphasics. *Cortex, 14,* 279-293.

De Renzi, E., & Vignolo, L. A. (1962). The Token Test: A sensitive test to detect disturbances in aphasics. *Brain, 85,* 665-678.

Detels, R., Clark, V. A., Valdiviezo, N. L., Visscher, B. R., Malmgren, R. M., & Dudley, J. P. (1982). Factors associated with a rapid course of multiple sclerosis. *Archives of Neurology, 39,* 337-341.

Devins, G. M., & Seland, T. P. (1987). Emotional impact of multiple sclerosis: Recent findings and suggestions for future research. *Psychological Bulletin, 101,* 363-375.

DeWardener, H. E., & Lennox, B. (1947). Cerebral beri beri (Wernicke's encephalopathy). *Lancet, i,* 249-252.

Dick, J. P. R., Guiloff, R. J., Stewart, A., Blackstock, J., Bielawska, C., Paul, E. A., & Marsden, C. D. (1984). Mini-Mental State examination in neurological patients. *Journal of Neurology, Neurosurgery, and Psychiatry, 47,* 496-499.

Diemling, G. T., & Bass, D. M. (1986). Symptoms of mental impairment among elderly adults and their effects on family caregivers. *Journal of Gerontology, 41,* 778-784.

Donnelly, E. F., & Chase, T. N. (1973). Intellectual and memory function in Parkinsonian and non-Parkinsonian patients treatment with L-Dopa. *Diseases of the Nervous System, 34,* 119-123.

Dowie, R., Povey, R., & Whitley, G. (1981). *Learning to live with multiple sclerosis.* London, England: Multiple Sclerosis Society of Great Britain and Northern Ireland.

Dubois, B., Pillon, B., Legault, F., Agid, Y., & Lhermitte, F. (1988). Slowing of cognitive processing in progressive supranuclear palsy. *Archives of Neurology, 45,* 1194-1199.

DuPont, E. (1976). Epidemiology of Parkinsonism: The Parkinson investigation, Arhus, Denmark. In J. Worm-Petersen & J. Bottcher (Eds.), *Symposium on Parkinsonism,* (pp. 65-75). Copenhagen, Denmark: Merck, Sharp & Dohme.

Dura, J. R., Bornstein, R. A., & Kiecolt-Glaser, J. K. (1990). Refinements in the assessment of dementia - related behaviors: Factor structure of the Memory and Behavior Problem Checklist. *Psychological Assessment: A Journal of Consulting and Clinical Psychology, 2,* 129-133.

Dura, J. R., Haywood-Niler, E., & Kiecolt-Glaser, J. K. (1990). Spousal caregivers of persons with Alzheimer's and Parkinson's disease dementia: A preliminary comparison. *Gerontologist, 30,* 332-336.

Durkheim, E. (1951). *Suicide: A study of sociology.* New York: Free Press.

Duvoisin, R. C., Gearing, F. R., Schweitzer, M. D., & Yahr, M. D. (1969). A family study of Parkinsonism. In A. Barbeau & J. R. Brunette (Eds.), *Progress in neurogenetics* (pp. 492-496). Amsterdam: Excerpta Medica.

D'Zurilla, T. J., & Goldfried, M. R. (1971). Problem solving and behavior modification. *Journal of Abnormal Psychology, 78,* 107-126.

Eisenson, J. (1954). *Examining for aphasia: A manual for the examination of aphasia and related disturbances.* New York: Psychological Corporation.

Elsass, P., & Zeeberg, I. (1983). Reaction time deficit in multiple sclerosis. *Acta Neurologica Scandinavica, 68,* 257-261.

Eppinger, M. G., Craig, P. L., Adams, R. L., & Parsons, O. A. (1987). The WAIS-R Index for estimating premorbid intelligence: Cross-validation and clinical utility. *Journal of Consulting and Clinical Psychology, 55,* 86-90.

Erickson, R. C., & Scott, M. L. (1977). Clinical memory testing: A review. *Psychological Bulletin, 84,* 1130-1149.

Evarts, E. V., Teravainen, H. & Calne, D. B. (1981). Reaction time in Parkinson's disease. *Brain, 104,* 167-186.

Fahy, M., Robbins, C., Bloch, M., Turnell, R. W., & Hayden, M. R. (1989). Different options for prenatal testing for Huntington's disease using DNA probes. *Journal of Medical Genetics, 26,* 353-357.

Fedio, P., Cox, C. S., Neophytides, A., Canal-Frederick, G., & Chase, T. N. (1979). Neuropsychological profile of Huntington's disease: Patients and those at risk. In T. N. Chase, N. Wexler, & A. Barbeau (Eds.), *Advances in neurology* (Vol. 23, pp. 239-271). New York: Raven.

Feehan, F. R., & Rudd, S. M. (1982). Clinical features that predict potentially reversible progressive intellectual deterioration. *Journal of the American Geriatrics Society, 30,* 449-451.

Feehan, M. J., Knight, R. G., & Partridge, F. M. (1991). Cognitive complaint and test performance in elderly patients suffering dementia and depression. *International Journal of Geriatric Psychiatry, 6,* 287-293.

Feier, C. D., & Leight, G. (1981). A communication-cognition program for elderly nursing home residents. *Gerontologist, 21,* 408-416.

Felton, B. J., & Revenson, T. A. (1984). Coping with chronic illness: A study of illness controllability and the influence of coping strategies on psychological adjustment. *Journal of Consulting and Clinical Psychology, 52,* 343-353.

Ferris, S. H., Crook, T., Clark, E., McCarthy, M., & Rae, D. (1980). Facial recognition memory deficits in normal aging and senile dementia. *Journal of Gerontology, 35,* 707-714.

Fillenbaum, G. G. (1980). Comparison of two brief tests of organic brain impairment: The MSQ and Short Portable MSQ. *Journal of the American Geriatrics Society, 27,* 381-384.

Fillenbaum, G. G., & Smyer, M. A. (1981). The development, validity, and reliability of the OARS Multidimensional Functional Assessment Questionnaire. *Journal of Gerontology, 36,* 428-434.

Filley, C. M., Heaton, R. K., Nelson, L. M., Burks, J. S., & Franklin, G. M. (1989). A comparison of dementia in Alzheimer's disease and multiple sclerosis. *Archives of Neurology, 46,* 157-161.

Filley, C. M., Kobayashi, J., & Heaton, R. K. (1987). Wechsler Intelligence Scale profiles, the cholinergic system, and Alzheimer's disease. *Journal of Clinical and Experimental Neuropsychology, 9,* 180-186.

Fink, S. L., & Houser, H. B. (1966). An investigation of physical and intellectual changes in multiple sclerosis. *Archives of Physical Medicine and Rehabilitation, 47,* 56-61.

Fischman, H. R. (1982). Multiple sclerosis: A new perspective on epidemiological patterns. *Neurology, 32,* 864-870.

Fisk, J. D., Goodale, M. A., Burkhart, G., & Barnett, H. J. (1982). Progressive supranuclear palsy: The relationship between ocular motor dysfunction and psychological test performance. *Neurology, 32,* 698-705.

Fitting, M., Rabins, P., Lucas, M. J., & Eastham, J. (1986). Caregivers for dementia patients: A comparison of husbands and wives. *Gerontologist, 26,* 248-252.

Flicker, C., Ferris, S. H., Crook, T., & Bartus, R. T. (1987). Implications of memory and language dysfunction in the naming deficit of senile dementia. *Brain & Language, 31,* 187-200.

Flowers, K. A. (1975). Ballistic and corrective movements on an aiming task: Intention tremor and Parkinsonian movement disorders compared. *Neurology, 25,* 413-421.

Flowers, K. A. (1976). Visual "closed-loop" and "open-loop" characteristics of voluntary movement in patients with Parkinsonism and intention tremor. *Brain, 99,* 259-310.

Flowers, K. A. (1978a). Some frequency response characteristics of Parkinsonism on pursuit tracking. *Brain, 101,* 19-34.

Flowers, K. A. (1978b). Lack of prediction in the motor behaviour of Parkinsonism. *Brain, 101,* 35-52.

Flowers, K. A., Pearce, I., & Pearce, J. M. S. (1984). Recognition memory in Parkinson's disease. *Journal of Neurology, Neurosurgery, and Psychiatry, 47*, 1174-1181.

Flowers, K. A., & Robertson, C. (1985). The effect of Parkinson's disease on the ability to maintain a mental set. *Journal of Neurology, Neurosurgery, and Psychiatry, 48*, 517-529.

Foley, F. W., Bedell, J. R., LaRocca, N. G., Scheinberg, L. C., & Reznikoff, M. (1987). Efficacy of stress-inoculation training in coping with multiple sclerosis. *Journal of Consulting and Clinical Psychology, 55*, 919-922.

Folkman, S., & Lazarus, R. S. (1985). If it changes, it must be a process: Study of emotion and coping during three stages of a college examination. *Journal of Personality and Social Psychology, 48*, 150-170.

Folsom, J. L. (1968). Reality orientation for the elderly mental patient. *Journal of Geriatric Psychiatry, 1*, 291-307.

Folstein, M. F., Folstein, S. E., & McHugh, P. R. (1975). Mini-Mental State: A practical method for grading the cognitive state of patients for the clinician. *Journal of Psychiatry Research, 12*, 189-198.

Folstein, S. E., Folstein, M. F., & McHugh, P. R. (1979). Psychiatric syndromes in Huntington's disease. In T. N. Chase, N. Wexler, & A. Barbeau (Eds.), *Advances in neurology* (Vol. 23, pp. 281-189). New York: Raven.

Forno, L. S. (1982). Pathology of Parkinson's disease. In C. D. Marsden & S. Fahn, (Eds.), *Movement disorders* (pp. 25-40). London: Butterworth.

Forsythe, E. (1979). *Living with multiple sclerosis.* London: Faber & Faber.

Frances, A., & Yudofsky, S. C. (1985). Prior cognitive problems as the key to treating a patient with resistant depression. *Hospital and Community Psychiatry, 36*, pp. 11-12, 21.

Franklin, G. M., Heaton, R. K., Nelson, L. M., Filley, C. M., & Seibert, C. (1988). Correlations of neuropsychological and MRI findings in chronic/progressive multiple sclerosis. *Neurology, 38*, 1826-1829.

Franklin, G. M., Nelson, L. M., Filley, C. M., & Heaton, R. K. (1989). Cognitive loss in multiple sclerosis. *Archives of Neurology, 46*, 162-167.

Freed, D., Corkin, S., & Cohen, N. J. (1984). Rate of forgetting in H.M.: A reanalysis. *Society for Neuroscience Abstracts, 10*, 383.

Freedman, M., Rivoira, P., Butters, N., Sax, D. S., & Feldman, R. G. (1984). Retrograde amnesia in Parkinson's disease. *Canadian Journal of Neurological Science, 11*, 297-301.

Friedman, A. P., & Davison, C. (1945). Multiple sclerosis with late onset of symptoms. *Archives of Neurology and Psychiatry, 54*, 348-360.

Frith, C. D., Bloxham, C. A., & Carpenter, K. N. (1986). Impairments in the learning and performance of a new manual skill in patients with Parkinson's disease. *Journal of Neurology, Neurosurgery, and Psychiatry, 49*, 661-668.

Fuld, P. A. (1981). *The Fuld Object-Memory Test.* Chicago, IL: The Stoelting Instrument Co.

Fuld, P. A. (1983). Psychometric differentiations of the dementias: An overview. In B. Reisberg (Ed.), *Alzheimer's disease: The standard reference* (pp. 201-210). New York: The Free Press.

Fuld, P. A. (1984). Test profile of cholinergic dysfunction and of Alzheimer-type dementia. *Journal of Clinical Neuropsychology, 6*, 380-392.

Gade, A. (1982). Amnesia after operations on aneurysms of the anterior communication artery. *Surgical Neurology, 18*, 46-49.

Galasko, D., Klauber, M. R., Hofstetter, C. R., Salmon, D. P., Lasker, B., & Thal, L. J. (1990). The Mini-Mental State Examination in the early diagnosis of Alzheimer's disease. *Archives of Neurology, 47*, 49-52.

Gallagher, J. P. (1989). Pathologic laughter and crying in amyotrophic lateral sclerosis: A search for their origin. *Acta Neurologica Scandinavica, 80*, 114-117.

Gallassi, R., Montagna, P., Ciardulli, C., Lorusso, S., Mussuto, V., & Stracciari, A. (1985). Cognitive impairment in motor neuron disease. *Acta Neurologica Scandinavica, 71*, 480-484.

Garland, H.G. (1952). Parkinsonism. *British Medical Journal, 1*, 153-155.

Gendron, C. E., Poitras, L. R., Engles, M. L., Dastoor, D. P., Sirota, M. A., Barza, S. L., Davis, J. C., & Levine, N. B. (1986). Skills training with supporters of the demented. *Journal of the American Geriatrics Society, 34*, 875-880.

George, L., & Gywther, L. (1986). Caregiver well-being: A multidimensional examination of family caregivers of demented adults. *Gerontologist, 26*, 253-259.

Gershon, S., & Herman, S. P. (1982). The differential diagnosis of dementia. *Journal of the American Geriatrics Society, 30*, 58-66.

Gewirth, L. R., Shindler, A. G., & Hier, D. B. (1984). Altered patterns of word associations in dementia and aphasia. *Brain & Language, 21*, 307-317.

Gibb, W. R. G. (1989). Neuropathology in the movement disorders. *Journal of Neurology, Neurosurgery, and Psychiatry, 52* (Special Supplement), 55-67.

Gibb, W. R. G., Mountjoy, C. Q., Mann, D. M. A., & Lees, A. J. (1989). A pathological study of the association between Lewy body disease and Alzheimer's disease. *Journal of Neurology, Neurosurgery, and Psychiatry, 52*, 701-708.

Gibbs, C. J., Gajdusek, D. C., Asher, D. M., Alpers, M. P., Beck, E., Daniel, P. M., & Matthews, W. B. (1968). Creutzfeldt-Jakob disease (spongiform encephalopathy): Transmission to the chimpanzee. *Science, 161*, 388-389.

Gibson, A. J., & Kendrick, D. C. (1979). *The Kendrick Battery for the Detection of Dementia in the Elderly.* Windsor, England: NFER.

Gilhooly, M. L. M. (1984). The impact of caregiving on caregivers: Factors associated with the psychological well-being of people supporting a dementing relative in the community. *British Journal of Medical Psychology, 57*, 35-44.

Gilleard, C. J., & Pattie, A. H. (1977). The Stockton Geriatric Rating Scale: A shortened version with British normative data. *British Journal of Psychiatry, 131*, 90-94.

Girotti, F., Soliveri, P., Carella, F., Piccolo, I., Caffarra, P., Musicco, M., & Caraceni, T. (1988). Dementia and cognitive impairment in Parkinson's disease. *Journal of Neurology, Neurosurgery, and Psychiatry, 51*, 1498-1502.

Glenner, G. G. (1989). The pathobiology of Alzheimer's disease. *Annual Review of Medicine, 40*, 45-51.

Glenner, G. G., & Wong, C. W. (1984). Alzheimer's disease and Down's syndrome: Sharing of a unique cerebrovascular amyloid fibril protein. *Biochemical and Biophysical Research Communications, 122*, 1131-1135.

Godfrey, H. P. D., & Knight, R. G. (1987). Interventions for amnesics: A review. *British Journal of Clinical Psychology, 26*, 83-91.

Godfrey, H. P. D., & Knight, R. G. (1988). Inpatient Memory Impairment Scale: A cross-validation and extension study. *Journal of Clinical Psychology, 55*, 783-786.

Godfrey, H. P. D., Partridge, F. M., Knight, R. G., & Bishara, S. N. (1991). *Course of insight disorder and emotional dysfunction following closed head injury: A controlled cross-sectional follow-up study*. Manuscript submitted for publication.

Goldman, L. S., & Luchins, D. J. (1984). Depression in the spouses of demented patients. *American Journal of Psychiatry, 141*, 1467-1468.

Goldman, M. S. (1983). Cognitive impairment in chronic alcoholics: Some cause for optimism. *American Psychologist, 10*, 1045-1053.

Goldstein, G., & Shelley, C. H. (1974). Neuropsychological diagnosis of multiple sclerosis in a neuropsychiatric setting. *Journal of Nervous and Mental Disease, 158*, 280-290.

Goldstein, G., Turner, S. M., Holzman, A., Kanagy, M., Elmore, S., & Barry, K. (1982). An evaluation of reality orientation therapy. *Journal of Behavioral Assessment, 4*, 165-178.

Goodglass, H., & Kaplan, E. (1972). *The assessment of aphasia and related disorders*. Philadelphia: Lea & Febiger.

Goodman, C. C., & Pynoos, J. (1988). Telephone networks connect caregiving families of Alzheimer's victims. *Gerontologist, 28*, 602-605.

Gotham, A. M., Brown, R. G., & Marsden, C. D. (1986). Depression in Parkinson's disease: A quantitative and qualitative analysis. *Journal of Neurology, Neurosurgery, and Psychiatry, 49*, 381-389.

Gotham, A. M., Brown, R. G., & Marsden, C. D. (1988). "Frontal" cognitive function in patients with Parkinson's disease "on" and "off" levodopa. *Brain, 111*, 299-321.

Gottleib, B. H. (1978). The development and application of a classification scheme of informal helping behaviors. *Canadian Journal of Science, 10*, 105-115.

Goudsmit, J. A., White, B. J., Weitkamp, L. R., Keats, B. J. B., Morrow, C. H., & Gajdusek, C. D. (1981). Familial Alzheimer's disease in two kindreds of the same enthic origin. *Journal of the Neurological Society, 49*, 79-89.

Gould, B. S. (1980). Psychiatric aspects. In D. W. Mulder (Ed.), *The diagnosis and treatment of amyotrophic lateral sclerosis* (pp. 157-168). Boston, MA: Houghton Mifflin.

Gould, J. (1982). Disabilities and how to live with them: Multiple sclerosis. *Lancet, 2*, 1208-1210.

Grady, C. L., Haxby, J. V., Horwitz, B., Sundaram, M., Berg, G., Schapiro, M., Friedland, R. P., & Rapoport, S. I. (1988). Longitudinal study of the early neuropsychological and cerebral metabolic changes in dementia of the Alzheimer type. *Journal of Clinical and Experimental Neuropsychology, 10*, 576-596.

Graf, P., Shimamura, A. P., & Squire, L. R. (1985). Priming across modalities and priming across category levels: Extending the domain of preserved function in amnesia. *Journal of Experimental Psychology: Learning, Memory, and Cognition, 11*, 385-395.

Graf, P., Squire, L. R., & Mandler, G. (1984). The information that amnesic patients do not forget. *Journal of Experimental Psychology: Learning, Memory, and Cognition, 10*, 164-178.

Graff-Radford, N., Tranel, D., Van Hoesen, G. W., & Brandt, J. P. (1990). Diencephalic amnesia. *Brain, 113*, 1-25.

Graham, F. K., & Kendall, B. S. (1960). Memory-for-Designs-Test: Revised general manual [Monograph]. *Perceptual and Motor Skills, 11*, 147-188.

Grant, I., McDonald, W. I., Trimble, M. R., Smith, E., & Reed, R. (1984). Deficient learning and memory in the early and middle phases of multiple sclerosis. *Journal of Neurology, Neurosurgery, and Psychiatry, 47,* 250-255.

Greene, J. G., Smith, R., Gardiner, M., & Timbury, G. C. (1982). Measuring behavioral disturbance of elderly dementing patients in the community and its effects on relatives: A factor analytic study. *Age and Aging, 11,* 121-126.

Gronwall, D. M. A. (1977). Paced auditory serial addition task: A measure of recovery from concussion. *Perceptual and Motor Skills, 44,* 367-373.

Gudmundsson, K. R. A. (1967). A clinical survey of Parkinsonism in Iceland. *Acta Neurologica Scandinavica, 43*(Suppl. 33), 9-61.

Gurd, J. M., & Ward, C. D. (1989). Retrieval from semantic and letter-initial categories in patients with Parkinson's disease. *Neuropsychologia, 27,* 743-746.

Gurel, L., Linn, M. W., & Linn, B. S. (1972). Physical and Mental Impairment-of-Function Evaluation in the aged: The PAMIE scale. *Journal of Gerontology, 27,* 83-90.

Gurland, B. J., Dean, L. L., Copeland, J., Gurland, R., & Golden, R. (1982). Criteria for the diagnosis of dementia in the community elderly. *Gerontologist, 22,* 180-186.

Gurland, B. J., Kuriansky, J., Sharpe, L., Simon, R., Stiller, P., & Birkett, P. (1977). The Comprehensive Assessment and Referral Evaluation (CARE): Rationale, development, and reliability. *International Journal of Aging and Human Development, 8,* 9-42.

Gusella, J. F., Wexler, N. S., Conneally, P. M., Naylor, S. L., Anderson, M. A., Tanzi, R. E., Watkins, P. C., Ottina, K., Wallace, M. R., Sakaguchi, A. Y., Young, A. B., Shoulson, I., Bonilla, E., & Martin, J. B. (1983). A polymorphic DNA marker genetically linked to Huntington's disease. *Nature, 306,* 234-238.

Hachinski, V. C., Iliff, L. D., Zilhka, E., DuBoulay, G. H., McAllister, V. L., Marshall, J., Russell, R. W. R., & Symon, L. (1975). Cebebral blood flow in dementia. *Archives of Neurology, 32,* 632-637.

Hachinski, V. C., Lassen, N. A., & Marshall, J. (1974). Multi-infarct dementia. A cause of mental deterioration in the elderly. *Lancet, ii,* 207-210.

Haley, W. E. (1983). A family behavioral approach to the treatment of the cognitively impaired elderly. *Gerontologist, 23,* 18-20.

Haley, W. E., Brown, S. L., & Levine, E. G. (1987). Experimental evaluation of the effectiveness of group intervention for dementia caregivers. *Gerontologist, 27,* 377-383.

Haley, W. E., Levine, E. G., Brown, S. L., & Bartolucci, A. A. (1987). Stress, appraisal, coping and social support as predictors of adaptational outcome among dementia caregivers. *Psychology and Aging, 2,* 323-330.

Haley, W. E., & Pardo, K. M. (1989). Relationship of severity of dementia to caregiving stressors. *Psychology and Aging, 4,* 389-392.

Hallett, M., & Khoshbin, S. (1980). A physiological mechanism of bradykinesia. *Brain, 103,* 301-304.

Hallett, M., Shahani, B. T., & Young, R. R. (1977). Analysis of stereotyped voluntary movements at the elbow in patients with Parkinson's disease. *Journal of Neurology, Neurosurgery, and Psychiatry, 40,* 1129-1135.

Halstead, W. C., & Wepman, J. M. (1959). The Halstead-Wepman aphasia screening test. *Journal of Speech and Hearing Disorders, 14,* 9-15.

Hamilton, M. (1967). Development of a rating scale for primary depressive illness. *British Journal of Social and Clinical Psychology, 6*, 278-296.

Hamsher, K. D., & Roberts, R. J. (1985). Memory for recent U.S. presidents in patients with cerebral disease. *Journal of Clinical and Experimental Neuropsychology, 7*, 1-13.

Hanley, J. R., Dewick, H. C., Davies, A. D. M., Playfer, J., & Turnbull, C. (1990). Verbal fluency in Parkinson's disease. *Neuropsychologia, 28*, 737-741.

Hanley, I. G., McGuire, R. J., & Boyde, W. D. (1981). Reality orientation and dementia: A controlled trial of two approaches. *British Journal of Psychiatry, 138*, 101-114.

Hannay, H. J., & Levin, H. S. (1985). Selective Reminding Test: An examination of the equivalence of four forms. *Journal of Clinical and Experimental Neuropsychology, 7*, 251-263.

Harrington, D. L., Haaland, K. Y., Yeo, R. A., & Marder, E. (1990). Procedural memory in Parkinson's disease: Impaired motor but not visuoperceptual learning. *Journal of Clinical and Experimental Neuropsychology, 12*, 323-329.

Harris, C. S., & Ivory, P. B. (1976). An evaluation of reality orientation therapy with geriatric patients in state mental hospitals. *Gerontologist, 16*, 496-503.

Hart, S. (1988). Language and dementia: A review. *Psychological Medicine, 18*, 99-112.

Hayden, M. R., & Leighton, P. (1982). Genetic aspects of Huntington's chorea: Results of a national survey. *American Journal of Medical Genetics, 11*, 135-141.

Hayden, M. R., Robbins, C., Allard, D., Haines, J., Fox, S., Wasmuth, J., Fahy, M., & Bloch, M. (1988). Improved predictive testing for Huntington disease by using three linked DNA markers. *American Journal of Human Genetics, 43*, 689-694.

Heaton, R. K. (1981). *Wisconsin Card Sorting Test.* Odessa, FL: Psychological Assessment Resources.

Heaton, R. K., Nelson, L. M., Thompson, D. S., Burks, J. S., & Franklin, G. M. (1985). Neuropsychological findings in relapsing-remitting and chronic-progressive multiple sclerosis. *Journal of Consulting and Clinical Psychology, 53*, 103-110.

Hefti, E., & Weiner, W. J. (1986). Nerve growth factor and Alzheimer's disease. *Annals of Neurology, 20*, 275-281.

Heilman, K. M., Bowers, D., Watson, R. T., & Greer, M. (1976). Reaction times in Parkinson's disease. *Archives of Neurology, 33*, 139-140.

Heindel, W. C., Salmon, D. P., & Butters, N. (1990). Pictorial priming and cued recall in Alzheimer's and Huntington's disease. *Brain & Cognition, 13*, 282-295.

Heindel, W. C., Salmon, D. P., Shults, C. W., Walicke, P. A., & Butters, N. (1989). Neuropsychological evidence for multiple implicit memory systems: A comparison of Alzheimer's, Huntington's and Parkinson's disease patients. *Journal of Neuroscience, 9*, 582-587.

Heinrichs, R. W., & Celinski, M. J. (1987). Frequency of occurrence of a WAIS dementia profile in male head trauma patients. *Journal of Clinical and Experimental Neuropsychology, 9*, 187-190.

Heller, K. (1979). The effects of social support: Prevention and treatment implications. In A. P. Goldstein & F. H. Kanfer (Eds.), *Maximizing treatment gains: Transfer enhancement in psychotherapy* (pp. 353-382). New York: Academic Press.

Heller, K., Swindle, R. W., & Dusenbury, L. (1986). Component social support processes: Comments and integration. *Journal of Consulting and Clinical Psychology, 54*, 466-467.

Henderson, A. S. (1983). The coming epidemic of dementia. *Australian and New Zealand Journal of Psychiatry, 17*, 117-121.

Henderson, A. S. (1988). The risk factors for Alzheimer's disease: A review and hypothesis. *Acta Psychiatrica Scandinavica, 78*, 257-275.

Henderson, A. S., Duncan-Jones, P., & Finlay-Jones, R. A. (1983). The reliability of the Geriatric Mental State Examination. *Acta Psychiatrica Scandinavica, 67*, 281-285.

Herndon, R. M., & Rudnick, R. A. (1983). Multiple sclerosis: The spectrum of severity. *Archives of Neurology, 40*, 531-532.

Heston, L. L., Mastri, A. R., Anderson, V. E., & White, J. (1981). Dementia of the Alzheimer type: Clinical genetics, natural history, and associated conditions. *Archives of General Psychiatry, 38*, 1085-1090.

Heyman, A., Wilkinson, W. E., Hurwitz, B. J., Schmechel, D., Sigmon, A. H., Weinberg, T., Helms, M. J., & Swift, M. (1983). Alzheimer's disease: Genetic aspects and associated clinical disorders. *Annals of Neurology, 14*, 507-515.

Hier, D. B., Hagenlocker, K., & Shindler, A. G. (1985). Language disintegration in dementia: Effects of etiology and severity. *Brain & Language, 25*, 117-133.

Hines, T. M., & Volpe, B. T. (1985). Semantic activation in patients with Parkinson's disease. *Experimental Aging Research, 11*, 105-107.

Hirai, S. (1968). Aging of the substantia nigra. *Advances in Neurological Sciences, 12*, 845-849.

Hirst, W. (1982). The amnesic syndrome: Description and explanations. *Psychological Bulletin, 91*, 435-460.

Hoehn, M. M., Crowley, T. J., & Rutledge, C. O. (1976). Dopamine correlates of neurological and psychological status in untreated Parkinsonism. *Journal of Neurology, Neurosurgery, and Psychiatry, 39*, 941-951.

Hoehn, M. M., & Yahr, M. D. (1967). Parkinsonism: Onset, progression, and mortality. *Neurology, 17*, 427-442.

Hogstel, M. O. (1979). Use of reality orientation with aging confused patients. *Nursing Research, 28*, 161-165.

Holmes, T. M., & Rahe, R. H. (1967). The social readjustment rating scale. *Journal of Psychosomatic Research, 11*, 213-218.

Hooper, H. E. (1958). *The Hooper Visual Organization Test*. Los Angeles, CA: Western Psychological Services.

Horn, S. (1974). Some psychological factors in Parkinsonism. *Journal of Neurology, Neurosurgery, and Psychiatry, 37*, 27-31.

Hornabrook, R. W., & Moir, D. J. (1970). Kuru: Epidemiological trends. *Lancet, 2*, 1175-1179.

Houpt, J. L., Gould, B. S., & Norris, F. H. (1977). Psychological characteristics of patients with amyotrophic lateral sclerosis. *Psychosomatic Medicine, 39*, 299-303.

House, J. S., Robbins, C., & Metzner, H.L. (1982). The association of social relationships and activities with mortality: Prospective evidence from the Tecumseh Community Health Study. *American Journal of Epidemiology, 116*, 123-140.

Hovestadt, A., de Jong, G. J., & Meerwaldt, J. D. (1987). Spatial disorientation as an early symptom of Parkinson's disease. *Neurology, 37*, 485-487.

Huber, S.J., Friedenberg, D. L., Paulson, G. W., Shuttleworth, E. C., & Christy, J. A. (1990). The pattern of depressive symptoms varies with progression of Parkinson's disease. *Journal of Neurology, Neurosurgery, and Psychiatry, 53*, 275-278.

Huber, S. J., & Paulson, G. W. (1985). The concept of subcortical dementia. *American Journal of Psychiatry, 142,* 1312-1317.

Huber, S. J., & Paulson, G. W. (1987). Memory impairment associated with progression of Huntington's disease. *Cortex, 23,* 275-283.

Hudson, A. J. (1981). Amyotrophic lateral sclerosis and its association with dementia, Parkinsonism, and other neurological disorders: A review. *Brain, 104,* 217-247.

Huff, F. J., Corkin, S., & Growden, J. H. (1986). Semantic impairment and anomia in Alzheimer's disease. *Brain & Language, 28,* 235-249.

Huff, F. J., Mack, L., Mahlmann, J., & Greenberg, S. (1988). A comparison of lexical-semantic impairments in left hemisphere stroke and Alzheimer's disease. *Brain & Language, 34,* 262-278.

Huggins, M., Bloch, M., Kanani, S., Quarrell, O. W. J., Theilman, J., Hendrick, A., Dickens, B., Lynch, A., & Hayden, M. (1990). Ethical and legal dilemmas arising during predictive testing for adult-onset disease: The experience of Huntington's disease. *American Journal of Human Genetics, 47,* 4-12.

Huntington, G. (1973). On chorea. *Advances in Neurology, 1,* 33-39. (Original work published 1872)

Huppert, F. A., & Piercy, M. (1978). Disassociation between learning and remembering in organic amnesia. *Nature, 275,* 317-318.

Huppert, F. A., & Tym, E. (1986). Clinical and neuropsychological assessment of dementia. *British Medical Bulletin, 42,* 11-18.

Ikuta, F., & Zimmerman, H. M. (1976). Distribution of plaques in seventy autopsy cases of multiple sclerosis in the United States. *Neurology, 26,* 26-28.

Inglis, J. (1957). An experimental study of learning and "memory function" in elderly psychiatric patients. *Journal of Mental Science, 103,* 796-803.

Inglis, J. (1959). Learning, retention, and conceptual usage in elderly patients with memory disorder. *Journal of Abnormal and Social Psychology, 59,* 210-215.

Ivnik, R. J. (1978a). Neuropsychological stability in multiple sclerosis. *Journal of Consulting and Clinical Psychology, 46,* 913-923.

Ivnik, R. J. (1978b). Neuropsychological test performance as a function of the duration of MS-related symptomatology. *Journal of Clinical Neurology, 39,* 304-312.

Ivnik, R. J., Malec, J. F., Tangalos, E. G., Peterson, R. C., Kokmen, E., & Kurland, L. T. (1990). The Auditory-Verbal Learning Test (AVLT): Norms for ages 55 years and older. *Psychological Assessment: A Journal of Consulting and Clinical Psychology, 2,* 304-312.

Iwasaki, Y., Kinoshita, M., Ikeda, K., Takamiya, K., & Shiojima, Y. (1990). Cognitive impairment in amyotrophic lateral sclerosis and its relation to motor disabilities. *Acta Neurologica Scandinavica, 81,* 141-143.

Jacobson, R. R., & Lishman, W. A. (1987). Selective memory loss and global intellectual deficits in alcoholic Korsakoff's syndrome. *Psychological Medicine, 17,* 649-655.

Jacoby, L. L. (1983). Perceptual enhancement: Persistent effects of an experience. *Journal of Experimental Psychology: Learning, Memory, and Cognition, 9,* 21-38.

Jacoby, L. L. (1984). Incidental versus intentional retrieval: Remembering and awareness as separate issues. In L. R. Squire & N. Butters (Eds.), *Neuropsychology of memory* (pp. 145-156). New York: Guilford Press.

Jacoby, L. L., & Witherspoon, D. (1982). Remembering without awareness. *Canadian Journal of Psychology, 36,* 300-324.

Jambor, K. L. (1969). Cognitive functioning in multiple sclerosis. *British Journal of Psychiatry, 115*, 765-775.

James, W. (1890). *The principles of psychology*. New York: H. Holt & Co.

Janowsky, J. S., Shimamura, A. P., Kritchevsky, M., & Squire, L. R. (1989). Cognitive impairment following frontal lobe damage and its relevance to human amnesia. *Behavioral Neuroscience, 103*, 548-560.

Javoy-Agid, F., & Agid, Y. (1980). Is the mesocortical dopaminergic system involved in Parkinson's disease? *Neurology, 30*, 1326-1330.

Jersild, C., Svejgaard, A., & Fog, T. (1972). HLA antigens and multiple sclerosis. *Lancet, 1*, 1240-1241.

Joffe, R. T., Lippert, G. P., Gray, T. A., Sawa, G., & Hovarth, Z. (1987). Mood disorder in multiple sclerosis. *Archives of Neurology, 44* 376-378.

Johnson, M. K., & Hasher, L. (1987). Human learning and memory. *Annual Review of Psychology, 38*, 631-638.

Johnson, R. T. (1975). The possible viral aetiology of multiple sclerosis. *Advances in Neurology, 3*, 1-46.

Jolliffe, N., Wortis, H., & Fein, H.D. (1941). The Wernicke syndrome. *Archives of Neurology and Psychiatry, 46*, 569-597.

Jorm, A. F. (1986). Controlled and automatic information processing in senile dementia: A review. *Psychological Medicine, 16*, 77-88.

Jorm, A. F., & Korten, A. E. (1988). Assessment of cognitive decline in the elderly by informant interview. *British Journal of Psychiatry, 152*, 209-213.

Jorm, A. F., Scott, R., & Jacomb, P.A. (1989). Assessment of cognitive decline in dementia by informant questionnaire. *International Journal of Geriatric Psychiatry, 4*, 35-39.

Josiassen, R. C., Curry, L. M., & Mancall, E. L. (1982). Patterns of intellectual deficit in Huntington's disease. *Journal of Clinical Neuropsychology, 4*, 173-183.

Kahan J., Kemp, B., Staples, F. R., & Brummell-Smith, K. (1985). Decreasing the burden in families caring for a relative with a dementing illness: A controlled study. *Journal of the American Geriatrics Society, 33*, 664-670.

Kahn, R. L., Goldfarb, A. I., Pollack, M., & Beck, A. (1960). Brief objective measures for the determination of mental status in the aged. *American Journal of Psychiatry, 117*, 326-328.

Kane, R. L., Bell, R., Reigler, S., Wilson, A., & Kane, R. A. (1983). Assessing the outcomes of nursing-home patients. *Journal of Gerontology, 38*, 385-393.

Kanner, A., Coyne, J., Schaefer, C., & Lazarus, R. (1981). Comparisons of two modes of stress measurement: Daily hassles and uplifts versus major life events. *Journal of Behavioral Medicine, 4*, 1-39.

Kaplan, E., Goodglass, H., & Weintraub, S. (1983). *Boston Naming Test*. Philadelphia: Lea & Febiger.

Kaszniak, A. W., Fox, J., Gandell, D. L., Garron, D. L., Huckman, M. S., & Ramsay, R. G. (1978). Predictors of mortality in presenile and senile dementia. *Annals of Neurology, 3*, 246-252.

Kaszniak, A. W., Garron, D. L., & Fox, J. (1979). Differential effects of age and cerebral atrophy upon span of immediate recall and paired-associate learning in older patients suspected of dementia. *Cortex, 15*, 285-295.

Katz, S., Ford, A. B., Moskowitz, R. W., Jackson, B. W., & Jaffe, M. (1963). Studies of illness in the aged: The index of ADL, a standardized measure of biological and psychological function. *Journal of the American Medical Association, 185,* 914-919.

Katzman, R., Brown, T., Fuld, P., Peck, A., Schechter, R., & Schimmel, H. (1983). Validation of a short orientation-memory-concentration test of cognitive impairment. *American Journal of Psychiatry, 140,* 734-739.

Katzman, R., Brown, T., Thal, L. J., Fuld, P., Aronson, M., Butters, N., Klauber, M. R., Wiederholt, W., Pay, M., Renbing, X., Ooi, W. L., Hofstetter, R., & Terry, R. D. (1988). Comparison of rate of annual changes of mental status score in four independent studies of patients with Alzheimer's disease. *Annals of Neurology, 24,* 384-389.

Kay, D. W. K. (1962). Outcome and cause of death in mental disorders of old age: A long-term follow-up of functional and organic psychoses. *Acta Psychiatrica Scandinavica, 38,* 249-276.

Kay, D. W. K. (1977). The epidemiology and identification of brain deficit in the elderly. In C. Eisdorfer & R. O. Friedel (Eds.), *Cognitive and emotional disturbances in the elderly* (pp. 11-26). Chicago: Year Book Medical Publishers.

Kay, D. W. K., Henderson, A. S., Scott, R., Wilson, J., Rickwood, D., & Grayson, D. A. (1985). Dementia and depression among the elderly living in the Hobart community: The effect of the diagnostic criteria on the prevalence rates. *Psychological Medicine, 15,* 771-788.

Kendrick, D. (1985). *Kendrick Cognitive Tests for the Elderly.* Oxford, England: NFER-Nelson.

Kendrick, D. C., Parboosingh, R. C., & Post, F. (1965). A synonym learning test for use with elderly psychiatric patients: A validation study. *British Journal of Social and Clinical Psychology, 4,* 63-71.

Kendrick, D. C., & Post, F. (1967). Differences in cognitive status between healthy psychiatrically ill and diffusely brain damaged elderly subjects. *British Journal of Psychiatry, 113,* 75-81.

Kertesz, A. (1979). *Aphasia and associated disorders.* New York: Grune & Stratton.

Kessler, S., Field, T., Worth, L., & Mosbarger, H. (1987). Attitudes of persons at risk for Huntington disease toward predictive testing. *American Journal of Medical Genetics, 26,* 259-270.

Kimura, D. (1963). Right temporal lobe damage. *Archives of Neurology, 8,* 264-271.

Kimura, D., Barnett, H. J. M., & Burkhart, G. (1981). The psychological test pattern in progressive supranuclear palsy. *Neuropsychologia, 19,* 301-306.

Kinnunen, E. (1984). Multiple sclerosis in Finland: Evidence of increasing frequency and uneven geographic distribution. *Neurology, 34,* 457-461.

Kinsbourne, M., & Wood, F. (1975). Short-term memory processes and the amnesic syndrome. In D. Deutsch & J. A. Deutsch (Eds.), *Short-term memory* (pp. 258-285). New York: Academic Press.

Kirshner, H. S., Webb, W. G., & Kelly, M. P. (1984). The naming disorder of dementia. *Neuropsychologia, 22,* 23-30.

Kishimoto, K., Nakamura, M., & Sotokawa, Y. (1957). On population genetics of Huntington's chorea in Japan. *Annual Reports of the Research on Environmental Medicine, 9,* 84-90.

Knehr, C. (1962). Differential impairment in multiple sclerosis. *Journal of Psychology, 54,* 443-451.

304

Knight, R. (1989). Creutzfeldt-Jakob disease. *British Journal of Hospital Medicine, 41,* 165-171.

Knight, R. G. (1983). On interpreting the several standard errors of the WAIS-R: Some further tables. *Journal of Consulting and Clinical Psychology, 51,* 671-673.

Knight, R. G., & Godfrey, H. P. D. (1984a). Assessing the significance of differences between subtests on the WAIS-R. *Journal of Clinical Psychology, 40,* 808-810.

Knight, R. G., & Godfrey, H. P. D. (1984b). The reliability and validity of a scale for rating memory impairment in hospitalized amnesiacs. *Journal of Consulting and Clinical Psychology, 52,* 769-773.

Knight, R. G., & Godfrey, H. P. D. (1985). The assessment of memory impairment: The relationship between different methods of evaluating dysmnesic deficits. *British Journal of Clinical Psychology, 24,* 125-131.

Knight, R. G., Godfrey, H. P. D., & Shelton, E. J. (1988). The psychological deficits associated with Parkinson's disease. *Clinical Psychology Review, 8,* 391-410.

Knight, R. G., & Longmore, B. E. (1991). What is an amnesic? In M. C. Corballis, K. G. White, & W. C. Abraham (Eds.), *Memory mechanisms: A tribute to G. V. Goddard* (pp. 149-174). Hillsdale, NJ: Lawrence Erlbaum Associates.

Knight, R. G., & Wooles, I. M. (1980). Experimental investigation of chronic organic amnesia: A review. *Psychological Bulletin, 88,* 753-771.

Kokmen, E., Chandra, V., & Schoenberg, B. S. (1988). Trends in incidence of dementing illness in Rochester, Minnesota, in three quinquennial periods: 1960-1974. *Neurology, 38,* 975-980.

Kopelman, M. D. (1985). Rates of forgetting in Alzheimer-type dementia and Korsakoff's syndrome. *Neuropsychologia, 23,* 623-638.

Kowall, N. W., Ferrante, R. J., & Martin, J. B. (1987). Patterns of cell loss in Huntington's disease. *Trends in the Neurosciences, 10,* 24-29.

Kraemer, H. C., Peabody, C. A., Tinklenberg, J. R., & Yesavage, J. A. (1983). Mathematical and empirical development of a test of memory for clinical and research use. *Psychological Bulletin, 94,* 367-380.

Kramer, J. H. (1990). Guidelines for interpreting WAIS-R subtest scores. *Psychological Assessment: A Journal of Consulting and Clinical Psychology, 2,* 202-205.

Kristensen, M. (1985). Progressive supranuclear palsy: Twenty years later. *Acta Neurologica Scandinavica, 71,* 177-189.

Krupp, L. B., LaRocca, N. G., Muir-Nash, J., & Steinberg, A. D. (1989). The Fatigue Severity Scale. *Archives of Neurology, 46,* 1121-1123.

Kuriansky, J. B., & Gurland, B. J. (1976). The performance test of activities of daily living. *International Journal of Aging and Human Development, 7,* 343-352.

Kurland, L. T. (1988). Amyotrophic lateral sclerosis and Parkinson's disease complex on Guam linked in an environmental neurotoxin. *Trends in the Neurosciences, 11,* 51-54.

Kurtzke, J. F. (1955). A new scale for evaluating disability in multiple sclerosis. *Neurology, 5,* 580-583.

Kurtzke, J. F. (1961). On the evaluation of disability in multiple sclerosis. *Neurology, 11,* 686-694.

Kurtzke, J. F. (1970). Epidemiology of multiple sclerosis. In P. J. Vinken & G. W. Bruyn (Eds.), *Handbook of clinical neurology* (Vol. 9, pp. 259-288). New York: Elsevier.

Kurtzke, J. F. (1979). Huntington's disease: Mortality and morbidity data from outside the United States. In T. N. Chase, N. Wexler, & A. Barbeau (Eds.), *Advances in Neurology* (Vol. 23, pp. 13-25). New York: Raven.

Kurtzke, J. F. (1983a). Rating neurologic impairment in multiple sclerosis: An Expanded Disability Status Scale (EDSS). *Neurology, 33,* 1444-1452.

Kurtzke, J. F. (1983b). Some epidemiological trends in multiple sclerosis. *Trends in the Neurosciences, 6,* 75-80.

Kurtzke, J. F., Beebe, G. W., Nagler, B., Auth, T. L., Kurland, L. T., & Nefzger, M. D. (1968). Studies on the natural history of multiple sclerosis: 4 Clinical features of the onset bout. *Acta Neurologica Scandinavica, 44,* 467-499.

Kurtzke, J. F., Beebe, G. W., Nagler, B., Nefzger, M. D., Auth, T. L., & Kurland, L. T. (1970). Studies on the natural history of multiple sclerosis: 5. Long-term survival in young men. *Archives of Neurology, 22,* 215-225.

Lang, C. (1989). Is Wilson's disease a dementing condition? *Journal of Clinical and Experimental Neuropsychology, 14,* 569-570.

Langston, J. W. (1989). Current theories on the cause of Parkinson's disease. *Journal of Neurology, Neurosurgery, and Psychiatry, 52*(Special Suppl.), 13-17.

Langston, J. W., Ballard, P., Tetrud, J. W., & Irwin, I. (1983). Chronic Parkinsonism in humans due to a product of Meperidine-analog synthesis. *Science, 219,* 979-980.

Larabee, G. J., & Crook, T. H. (1989). Dimensions of everyday memory in age-associated memory impairment. *Psychological Assessment: A Journal of Consulting and Clinical Psychology, 1,* 92-97.

Larabee, G. J., Largen, J. W., & Levin, H. S. (1985). Sensitivity of age-decline resistant ("hold") WAIS subtests to Alzheimer's disease. *Journal of Clinical and Experimental Neuropsychology, 7,* 497-504.

Larcombe, N. A., & Wilson, P. H. (1984). An evaluation of cognitive behavior therapy for depression in patients with multiple sclerosis. *British Journal of Psychiatry, 145,* 366-371.

Larsson, T., Sjogren, T., & Jacobson, G. (1963). Senile dementia: A clinical, sociomedical and genetic study. *Acta Psychiatrica Scandinavica, 167,* 1-259.

LaRocca, N. G. (1984). Psychosocial factors in multiple sclerosis and the role of stress. *Annals of the New York Academy of Sciences, 436,* 435-453.

La Rue, A. (1989). Patterns of impairment on the Fuld Object Memory Evaluation in elderly inpatients with depression or dementia. *Journal of Clinical and Experimental Neuropsychology, 11,* 409-422.

Lawton, M. O., Brody, E. M., & Saperstein, A. R. (1989). A controlled study of respite service for caregivers of Alzheimer patients. *Gerontologist, 29,* 8-16.

Lazarus, L. W., Stafford, B., Cooper, K., Cohler, B., & Dysken, M. (1981). A pilot study of an Alzheimer patients' relatives discussion group. *Gerontologist, 21,* 353-358.

Lazarus, R. S., & Folkman, S. (1984). *Stress, appraisal, and coping.* New York: Springer Publishing Co.

Lees, A. J. (1989). The on-off phenomenon. *Journal of Neurology, Neurosurgery, and Psychiatry, 52(Special Suppl.),* 29-37.

Lees, A. J., & Smith, E. (1983). Cognitive deficits in the early stages of Parkinson's disease. *Brain, 106,* 257-270.

Lehman, D. R., Ellard, J. H., & Wortman, G. B. (1986). Social support for the bereaved recipient and providers: Perspectives on what is helpful. *Journal of Consulting and Clinical Psychology, 54,* 438-446.

306

Leibowitz, U. (1971). Multiple sclerosis: Progress in epidemiological and experimental research: A review. *Journal of Neurological Science, 12,* 307-318.

Leng, N. R. C., & Parkin, A. J. (1988). Double dissociation of frontal dysfunction in organic amnesia. *British Journal of Clinical Psychology, 27,* 359-362.

Leng, N. R. C., & Parkin, A. J. (1989). Aetiological variation in the amnesic syndrome: Comparisons using the Brown-Peterson task. *Cortex, 25,* 251-260.

Levine, N.B., Dastooor, D. P., & Gendron, C. E. (1983). Coping with dementia: A pilot study. *Journal of the American Geriatrics Society, 31,* 12-18.

Lezak, M. D. (1983). *Neuropsychological assessment* (2nd ed.). New York: Oxford University Press.

Lichter, D. G., Corbett, A. J., Fitzgibbon, G. M., Davidson, O. R., Hope, A. J., Goddard, G. V., Sharples, K. J., & Pollock, M. (1988). Cognitive and motor dysfunction in Parkinson's disease. *Archives of Neurology, 45,* 854-860.

Lieberman, A., Dziatolowski, M., Neophytides, A., Kupersmith, M., Aleksic, S., Serby, M., Korein, J., & Goldstein, H. (1979). Dementias of Huntington's and Parkinson's diseases. In T. N. Chase, N. Wexler, & A. Barbeau (Eds.), *Advances in neurology* (Vol. 23, pp. 273-289). New York: Raven.

Lieberman, A. N., Leibowitz, M., Gobinathan, G., Walker, R., Hiesiger, E., Nelson, J., & Goldstein, M. (1985). Review: The use of pergolide and lisuride, two experimental dopamine agonists, in patients with advanced Parkinson disease. *American Journal of Medical Sciences, 290,* 102-106.

Lieberman, P., Friedman, J., & Feldman, L.S. (1990). Syntax comprehension deficits in Parkinson's disease. *Journal of Nervous and Mental Disease, 178,* 360-365.

Lilius, H. G., Valtonen, E. J., & Wikstrom, J. (1976). Sexual problems in patients suffering from multiple sclerosis. *Journal of Chronic Diseases, 29,* 643-647.

Lindvall, O., Brundin, P., Widner, H., Rehncrona, S., Gustavii, B., Frackowiak, R., Leenders, K.L., Swale, G., Rothwell, J. C., Marsden, C. D., & Bjorklund, A. (1990). Grafts of fetal dopamine neurons survive and improve motor function in Parkinson's disease. *Science, 247,* 574-577.

Linn, M. W., & Linn, B. S. (1982). The Rapid Disability Rating Scale - 2. *Journal of the American Geriatrics Society, 30,* 378-382.

Lishman, W. A. (1978). *Organic psychiatry: The psychological consequences of cerebral disorder.* Oxford, England: Blackwell Scientific Publications.

Lishman, W. A. (1981). Cerebral disorder in alcoholism. *Brain, 104,* 1-20.

Litvan, I., Grafman, J., Gomez, C., & Chase, T. N. (1986). Memory impairment in patients with supranuclear palsy. *Archives of Neurology, 46,* 765-767.

Litvan, I., Grafman, J., Vendrell, P., Martinez, J. M., Junque, C., Vendrell, J. M., & Barraquer-Bordas, J. L. (1988). Multiple memory deficits in patients with multiple sclerosis. *Archives of Neurology, 45,* 607-610.

Loewenstein, D. A., Amigo, E., Duara, R., Guterman, A., Hurwitz, D., Berkowitz, N., Wilkie, F., Weinberg, G., Black, B., Gittleman, B., & Eisdorfer, C. (1989). A new scale for the assessment of functional status in Alzheimer's disease and related disorders. *Journal of Gerontology: Psychological Sciences, 44,* 114-121.

Logsdon, R. G., Teri, L., Williams, D. E., Vitiello, M. V., & Prinz, P. N. (1989). The WAIS-R profile: A diagnostic tool for Alzheimer's disease? *Journal of Clinical and Experimental Neuropsychology, 11,* 892-898.

Longmore, B. E., & Knight, R. G. (1988). The effect of intellectual deterioration on retention deficits in amnesic alcoholics. *Journal of Abnormal Psychology, 97,* 448-454.

Longmore, F. J., Knight, R. G., & Longmore, B. E. (1990). A test of remote memory for use with New Zealand subjects. *New Zealand Journal of Psychology, 19* 17-23.

Loranger, A. W., Goddell, H., McDonald, F. H., Lee, J. E., & Sweet, R. H. (1972). Intellectual impairment in Parkinson's syndrome. *Brain, 95,* 405-412.

Loring, D. W., Lee, G. P., Martin, R. C., & Meador, K. J. (1989). Visual and verbal memory index discrepancies from the Wechsler Memory Scale - Revised: Cautions in interpretation. *Psychological Assessment: A Journal of Consulting and Clinical Psychology, 1,* 198-202.

Loring, D. W., & Papanicolaou, A. C. (1987). Memory assessment in neuropsychology: Theoretical considerations and practical utility. *Journal of Clinical and Experimental Neuropsychology, 9,* 340-358.

Luloff, P. B. (1986). Reactions of patients, family, and staff in dealing with amyotrophic lateral sclerosis. In J. Caroscio (Ed.), *Amyotrophic lateral sclerosis: A guide to patient care* (pp. 266-271). New York: Thieme Publishers.

Lumsden, C. E. (1970). The neuropathology of multiple sclerosis. In P. J. Vinken & G. W. Bruyn (Eds.), *Handbook of clinical neurology: Vol. 9. Multiple sclerosis and other demyelinating diseases* (pp. 217-309). Amsterdam, Holland: Elsevier North Holland.

Lyle, O. E., & Gottesmann, I. I. (1979). Subtle cognitive deficits as 15- to 20-year precursors of Huntington's disease. *Advances in Neurology, 23,* 227-238.

Mace, N. L., & Rabins, P. V. (1981). *The 36-hour day.* Baltimore, MD: Johns Hopkins University Press.

Maher, E. R., Smith, E. M., & Lees, A. J. (1985). Cognitive deficits in the Steele-Richardson-Olszewski syndrome (progressive supranuclear palsy). *Journal of Neurology, Neurosurgery, and Psychiatry, 48,* 1234-1239.

Mair, W. G. P., Warrington, E. K., & Weiskrantz, L. (1979). Memory disorder in Korsakoff psychosis. A neuropathological and neuropsychological investigation in two cases. *Brain, 102,* 749-783.

Malmud, N. (1972). Neuropathology of organic brain syndromes associated with aging. In C. M. Gaitz (Ed.), *Aging and the brain* (pp. 63-87). New York: Plenum.

Markowitsch, H. J., & Pritzel, M. (1985). The neuropathology of amnesia. *Progress in Neurobiology, 25,* 189-287.

Marsden, C. D. (1982). The mysterious motor function of the basal ganglia: The Robert Wartenberg lecture. *Neurology, 32,* 514-539.

Marsh, G. (1980). Disability and intellectual function in multiple sclerosis. *Journal of Nervous and Mental Disease, 168,* 758-762.

Martilla, R. J., & Rinne, U. K. (1976). Epidemiology of Parkinson's disease in Finland. *Acta Neurologica Scandinavica, 54,* 81-102.

Martilla, R. J., Rinne, U. K., Siirtola, T., & Sonninen, V. (1977). Mortality of patients with Parkinson's disease treated with levodopa. *Journal of Neurology, 216,* 147-153.

Martin, A., Brouwers, P., Cox, C., & Fedio, P. (1985). On the nature of the verbal memory deficit in Alzheimer's disease. *Brain & Language, 25,* 323-341.

Martin, A., & Fedio, P. (1983). Word production and comprehension in Alzheimer's disease: The breakdown of semantic knowledge. *Brain & Language, 19,* 124-141.

Martin, W. E., Loewenson, R. B., Resch, J. A., & Baker, A. B. (1973). Parkinson's disease: Clinical analysis of 100 patients. *Neurology, 23,* 783-790.

Martin, W. E., Young, W. I., & Anderson, V. E. (1973). Parkinson's disease: A genetic study. *Brain, 96,* 495-506.

Martone, M., Butters, N., Payne, M., Becker, J., & Sax, D. (1984). Dissociations between skill learning and verbal recognition in amnesia and dementia. *Archives of Neurology, 41,* 965-970.

Mastromauro, C., Myers, R. H., & Berkman, B. (1987). Attitudes towards presymptomatic testing in Huntington disease. *American Journal of Medical Genetics, 26,* 271-282.

Matison, R., Mayeux, R., Rosen, J., & Fahn, S. (1982). "Tip-of-the-tongue" phenomenon in Parkinson disease. *Neurology, 32,* 567-570.

Matarazzo, J. D., & Prifitera, A. (1989). Subtest scatter and premorbid intelligence: Lessons from the WAIS-R standardization sample. *Psychological Assessment: A Journal of Consulting and Clinical Psychology, 1,* 186-191.

Matthews, C. G., Cleeland, C. S., & Hopper, C. L. (1970). Neuropsychological patterns in multiple sclerosis. *Diseases of the Nervous System, 31,* 161-170.

Matthews, C. G., & Haaland, K. Y. (1979). The effect of symptom duration on cognitive and motor performance in Parkinsonism. *Neurology, 29,* 951-956.

Mattis, S. (1976). Mental status examination for organic mental syndrome in the elderly patient. In L. Bellack & T. B. Karasu (Eds.), *Geriatric psychiatry* (pp. 77-121). New York: Grune & Stratton.

Maybury, C. P., & Brewin, C. R. (1984). Social relationships, knowledge and adjustment to multiple sclerosis. *Journal of Neurology, Neurosurgery, and Psychiatry, 47,* 372-376.

Mayer-Gross, W., Slater, E., & Roth, M. (1969). *Clinical psychiatry.* Baltimore, MD: Williams & Wilkins.

Mayes, A. R., Meudell, P., Mann, D., & Pickering, A. (1988). Lesions in Korsakoff's syndrome: Neuropsychological and neuropathological data on two patients. *Cortex, 24,* 367-388.

Mayes, A. R., Pickering, A., & Fairbairn, A. (1987). Amnesic sensitivity to proactive interference: Its relationship to priming and the causes of amnesia. *Neuropsychologia, 25,* 211-220.

Mayeux, R., Stern, Y., Rosen, J., & Benson, D. F. (1983). Is "subcortical dementia" a recognizable clinical entity? *Annals of Neurology, 14,* 278-283.

Mayeux, R., Stern, Y., Rosen, J., & Leventhal, J. (1981). Depression, intellectual impairment, and Parkinson's disease. *Neurology, 31,* 645-650.

McAlpine, D. (1961). The benign form of multiple sclerosis: A study based on 241 cases seen within three years of onset and followed up until the tenth year or more of the disease. *Brain, 84,* 186-203.

McAlpine, D. (1972). Symptoms and signs. In D. McAlpine, C. E. Lumsden, & E. D. Acheson (Eds.), *Multiple sclerosis: A reappraisal* (pp. 132-196). Edinburgh: Churchill-Livingston.

McAlpine, D., Lumsden, C. E., & Acheson, E. D. (1972). *Multiple sclerosis: A reappraisal.* Edinburgh: Churchill-Livingstone.

McDonald, M. L., & Stettin, J. M. (1978). Reality orientation versus sheltered workshops as treatment for the institutionalized aging. *Journal of Gerontology, 33,* 416-421.

McDonald, W. I. (1983). Multiple sclerosis: The present position. *Acta Neurologica Scandinavica, 68,* 65-72.

McHugh, P. R., & Folstein, M. F. (1975). Psychiatric syndromes of Huntington's chorea: A clinical and phenomenologic study. In D. F. Benson & D. Blumer (Eds.), *Psychiatric aspects of neurologic disease* (pp. 267-286). New York: Grune & Stratton.

McIvor, G. P., Riklan, M., & Reznikoff, M. (1984). Depression in multiple sclerosis as a function of length and severity of illness, age, remissions, and perceived social support. *Journal of Clinical Psychology, 40,* 1028-1033.

McKhanna, G. M. (1982). Multiple sclerosis. *Annual Review of the Neurosciences, 5,* 219-239.

MacCarthy, B., & Brown, R. G. (1989). Psychosocial factors in Parkinson's disease. *British Journal of Clinical Psychology, 28,* 41-52.

Meer, B., & Baker, I. A. (1965). The Stockton Geriatric Rating Scale. *Journal of Gerontology, 21,* 392-403.

Meissen, G. J., Myers, R. H., Mastromauro, C. A., Koroshetz, W. J., Klinger, K. W., Farrer, L. A., Watkins, P. A., Gusella, J. F., Bird, E. D., & Martin, J. B. (1988). Predictive testing for Huntington's disease with use of a linked DNA marker. *New England Journal of Medicine, 318,* 535-542.

Meudell, P., Butters, N., & Montgomery, K. (1978). Role of rehearsal in the short-term memory performance of patients with Korsakoff's and Huntington's disease. *Neuropsychologia, 16,* 507-510.

Milberg, W., & Albert, M. S. (1989). Cognitive differences between patients with supranuclear palsy and Alzheimer's disease. *Journal of Clinical and Experimental Neuropsychology, 11,* 605-614.

Miller, E. (1971). On the nature of the memory disorder in presenile dementia. *Neuropsychologia, 9,* 75-78.

Miller, E. (1973). Short- and long-term memory in presenile dementia. *Psychological Medicine, 3,* 221-224.

Miller, E. (1975). Impaired recall and the memory disturbance in presenile dementia. *British Journal of Social and Clinical Psychology, 14,* 73-79.

Miller, E. (1977). *Abnormal aging: The psychology of senile and presenile dementia.* London: Wiley.

Miller, E. (1978). Retrieval from long-term memory in presenile dementia: Two tests of an hypothesis. *British Journal of Social and Clinical Psychology, 17,* 143-148.

Milner, B., Corkin, S., & Teuber, H-L. (1968). Further analyses of the hippocampal amnesic syndrome: A 14-year follow-up study of H. M. *Neuropsychologia, 6,* 215-234.

Minden, S. L., & Schiffer, R. B. (1990). Affective disorders in multiple sclerosis. *Archives of Neurology, 47,* 98-104.

Mindham, R. H. S., Steele, C., Folstein, M., & Lucas, J. (1985). A comparison of the frequency of major affective disorder in Huntington's disease and Alzheimer's disease. *Journal of Neurology, Neurosurgery, and Psychiatry, 48,* 1172-1174.

Mishkin, M. (1978). Memory in monkeys severely impaired by combined but not by separate removals of amygdala and hippocampus. *Nature, 273,* 297-298.

Mishkin, M. (1982). A memory system in the monkey. *Philosophical Transactions of the Royal Society of London, Series B, 298,* 85-95.

Mishkin, M., Malamut, B., & Bachevalier, J. (1984). Memories and habits: Two neural systems. In G. Lynch, J. L. McGaugh, & N. Wernberger (Eds.), *Neurobiology of learning and memory.* New York: Guilford Press.

Mjones, H. (1949). Paralysis agitans: A clinical and genetic study. *Acta Psychiatrica Scandinavica, 25*(Suppl. 54), 1-195.

Mohide, E. A., Pringle, D. M., Streiner, D. L., Gilbert, J. R., Muir, G., & Tew, M. (1990). A randomized trial of family caregiver support in the management of dementia. *Journal of the American Geriatrics Society, 38,* 446-454.

Mohr, E., Juncos, J., Cox, C., Litvan, I., Fedio, P., & Chase, T. N. (1990). Selective deficits in cognition and memory in high-functioning Parkinsonian patients. *Journal of Neurology, Neurosurgery, and Psychiatry, 53,* 603-606.

Molsa, P. K., Marttila, R. J., & Rinne, U. K. (1982). Epidemiology of dementia in a Finnish population. *Acta Neurologica Scandinavica, 86,* 541-552.

Morris, J. C., Heyman, A., Mohs, R. C., Hughes, J. P., van Belle, G., Fillenbaum, G., Mellitts, E. D., & Clark, C. (1989). The Consortium to Establish a Registry for Alzheimer's disease (CERAD): Part I. Clinical and neuropsychological assessment of Alzheimer's disease. *Neurology, 39,* 1159-1165.

Morris, J. C., McKeel, D. W., Jr., Fulling, K., Torack, R. M., & Berg, L. (1988). Validation of clinical diagnostic criteria for Alzheimer's disease. *Annals of Neurology, 24,* 17-22.

Morris, L. W., Morris, R. G., & Britton, P. G. (1988). The relationship between marital intimacy, perceived strain and depression in spouse carers of dementia sufferers. *British Journal of Medical Psychology, 61,* 231-236.

Morris, R., Wheatley, J., & Britton, P. (1983). Retrieval from long-term memory in senile dementia: Cued recall revisited. *British Journal of Clinical Psychology, 22,* 141-142.

Morris, R. G. (1984). Dementia and the functioning of the articulatory loop system. *Cognitive Neuropsychology, 1,* 143-157.

Morris, R. G. (1986). Short-term forgetting in senile dementia of the Alzheimer's type. *Cognitive Neuropsychology, 3,* 77-97.

Morris, R. G., & Baddeley, A. D. (1988). Primary and working memory functioning in Alzheimer-type dementia. *Journal of Clinical and Experimental Neuropsychology, 10,* 279-296.

Morris, R. G., Morris, L. W., & Britton, P. G. (1988). Factors affecting the emotional wellbeing of the caregivers of dementia sufferers. *British Journal of Psychiatry, 151,* 260-263.

Murdoch, B. B., Jr. (1974). *Human memory: Theory and data.* Hillsdale, NJ: Lawrence Erlbaum Associates.

Murdoch, B. E., Chenery, H. J., Wilks, V., & Boyle, R. S. (1987). Language disorders in dementia of the Alzheimer type. *Brain & Language, 31,* 122-137.

Naville, F. (1922). Les complications et les sequelles mentales de l'encephalite epidemique [The complications and psychological sequelae of the encephalitis epidemic]. *Encephale, 17,* pp. 369-375, 423-436.

Nebes, R. D. (1989). Semantic memory in Alzheimer's disease. *Psychological Bulletin, 106,* 377-394.

Nebes, R. D., Boller, F., & Holland, A. (1986). Use of semantic context by patients with Alzheimer's disease. *Psychology and Aging, 1,* 261-269.

Nebes, R. D., Brady, C. B., & Huff, F. J. (1989). Automatic and attentional mechanisms of semantic priming in Alzheimer's disease. *Journal of Clinical and Experimental Neuropsychology, 11,* 219-230.

Nebes, R. D., Martin, D.C., & Horn, L. C. (1984). Sparing of semantic memory in Alzheimer's disease. *Journal of Abnormal Psychology, 93,* 321-330.

Nee, L. E., Polinsky, R. J., Eldridge, R., Weingartner, H., Smallberg, S., & Ebert, M. (1983). A family with histologically confirmed Alzheimer's disease. *Archives of Neurology, 40,* 203-208.

Nelson, H. E.(1982). *The National Adult Reading Test.* Windsor, England: NFER-Nelson.

Newcombe, R. G. (1981). A life-table for onset of Huntington's chorea. *Annals of Human Genetics, 45,* 375-385.

Novak, M., & Guest, C. (1989). Caregiver response to Alzheimer's disease. *International Journal of Aging and Human Development, 28,* 67-79.

Ober, B. A., Dronkers, N. F., Koss, E., Delis, D. C., & Friedland, R. P. (1986). Retrieval from semantic memory in Alzheimer-type dementia. *Journal of Clinical and Experimental Neuropsychology, 8,* 75-92.

O'Grady, K. E. (1983). A confirmatory maximum likelihood factor analysis of the WAIS-R. *Journal of Consulting and Clinical Psychology, 51,* 826-831.

Okinawa, S., McAlpine, D., Miyagawa, K., Suwa, N., Kuroiwa, Y., Shiraki, H., Araki, S., & Kurland, L. T. (1960). Multiple sclerosis in northern and southern Japan. *World Neurology, 1,* 22-38.

Ortof, E., & Crystal, H. A. (1989). Rate of progression of Alzheimer's disease. *Journal of the American Geriatrics Society, 37,* 511-514.

Osato, S. S., Van Gorp, W. G., Kern, R. S., Satz, P., & Steinman, L. (1989). The Satz-Mogel short form of the WAIS in an elderly demented population. *Psychological Assessment: A Journal of Consulting and Clinical Psychology, 1,* 339-341.

Oscar-Berman, M. (1973). Hypothesis testing and focusing behavior during concept formation by amnesic Korsakoff patients. *Neuropsychologia, 11,* 191-198.

Osterrieth, P. A. (1944). Le test de copie d'une figure complexe [Test of copying a complex figure]. *Archives de Psychologie, 30,* 206-356.

Overall, J. E. (1989). A guide to the main instruments. In T. Hovaguimian, S. Henderson, Z. Khachaturian, & J. Orley (Eds.), *Classification and diagnosis of Alzheimer's disease: An international perspective* (pp. 65-77). Toronto: Hogrefe & Huber.

Pagel, M. D., Becker, J., & Coppel, D. B. (1985). Loss of control, self-blame, and depression: An investigation of spouse caregivers of Alzheimer's disease patients. *Journal of Abnormal Psychology, 94,* 169-182.

Parkin, A. J. (1984). Amnesic syndrome: A lesion-specific disorder? *Cortex, 20,* 479-508.

Parkin, A. J. (1990). Recent advances in the neuropsychology of memory. In J. Weinmann & J. Hunter (Eds.), *Clinical and biochemical contributions to the study of human memory function* (pp. 141-161). London: Harwood.

Parkin, A. J., Bell, W. P., & Leng, N. R. C. (1988). Metamemory in amnesic and normal subjects. *Cortex, 24,* 141-147.

Parkinson, J. (1955). *An essay on the shaking palsy.* In M. Critchley, W. H. McMenemey, F. M. R. Walshe, & J. G. Greenfield (Eds.), *James Parkinson (1755-1824): A bicentenary volume of dealing with Parkinson's disease* (pp. 145-218). London: Macmillan. (Original work published 1817)

Partridge, F. M., Knight, R. G., & Feehan, M. J. (1990). Memory performance and semantic priming in patients with senile dementia. *Psychological Medicine, 20,* 111-118.

Pattie, A. H., & Gilleard, C. J. (1975). A brief psychogeriatric assessment schedule: Validation against psychiatric diagnosis and discharge from hospital. *British Journal of Psychiatry, 127*, 489-493.

Paulson, G. W. (1979). Diagnosis of Huntington's disease. *Advances in Neurology, 23*, 177-184.

Penney, J. B., & Young, A. B. (1986). Striatal inhomogeneties and basal ganglia function. *Movement Disorders, 1*, 3-15.

Pepin, E. P., & Eslinger, P. J. (1989). Verbal memory decline in Alzheimer's disease: A multiple-processes deficit. *Neurology, 39*, 1477-1482.

Perl, D. P., & Brody, A. R. (1980). Alzheimer's disease: X-ray spectometric evidence of aluminium accumulation in neurofibrillary tangle bearing neurons. *Science, 208*, 207-209.

Perret, E., Eggenberger, E., & Siegfried, J. (1970). Simple and complex finger movement performance of patients with Parkinsonism before and after a unilateral stereotaxic thalamotomy. *Journal of Neurology, Neurosurgery, and Psychiatry, 33*, 16-21.

Perry, E. K., Perry, R. H., Blessed, G., & Tomlinson, B. E. (1977). Necropsy evidence of central cholinergic deficits in senile dementia. *Lancet, i*, 189.

Peters, P. K., Wedell, M. S., & Mulder, P. W. (1977). Is there a characteristic personality profile in amyotrophic lateral sclerosis? *Archives of Neurology, 35*, 321-322.

Peters, R. A. (1936). The biochemical lesion in Vitamin B1 deficiency. *Lancet, i*, 1161-1165.

Peterson, L. R., & Peterson, M. J. (1959). Short-term retention of individual verbal items. *Journal of Experimental Psychology, 58*, 193-198.

Petry, S., Cummings, J. L., Hill, M. A., & Shapira, J. (1988). Personality alterations in dementia of the Alzheimer type. *Archives of Neurology, 45*, 1187-1190.

Peyser, J., Rao, S. M., LaRocca, N. G., & Kaplan, E. (1990). Guidelines for neuropsychological research in multiple sclerosis. *Archives of Neurology, 47*, 94-97.

Peyser, J. M., Edwards, K. R., Poser, C. M., & Filskov, S. M. (1980). Cognitive function in patients with multiple sclerosis. *Archives of Neurology, 37*, 577-579.

Pfeiffer, E. (1975). A short portable mental status questionnaire for the assessment of organic brain deficit in elderly patients. *Journal of the American Geriatrics Society, 23*, 433-441.

Philippopoulos, G. S., Wittkower, E. D., & Cousineau, A. (1958). The etiologic significance of emotional factors in onset and exacerbations of multiple sclerosis. *Psychosomatic Medicine, 20*, 458-474.

Pillon, B., Dubois, B., Lhermitte, F., & Agid, Y. (1986). Heterogeneity of cognitive impairment in progressive supranuclear palsy: Parkinson's disease and Alzheimer's disease. *Neurology, 36*, 1179-1185.

Pinkerton, P., & Kelly, J. (1952). An attempted correlation between clinical and psychometric findings in senile arteriosclerotic dementia. *Journal of Mental Science, 98*, 244-255.

Pirozzolo, F. J., Hansch, E. C., Mortimer, J. A., Webster, D. A., & Kuskowski, M. A. (1982). Dementia in Parkinson's disease: A neuropsychological analysis. *Brain & Cognition, 1*, 71-83.

Plutchik, R., Conte, H., Lieverman, M., Bakur, M., Grossman, J., & Lehrman, N. (1970). Reliability and validity of a scale for assessing the functioning of geriatric patients. *Journal of the American Geriatrics Society, 18*, 491-500.

Poloni, M., Capitani, E., Mazzini, L., & Ceroni, M. (1986). Neuropsychological meas ures in amyotrophic lateral sclerosis and their relationship with CT-scan assessed cerebral atrophy. *Acta Neurologica Scandinavica, 74,* 257-260.

Poon, L. W. (1988). *Handbook for clinical memory assessment of older adults.* Washington, DC: American Psychological Association.

Popkin, S. J., Gallagher, D., Thompson, L. W., & Moore, M. (1982). Memory complaint and performance in normal and depressed older adults. *Experimental Aging Research, 8,* 141-145.

Porch, B. (1971). *Porch Index of Communicative Ability: Administration, scoring, and interpretation.* Palo Alto, CA: Consulting Psychologists Press.

Porch, B. E. (1967). *Porch Index of Communicative Ability.* Palo Alto, CA: Consulting Psychologists Press.

Poser, C. M., Paty, D. W., Scheinberg, L., MacDonald, W. I., Davis, F. A., Ebers, G. C., Johnson, K. P., Sibley, W. A., Silberberg, D. H., & Tourtellotte, W. W. (1983). New diagnostic criteria for multiple sclerosis: Guidelines for research protocols. *Annals of Neurology, 13,* 227-231.

Poskanzer, D. C., Schapira, K., & Miller, H. (1963). Epidemiology of multiple sclerosis in the counties of Northumberland and Durham. *Journal of Neurology, Neurosurgery, and Psychiatry, 26,* 368-376.

Potegal, M. (1971). A note on spatial-motor deficits in patients with Huntington's disease: Test of a hypothesis. *Neuropsychologia, 9,* 233-235.

Powell, G. E., Bailey, S., & Clark, E. (1980). A very short version of the Minnesota Aphasia Test. *British Journal of Social and Clinical Psychology, 19,* 189-194.

Powell-Proctor, L., & Miller, E. (1982). Reality orientation: A critical appraisal. *British Journal of Psychiatry, 140,* 457-463.

Pratt, R. T. C. (1951). An investigation of the psychiatric aspects of disseminated sclerosis. *Journal of Neurology, Neurosurgery, and Psychiatry, 14,* 326-335.

Prifitera, A., & Barley, W. D. (1985). Cautions in the interpretation of comparisons between the WAIS-R and the Wechsler Memory Scale. *Journal of Consulting and Clinical Psychology, 53,* 564-565.

Prigatano, G. (1977). Wechsler Memory Scale is a poor screening test for brain dysfunction. *Journal of Clinical Psychology, 33,* 772-776.

Procidano, M. E., & Heller, K. (1983). Measures of perceived social support from friends and from family: Three validation studies. *American Journal of Community Psychology, 11,* 1-24.

Proctor, F., Riklan, M., Cooper, S. T., & Teuber, H. L. (1964). Judgement of visual and postural vertical by Parkinsonism patients. *Neurology, 14,* 287-293.

Pruchno, R. A., & Resch, N. L. (1989a). Husbands and wives as caregivers: Antecedents of depression and burden. *Gerontologist, 29,* 159-165.

Pruchno, R. A., & Resch, N. L. (1989b). Aberrant behaviors and Alzheimer's disease: Mental health effects on spouse caregivers. *Journal of Gerontology, 44,* 177-182.

Quayhagen, M. P., & Quayhagen, M. (1988). Alzheimer's stress: Coping with the caregiving role. *Gerontologist, 28,* 391-396.

Quinn, N. P., Rossor, M. N., & Marsden, C. D. (1986). Dementia and Parkinson's disease: Pathological and neurochemical considerations. *British Medical Bulletin, 42,* 86-90.

Rabin, A. I. (1945). Psychometric trends in senility and psychoses of the senium. *Journal of General Psychology, 32,* 149-162.

Rabins, P., Mace, N., & Lucas, M. (1982). The impact of dementia on the family. *Journal of the American Medical Association, 248,* 333-335.

Radloff, L. S. (1977). The CES-D scale: A self-report depression scale for research in the general population. *Applied Psychological Measurement, 1,* 385-401.

Rafal, R. D., Posner, M. I., Walker, J. A., & Friedrich, F. J. (1984). Cognition and the basal ganglia: Separating mental and motor components of performance in Parkinson's disease. *Brain, 107,* 1083-1094.

Rajput, A. H., Offord, K. P., Beard, C. M., & Kurland, L. T. (1984). Epidemiology of Parkinsonism: Incidence, classification, and mortality. *Annals of Neurology, 16,* 278-282.

Rao, S. M. (1986). Neuropsychology of multiple sclerosis: A critical review. *Journal of Clinical and Experimental Neuropsychology, 8,* 503-542.

Rao, S. M., & Hammeke, T. A. (1984). Hypothesis testing in patients with chronic progressive multiple sclerosis. *Brain & Cognition, 3,* 94-104.

Rao, S. M., Hammeke, T. A., McQuillen, M. P., Khatri, B. O., & Lloyd, D. (1984). Memory disturbance in chronic progressive multiple sclerosis. *Archives of Neurology, 41,* 625-631.

Rao, S. M., Hammeke, T. A., & Speech, T. F. (1987). Wisconsin Card-Sorting Test performance in relapsing-remitting and chronic progressive multiple sclerosis. *Journal of Consulting and Clinical Psychology, 55,* 263-265.

Rao, S. M., Leo, G. J., & St. Aubin-Faubert, P. (1989). On the nature of memory disturbance in multiple sclerosis. *Journal of Clinical and Experimental Neuropsychology, 11,* 699-712.

Raven, J. C. (1960). *Guide to the Standard Progressive Matrices.* London, England: H. K. Lewis.

Reisberg, B. (1986). Dementia: A systematic approach to identifying reversible causes. *Geriatrics, 41,* 30-46.

Reisberg, B., Ferris, S. H., deLeon, M. J., & Crook, T. (1982). The Global Deterioration Scale for assessment of primary degenerative dementia. *American Journal of Psychiatry, 139,* 1136-1139.

Reisberg, B., Ferris, S. H., deLeon, M. J., & Crook, T. (1988). Global Deterioration Scale (GDS). *Psychopharmacology Bulletin, 24,* 661-663.

Reisberg, B., Ferris, S. H., deLeon, M. J., Kluger, A., Franssen, E., Borenstein, J., & Alba, R. C. (1989). The stage-specific temporal course of Alzheimer's disease: Functional and behavioral concomitants based upon cross-sectional and longitudinal observation. *Progress in Clinical and Biological Research, 317,* 23-41.

Reitan, R. H., & Boll, T. J. (1971). Intellectual and cognitive functions in Parkinson's disease. *Journal of Consulting and Clinical Psychology, 37,* 364-369.

Reitan, R. H., Reed, J. C., & Dyken, M. L. (1971). Cognitive, psychomotor and motor correlates of multiple sclerosis. *Journal of Nervous and Mental Disease, 153,* 218-224.

Richardson-Klavehn, A., & Bjork, R. A. (1988). Measures of memory. *Annual Review of Psychology, 39,* 475-543.

Riege, W. (1977). Inconstant nonverbal recognition memory in Korsakoff patients and controls. *Neuropsychologia, 15,* 269-276.

Riklan, M., Whelihan, W., & Cullinan, T. (1976). Levodopa and psychometric test performance in Parkinsonism: Five years later. *Neurology, 26,* 173-179.

Ringel, S. P. (1987). *Neuromuscular disorders.* New York: Raven.

Rissenberg, M., & Glanzer, M. (1987). Free recall and word finding ability in normal aging and senile dementia of the Alzheimer's type: The effect of item concreteness. *Journal of Gerontology, 42,* 318-322.

Robertson, C., & Flowers, K. A. (1990). Motor set in Parkinson's disease. *Journal of Neurology, Neurosurgery, and Psychiatry, 53,* 583-592.

Robertson, W. D., Li, D., Mayo, J., & Paty, D. W. (1984). Clinical versus magnetic resonance imaging: Diagnosis of multiple sclerosis. *Annals of Neurology, 16,* 140.

Robins, A. H. (1976). Depression in patients with Parkinsonism. *British Journal of Psychiatry, 128,* 141-145.

Robinson, B. C. (1983). Validation of a caregiver strain index. *Journal of Gerontology, 38,* 344-348.

Rocca, W. A., Amaducci, L. A., & Schoenberg, B. S. (1986). Epidemiology of clinically diagnosed Alzheimer's disease. *Annals of Neurology, 19,* 415-424.

Rogers, D. (1986). Bradyphrenia in Parkinsonism: A historical review. *Psychological Medicine, 16,* 257-265.

Rogers, D., Lees, A. J., Smith, E., Trimble, M., & Stern, G. M. (1987). Bradyphrenia in Parkinson's disease and psychomotor retardation in depressive illness: An experimental study. *Brain, 110,* 761-776.

Rosen, W. G., Mohs, R. C., & Davis, K. L. (1984). A rating scale for Alzheimer's disease. *American Journal of Psychiatry, 141,* 1356-1364.

Rosen, W. G., Terry, R. D., Fuld, P. A., Katzman, R., & Peck, A. (1980). Pathological verification of ischemic score in differentiation of the dementias. *Annals of Neurology, 7,* 486-488.

Ross, A. T., & Reitan, R. M. (1955). Intellectual and affective functions in multiple sclerosis. *Archives of Neurology and Psychiatry, 73,* 663-677.

Rosselli, M., Lorenzana, P., Rosselli, A., & Vergara, I. (1987). Wilson's disease: A reversible dementia. Case report. *Journal of Clinical and Experimental Neuropsychology, 9,* 399-406.

Roth, M., Tym, E., Mountjoy, C. Q., Huppert, F. A., Hendrie, J., Verma, S., & Goddard, R. (1986). CAMDEX: A standardized instrument for the diagnosis of mental disorder in the elderly with special reference to the early detection of dementia. *British Journal of Psychiatry, 148,* 698-709.

Rowland, L. P. (1987). Motor neuron diseases and amyotrophic lateral sclerosis: Research progress. *Trends in Neurosciences, 10,* 393-397.

Ruff, R. M., Light, R. H., & Quayhagen, M. (1988). Selective reminding tests: A normative study of verbal learning in adults. *Journal of Clinical and Experimental Neuropsychology, 11,* 539-550.

Russell, E. W. (1975). A multiple scoring method for the assessment of complex memory functions. *Journal of Clinical and Consulting Psychology, 55,* 800-809.

Russell, E. W. (1982). Factor analysis of the Revised Wechsler Memory scale tests in a neuropsychological battery. *Perceptual and Motor Skills, 54,* 971-974.

Russell, E. W. (1988). Renorming Russell's version of the Wechsler Memory Scale. *Journal of Clinical and Experimental Neuropsychology, 10,* 235-249.

Ryan, C., & Butters, N. (1980). Further evidence for a continuum-of-impairment encompassing male alcoholic Korsakoff patients and chronic alcoholic men. *Alcoholism: Clinical and Experimental Research, 4,* 190-197.

Ryan, J. J., Geisser, M. E., Randall, D. M., & Georgemiller, R. J. (1986). Alternate form reliability and equivalency of the Rey Auditory Verbal Learning Test. *Journal of Clinical and Experimental Neuropsychology, 8,* 611-616.

Ryan, J. J., Paola, A. M., & Brungardt, T. M. (1990). Standardization of the Wechsler Adult Intelligence Scale-Revised for persons 75 years and older. *Psychological Assessment: A Journal of Consulting and Clinical Psychology, 2,* 404-411.

Ryan, J. J., Rosenberg, S. J., & De Wolfe, A. S. (1984). Generalization of the WAIS-R factor structure with a vocational rehabilitation sample. *Journal of Consulting and Clinical Psychology, 52,* 311-312.

Safford, F. (1980). A program for families of the mentally impaired elderly. *Gerontologist, 20,* 656-660.

Sagar, H. J., Cohen, N. J., Sullivan, E. V., Corkin, S., & Growdon, J. H. (1988). Remote memory function in Alzheimer's disease and Parkinson's disease. *Brain, 111,* 185-206.

Sagar, H. J., Gabrieli, J. D. E., Sullivan, E. V., & Corkin, S. (1990). Recency and frequency discrimination in the amnesic patient H. M. *Brain, 113,* 581-602.

Sagar, H. J., Sullivan, E. V., Gabrieli, J. D. E., Corkin, S., & Growdon, J. H. (1988). Temporal ordering and short-term memory deficits in Parkinson's disease. *Brain, 111,* 525-539.

Saint-Cyr, J. A., Taylor, A. E., & Lang, A. E. (1988). Procedural learning and neostriatal dysfunction in man. *Brain, 111,* 941-959.

Salmon, D. P., Kwo-on-Yuen, P. F., Heindel, W. C., Butters, N., & Thal, L. J. (1989). Differentiation of Alzheimer's disease and Huntington's disease with the Dementia Rating Scale. *Archives of Neurology, 46,* 1204-1208.

Salmon, D. P., Shimamura, A. P., Butters, N., & Smith, S. (1988). Lexical and semantic priming deficits in patients with Alzheimer's disease. *Journal of Clinical and Experimental Neuropsychology, 10,* 477-494.

Sanders, H. I., & Warrington, E. K. (1971). Memory for remote events in amnesic patients. *Brain, 94,* 661-668.

Sanes, J. N. (1985). Information processing deficits in Parkinson's disease during movement. *Neuropsychologia, 23,* 381-392.

Satz, P., Hynd, G. W., D'Elia, L., Daniel, M. H., Van Gorp, W., & Connor, R. (1990). A WAIS-R marker for accelerated aging and dementia, Alzheimer's type? Base rates of the Fuld formula in the WAIS-R standardization sample. *Journal of Clinical and Experimental Neuropsychology, 12,* 759-765.

Satz, P., & Mogel, S. (1962). An abbreviation of the WAIS for clinical use. *Journal of Consulting Psychology, 18,* 77-79.

Satz, P., Van Gorp, W. G., Soper, H. V., & Mitrushina, M. (1987). A WAIS-R marker for dementia of the Alzheimer type? *Journal of Clinical and Experimental Neuropsychology, 9,* 767-774.

Saugstad, L., & Odegard, O. (1986). Huntington's chorea in Norway. *Psychological Medicine, 16,* 39-48.

Savage, R. D., Britton, P. G., Bolton, N., & Hall, E. H. (1973). *Intellectual functioning in the aged.* New York: Harper & Row.

Saxton, J., McGonigle-Gibson, K. L., Swihart, A. A., Miller, V. J., & Boller, F. (1990). Assessment of severely impaired patient: Description and validation of a new neuropsychological test battery. *Psychological Assessment: A Journal of Consulting and Clinical Psychology, 2,* 298-303.

Schacter, D. L. (1985). Priming of old and new knowledge in amnesic patients and normal subjects. *Annals of the New York Academy of Sciences, 444,* 41-53.

Schacter, D. L. (1987). Implicit memory: History and current status. *Journal of Experimental Psychology: Learning, Memory, and Cognition, 13,* 501-518.

317

Schacter, D. L., Harbluk, J. L., & McLachlan, D. R. (1984). Retrieval without recollection: An experimental analysis of source amnesia. *Journal of Verbal Learning and Verbal Behavior, 28,* 593-611.

Schiffer, R. B., & Babigian, H. M. (1984). Behavioral disorders in multiple sclerosis, temporal lobe epilepsy, and amyotrophic lateral sclerosis: An epidemiological study. *Archives of Neurology, 41,* 1067-1069.

Schiffer, R. B., Caine, E. D., Bamford, K. A., & Levy, S. (1983). Depressive episodes in patients with multiple sclerosis. *American Journal of Psychiatry, 140,* 1498-1500.

Schiffer, R. B., Herndon, R. M., & Rudnick, R. A. (1985). Treatment of pathologic laughing and weeping with amitriptyline. *New England Journal of Medicine, 312,* 1480-1482.

Schiffer, R. B., Wineman, M., & Weitkamp, L. R. (1986). Association between bipolar affective disorder and multiple sclerosis. *American Journal of Psychiatry, 143,* 94-95.

Schoenberg, B. S., Kokmen, E., & Okazaki, H. (1987). Alzheimer's disease and other dementing illnesses in a defined United States population: Incidence rates and clinical features. *Annals of Neurology, 22,* 724-729.

Scholz, O. M., & Shastry, M. (1985). Memory characteristics in Parkinson's disease. *International Journal of Neuroscience, 27,* 229-234.

Schuell, H. (1972). *Differential diagnosis of aphasia with the Minnesota Test* (2nd ed.). Minneapolis: University of Minnesota Press.

Schwab, R. S., Chafetz, M. E., & Walker, S. (1954). Control of two simultaneous voluntary motor acts in normals and in Parkinsonism. *Archives of Neurology and Psychiatry, 72,* 591-598.

Scott, S., Caird, F. I., & Williams, B. O. (1984). Evidence for an apparent sensory speech disorder in Parkinson's disease. *Journal of Neurology, Neurosurgery, and Psychiatry, 47,* 840-843.

Scoville, W. B., & Milner, B. (1957). Loss of recent memory after bilateral hippocampal lesions. *Journal of Neurology, Neurosurgery, and Psychiatry, 20,* 11-21.

Seltzer, B., & Sherwin, I. (1983). A comparison of clinical features in early- and late-onset primary degenerative dementia: One entity or two? *Archives of Neurology, 40,* 143-146.

Shader, R. I., Harmatz, J.S., & Salzman, C. (1974). A new scale for clinical assessment in geriatric populations: Sandoz Clinical Assessment—Geriatric. *Journal of the American Geriatrics Society, 22,* 107.

Shallice, T., & Warrington, E. K. (1970). The independence of the verbal memory stores: A neuropsychological study. *Quarterly Journal of Experimental Psychology, 22,* 261-273.

Shimamura, A. P., Salmon, D. P., Squire, L. R., & Butters, N. (1987). Memory dysfunction and word priming in dementia and amnesia. *Behavioral Neuroscience, 101,* 347-351.

Shimamura, A. P., & Squire, L. R. (1984). Paired-associate learning and priming effects in amnesia: A neuropsychological study. *Journal of Experimental Psychology: General, 113,* 556-570.

Shimamura, A. P., & Squire, L. R. (1986a). Memory and metamemory: A study of the feeling-of-knowing phenomenon in amnesic patients. *Journal of Experimental Psychology: Learning, Memory, and Cognition, 12,* 452-460.

Shimamura, A. P., & Squire, L. R. (1986b). Korsakoff's syndrome: A study of the relation between anterograde amnesia and remote memory impairment. *Behavioral Neuroscience, 100*, 165-170.

Shimamura, A. P., & Squire, L. R. (1989). Impaired priming of new associations in amnesia. *Journal of Experimental Psychology: Learning, Memory, and Cognition, 15*, 721-728.

Shoulson, I., & Fahn, S. (1979). Huntington's disease: Clinical care and evaluation. *Neurology, 29*, 1-3.

Silverstein, A. B. (1982). Two- and four-subtest short forms of the Wechsler Adult Intelligence Scale-Revised. *Journal of Consulting and Clinical Psychology, 50*, 415-418.

Simons, A. (Ed.). (1984). *Multiple sclerosis: Psychological and social aspects.* New York: Heinemann Medical Books.

Singer, E. (1973). Social costs of Parkinson's disease. *Journal of Chronic Diseases, 26*, 243-254.

Singer, E. (1974a). The effect of treatment with levodopa on Parkinson patients' social functioning and outlook on life. *Journal of Chronic Diseases, 27*, 581-594.

Singer, E. (1974b). Premature social aging: The social-psychological consequences of a chronic illness. *Social Science and Medicine, 8*, 143-151.

Singer, E. (1976). Sociopsychological factors influencing response to levodopa therapy for Parkinson's disease. *Archives of Physical Medicine and Rehabilitation, 57*, 328-334.

Sjogren, T., Sjogren, H., & Lindgren, A. G. H. (1952). Morbus Alzheimer and morbus Pick: A general, clinical, and pathoanatomical study. *Acta Psychiatrica et Neurologica Scandinavia,*(Suppl. 82), 1-152.

Skelton-Robinson, M., & Jones, S. (1984). Nominal dysphasia and the severity of senile dementia. *British Journal of Psychiatry, 145*, 168-171.

Skurla, E., Rogers, J. C., & Sunderland, T. (1988). Direct assessment of activities of daily living in Alzheimer's disease. *Journal of the American Geriatrics Society, 36*, 97-103.

Slater, R. J., LaRocca, N.G., & Scheinberg, L. C. (1984). Development and testing of a minimal record of disability in multiple sclerosis. *Annals of the New York Academy of Sciences, 436*, 453-468.

Smith, A. (1973). *Symbol Digit Modalities Test.* Los Angeles, CA: Western Psychological Services.

Spellman, G. G. (1962). Report of familial cases of Parkinsonism. *Journal of the American Medical Association, 179*, 160-162.

Spitzer, R. L., & Endicott, J. (1978). *NIMH Clinical Research Branch Collaborative Program on the Psychobiology of Depression: Schedule for Affective Disorders and Schizophrenia (SADS).* New York: NY State Psychiatric Institute, Biometrics Research Division.

Spitzer, R. L., Fleiss, J. L., Burdock, E. I., & Hardesty, A. S. (1964). The Mental Status Schedule: Rationale, reliability, and validity. *Comprehensive Psychiatry, 5*, 384-395.

Spokes, E. G. S. (1981). The neurochemistry of Huntington's chorea. *Trends in the Neurosciences, 4*, 115-118.

Spreen, O., & Benton, A. L. (1969). *Neurosensory Centre Comprehensive Examination for Aphasia.* Victoria, BC: Department of Psychology, University of Victoria.

Squire, L. R. (1974). Remote memory as affected by aging. *Neuropsychologia, 12,* 429-435.

Squire, L. R. (1982). Comparisons between forms of amnesia: Some deficits are unique to Korsakoff's syndrome. *Journal of Experimental Psychology: Learning, Memory, and Cognition, 8,* 56-571.

Squire, L. R. (1986). Mechanisms of memory. *Science, 232,* 1612-1619.

Squire, L. R., & Cohen, N. J. (1984). Human memory and amnesia. In J. McGaugh, G. Lynch, & N. Weinberger (Eds.), *Proceedings of the Conference on the Neurobiology of Learning and Memory* (pp. 3-64). New York: Guilford Press.

Squire, L. R., & Shimamura, A. P. (1986). Characterizing amnesic patients for neurobehavioral study. *Behavioral Neuroscience, 100,* 866-877.

Squire, L. R., Wetzel, C. D., & Slater, P.C. (1978). Anterograde amnesia following ECT: An analysis of the beneficial effects of partial information. *Neuropsychologia, 16,* 339-348.

Squire, L. R., & Zouzounis, J A. (1988). Self-rating of memory dysfunction: Different findings in depression and amnesia. *Journal of Clinical and Experimental Neuropsychology, 10,* 727-738.

Staples, D., & Lincoln, N. B. (1979). Intellectual impairment in multiple sclerosis and its relation to functional abilities. *Rheumatology and Rehabilitation, 18,* 153-160.

Starkstein, S. E., Bolduc, P. L., Mayberg, H. S., Preziosi, T. J., & Robinson, R. G. (1990). Cognitive impairments and depression in Parkinson's disease: A follow-up study. *Journal of Neurology, Neurosurgery, and Psychiatry, 53,* 597-602.

Starkstein, S. E., Leiguarda, R., Gershanik, O., & Berthier, M. (1987). Neuropsychological disturbances in hemiParkinson's disease. *Neurology, 37,* 1762-1764.

Starkstein, S. E., Preziosi, T. J., Berthier, M. L., Bolduc, P. L., Mayberg, H. S., & Robinson, R. G. (1989). Depression and cognitive impairment in Parkinson's disease. *Brain, 112,* 1141-1153.

Steck, H. (1931). Les syndromes mentaux postencephalitiques [Post-encephalitic psychiatric syndromes]. *Schweizer Archiv fur Neurologie und Psychiatrie, 27,* 137-173.

Steele, J. C., Richardson, J. C., & Olszewski, J. (1964). Progressive supranuclear palsy: A heterogeneous degeneration involving the brainstem, basal ganglia, and cerebellum with vertical gaze pseudobulbar palsy, muchal dystonia, and dementia. *Archives of Neurology, 10,* 333-359.

Stern, Y., & Langston, J. W. (1985). Intellectual changes in patients with MPTP-induced Parkinsonism. *Neurology, 35,* 1506-1509.

Stern, Y., Mayeux, R., & Rosen, J. (1984). Contribution of perceptual motor dysfunction to construction and tracing disturbances in Parkinson's disease. *Journal of Neurology, Neurosurgery, and Psychiatry, 47,* 983-989.

Stern, Y., Mayeux, R., Rosen, J., & Ilson, J. (1983). Perceptual-motor dysfunction in Parkinson's disease: A deficit in sequential and predictive voluntary movement. *Journal of Neurology, Neurosurgery, and Psychiatry, 46,* 145-151.

St. George-Hyslop, P. H., Tanzi, R. E., Polinsky, R. J., Haines, J. L., Nee, L., Watkins, P. C., Myers, R. H., Feldman, R. G., Pollen, D., Drachman, D., Growdon, J., Bruni, A., Foncin, J., Salmon, D., Frommelt, P., Amaducci, L., Scorbi, S., Piancentini, S., Stewart, G. D., Hobbs, W. J., Conneally, P. M., & Gusella, J. F. (1987). The genetic defect causing familial Alzheimer's disease maps on chromosome 21. *Science, 235,* 885-887.

Stone, R., Cafferata, G. L., & Sangl, J. (1987). Caregivers of the frail elderly: A national profile. *Gerontologist, 27,* 616-626.

Storandt, M., Botwinick, J., Danziger, W. L., Berg, L., & Hughes, C. P. (1984). Psychometric differentiation of mild senile dementia of the Alzheimer type. *Archives of Neurology, 41*, 497-499.

Storandt, M., & Hill, R. D. (1989). Very mild senile dementia of the Alzheimer type: II. Psychometric test performance. *Archives of Neurology, 46*, 383-386.

Strauss, M. E., & Brandt, J. (1986). Attempt at preclinical identification of Huntington's disease using the WAIS. *Journal of Clinical and Experimental Neuropsychology, 8*, 210-218.

Stroop, J. R. (1955). Studies of interference in serial verbal reactions. *Journal of Experimental Psychology, 18*, 643-662.

Stuss, D. T., & Benson, D. F. (1984). Neuropsychological studies of the frontal lobes. *Psychological Bulletin, 95*, 3-28.

Sullivan, E. V., & Sagar, H. J. (1989). Nonverbal recognition and recency discrimination deficits in Parkinson's disease and Alzheimer's disease. *Brain, 112*, 1503-1517.

Sullivan, E. V., Sagar, H. J., Gabrieli, J. D. E., Corkin, S., & Growdon, J. H. (1985). Sequencing deficits in Parkinson's disease. *Journal of Clinical and Experimental Neuropsychology, 7*, 160-168.

Sunderland, A., Harris, J. E., & Baddeley, A. D. (1983). Do laboratory tests predict everyday memory? A neuropsychological study. *Journal of Verbal Learning and Verbal Behavior, 22*, 341-357.

Surridge, D. (1969). An investigation into some aspects of multiple sclerosis. *British Journal of Psychiatry, 114*, 749-764.

Sutcliffe, R. L., Prior, R., Mawby, B., & McQuillan, W. J. (1985). Parkinson's disease in the district of the Northampton Health Authority, UK: A study of prevalence and disability. *Acta Neurologica Scandinavica, 72*, 363-379.

Swearer, J. M., Drachman, D. A., O'Donnell, B. F., & Mitchell, A. L. (1988). Troublesome and disruptive behaviors in dementia: Relationships to diagnosis and disease severity. *Journal of the American Geriatrics Society, 36*, 784-790.

Sweet, J. J., Moberg, P. J., & Tovian, S. M. (1990). Evaluation of Wechsler Adult Intelligence Scale-Revised premorbid IQ formulas in clinical populations. *Psychological Assessment: A Journal of Consulting and Clinical Psychology, 2*, 41-44.

Szasz, G., Paty, D. W., & Maurice, W. L. (1984). Sexual dysfunction in multiple sclerosis. *Annals of the New York Academy of Sciences, 436*, 443-452.

Talland, G. A. (1962). Cognitive function in Parkinson's disease. *Journal of Nervous and Mental Disease, 135*, 196-205.

Talland, G. A. (1963). Manual skill in Parkinson's disease. *Geriatrics, 181*, 613-620.

Talland, G. A. (1965). *Deranged memory*. New York: Academic Press.

Talland, G. A., & Schwab, R. S. (1964). Performance with multiple sets in Parkinson's disease. *Neuropsychologia, 2*, 45-53.

Tandan, R., & Bradley, W. G. (1985). Amyotrophic lateral sclerosis: Part 1. Clinical features, pathology, and ethical issues in management. *Annals of Neurology, 18*, 271-280.

Tanzi, R. E., Bird, E. D., Latt, S.A., & Neve, R. L. (1987). The amyloid beta protein gene is not duplicated in brains from patients with Alzheimer's disease. *Science, 238*, 666-669.

Taylor, A. E., Saint-Cyr, J. A., & Lang, A. E. (1986). Frontal lobe dysfunction in Parkinson's disease: The cortical focus of neostriatal outflow. *Brain, 109*, 845-883.

Taylor, A. E., Saint-Cyr, J. A., & Lang, A. E. (1987). Parkinson's disease: Cognitive changes in relation to treatment response. *Brain, 110*, 35-51.

Taylor, A. E., Saint-Cyr, J. A., Lang, A. E., & Kenny, F. T. (1986). Parkinson's disease and depression: A critical re-evaluation. *Brain, 109*, 279-292.

Teng, E. L., Chui, H. C., Schneider, L. S., & Metzger, L. E. (1987). Alzheimer's dementia: Performance on the Mini-Mental State Examination. *Journal of Consulting and Clinical Psychology, 55*, 96-100.

Teng, E. L., Wimer, C., Roberts, E., Damasio, A. R., Eslinger, P. J., Folstein, M. F., Tune, L. E., Whitehouse, P., Bardolph, E. L., Chui, H. C., & Henderson, V. W. (1989). Alzheimer's dementia: Performance on parallel forms of the Dementia Assessment Battery. *Journal of Clinical and Experimental Neuropsychology, 11*, 899-912.

Teri, L., Borson, S., Kiyak, H. A., & Yamagishi, M. (1989). Behavioral disturbance, cognitive dysfunction, and functional skill: Prevalence and relationship in Alzheimer's disease. *Journal of the American Geriatrics Society, 37*, 109-116.

Teri, L., Larson, E. B., & Reifler, B. V. (1988). Behavioral disturbance in dementia of the Alzheimer's type. *Journal of the American Geriatrics Society, 36*, 1-6.

Terry, R., & Katzman, R. (1983). Senile dementia of the Alzheimer type. *Annals of Neurology, 14*, 497-506.

Terry, R. D., & Pena, C. (1965). Experimental production of neurofibrillary degeneration: II. Electron microscopy, phosphate histochemistry and electron probe analysis. *Journal of Neuropathology and Experimental Neurology, 24*, 200-210.

Teuber, H-L., Milner, B., & Vaughan, H. G. (1968). Persistent anterograde amnesia after a stab wound of the basal forebrain. *Neuropsychologia, 6*, 276-282.

Thal, L. J., Grundman, M., & Golden, R. (1986). Alzheimer's disease: A correlational analysis of the Blessed Information-Memory-Concentration Test and the Mini-Mental State Exam. *Neurology, 36*, 262-264.

Thoits, P. A. (1983). Dimensions of life events as influences upon the genesis of psychological distress and associated conditions: An evaluation and synthesis of the literature. In H. B. Kaplan (Ed.), *Psychosocial stress: Trends in theory and research* (pp. 33-103). New York: Academic.

Thoits, P. A. (1986). Social support as coping assistance. *Journal of Consulting and Clinical Psychology, 54*, 416-423.

Thompson, L. W. (1988). Measurement of depression: Implications for assessment of cognitive function in the elderly. In L. W. Poon (Ed.), *Handbook for clinical memory assessment of older adults* (pp. 199-202). Washington, DC: American Psychological Association.

Thompson, P. D., Berardelli, A., Rothwell, J. C., Day, B. L., Dick, J. P. R., Benecke, R., & Marsden, C. D. (1988). The coexistence of bradykinesia and chorea in Huntington's disease and its implications for theories of basal ganglia control of movement. *Brain, 111*, 223-244.

Tierney, M. C., Fisher, R. H., Lewis, A. J., Zorzitto, M., Snow, W. G., Reid, D. W., & Nieuwstraten, P. (1988). The NINCDS-ADRDA Work Group criteria for the clinical diagnosis of probable Alzheimer's disease: A clinicopathologic study of 57 cases. *Neurology, 38*, 359-364. '

Tiwari, J. L., Hodge, S. E., Teraski, P. I., & Spence, M. A. (1980). HLA and the inheritance of multiple sclerosis: Linkage analysis of 72 pedigrees. *American Journal of Human Genetics, 32*, 103-111.

Tomlinson, B. E. (1977). Morphological changes and dementia in old age. In W. L. Smith & M. Kinsbourne (Eds.), *Aging and dementia* (pp. 25-56). New York: Spectrum.

Tomlinson, B. E., Blessed, G., & Roth, M. (1968). Observations on the brains of non-demented old people. *Journal of Neurological Science, 7*, 331.

Tomlinson, B. E., Blessed, G., & Roth, M. (1970). Observations on the brains of demented old people. *Journal of Neurological Science, 11*, 205.

Tomlinson, B. E., & Henderson, G. (1976). Some quantitative cerebral findings in normal and demented old people. In R. D. Terry & S. Gershon (Eds.), *Neurobiology of Aging* (pp. 183-204). New York: Raven.

Trimble, M. R., & Grant, I. (1982). Psychiatric aspects of multiple sclerosis. In D. F. Benson & D. Blumer (Eds.), *Psychiatric aspects of neurologic disease* (Vol. 2, pp. 279-299). New York: Grune & Stratton.

Tulving, E. (1983). *Elements of episodic memory.* Oxford, England: Clarendon.

Tuokko, H., & Crockett, D. (1987). Central cholinergic deficiency: WAIS profiles in a nondemented aged sample. *Journal of Clinical and Experimental Neuropsychology, 9*, 225-227.

Tuokko, H., & Crockett, D. (1989). Cued recall and memory disorders in dementia. *Journal of Clinical and Experimental Neuropsychology, 11*, 278-294.

Turney, J. (1990, April 6). A lifeline tied to embryo cord. *Times Higher Education Supplement*, p. 14.

Tweedy, J. R., Langer, K. G., & McDowell, F. H. (1982). The effect of semantic relations on the memory deficit associated with Parkinson's disease. *Journal of Clinical Neuropsychology, 4*, 235-247.

Van den Burg, W., Van Zomeren, A. H., Minderhoud, J. M., Prange, A. J. A., & Meijer, N. S. A. (1987). Cognitive impairment in patients with multiple sclerosis and mild physical disability. *Archives of Neurology, 44*, 494-501.

VanderPlate, C. (1984). Psychological aspects of multiple sclerosis and its treatment: Towards a biopsychosocial perspective. *Health Psychology, 3*, 253-272.

Vessie, B. R. (1932). On the transmission of Huntington's chorea for 300 years: The Bures family group. *Journal of Nervous and Mental Disease, 76*, 553-573.

Victor, M., Adams, R. D., & Collins, G. H. (1971). *The Wernicke-Korsakoff syndrome.* Oxford: Blackwell Scientific Publications.

Vonsattel, J-P., Myers, R. H., Stevens, T. J., Ferrante, R. J., Bird, E. D., & Richardson, E. P. (1985). Neuropathological classification of Huntington's disease. *Journal of Neuropathology and Experimental Neurology, 44*, 559-577.

Wade, J. P. H., Mirsen, T. R., Hachinski, V. C., Fisman, M., Lau, C., & Merskey, D. M. (1987). The clinical diagnosis of Alzheimer's disease. *Archives of Neurology, 44*, 24-29.

Waksman, B. H. (1983). Rationales of current therapies for multiple sclerosis. *Archives of Neurology, 40*, 671-672.

Waller, N. G., & Waldman, I. D. (1990). A reexamination of the WAIS-R factor structure. *Psychological Assessment: A Journal of Consulting and Clinical Psychology, 2*, 139-144.

Walton, D., & Black, D. A. (1957). The validity of a psychological test of brain damage. *British Journal of Medical Psychology, 30*, 270-279.

Wang, H. A., & Whanger, A. (1971). Brain impairment and longevity. In E. Palmore & F. C. Jeffers (Eds.), *Prediction of life-span* (pp. 95-105). Lexington, MA: Heath & Co.

Warburton, J. W. (1967a). Depressive symptoms in Parkinsonian patients referred for thalamotomy. *Journal of Neurology, Neurosurgery, and Psychiatry, 30,* 368-370.

Warburton, J. W. (1967b). Memory disturbance and the Parkinson syndrome. *British Journal of Medical Psychology, 40,* 169-171.

Warren, S., Greenhill, S., & Warren, K. G. (1982). Emotion, stress, and the development of multiple sclerosis: Case control evidence of a relationship. *Journal of Chronic Diseases, 35,* 821-831.

Warrington, E. K. (1975). The selective impairment of semantic memory. *Quarterly Journal of Experimental Psychology, 27,* 635-657.

Warrington, E. K. (1982). The double dissociation of short- and long-term memory deficits. In L. S. Cermak (Ed.), *Human memory and amnesia* (pp. 61-76). Hillsdale, NJ: Lawrence Erlbaum Associates.

Warrington, E. K. (1984). *Recognition Memory Test.* Windsor, England: NFER-Nelson.

Warrington, E. K., & Baddeley, A. D. (1974). Amnesia and memory for visual location. *Neuropsychologia, 12,* 257-263.

Warrington, E. K., & Weiskrantz, L. (1968). A new method of testing long-term retention with special reference to amnesic patients. *Nature, 217,* 972-974.

Warrington, E. K., & Weiskrantz, L. (1970). Amnesic syndrome: Consolidation or retrieval? *Nature, 228,* 628-630.

Warrington, E. K., & Weiskrantz, L. (1978). Further analysis of the prior learning effect in amnesic patients. *Neuropsychologia, 11,* 169-177.

Warrington, E. K., & Weiskrantz, L. (1982). Amnesia: A disconnection syndrome? *Neuropsychologia, 20,* 233-248.

Wechsler, D. A. (1945). A standardized memory scale for clinical use. *Journal of Psychology, 19,* 87-95.

Wechsler, D. (1987). *Manual for the Wechsler Memory Scale-Revised.* New York: The Psychological Corporation.

Weingartner, H., Burns, S., Diebel, R., & LeWitt, P. (1984). Cognitive impairment in Parkinson's disease: Distinguishing between effort demanding and automatic cognitive processes. *Psychiatry Research, 11,* 223-235.

Weingartner, H., Caine, E., & Ebert, M. H. (1979). Imagery, encoding, and retrieval of information from memory: Some specific encoding - retrieval changes in Huntington's disease. *Journal of Abnormal Psychology, 73,* 52-58.

Weingartner, H., Grafman, J., Boutelle, W., Kaye, W., & Martin, P. R. (1983). Forms of memory failure. *Science, 221,* 380-382.

Weingartner, H., Kaye, W., Smallberg, S. A., Ebert, M. H., Gillin, J. C., & Sitaram, N. (1981). Memory failures in progressive idiopathic dementias. *Journal of Abnormal Psychology, 90,* 187-196.

Weinstock, C., & Bennett, R. (1971). From "waiting on the list" to becoming a "newcomer" and an "old timer" in a home for the aged: Two studies of socialization and its impact upon cognitive functioning. *Aging and Human Development, 2,* 45-58.

Weiskrantz, L. (1985). Issues and theories in the study of the amnesic syndrome. In N. M. Weinberger, J. L. McGaugh & G. Lynch (Eds.), *Memory systems of the brain* (pp. 380-415). New York: Guilford Press.

Weiskrantz, L., & Warrington, E. K. (1979). Conditioning in amnesic patients. *Neuropsychologia, 17,* 187-194.

Welsh, K. A., Butters, N., Hughes, J., Mohs, R., & Heyman, A. (1991). Detection of abnormal memory decline in mild cases of Alzheimer's disease using CERAD neuropsychological measures. *Archives of Neurology, 48,* 278-281.

Wernicke, C. (1973). Acute hemorrhagic superior polioencephalitis. In R. H. Wilkins & I. A. Brody (Eds.), *Neurological classics* (pp. 45-48). New York: Johnson Reprint Corporation. (Original work published 1881)

Wetzel, C. D., & Squire, L. R. (1982). Cued recall in anterograde amnesia. *Brain & Language, 15,* 70-81.

Wexler, N. S. (1985). Genetic jeopardy and the new clairvoyance. In A. Bean, A. Motulsky, & B. Childs (Eds.), *Progess in medical genetics* (pp. 277-304). Philadelphia: Praeger.

Wexler, N. S. (1989). The oracle of DNA. In L. P. Rowland, D. S. Wood, E. A. Schon, & Di Mauro (Eds.), *Molecular genetics in diseases of brain, nerve, and muscle* (pp. 429-442). New York: Oxford University Press.

Whelihan, W. M., Lesher, E. L., Kleban, M. H., & Granick, S. (1984). Mental status and memory assessment as predictors of dementia. *Journal of Gerontology, 39,* 572-576.

Whitehouse, P. J., Hedreen, J. C., White, C. L., & Price, D. L. (1983). Basal forebrain neurons in the dementia of Parkinson's disease. *Annals of Neurology, 13,* 243-248.

Whitehouse, P. J., Price, D. L., Struble, R. G., Clark, A. W., & Coyle, J. T. (1982). Alzheimer's disease and senile dementia: Loss of neurons in the basal forebrain. *Science, 215,* 1237-1239.

Whitlock, F. A., & Siskind, M. M. (1980). Depression as a major symptom of multiple sclerosis. *Journal of Neurology, Neurosurgery, and Psychiatry, 43,* 861-865.

Wickens, D. D. (1970). Encoding categories of words: An empirical approach to meaning. *Psychological Review, 77,* 1-15.

Williams, B. W., Mack, W., & Henderson, V. W. (1989). Boston Naming Test in Alzheimer's disease. *Neuropsychologia, 27,* 1073-1079.

Wilson, B., Cockburn, J., Baddeley, A., & Hiorns, R. (1989). The development and validation of a test battery for detecting and monitoring everyday memory problems. *Journal of Clinical and Experimental Neuropsychology, 11,* 855-870.

Wilson, R. S., Como, P. G., Garron, D. C., Klawans, H. L., Barr, A., & Klawans, D. (1987). Memory failure in Huntington's disease. *Journal of Clinical and Experimental Neuropsychology, 9,* 147-154.

Wilson, R. S., Kaszniak, A. W., Bacon, L. D., Fox, J. H., & Kelly, M. P. (1982). Facial recognition memory in dementia. *Cortex, 18,* 329-336.

Wilson, R. S., Kaszniak, A. W., & Fox, J. H. (1981). Remote memory in senile dementia. *Cortex, 17,* 41-48.

Wilson, R. S., Kaszniak, A. W., Klawans, H. L., & Garron, D. C. (1980). High speed memory scanning in Parkinsonism. *Cortex, 16,* 67-72.

Wilson, R. S., Rosenbaum, G., Brown, G., Rourke, D., Whitman, D., & Grissell, J. (1978). An index of premorbid intelligence. *Journal of Consulting and Clinical Psychology, 46,* 1554-1555.

Wilson, S. A. K. (1912). Progressive leuticular degeneration: A familial nervous disease associated with cirrhosis of the liver. *Brain, 34,* 295-509.

Wilson, S. A. K. (1925). The Croonian lectures on some disorders of motility and of muscle tone, with special reference to the corpus striatum. *Lancet, 2,* pp. 1-10, 53-62, 169-178, 215-276.

Wing, J. K., Cooper, J. E., & Sartorius, N. (1974). *The measurement and classification of psychiatric symptoms.* Cambridge: Cambridge University Press.

Winocur, G., Kinsbourne, M., & Moscovitch, M. (1981). The effect of cuing on release from proactive interference in Korsakoff amnesic patients. *Journal of Experimental Psychology: Human Learning and Memory, 7,* 56-65.

Winogrond, I., Fisk, A., Kirsling, R., & Keyes, B. (1987). The relationship of caregiver burden and morale to Alzheimer's disease patients' function in a therapeutic setting. *Gerontologist, 27,* 336-342.

Wisniewski, H. M., Moretz, R. C., & Iqbal, K. (1986). No evidence for aluminium in etiology and pathogenesis of Alzheimer's disease. *Neurobiology and Aging, 7,* 532-535.

Wolff, M. L. (1982). Reversible intellectual impairment: An internist's perspective. *Journal of the American Geriatrics Society, 30,* 647-650.

Woods, R. T. (1979). Reality orientation and staff attention: A controlled study. *British Journal of Psychiatry, 34,* 502-507.

Woods, R. T. (1982). The psychology of aging: Assessment of defects and their management. In R. Levy & F. Post (Eds.), *The psychiatry of late life* (pp. 68-113). Oxford, England: Blackwell Scientific Publications.

Woods, R. T. (1983). Specificity of learning in reality orientation sessions: A single case study. *Behaviour Research and Therapy, 21,* 173-175.

Yesavage, J. A., Brink, T. L., Rose, T. L., & Adey, M. (1983). The Geriatric Depression Rating Scale: Comparison with other self-report and psychiatric rating scales. In T. Crook, S. Ferris, & R. Bartus (Eds.), *Assessment in geriatric psychopharmacology* (pp. 153-167). New Canaan, CT: Mark Powley.

Zarit, S. H. (1989). Do we need another "stress and caregiving" study? *Gerontologist, 29,* 147-148.

Zarit, S. H., Anthony, C. R., & Boutselis, M. (1987). Interventions with caregivers of dementia patients: Comparison of two approaches. *Psychology and Aging, 2,* 225-232.

Zarit, S. H., Orr, N. K., & Zarit, J. M. (1985). *The hidden victims of Alzheimer's disease: Families under stress.* New York: New York University Press.

Zarit, S. H., Reever, K. E., & Bach-Peterson, J. (1980). Relatives of the impaired elderly: Correlates of feelings of burden. *Gerontologist, 20,* 649-654.

Zarit, S. H., Todd, P., & Zarit, J. (1986). Subjective burden of husbands and wives as caregivers: A longitudinal study. *Gerontologist, 26,* 260-266.

Zarit, S. H., Zarit, J. M., & Reever, K. E. (1982). Memory training for severe memory loss: Effects on senile dementia patients and their families. *Gerontologist, 22,* 373-377.

Zeigler, L. H. (1928). Follow-up studies on persons who have had epidemic encephalitis. *Journal of the American Medical Association, 91,* 138-140.

Zola-Morgan, S., Squire, L. R., & Amaral, D. G. (1986). Human amnesia and medical temporal region: Enduring memory impairment following a bilateral lesion limit to field CA1 of the hippocampus. *Journal of Neuroscience, 6,* 2950-2967.

Zola-Morgan, S., Squire, L. R., & Amaral, D. G. (1989). Lesions of the amygdala that spare adjacent cortical regions do not impair memory or excerbate the impairment following lesions of the hippocampal formation. *Journal of Neuroscience, 9,* 1922-1936.

Zung, W. W. K. (1965). A self-rating depression scale. *Archives of General Psychiatry, 12,* 63-70.

AUTHOR INDEX

328

SUBJECT INDEX